3G Wireless Demystified

Lawrence Harte
Roman Kitka
Richard Levine

McGraw-Hill

New York   Chicago   San Francisco   Lisbon   London
Madrid   Mexico City   Milan   New Delhi   San Juan   Seoul
Singapore   Sydney   Toronto

Cataloging-in-Publication Data is on file with the Library of Congress

McGraw-Hill

A Division of The McGraw·Hill Companies

1 2 3 4 5 6 7 8 9   AGM/AGM   0 7 6 5 4 3 2 1

ISBN 0-07-136301-7

The sponsoring editor for this book was Steve Chapman, the editing supervisor was Carol Levine, and the production supervisor was Pamela Pelton.

Printed and bound by Quebecor / Martinsburg.

McGraw-Hill books are available at special quantity discounts to use as premiums and sales promotions, or for use in corporate training programs. For more information, please write to the Director of Special Sales, Professional Publishing, McGraw-Hill, Two Penn Plaza, New York, NY 10121-2298. Or contact your local bookstore.

 This book is printed on recycled, acid-free paper containing a minimum of 50% recycled, de-inked fiber.

Dedication

"I dedicate this book to my love Tara and my children Lawrence, William, and Danielle Elizabeth. To Tara, I love you to infinity and beyond."
Lawrence

"I dedicate this book to Robert J. Charles, a telecommunications industry veteran who's bringing xDSL broadband access services to the United Kingdom, for his perseverance, dedication, and inspiration."
Roman

"I dedicate this book to my wife Sara and the next generations: Naomi, Yossi, Kyle, Kyle's forthcoming younger sister or brother, Susan, Earl, Rael, Annika, and David. May you all live in a still better world. Love and Thanks."
Richard

Table of Contents

Foreword

At the beginning of 2001, almost 1 person in 7 worldwide had a wireless phone. To connect people and improve the overall quality of life, new third generation wireless systems have been developed that offer new multimedia capabilities, better reliability, improved battery life, and efficient and more cost-effective solutions.

Since the first second generation mobile telephones were introduced into the marketplace in 1991, the demand for digital mobile telephones and service continues to grow at over 40% per year. At the end of 2000, there were more than 680 million mobile subscribers throughout the world. Third generation systems will rapidly replace second generation systems as second generation digital mobile telephone systems have rapidly replaced first generation analog systems.

Third generation (3G) wireless systems are an evolution of second generation wireless technologies, and they will use much of the existing second generation infrastructure and radio systems. 3G systems will become the leading communication technology because they provide more cost effective solutions and new broadband multimedia services. In comparison to second generation systems, 3G systems available in 2001 allow for a 70% increase in network capacity while reducing the cell sites needed by over 30%.

The main issues for both users and operators will be capacity and security. Revenue from radio airtime usage is declining. To increase the value of a customer to a wireless operator, new services can be offered that will increase airtime usage, and content delivery and advertising revenues will supplement basic service revenues. Creative mobile operators offer thousands of services through Internet hypermarketing that will prompt greater wireless usage.

Third generation systems were designed for secure, efficient interconnection with the Internet. By designing the network to take advantage of Internet Protocol (IP), third generation networks provide cost savings for system operators and end users. Third generation systems are less complex networks with fewer nodes, with a single core network that allows standard Internet-based software applications such as email and web browsing.

The twenty-first century will see new lifestyles that are enabled by the advanced capabilities of digital wireless communication. Third generation systems offer the potential for many new content-based services to take advantage of efficient high-speed data services that can reach up to 2 Mbps. The key applications can be classified as person-to-person communications, mobile entertainment, wireless advertising, mobile transactions, location-based services, mobile information, and business solutions. By focusing on these key applications and establishing partnerships with content providers, operators will be able to increase profits and customers will improve their lifestyle.

Industry standards are necessary to allow common technology to be shared among many manufacturers. Hundreds of manufacturers, carriers, and associations have participated in the development of third generation industry standards. In an unprecedented move by the different national standards committees, a harmonization effort produced a single source of third generation standards. The third generation partnership program (3GPP) was composed of national standards committees that balanced their individual country's interests with the global needs of the third generation systems. These groups worked together to create the specification for the third generation universal mobile telecommunications system (UMTS).

This book arrives at a fortunate time for the wireless industry. The amount of new technology, human resources, and capital that will be invested in third generation wireless technology is huge. While second generation digital wireless technology has been successful, to sustain the rapid growth and maintain a competitive advantage, new third generation capabilities are essential for new emerging markets. A balanced understanding between market needs and technology availability is required to achieve success. This book describes the new services and technologies third generation digital systems can provide along with the financial considerations for its deployment.

Preface

The cellular or PCS industry changed dramatically in the year 2001. Second generation cellular systems have begun to migrate into new multimedia wireless systems and new competing third generation wireless systems are being deployed. These new changes allow cellular systems to provide new information content services, high-speed wireless data services, digital video, advanced messaging, and fixed wireless access, in addition to traditional mobile telephone services.

Since the first cellular telephones were introduced into the marketplace in 1979, the market demand for mobile telephones and services continues to grow at over 20% per year. At the beginning of the year 2001, there were over 680 million cellular and PCS telephones in use worldwide.

There have been many claims of advanced features and economic benefits for third generation cellular technologies. The reality is that existing systems must be changed to allow for advanced features, and new competitors will enter the wireless marketplace. This book provides a semi-technical understanding of the different third generation cellular systems, their economics, and the new advanced services they can provide. Third generation cellular technologies offer the advantages of traditional mobile telephone service with the added benefits of high bandwidth and advanced intelligent network features.

Third generation systems offer new features but have limitations that result in important choices for managers, technicians, and others involved with cellular and PCS telephones and systems. *3G Wireless Demystified* provides a description of third generation wireless technologies, shows their economic benefits, and provides references of associations and industry specifications.

3G Wireless Demystified uses over 150 illustrations and tables to explain third generation cellular and PCS technologies and their services. More than 100 industry experts have helped create and reviewed the technical content of this book. Industry terminology is explained and chapters in this book are organized to help find the needed detailed information quickly. These chapters are divided to cover specific parts or applications of third generation technology and may be read either consecutively or individually.

Chapter 1. Provides a basic introduction to third generation wireless technologies including cellular, PCS, wireless office, cordless, messaging, wireless LAN and high bandwidth services. Advanced wireless messaging and high bandwidth services such as advertising, digital video, imaging, and monitoring are identified and explained. This chapter is an excellent introduction for newcomers to mobile wireless technology.

Chapter 2. Covers first generation analog cellular systems. A history of world cellular systems is provided along with systems overview, basic cellular operation, and descriptions of the leading cellular systems deployed throughout the world.

Chapter 3. Explains digital wireless technology in simple terms. This chapter teaches the basics of radio channel structures, signaling methods, system measurements (parameters), power control techniques, call transfers (handoff/handover), modulation, frequency and time diversity techniques, digital speech coding, data compression, and other important aspects of digital wireless technology.

Chapter 4. Provides an overview of enhanced data rates for global evolution (EDGE) and also describes how the North American IS-136 TDMA system is in transition to this system. Included is the history of the original IS-54 TDMA standard, its evolution to the IS-136 system, and how the transition to EDGE is occurring. A system overview is provided and the new modulation and radio channel structure proposed for its evolution into a third generation system is presented.

Chapter 5. This chapter explains the CDMA2000 system and how it evolved from IS-95 Code Division Multiple Access (CDMA). Included is the history of CDMA, a system overview, system attributes, and basic operation.

Chapter 6. Find out how the WCDMA system developed from the Global System for Mobile (GSM) communications system. This chapter includes GSM's history, system overview, system attributes, basic operation, and 3rd generation enhancements.

Chapter 7. This chapter describes mobile telephones and wireless devices and which devices will be used in third generation systems. These include mobile telephones, video displays, telemetry monitoring devices, and others. The user interface, radio frequency section, signal processing, power supply, and accessories will be covered.

Chapter 8. This chapter describes third generation network systems. These include base stations, network databases, intelligent networks, public switched telephone network, wireless system planning, and network options.

Chapter 9. Economics for third generation systems is different from traditional cellular systems. Discover the costs of wireless telephones, system equipment costs, network capital costs, and operational costs in this chapter.

Chapter 10. Covers key applications that benefit from third generation wireless. These applications require the high-speed (broadband) data transmission capability or mobility that third generation systems offer. Described are distance education, information services, entertainment, telemedicine, security monitoring, and many others.

Appendix. Lists and defines third generation wireless related acronyms and abbreviations that appear in this book.

Acknowledgments

We thank the many gifted people who gave their technical and emotional support for the creation of this book. In many cases, published sources were not available on this subject area. Experts from manufacturers, service providers, trade associations, and other telecommunications-related companies gave their personal precious time to help us and for this we sincerely thank and respect them.

We thank the many manufacturing experts that helped us validate technology information including: Tom Margetis from Anritsu; Gursel Ilipinar from Bellsouth; Vijay Deokar from Californinia Polytechnic University; Yas Mochizuki with Casio; Pat Kennedy at CellPort Laboratories; Shahin Hatamian with Denso Wireless Communications; Gabriel Hilevitz of DSPC Israel Ltd.; Eric Stasik from Ericsson Radio Systems AB; Osmo Hautanen at Formus Communications; Richard Holder with HebCom; Beth Eurotas of Hewlett Packard; Bob Sarwacinski from Insight Technologies; Mat Kirimura at Japan Radio Company; Ronald Koppel and Vijay Garg, Ph.D. with Lucent Technologies; Greg Foss, Mark Worthey, Sherri Haupert, and YS Cho of Maxon; Brian Walker, Joshua Kiem, and Robert Dunnigan from Motorola; Kim Kennedy at NEC America, Inc.; Denise Borel with Nortel Networks; Mike Wise of Oki Telecom-GA; Bob Roth, Christine Trimble, Gill Harneet, Joanne Coleman, Kevin Kelly, and Michelle French from Qualcomm; Ram Velidi, Ph.D. at Raytheon TI Systems, Inc.; Kurt Siem and Rich Conlon with Repeater Technologies; Dawn McLain of Samsung; Dan Fowler at SCALA; Elliot Hamilton at Strategis; and Stuart Creed with Tektronix.

Special thanks to the people who assisted with the production of this book including Dave Richardson and Amy Case (project managers), Tom Pazderka (illustator), and Karen Bunn (editor). Special thanks to Steve Chapman at McGraw-Hill who helped ensure this book was at the highest industry standard and that the book contained valuable and quality information. And thanks to our financial supporters including Linda Plano, Konny Zsigo, Mike Cromie, Ted Ericsson, Eric Stasik, Micheal Zapata, Elliott Hamilton, Quincy Scott, and Virginia Harte.

About the Authors

Lawrence Harte is the president of APDG, a provider of expert information to the telecommunications market.

Mr. Harte has over 23 years of experience in the electronics industry including company leadership, product management, development, marketing, design, and testing of telecommunications (cellular), radar, and microwave systems. He has been issued patents relating to cellular technology. He has authored over 75 articles on related subjects and has been a speaker and panel moderator at industry trade events.

Mr. Harte earned an executive MBA at Wake Forest University and received his B.A. from the University of the State of New York. During the TDMA digital cellular standard development process, Mr. Harte served as an editor and voting company representative for the Telecommunications Industries Association (TIA) TR45.3, digital cellular standards committee.

As of 2001, Mr. Harte had authored and co-authored over 20 books relating to telecommunications technology. He has served as a consultant and expert witness for leading companies including Ericsson, Siemens, VLSI, AMD, Casio, Samsung, Sony, ATT, Nokia, Hughes, and many others.

Roman Kikta is the Director, Strategy & Business Creation, Nokia Ventures Organization. He is a seasoned wireless communications industry veteran, innovator, and visionary.

During his 17+ years in wireless communications, he has held product planning & development, marketing, and market/business development positions with leading wireless manufacturers including Nokia Mobile Phones, Panasonic, GoldStar, and OKI Telecom. Mr. Kikta has influenced several cellular mobile, transportable, and portable phone model designs, features, and functionality. His efforts have resulted in the first cellular payphone, first cellular PBX adjunct "Business Link," voice recognition dialers, as well as the first PCS product launch in the U.S.

Mr. Kikta possesses exceptional foresight and understanding of global market needs, both from anthropological and psychological aspects, as well as the opportunities provided by existing and future wireless communications, Internet and related technologies, and businesses.

Mr. Kikta, a graduate of Rutgers University in New Jersey, is a co-author of the books *CDMA IS-95 for Cellular and PCS: Technology, Economics & Services*; *Delivering xDSL*; *3G Cellular and PCS Demystified*; and *WAP Demystified*. He has also written several articles published in industry magazines. Mr. Kikta has been a speaker at several wireless communications and Internet conferences and events, both in the U.S. and internationally.

Richard Levine is the founder and principal engineer of Beta Scientific Laboratory and is also Adjunct Professor of Electrical Engineering at Southern Methodist University. He is active as a technology consultant to many firms developing new cellular and PCS systems and products used in Brazil, Canada, England, France, Germany, Israel, Korea, Mexico, and the United States.

Mr. Levine is a well-known teacher of cellular and PCS technology to people in the industry. He was formerly the chairman of several working groups in the North American digital cellular standards development.

Mr. Levine earned the Bachelor, Master, and Doctor of Science degrees from M.I.T., is licensed as a Professional Engineer, and has earned both amateur and professional radio operator licenses. He has been issued several patents on telecommunications, computer systems, and related technologies.

Chapter 1

Introduction to Mobile Wireless

At the beginning of 2001, more than one out of 10 people in the world (over 680 million customers) had a mobile telephone [1]. Over the past 15 years, wireless telephony end-user equipment size, weight, and costs have dropped over 20% per year. This incredible industry growth can be attributed to advancements in wireless communications technologies.

Mobile wireless technology and products have evolved through multiple generations. First generation (1G) technology was analog (many analog systems are being eliminated now). Second generation (2G) technology is digital (these systems will likely remain operational until 2010). Third generation (3G) technology integrates mobile wireless communications with services traditionally offered by wired telecommunications systems.

The use of the radio spectrum can be divided into licensed and unlicensed frequency bands. Licensed frequency bands require that the user (or service provider) apply for the right to transmit radio energy. Unlicensed frequency bands allow users (or service providers) to communicate without applying for a license. Unlicensed radio transmission must conform, however, to pre-established regulations that specify the frequency bands and amount of radio energy that can be used. Unlicensed users typically have very limited (or none at all) rights when they experience radio interference.

The ability to transmit information through the air is considered a natural resource and is, therefore, regulated by national government agencies. Frequency bands that are used by wireless communication devices are assigned by the International Telecommunications Union (ITU). The ITU is part of the United Nations. Although the ITU coordinates the general frequency assignments, it is up to the department of communication (DOC) in each country to regulate and assign the specific frequency bands to individual companies or users.

Each country has its own regulatory agency. In the United States, Federal Communications Commission (FCC) regulates the use of radio spectrum, while the Department of Communications (DOC) regulates it in Canada.

Wireless Systems

Wireless systems link customers and information services via a wireless communication path or channel. A typical wireless communications system uses mobile or fixed radios that communicate with a fixed radio tower (called a base station),which connects to the public switched telephone network (PSTN) or a data network (such as the Internet).

Traditionally, different types of wireless systems have been used for different types of services. Cellular systems provide radio coverage to a wide area, such as a city, through the use of many radio towers (25 to 500 per city). Wireless office telephone systems (WOTS) typically use 5 to 20 small radio base stations to offer radio coverage in small areas such as a school campus or hospital building. Cordless telephones (often called "residential cordless" or "home cordless") usually allow one handset to communicate with a single radio base station within a home. Wireless local area network (WLAN) systems allow computers and workstations to communicate with each other using radio signals to transfer high-speed digital information. Satellite systems provide low-speed digital voice and high-speed broadcast services to a large geographic region. Third generation wireless is considered an integration of cellular, wireless office, cordless, wireless local area network and satellite systems with the addition of advanced information services. Regardless of the type of system, wireless systems all use radio channels to communicate with wireless telephones.

Cellular and PCS/PCN

The cellular concept originated at Bell Laboratories in 1947 [2]; the first automatic cellular system started operation in Japan in 1979; and the first cellular system in the United States started in Chicago in October 1983. All mobile radio systems use cellular technology, and this includes personal communication services (PCS) and personal communications network (PCN) systems. PCS/PCN systems are names that are used to refer to cellular systems that operate at higher frequency bands.

A single cellular system interconnects many small radio coverage areas (called "cells") to serve hundreds of square miles. Radio frequencies in cellular systems are reused in distant cells, and telephone calls are automatically switched between neighboring cell sites when the wireless telephone moves out of range of the serving cell. The wireless telephone is called user equipment (UE) in 3rd generation systems, is called mobile equipment (ME) or mobile station (MS) in 2nd generation systems, and mobile radio in some first generation systems.

Neighboring cellular systems often allow customers from other cellular systems to use their service, a practice called roaming. The basic goals for cellular systems include affordability, nationwide (and possibly global) compatibility, the ability to provide efficient service to many customers, and the ability to serve many types of telephones (fixed, mobile and portable) at the same time.

The cellular concept employs a central switching office called a mobile-service switching center (MSC) to interconnect the small radio coverage areas into a larger system. To maintain a call when the cellular telephone moves to another coverage area, the cellular system switches the phone's radio channel frequency to a frequency in use at an adjacent cell site. The cellular concept also allows a frequency to be used by more than one customer (commonly called a "subscriber") at a time so that one subscriber who is using the same radio channel frequency as another subscriber will not interfere with each other because they are far enough apart.

Cellular systems take advantage of frequency reuse by breaking the coverage area into many small cells. Each cell site base station can simultaneously transmit on several different radio channel frequencies or codes. Adjacent cells use different frequencies or codes to avoid interference. Widely separated cells can reuse the same frequencies or codes without interference. This allows the system to repeatedly reuse radio channels and increase the number of subscribers it can serve. The amount of geographic radio coverage area for each cell is determined by the base station's transmitter power. Consequently, lowering power decreases the coverage area.

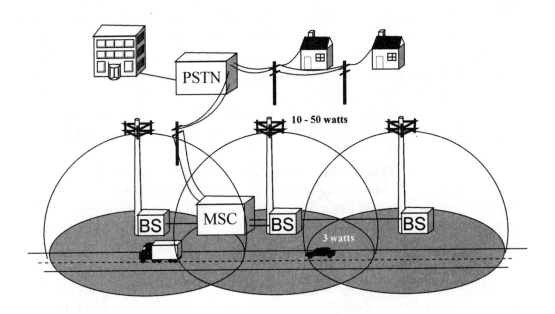

Figure 1.1. Basic Cellular System.

Figure 1.1 shows the basic parts of a cellular system. The mobile telephone has the ability to tune in to many different radio channel frequencies or codes. The base station (BS) commands the mobile telephone on which frequency to use in order to communicate with another base station from two to 15 miles away. The base station routes the radio signal to the MSC by either wire (e.g., a leased telephone line), microwave radio link, or fiber-optic line. The MSC connects the call to the public switched telephone network (PSTN), and the PSTN then connects the call to its designation (e.g., office telephone.)

Since each base station typically has several different radio frequencies or codes available for use, a single base station is able to communicate with several mobile stations at the same time. When a base station has reached its capacity or maximum number of radio channels, additional customers cannot access the cellular system through that base station. The cellular system can expand by adding more radio channels to the base station or by adding more cell sites with smaller coverage areas.

To maintain a call while a subscriber is moving throughout several cell site areas, the call is transferred between adjacent cells while the call is in progress. This call transfer is termed "handover" or "handoff." The trends in cellular systems include changing from analog (FM radio transmission) to digital technology and in providing advanced information services such as short message delivery.

Wireless Office Telephone System (WOTS)

A wireless office telephone system (WOTS) is similar to a miniature (mini) cellular system. Because there are usually a limited number of users associated with WOTS systems and small radio coverage areas, they often offer advanced features such as closed user groups (three- or four-digit dialing), internal paging and messaging, smaller handset size, and long battery life. Over the past three to four years, the trend has been to use the same type of phone for both office and cellular systems.

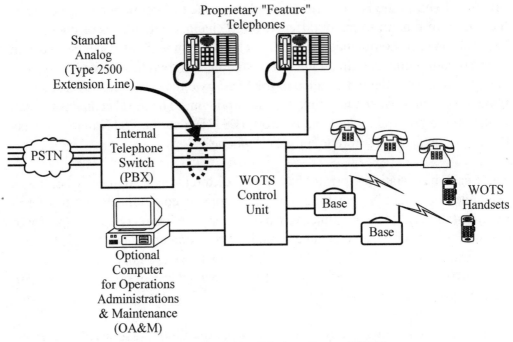

Figure 1.2. Wireless Office Telephone System (WOTS).

Figure 1.2 shows the basic parts of a wireless office telephone system. Micro base stations are located throughout a building or area to provide radio coverage. These micro base stations are connected to a switch that is similar to a miniature cellular MSC. While this switch is connected to the PSTN, interoffice calls can be directly routed to each other without connecting to the PSTN.

Residential Cordless

Residential (home) cordless telephones transmit at very low radio power to a base station that interconnects it to the public telephone network. Similar to cellular systems, residential cordless telephone technology has evolved through multiple generations. The first generation cordless telephones used a single radio frequency (RF) channel, and many 1G cordless telephones used amplitude modulation (AM). This resulted in poor voice quality. Second generation cordless

6

used multiple channels that could be independently assigned and most used analog frequency modulation (FM) technology. This greatly improved voice quality. Third generation cordless telephony systems improved by using digital radio and roaming into other public places (other home base stations). Multiple radio channel capability and digital transmission have led to some cordless phones being produced that allow customers to use the same phone in the home as in the cellular system.

Figure 1.3 shows the basic parts of a cordless telephone system. Typically, a single cordless base station located in a building or home provides a limited amount of radio coverage at a distance of up to approximately 1000 feet. These cordless base stations are connected to a standard phone line to allow for connecting to the PSTN. Most cordless telephones currently sold have the capability to retune to different radio channel frequencies. When the cordless telephone senses interference from another phone, it will automatically change to a new frequency.

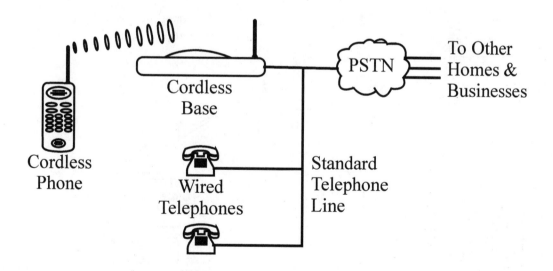

Figure 1.3. Cordless Telephone System.

Because cordless telephones typically do not have handoff capability, the call will be disconnected when the cordless phone moves far enough away from its base station.

Wireless Local Area Network (WLAN)

Wireless local area networks (WLANs) provide all the functionality of traditional wired LANs, but without the physical constraints of the wire itself. WLAN systems typically have a limited maximum geographic distance of a few hundred feet between computers. To extend the range of WLAN systems, they may be connected to other WLANs or traditional LAN systems through a bridge or gate-

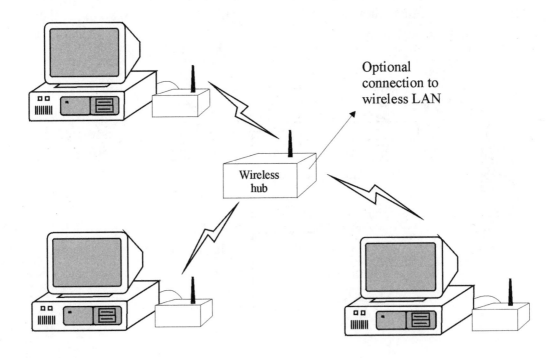

Optional connection to wireless LAN

Wireless hub

Figure 1.4. Wireless LAN System.

way network adapter. Typical data rates for WLAN systems are around 2 Mbps compared to 10 Mbps - 100 Mbps for wired LAN systems.

Figure 1.4 shows a typical wireless local area network (WLAN) system. In this diagram, several computers communicate data information with a wireless hub. The wireless hub receives, buffers, and retransmits the information to other computers. Optionally, the hub may be connected to other networks (possibly other wireless network hubs) by wires.

Satellite Systems

Satellite systems are able to provide communication services to very large geographic areas and areas that do not have access to terrestrial (land based) systems. Satellite systems have been used for many years to communicate between ships and a landline telephones. Satellites orbit in free space, where there is little or no air. In such an environment, there is little to slow the satellites down or wear them out once they are sent into orbit.

Figure 1.5 shows that satellites are usually classified by either the service type or the height of the orbit where they have been placed around the earth orbit. There are three classes of satellites in orbit today: geosynchronous earth orbit (GEO), medium earth orbit (MEO), and low earth orbit (LEO). GEO satellites are positioned high above the earth (approximately at 22,300 miles) and a single satellite can cover one third of the surface of the earth. MEO satellites are commonly positioned up to 6,000 miles above the earth, and a single one can cover several thousand miles. LEO systems are located at approximately 500--1,000 miles above the earth, and a single one can cover a thousand miles.

There are three basic types of satellite telecommunications services: broadcast (e.g., satellite television), very small aperture satellite terminal (VSAT), and mobile satellite service (MSS). GEO satellites are the only type of satellite that appears stationary (fixed in location) to receivers on earth compared to MEO and

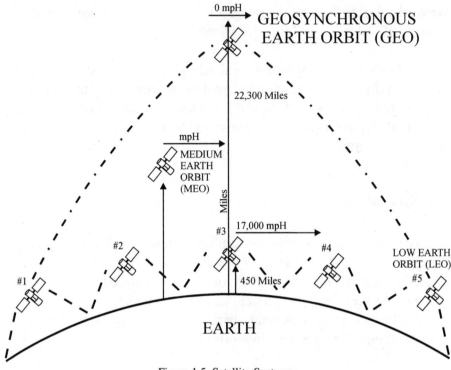

Figure 1.5. Satellite Systems.

LEO satellites, which regularly move across the horizon. There are three key portions to satellite systems: satellite section, ground section, and end-user equipment.

Until recent times, mobile satellite telephones have been relatively large (briefcase size) and expensive. Due to the long distance to reach GEO satellites, mobile satellite phones had to use high-power amplifiers and large directional antennas. With the introduction of LEO and MEO systems, it is now possible to use handheld portable satellite telephones.

Some mobile telephones have dual mode satellite and terrestrial cellular service capability. This allows mobile telephones to use a low-cost cellular system for service if it is available. If the cellular system is not available or costs more than satellite access, the mobile telephone will access the satellite system.

First Generation Cellular

First generation analog cellular systems were actually a hybrid of analog voice channels and digital control channels. The analog voice channels typically used FM and the digital control channels used simple frequency shift keying (FSK) modulation. The first commercial analog cellular systems include Nippon Telephone and Telegraph (NTT) cellular, Advanced Mobile Phone Service (AMPS), Total Access Communications System (TACS), and Nordic Mobile Telephone (NMT). Dozens of other analog systems use similar technologies to these systems.

Analog cellular systems can send digital messages and provide advanced services such as short messaging. However, these messaging services are usually limited to very slow data rates, and new features generally require hardware changes to both the mobile telephones and cellular networks.

The limited digital signaling rates and the transmission of complex analog voice signals limit the ability of analog systems to offer advanced authentication techniques and voice encryption services. Most 1G analog phones only have processing capability of about 500,000 instructions per second. Compare this to the processing power of 2G digital phones of 10 million to 40 million instructions per second (MIPS) and one will see why it is not possible for 1G phones to use advanced security procedures or voice scrambling (encryption).

Second Generation Cellular and PCS/PCN

Second generation digital systems use digital radio channels for both voice (digital voice) and digital control channels. 2G digital systems typically use more efficient modulation technologies, including global system for mobile communications (GSM), IS-95 code division multiple access (CDMA), and IS-136 time division multiple access (TDMA).

Digital radio channels offer a universal data transmission system, which can be divided into many logical channels that can perform different services. Some of these logical channels are used for control purposes and some channels for voice and data transmission.

Second generation systems use multiple access technologies to allow more customers to share individual radio channels or use narrow channels to allow more radio channels into a limited amount of radio spectrum band. There are three basic types of access technologies used in 2G systems: frequency division multiple access (FDMA), time division multiple access (TDMA), and code division multiple access (CDMA). These technologies either reduce the RF channel bandwidth (FDMA), share a radio channel by assigning users to brief time slots, or divide a wide RF channel into many different coded channels.

Because digital systems use a common data communication channel, this allows advanced features to be added more easily. New features such as short messaging service and web browsing (microbrowsers) can often be added by simple software changes to the system or the wireless telephone. When the software of the wireless telephone requires updating, some of the software feature upgrades can be directly transmitted to the wireless telephone without involving the customer.

All 2G systems have improved authentication and voice privacy capability. This has dramatically reduced fraudulent use of mobile telephones and reduced the incidents of media exploitation of unauthorized recording of private conversations. The advanced digital signal processing of digital mobile radios can easily process the authentication (identity validation) and encryption codes necessary to ensure that authorized customers are using the service and other people cannot listen to conversations.

Enhanced 2nd Generation Digital Cellular and PCS/PCN (2.5G)

2.5G (also called "two and a half G") is a term that is commonly used to describe enhancements to 2nd generation cellular and PCS/PCN technologies that provide significantly new and improved capabilities but don't quite satisfy 3rd generation wireless requirements. The 2.5G systems use improved digital radio technology to increase their data transmission rates and new packet-based technology to increase the system efficiency for data users. Some of these needs included high-speed data transmission service, efficient packet data transmission, and more efficient radio channel capacity through the use of new modulation technology.

High-Speed Circuit-Switched Data (HSCSD)

High-speed circuit-switched data (HSCSD) was developed to overcome the limited maximum user data transfer rate of 9.6 kbps in the original GSM system. Higher data transfer speeds are achieved by combining more than one traffic channel (TCH/F) for data services. The maximum HSCSD data transfer rate on the GSM system is 64 kbps but it is possible to increase this by a factor of 2--4 through the added use of GSM data compression technology (using the V.42 bis GSM algorithm).

The HSCSD network primarily involves an upgrade to network software and the addition of gateways that allow connection to data networks (such as the Internet). The required upgrades include enhancements to the mobile telephone's software, base station controller (BSC) software, and an interworking function (IWF) between the MSC and the data network (e.g., the Internet).

Figure 1.6 shows how GSM can provide HSCSD service. This diagram shows that asynchronous operation is permitted where there can be a higher data trans-

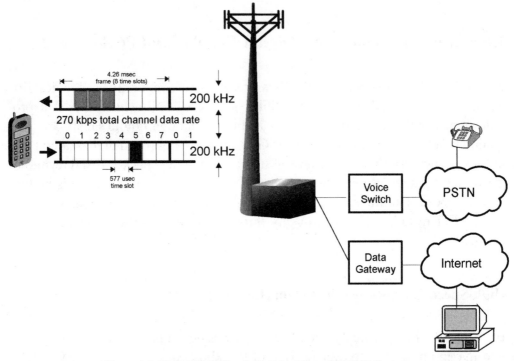

Figure 1.6. High-Speed Circuit-Switched Data (HSCSD) System.

fer rate in one direction (typically in the downlink when the user is downloading files or images from the Internet) than the other direction. This diagram also shows that this mobile telephone must have an available time slot to measure other channels for handoff.

General Packet Radio Service (GPRS)

General packet radio service provides high-speed packet data service on a GSM network. The GPRS system dynamically assigns time slots on GSM radio channels to allow quick and efficient transfer small packets of data. GPRS allows point-to-point and point-to-multipoint packet data transmission. GPRS provides a maximum data transmission capacity of 171.2 kbps.

To provide GPRS service, additional equipment is added to the GSM network. Figure 1.7 shows some of the key GPRS network elements that include a gateway GPRS support node (GGSN), a serving GPRS support node (SGSN), and a GPRS backbone network. The SGSN uses a process similar to that of a MSC and a VLR (visited location register), except the SGSN performs packet switching instead of circuit switching. The SGSN registers and maintains a list of active packet data radios in its network and coordinates the packet transfer between the mobile radios. The GGSN is a packet-switching system that is used to connect a GSM mobile communication network (GPRS support nodes) to other packet networks such as the Internet.

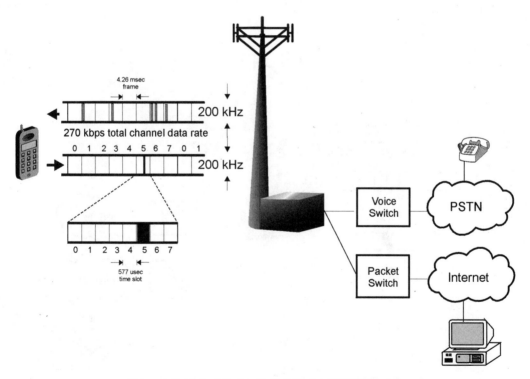

Figure 1.7. General Packet Radio Service (GPRS) System.

Enhanced Data Rates for Global Evolution (EDGE)

The enhanced data rates for global evolution (EDGE) system is an evolved version of the global system for mobile (GSM) radio channel that uses new phase modulation and packet transmission to provide for advanced high-speed data services. The EDGE system uses 8-level phase shift keying (8PSK) to allow one symbol change to represent 3 bits of information. This is three times the amount of information that is transferred by a standard 2-level GMSK signal used by the first generation of GSM system. This results in a radio-channel data-transmission rate of 604.8 kbps and a net maximum delivered data transmission rate of approximately 474 kbps. The advanced packet transmission control system allows for constantly varying data transmission rates in either direction between mobile radios.

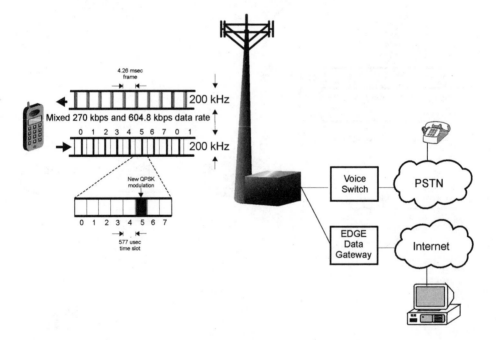

Figure 1.8. Enhanced Data rates for Global Evolution (EDGE) System.

Figure 1.8 shows an EDGE system. This diagram shows that a standard GSM radio channel is modified to use a new, more efficient modulation technology. The quadrature phase shift keying (QPSK) modulation using EDGE modulation can be inserted on a slot-by-slot basis on the GSM channel. EDGE systems can be mixed with existing GSM systems because standard GSM mobile telephones will ignore the EDGE modulated time slots that they cannot demodulate and decode.

EDGE compact is a version of EDGE that allows the close packing of GSM radio channel frequencies to allow an overlay of GSM technology into other systems (such as IS-136 TDMA) with a minimum loss of existing channel frequencies. Because EDGE compact reuses frequencies in nearby cells, the average interference level for each time slot is higher. Although it is acceptable to discard data packets that experience high levels of interference, discarding packets that contain control messages (such as handoff or packet-data paging messages) is unacceptable. To help ensure that most control messages reach their destination, EDGE compact inhibits the transmission of messages on the same frequency and time slot in nearby cell sites. As customers are converted from the other system (e.g., IS-136 TDMA) and radio channels become lightly loaded, more of those radio channels can be removed and additional EDGE channels can be added. This allows the gradual conversion from one technology to compatible GSM/EDGE technology.

Third Generation Requirements

In the early 1990s, the success of 2G digital cellular and PCS/PCN systems (dramatic growth in the number of customers) led to demand for new features and more efficient services. It became apparent that robust high-capacity and lower-cost wireless systems were needed to better service customers that 2nd generation systems could not easily provide. To satisfy these needs, a new 3rd generation wireless system was needed.

The 3rd generation system is called universal mobile telecommunications system (UMTS). In 1992, the world administrative radio conference (WARC) defined the frequency bands that would be used for 3rd generation systems. The ITU then defined new requirements for the 3rd generation systems. The original requirements for the 3rd generation system were defined in the international mobile telecommunications 2000 (IMT-2000) system. IMT-2000 key requirements included high-speed (broadband) data services, multimedia support (simultaneous voice and data), improved system efficiency (cost reduction), and backward compatibility with 2nd generation systems.

Figure 1.9 shows the different frequency bands that have been identified for UMTS use. It is likely that additional frequency bands will be added in the future to allow increased competition and cost-effective system capacity expansion. Some countries already use frequency bands that have been designated as UMTS. These include part of the personal communication service (PCS) systems in the United States. These bands may be converted to UMTS systems.

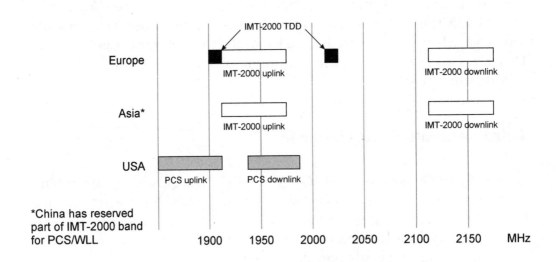

Figure 1.9. Universal Mobile Telecommunications System (UMTS) Frequency Bands.

The creation of the UMTS system required the participation of many companies. Because the system specifications are global standards, the development of this system was performed with the cooperation of the leading standards committees of most countries. To help coordinate this process, a global committee was created called the Third Generation Partnership Program (3GPP). Some of the key standard groups that are part of the 3GPP include European Telecommunications Standards Institute (ETSI); Research Institute of Telecommunications Transmission (RITT), China; Association of Radio Industry and Business (ARIB), Japan; Telecommunications Technologies Association (TTA), Korea; Telecommunications Industry Association (TIA), United States.

The basic structure of the UMTS system provides high capacity communication service (up to 2 Mbps) for in-building users. As subscribers move into urban areas (pedestrian), they have access to medium capacity services (up to 384 kbps). Capacity is moderate (up to 144 kbps) in wide area mobile services. And finally, in large geographic area systems (satellite), the data rates are variable.

Multimedia Services

Multimedia is a term that is used to describe the delivery of different types of information such as voice, data, and video. Communication systems may deliver media services separately or simultaneously. Second generation systems were primarily limited to low-speed single channel (nonsimultaneous) communication. Third generation systems can provide simultaneous channels with data rates up to 2 Mbps, and each of them can have a different quality of service (QoS) capability. For example, a 3G handset can be participating in a video conference call while downloading an email file from the Internet. The real time video clip requires a high-speed data transfer rate that needs to be real time but can tolerate errors, while the email file download can tolerate large delays but errors are not acceptable.

Multisystem Compatibility

The multisystem compatibility of 3rd generation systems allows customers to roam globally (different frequency bands) and be able to hand off to 2nd generation systems (backward compatibility). It is possible for existing 2nd generation service providers to upgrade their systems to 3rd generation technology and to connect 2nd and 3rd generation systems together.

Increased System Efficiency

Third generation systems must be more cost effective than 2nd generation systems. All of the advancements in technology and services have little chance of achieving market success if the cost of 3G basic telecommunications services is higher than that of 2nd generation systems. Third generation systems use the available radio spectrum more efficiently, and the implementation offers cost savings through the reduction of cell sites and equipment and simplified operational service support.

Most wireless service providers continually add new customers. As the number of subscribers increases, more communication channels will be needed. If the service provider's cell sites are not filled to capacity with radio (RF) channels, (approximately 5--10 wide radio channels per site), the wireless service provider simply adds more radio channels. If cell sites are filled with radio channels, more cell sites must be added to accommodate the increased capacity. Either way, to expand the system capacity, wireless service providers must add communication channels.

Second and third generation digital cellular technologies allow for capacity increases by allowing more subscribers to share the same radio channel spectrum. The intensified use of radio spectrum is accomplished by allowing more subscribers to share the same radio channel. To simultaneously serve multiple subscribers on the same radio channel, new technologies assign either specific time slots or unique codes to each call. These techniques reduce the amount of radio spectrum needed and allow more subscribers to use a wireless service provider's radio coverage area. In this way, 3rd generation UMTS reduces the average system equipment cost per customer.

Wireless service providers can evaluate the potential system capacity factors of the new cellular technologies by reviewing two types of efficiency: radio channel and infrastructure . Radio channel, or spectral, efficiency is measured by the number of conversations (voice paths) that can be assigned per frequency bandwidth. Geographic spectral efficiency can be defined by measuring the number of conversations per frequency bandwidth per unit of service area. Infrastructure efficiency is measured by the wireless system equipment and operating costs, calculated on a per-subscriber basis, or per available channel per unit of service area.

Figure 1.10 illustrates how wireless systems allow many users to share a single cell site. The number of subscribers who can share a cell site is much greater than the number of available radio channels but, because not everyone places calls at exactly the same time (except during traffic jams), many users can share a single radio channel. For analog systems that can allow only one conversation per radio channel, a typical analog system may add 20--32 customers to the system for each available voice/radio channel. If an analog cell site has 50 radio channels installed, this has enough capacity to serve about 1000 customers. Second generation digital technologies can multiply this number by 3--20 times. A single 2nd generation cell site can serve approximately 3,000 to 20,000 customers. Third generation UMTS systems increase the overall efficiency by 2--4 times compared to 2nd generation systems. This means if a 2nd generation cell site is completely converted to UMTS channels, that cell site can serve approximately 6,000 to 80,000 customers.

The original viewpoint of the ITU for IMT-2000 (International Mobile Telephony) in 1986 was to develop a completely new system for UMTS. In 1996, this viewpoint changed to allow the existing networks developed to integrate with UMTS systems. This is very important as it allows existing wireless operators to cost-effectively upgrade their systems and network equipment man-

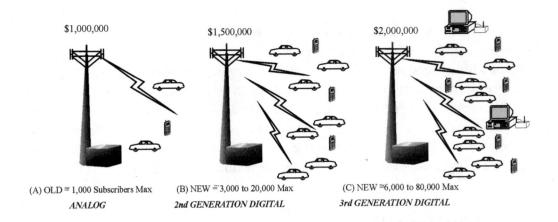

$1,000,000 $1,500,000 $2,000,000

(A) OLD ≅ 1,000 Subscribers Max   (B) NEW ≅ 3,000 to 20,000 Max   (C) NEW ≅6,000 to 80,000 Max

ANALOG   *2nd GENERATION DIGITAL*   *3rd GENERATION DIGITAL*

Figure 1.10. Serving More Users.

ufacturers to offer existing field-proven network equipment to new operators without having to invest billions of dollars into research and new product development.

Figure 1.11 shows how a 3rd generation wireless system integrates several types of services. This system interconnects cellular, wireless office, cordless telephone, wireless LAN, and satellite systems through the use of flexible radio communication technology and an underlying advanced intelligent network (AIN).

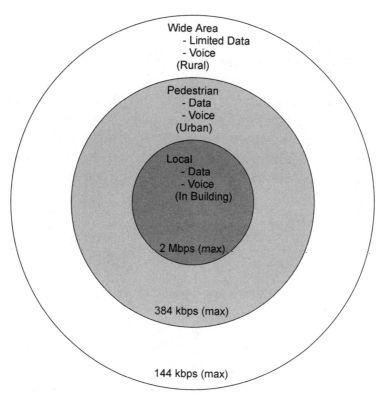

Figure 1.11. 3rd Generation Wireless System.

Third Generation Wireless Systems

Third generation wireless systems combine cellular, wireless office telephone systems, cordless telephone systems, and advanced intelligent features into one portable device. In 2001, there were three different system specifications for 3rd generation wireless systems: wideband code division multiple access (WCDMA), time division CDMA (TD/CDMA), and CDMA2000.

Wideband Code Division Multiple Access (WCDMA)

The WCDMA system uses a wide RF channel, efficient coding, and multiple channels to provide for both low-speed circuit and high-speed packet services. The WCDMA system uses direct sequence code division multiple access (DS-CDMA) technology, efficient QPSK modulation, paired frequency division duplex (FDD) RF channels, and variable bandwidth control.

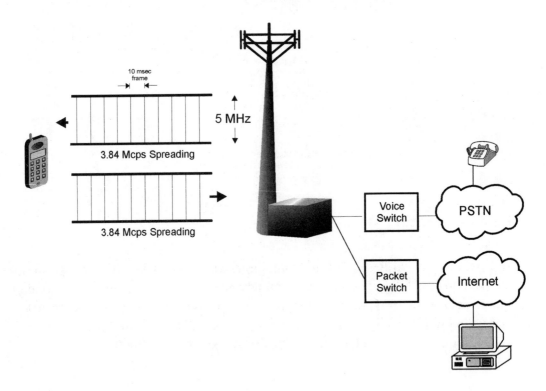

Figure 1.12. Wideband Code Division Multiple Access (WCDMA) System.

Figure 1.12 shows a WCDMA system. This diagram shows the WCDMA system has paired 5 MHz channels (FDD). Multiple physical channels can coexist in the same frequency band by using different spreading codes (4--256). The spreading code is used to create several chips per bit of information. These codes are chosen to be orthogonal (noninterfering) with each other. The code chip rate is 3.84 Mcps, and each coded channel is divided into frames of 10 msec each. The WCDMA system can dynamically change its spreading codes to provide bandwidth on demand (BoD) services.

Time Division Duplex/Code Division Multiple Access (TD/CDMA)

TDD is a process of allowing two way communications between two devices by timesharing. The TD/CDMA system uses time division duplex (TDD) technology to overcome the requirement of paired frequencies that the WCDMA system has. In some countries, paired frequencies are not available. When using TDD, one device transmits (device 1), then the other device listens (device 2) for a short period of time. After the transmission is complete, the devices reverse their roles, so device 1 becomes a receiver and device 2 becomes a transmitter. The process continually repeats itself, so data appears to flow in both directions simultaneously.

The TD/CDMA system uses the same DS-CDMA channel-coding technology to maintain compatibility with the WCDMA system. It is anticipated that TD/CDMA systems will be used for indoor environments and WCDMA systems will be used for wide area mobile operation.

Figure 1.13 shows a TD/CDMA system. This diagram shows the TD/CDMA system divides the 5 MHz radio channel into short 666 msec time slots. Fifteen of these time slots are grouped together to form 10 msec frames. Each time slot can be transmitted in either direction between the mobile telephone and node B. The assignment of time slots can be asymmetrical so that high data rates can occur in one direction (e.g., for high-speed file downloads)

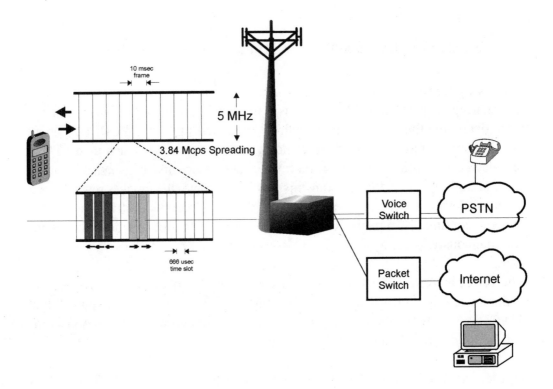

Figure 1.13. TD/CDMA System.

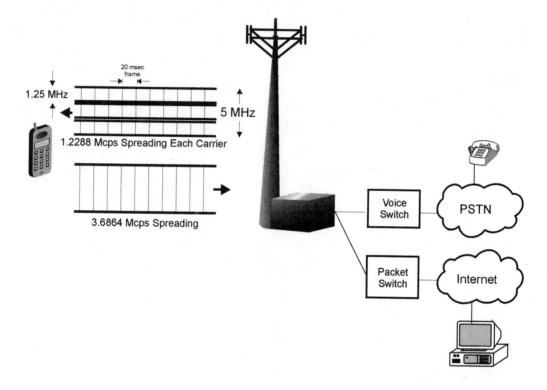

Figure 1.14. CDMA2000 System.

Code Division Multiple Access 2000 (CDMA2000)

Code division multiple access 2000 (CDMA2000) is an evolved version of the 2nd generation IS-95 code division multiple access (CDMA) system. The CDMA2000 system combines multiple IS-95 radio channels (called multi-carrier transmission) with enhanced packet transmission protocols to provide for advanced high-speed data services.

Figure 1.14 shows how the CDMA2000 system uses multiples of the standard IS-95 radio channels. These multiples are 3, 6, 9, or 12 times the standard 1.25

MHz wide bandwidth. To upgrade 2nd generation IS-95 systems to 3rd generation capability, IS-95 radio channels in the base station can be enhanced with new protocols, and new 3rd generation mobile telephones are required.

References:

1. GSM MoU, www.GSMWorld.com, February 22, 2001.
2. Bell Systems Technical Journal, Vol. 58, No. 1, American Telephone and Telegraph Company, Murray Hill, NJ, January 1979.

Chapter 2

First Generation Analog Cellular

The first generation of cellular systems used analog radio technology. Analog cellular systems consist of three basic elements: a mobile telephone (mobile radio), cell sites, and a mobile switching center (MSC). Figure 2.1 shows a basic cellular system in which a geographic service area such as a city is divided into smaller radio coverage area cells. A mobile telephone communicates by radio signals to the cell site within a radio coverage area. The cell site's base station (BS) converts these radio signals for transfer to the MSC via wired (landline) or wireless (microwave) communications links. The MSC routes the call to another mobile telephone in the system or the appropriate landline facility. These three elements are integrated to form a ubiquitous coverage radio system that can connect to the public switched telephone network (PSTN).

History

Nippon Telephone and Telegraph (NTT) in Tokyo started the first commercial analog cellular system on December, 1979 [1]. In 1981, the commercial Nordic Mobile Telephone (NMT) system was started in the Nordic countries [2]. Although there was an Advanced Mobile Phone Service (AMPS) test system operating in 1979, the first commercial AMPS system was not introduced in the United States until 1983. By 1985, a commercial TACS system began in the

Base Station

Radio Coverage Area

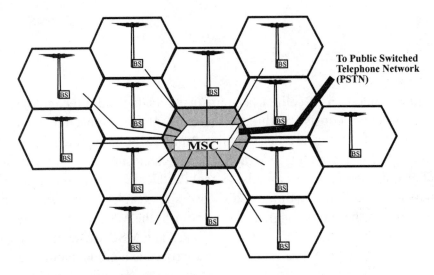

Figure 2.1. Basic Cellular System.

United Kingdom [3]. Since their introduction, these first generation analog cellular technologies have evolved to provide higher system capacity and advanced features.

Mobile Telephone

A mobile telephone (commonly called a mobile station) contains a radio transceiver, user interface, and antenna assembly (see Figure 2.2) in one physical package. The radio transceiver converts audio to radio frequency (RF) signals and RF signals into audio. A user interface provides the display and keypad that allow the subscriber to communicate commands to the transceiver. The antenna assembly couples RF energy between the electronics within the mobile telephone and the outside "air" for transmission and reception.

Analog mobile cellular telephones have many industry names. These names sometimes vary by the type of cellular radio. Handheld cellular radios are often referred to as "portables." Cellular radios that are installed in cars are typically called "mobiles." Cellular radios mounted in bags are often called "bag phones." In most cases, these three types and sizes also correspond to three distinct maximum power levels: 600 milliwatts, 1.6 watts, and 3 watts, or classes I, II, and III.

To make each mobile telephone unique, several types of information are stored into its internal memory. This internal memory is called a number assignment

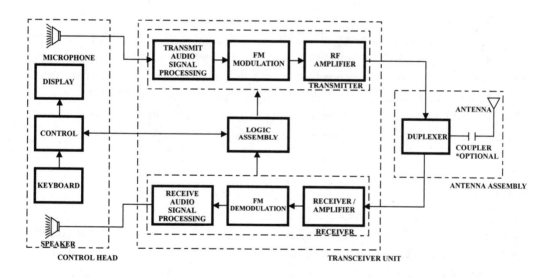

Figure 2.2. Mobile Telephone Block Diagram.

module (NAM). The NAM contains the mobile identification number (MIN), which is the telephone number, home system identifier, access classification, and other customer features. The internal memory, which stores the telephone number and system features, can be modified by either changing a chip stored inside the mobile telephone or programming the phone number into memory through special keypad instructions.

Each mobile telephone also contains a unique electronic serial number (ESN), which is not supposed to be changed. If the ESN could be easily changed, it would be possible to duplicate another mobile telephone's identification (called cloning) to make fraudulent calls. Because duplication of mobile telephone numbers and ESNs is technically possible, advanced authentication programs that validate prestored information have been created to provide a more reliable unique identification system.

Initially, information stored in a NAM was programmed into a standard programmable read only memory (PROM) chip. Because of the cost of the chips and because special programming devices were required, manufacturers now make the NAM information programmable via the handset keypad. The information is stored internally in an electrically alterable PROM (EPROM). This is also referred to as a nonvolatile memory, since the information contents stay intact even if power is not available, such as when a battery is replaced.

Cell Site

A cell site is the link between the mobile telephone and the cellular mobile switching center (MSC). A cell site consists of a base station (BS), transmission tower, and antenna assembly. The base station is the radio portion of the cell site that converts radio signals to electrical signals for transfer to and from a switching center.

A base station contains amplifiers, radio transceivers, RF combiners, control sections, communications links, a scanning receiver, backup power supplies, and an

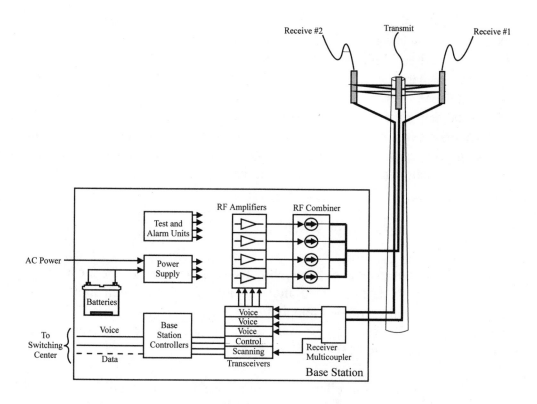

Figure 2.3. Cell Site and Base Station Block Diagram.

antenna assembly (see Figure 2.3). The transceiver sections are similar to the mobile telephone transceiver as they convert audio to RF signals and RF to audio signals. The transmitter output side of these radio transceivers is supplied to a high-power RF amplifier (typically 10 to 50 watts). The RF combiner allows separate radio channels to be combined onto one or several antenna assemblies without interfering with each other. This combined RF signal is routed to the transmitter antenna on top of the radio tower via low-energy-loss coaxial cable.

Cell sites typically have two receiver antennas to allow for selection of the strongest radio signal (minimizing radio signal fading). Receiver antennas are connected to the RF multicoupler via low-loss coaxial cable that splits the received signals to multiple transceivers. The receiver portion of the transceiver converts the RF signal to an audio signal that is routed to the communication links. Communication links route audio and control information between the base station and an MSC. A scanning receiver measures the signal strength on any of the cellular channel frequencies. The scanning receiver is used to monitor the signal level of mobile phones in adjacent cell sites. This signal level information helps to determine if a call transfer to this cell site is a good choice. The backup power supply maintains radio equipment and cooling system operation when primary power is interrupted. Many sections of the base station are duplicated to maintain functioning if equipment fails.

Mobile Switching Center (MSC)

The MSC is the control center of the cellular system. It monitors the location and call quality of mobile telephones, and it switches calls between mobile telephones and the public switched telephone network (PSTN). The MSC is sometimes called by different names, such as mobile telephone switching office (MTSO) or mobile telephone exchange (MTX).

The MSC consists of controllers, switching assembly, communications links, operator terminal, subscriber database, and backup energy sources (see Figure 2.4). The controllers, each of which are powerful computers, are the brains of the entire cellular system, guiding the MSC through the creation and interpretation of commands to and from the base stations. In addition to the main controller, secondary controllers devoted specifically to control of the cell sites (base stations) and to handling the signaling messages between the MSC and the PTSN. A switching assembly routes voice connections from the cell sites to each other or to the public telephone network. Communications links between cell sites and the MSC may be copper wire, microwave, or fiber optic. An operator terminal allows operations, administration, and maintenance of the system. A subscriber database contains features the customer has requested, along with billing records. Backup energy sources provide power when primary power is inter-

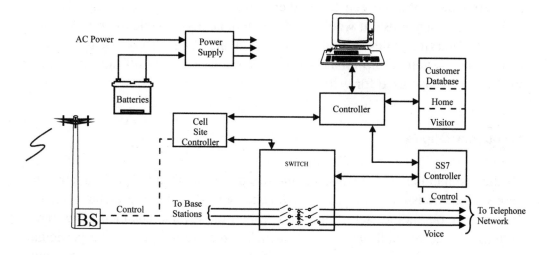

Figure 2.4. Cellular Mobile Switching Center.

rupted. As with the base station, the MSC has many standby duplicate circuits and backup power sources to allow system operation to be maintained when a failure occurs.

System Overview

The cellular system provides telephone service to many customers through duplex radio channels, frequency reuse, cost-effective capacity expansion, and coordinated system control. To conserve the limited amount of radio spectrum, cellular systems reuse the same channels many times within a geographic coverage area. The technique, called frequency reuse, makes it possible to expand system capacity by increasing the number of channels that are effectively available for subscribers. As the subscriber moves through the system, the MSC centrally transfers calls from one cell to another and maintains call continuity. In fact, without frequency reuse, it would not be economically feasible to provide cellular or PCS service, unless all other radio frequency bands (broadcasting, emergency radio systems, ship-to-shore, military, etc.) were shut off and their spectrum capacity also used for cellular/PCS.

Frequency Duplex

To allow simultaneous transmission and reception (no need for push to talk), the base stations transmit on one set of radio channels, called forward channels, and they receive on another set of channels, called the reverse channels. The transmitter and receiver radio channel frequencies that are assigned for a particular cell are separated by a fixed amount of frequency bandwidth. Figure 2.5 shows a system of radio channels that are separated by 45 MHz. Figure 2.5 displays a

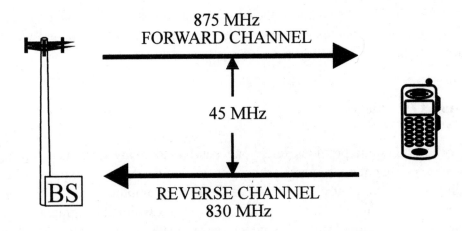

Figure 2.5. Duplex Radio Channel Spacing.

base station transmitting to the mobile telephone at 875 MHz on the forward channel. The mobile telephone then transmits to the base station at 830 MHz on the reverse channel.

Frequency Reuse

In early mobile radio systems, one high-power transmitter served a large geographic area. Because each radio channel requires a certain bandwidth, the resulting limited number of radio channels kept the serving capacity of such sys-

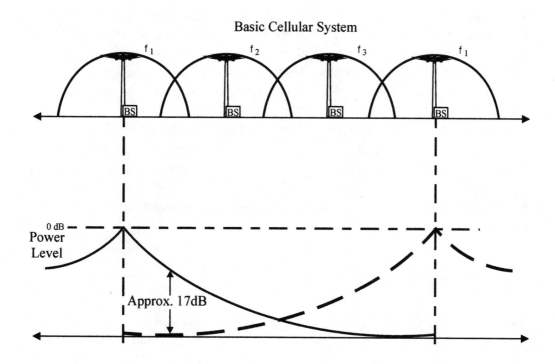

Figure 2.6. Frequency Reuse

tems low. The customer demand for the few available channels was very high. For example, in 1976, New York City had only 12 radio channels to support 545 subscribers (not all customers use a radio channel at the same time) and a two-year long waiting list of typically 3,700 [4].

To increase the number of radio channels in where the frequency spectrum allocation is limited, cellular providers must reuse frequencies. Because the radio channel signal strength decreases exponentially with distance, subscribers who are far enough apart can use the same radio channel frequency without interference (see Figure 2.6).

To minimize interference in this way, cellular system planners position the cell sites that use the same radio channel frequency far away from each other. The distances between sites are initially planned by general RF propagation rules, but it is difficult to account for enough propagation factors to precisely position the towers, so the cell site position and power levels are usually adjusted later.

The acceptable distance between cell sites that use the same channel frequencies are determined by the distance to radius (D/R) ratio. The D/R ratio is the ratio of the distance (D) between cells using the same radio frequency to the radius (R) of the cells. In analog systems, a typical D/R ratio is 4.6: a channel used in a cell with a 1 mile radius would not interfere with the same channel being reused at a cell 4.6 miles away.

Capacity Expansion

As cellular systems mature, they must serve more subscribers, by either adding more radio channels in a cell or adding new cells. To add radio channels, cellular systems use several techniques in addition to strategically locating cell sites that use the same frequencies. Directional antennas and underlay/overlay transmit patterns improve signal quality by focusing radio signals into one area and reducing the interference to other areas. The reduced interference allows more

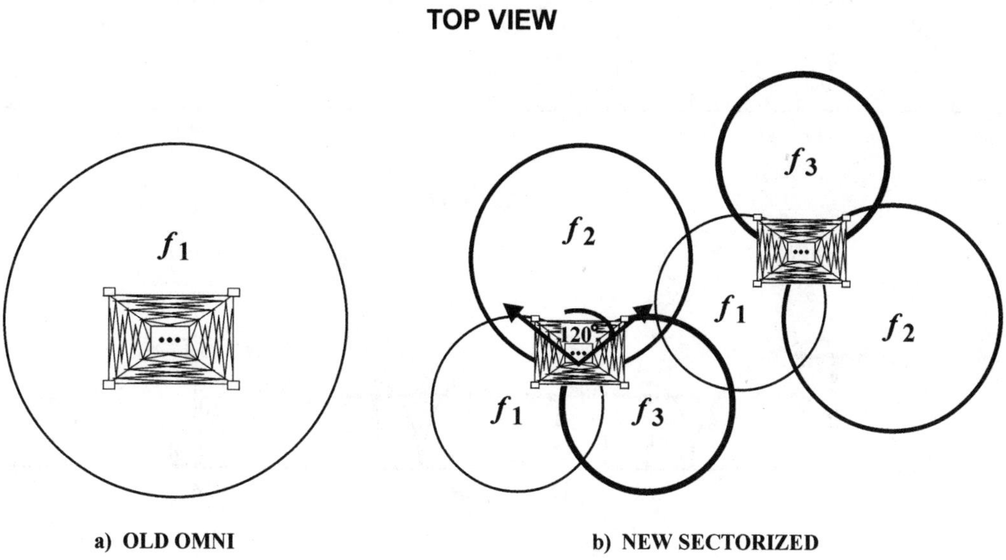

TOP VIEW

Figure 2.7. Cell Site Sectorization.

frequency reuse. Directional antennas can be used to sector a cell in to wedges so that only a portion of the cell area (e.g., 1/3, or 120 degrees) is used for a single radio channel. Such sectoring reduces interference with the other cells in the area. Figure 2.7 shows cells that are sectored into three 120-degree sectors.

Another technique, called cell splitting, helps to expand capacity gradually. The radio coverage area of a cell site is split by adjusting the power level and/or using reduced antenna height to cover a reduced area (see Figure 2.8). Reducing the radio coverage area of a cell site by changing the RF boundaries of a cell site has the same effect as placing cells farther apart, and allows new cell sites to be added. However, the boundaries of a cell site vary with the terrain and land con-

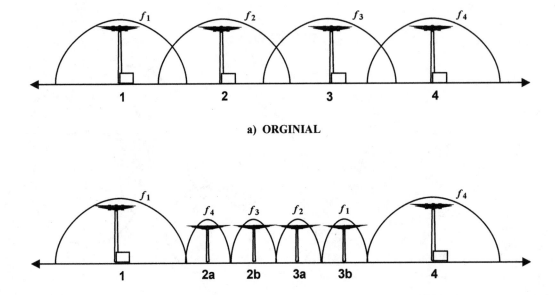

Figure 2.8. Cell Splitting.

ditions, especially with seasonal variations in foliage. Coverage areas actually increase in fall and winter as the leaves fall from the trees.

Current analog systems serve only one subscriber at a time on a radio channel, so the system's serving capacity is influenced by the number of available radio channels. However, a typical subscriber uses the system for only a few minutes a day so that, on a daily basis, many subscribers share a single channel. Typically, 20--32 subscribers share each radio channel [5], depending upon the average talk time per hour per subscriber. Generally, a cell site that has 50 installed radio channels can support 1000--1600 subscribers.

When a cellular system is first established, it can effectively serve only a limited number of callers. When that limit is exceeded, callers experience too many system busy signals (known as blocking) and their calls cannot be completed. More callers can be served by adding more cells with smaller coverage areas-- that is, by cell splitting. The increased number of smaller cells provides more available radio channels in a given area because it allows radio channels to be reused at closer geographical distances.

System planning must also account for present and future coverage requirements. After a cellular service provider is granted a license, it typically has only a few years to provide coverage to almost all of its licensed territory [6]. To accomplish this, and to ensure that the system will be efficient and competitive, cellular carriers must plan and design the system in advance.

Radio Interference

Radio interference limits the number of radio channels that can be used in a single cell site and how close nearby cell sites that use the same frequency can be located. The main types of interference are co-channel, adjacent channel, and alternate channel interference.

Co-channel Interference

Co-channel interference occurs when two nearby cellular radios operating on the same radio channel interfere with each other. Co-channel interference at a particular location can be measured by comparing the received radio signal power (signal strength) from the desired signal, to the signal strength of the interfering signal. Today's analog systems are designed to assure that interfering signal strength remains approximately less than 2% of desired signal strength. At this level, the desired signal is nearly undistorted.

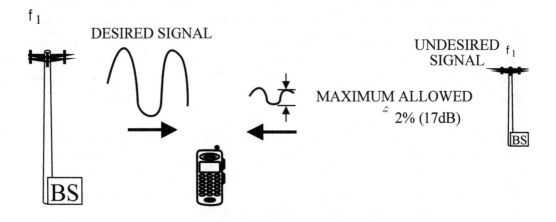

Figure 2.9. Co-Channel Interference.

To minimize interference, cellular carriers frequently monitor the received signal strength by regularly driving test equipment throughout the system. This testing determines whether the combined interference from cells using the same channel exceeds the 2% level of the desired channel (which is 17 dB below the desired signal). This information is used to determine whether radio channels and/or power levels at each cell need to be changed. Figure 2.9 shows how co-channel interference occurs.

Using a radio technology that provides a higher tolerance to co-channel interference (i.e., exceeding 2% with no distortion) would allow system operators to reuse the same frequencies more often, thus increasing the system capacity. This higher tolerance is an advantage of next-generation digital cellular technologies.

Adjacent Channel Interference

Adjacent channel interference occurs when one radio channel interferes with a channel next to it (e.g., channel 412 interferes with 413). Each radio channel has a limited amount of bandwidth (10 kHz to 30 kHz), but some radio energy is transmitted at low levels outside this band. A cellular radio operating at full power can produce enough low-level radio energy outside the channel bandwidth to interfere with cellular radios operating on adjacent channels. Because of alternate channel interference, radio channels cannot be spaced adjacent to each other in a single cell site (e.g., channels 115 and 116). A channel separation of three channels is typically sufficient to protect most radio channels from adjacent channel interference. However, for frequency planning reasons (discussed in Chapter 9), the radio channel frequencies at each cell site are selected so they are typically separated by 21 channels from other radio channels in that base station or sector. Figure 2.10 displays adjacent channel interference.

Alternate Channel Interference

Alternate channel interference occurs when radio energy from a transmitter frequency that is located two radio channel bandwidths away interferes with the desired signal.

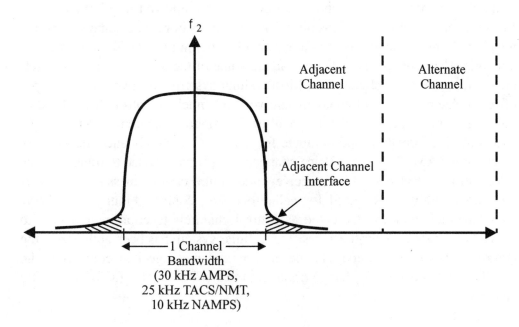

Figure 2.10. Adjacent Channel Interference.

Interleaved Radio Channels

Because a majority of the radio energy is in the center of the band, some cellular systems allow radio channels to be interleaved (offset) at fi channel bandwidth (e.g., 12.5 kHz offset in a 25 kHz channel) to allow radio channel spacing to be as close as possible. Since a goal of the cellular system is to reuse as many radio channel frequencies as possible, placing more radio channels in each cell site increases the capacity of the cellular system. By careful frequency planning, the use of interleaved radio channels can increase system capacity by more than 100% [7].

Basic Cellular Operation

In early mobile radio systems, a mobile telephone scanned the limited number of available channels until it found an unused one that allowed it to initiate a call. Because analog cellular systems often have hundreds of radio channels, a mobile telephone cannot scan them all in a reasonable amount of time. To quickly direct a mobile telephone to an available channel, some of the available radio channels are dedicated as control channels. Most cellular systems use two different types of radio channels: control channels and voice channels. Control channels carry only digital messages and signals that allow the mobile telephone to retrieve system control information and compete for access. Control channels never carry voice (in the AMPS system). Voice channels are primarily used to transfer voice information, but also send and receive some digital control messages, and certain super-audible tones used for call processing control. Figure 2.11 shows some channels that are dedicated as control channels to coordinate access to the cellular system. After the access to a cellular system has been authorized, the control channel sends out a channel assignment message that commands the mobile telephone to tune (change frequency) to a voice channel (a different radio channel).

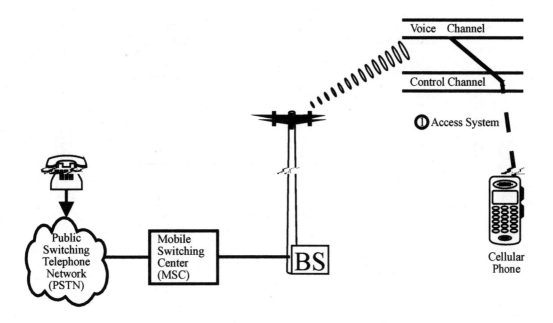

Figure 2.11. Control Channels and Voice Channels.

When a mobile telephone is first powered on, it initializes itself by scanning a predetermined set of control channels and then tuning to the strongest one. Figure 2.12 shows that during this initialization mode, it retrieves system identification and setup information.

After the mobile telephone initializes, it enters the idle mode where it waits to be paged for an incoming call and continually senses the keypad to determine if the user has initiated (dialed) a call (access). When a call begins to be received or initiated, the mobile telephone enters system access mode to try to access the system via a control channel. When it gains access, the control channel sends an

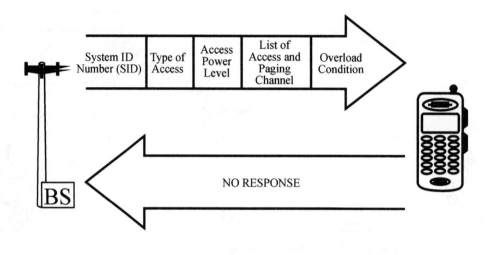

Figure 2.12. Cellular System Broadcast Information.

initial voice channel designation message indicating an open voice channel. The mobile telephone then tunes to the designated voice channel and enters the conversation mode. As the mobile telephone operates on a voice channel, the system uses frequency modulation (FM) similar to commercial broadcast FM radio. To send control messages on the voice channel, the voice information is either replaced by a short burst (blank and burst) message or, in some systems, control messages can be sent along with the audio signal.

Access

A mobile telephone's attempt to obtain service from a cellular system is referred to as "access." Mobile telephones compete on the control channel to obtain access from a cellular system. Access is attempted when a command is received by the mobile telephone indicating the system needs to service that mobile tele-

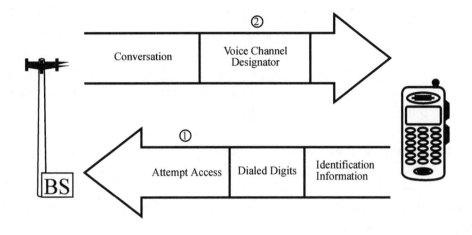

Figure 2.13. Cellular System Call Origination Radio Channel Access.

phone (such as a paging message indicating a call to be received) or as a result of a request from the user to place a call. The mobile telephone gains access by monitoring the busy/idle status of the control channel both before and during transmission of the access attempt message. If the channel is available, the mobile station begins to transmit and the base station simultaneously monitors the channel's busy status. Transmissions must begin within a prescribed time limit after the mobile station finds that the control channel access is free, or the access attempt is stopped on the assumption that another mobile telephone has possibly gained attention of the base station control channel receiver. Figure 2.13 shows a sample access process.

If the access attempt succeeds, the system sends out a channel assignment message commanding the mobile telephone to tune to a cellular voice channel. Figure 2.14 displays the access process when a call is placed from the mobile telephone to the cellular system (called "origination"). The access attempt message is called a Call Setup message and it contains the dialed digits and other information. The system will assign a voice channel by sending a voice channel designator message. If the access attempt fails, the mobile telephone waits a random amount of time before trying again. The mobile station uses a random-number-generating algorithm internally to determine the random time to wait. The design of the system minimizer the chance of repeated collisions between different mobile stations that are both trying to access the control channel, since each one waits a different random time interval before trying again if they have already collided on their first, simultaneous attempt.

An access overload class (ACCOLC) code is stored in the mobile telephone's memory, which can inhibit it from transmitting when the system gets too busy. When an access overload class category is sent on the control channel that matches its stored access overload class, the mobile telephone is inhibited from attempting to access the cellular system. This process allows the cellular system to selectively reduce the number of access attempts and only allow particular groups of mobile telephones to access the system. The assignment of high-level system access class codes to mobile telephones is reserved for emergency personnel.

Paging

To receive calls, a mobile telephone is notified of an incoming call by a process called paging. A page is a control channel message that contains the telephone's mobile identification number (MIN), and it responds automatically with a system access message of a type called a Page Response. This indicates that an incoming call is to be received. After the mobile telephone receives its own telephone number, the mobile telephone begins to ring. When the customer answers the call (user presses SEND), the mobile telephone transmits a service request to the system to answer the call. It does this by sending the telephone number and an electronic serial number to provide the user's identity. Figure 2.14 shows that if the mobile telephone is paged in the system and the customer wishes to receive the call (user presses SEND), it responds to the page by attempting access to the system.

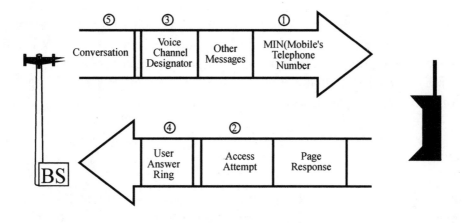

Figure 2.14. Cellular System Paging.

Discontinuous Reception

The use of discontinuous reception allows the mobile telephone's receiver to turn itself off ("sleep") for brief periods of time (typically less than 2 seconds) to save battery energy. Because the cellular system coordinates discontinuous reception, it knows when the mobile telephone has turned the receiver off and will hold pages until it knows the mobile telephone's receiver is turned back on ("awake").

Conversation

After a mobile telephone has been commanded to tune to a radio voice channel, it sends mostly voice or other customer information. Periodically, control messages may be sent between the base station and the mobile telephone. Control messages may command the mobile telephone to adjust its power level, change frequencies, or request a special service (such as three-way calling).

Discontinuous Transmission

To conserve battery life, a mobile phone may be permitted by the base station to only transmit when it senses the mobile telephone's user is talking. When there is silence, the mobile telephone may stop transmitting for brief periods of time (several seconds). When the mobile telephone user begins to talk again, the transmitter is turned on again.

Handoff

Handoff is a process where the cellular system automatically switches channels to maintain voice transmission when a mobile telephone moves from one cell radio coverage area to another. The MSC's switching equipment transfers calls from cell to cell and connects the call to other mobile telephones or the landline telephone network. The MSC creates and interprets the necessary command signals to control mobile telephones via base stations. This allows the switching from channel to channel as the mobile telephone moves from one coverage area to another.

Figure 2.15 shows the cellular handoff process. Initially, base station #1 is communicating with the mobile telephone (t1). Because the signal strength of the mobile telephone has decreased, it has become necessary to transfer the call to a neighboring cell, base station #2. This is accomplished by base station #1 sending a handoff command to the mobile telephone (t2). The mobile telephone tunes to the new radio channel (428) and begins to transmit a control tone, which indicates it is operating on the channel (t3). The system senses that the mobile telephone is ready to communicate on channel 428 and the MSC switches the call to base station #2 (t4). The conversation can then continue (t5). This entire process is usually accomplished in less than 1/4 of a second.

When a cellular radio moves far away from the cell that is serving it, the cellular system must transfer service to a closer cell. Figure 2.16 illustrates the process. To determine when handoff is necessary, the serving base station con-

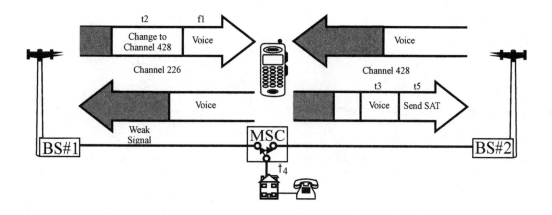

Figure 2.15. Cellular System Handoff.

tinuously monitors the signal strength of the cellular radio. When the cellular radio's signal strength falls below a minimum level of signal strength, the serving base station requests adjacent base stations to measure that radio's signal strength (step 1). The adjacent base stations tune to the cellular radio's current operating channel and measure the signal strength. When a closer adjacent base station measures sufficient signal strength (step 2), the serving base station commands the cellular radio to switch to the new base station (step 3). After the cellular radio starts communicating with the new base station, the communication link carrying the landline voice path is switched to the new serving base station to complete the handoff (step 4).

Mobile Reported Interference (MRI)

Some mobile telephones can transmit their radio channel quality information back to the base station to assist with handoff decisions. The process, called mobile reported interference (MRI), sends channel quality information via the

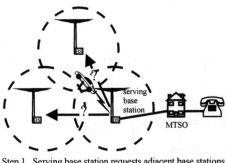

Step 1. Serving base station requests adjacent base stations
to measure cellular radio signal strength.

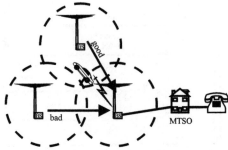

Step 2. Adjacent base stations return
cellular radio signal level.

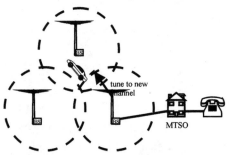

Step 3. Command mobile to new channel.

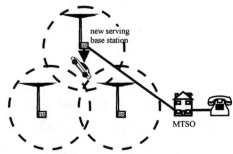

Step 4. Switch voice path. Handoff complete.

Figure 2.16. Handoff Messaging.

sub-band digital audio channel. Radio channel quality is measured using messsage parity bits to count the bits on the sub-band digital audio channel that are received in error. The base station sets a channel quality threshold level so that the mobile telephone can determine when the signal strength and interference levels become unacceptable. When signal levels fall below the threshold, the mobile telephone informs the cellular system of poor radio channel conditions, and a handoff request is processed.

Figure 2.17 illustrates the MRI process. The process begins as the serving base station sends the minimum acceptable signal strength level to the mobile telephone. This information sets a minimum signal strength threshold in the mobile telephone (step 1). The mobile telephone continues to monitor the received

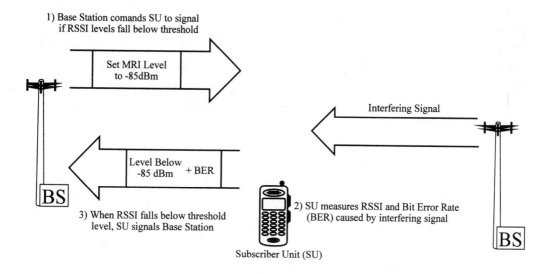

Figure 2.17. Mobile Reported Interference.

signal strength indicator (RSSI) and the bit error rate (BER) of the sub-band digital signaling channel until the threshold is reached (step 2). The BER is an indicator of co-channel interference. When the threshold is crossed, the mobile telephone sends a single message to the base station indicating that the received signal strength and BER rates are beyond tolerance. The base station then uses the information to assist the handoff decision. If the base station wants another measurement from the mobile telephone, it sends a new message indicating a new threshold level.

RF Power Control

Mobile telephones are typically classified by their maximum amount of power output, called the "power class." Mobile telephone power output is adjusted by commands received from the base station to reduce the transmitted power from the mobile telephone in smaller cells. This reduces interference to nearby cell sites. As the mobile telephone moves closer to the cell site, less power is required from the mobile telephone, and it is commanded to reduce its transmitter output power level. The base station transmitter power level can also be reduced although the base station RF output power is not typically reduced. While the maximum output power varies for different classes of mobile telephones, typically they have the same minimum power level. Figure 2.18 shows the power control process.

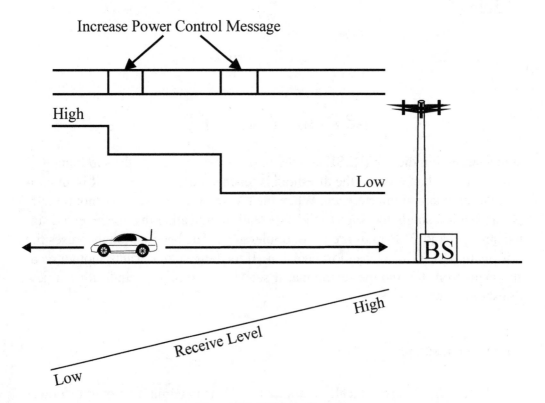

Figure 2.18. RF Power Control.

Roaming

A home system identifier code is stored in the mobile telephone's memory, which allows it to compare the home system identifier code to the system identifier code that is transmitted on the serving control channel. If they do not match, it means the subscriber is operating in a visited system and the mobile telephone will provide a ROAM indicator. The ROAM indicator display on the mobile telephone is typically used by subscribers to determine if their billing rates have changed. Visited systems often charge a premium for service usage.

Signaling

Signaling is the transferring of control messages between two points. There are basic two parts of signaling: the physical transport of the message and the actual content of the message. Control messages are sent on radio control channels and radio voice channels, and between the network parts of the cellular and telephone system.

Radio Control Channels

Most cellular systems have dedicated control channels that carry several types of messages to allow the mobile telephone to listen for pages and compete for access. These messages include:

1. *Overhead messages,* which continuously communicate the system identification (SID) number, power levels for initial transmissions, and other important system registration information
2. *Pages,* which tell a particular mobile telephone that a call is to be received
3. *Access information,* which is the information exchanged between the mobile telephone and the system to request service
4. *Channel assignment commands,* which establish the radio channels for voice communications.

The control channel sends information by frequency shift keying (FSK). To allow self-synchronization, the information is usually Manchester encoded, which forces a frequency shift (bit transition) for each bit input [8]. Orders are sent as messages composed of one or more words.

To help coordinate multiple mobile telephones accessing the system, busy idle indicator bits are typically interlaced with the other message bits. Before a mobile telephone attempts access to the system, it checks the busy/idle bits to see if the control channel is serving another mobile telephone. This system is called carrier sense multiple access (CSMA) and it helps to avoid collisions during access attempts.

When a mobile telephone begins to listen to a control channel, it must find the beginning of messages so that they can be decoded. Messages are preceded with an alternating pattern called a dotting sequence, which is easy to sense and identifies that a message will follow. Following the dotting sequence, a unique sequence of bits called a synchronization is sent, which allows the mobile telephone to match the exact start time of the message.

Radio channels can have rapid signal level fades that introduce errors, so the message words are repeated several times to ensure reliability (except the NMT system). Of the repeated words, the mobile telephone can use a majority vote system to eliminate corrupted messages. Message and signaling formats on the control channels vary between forward and reverse channels. The forward channel is synchronous, and the reverse channel is asynchronous.

Forward Control Channel

On the forward control channel, several message words follow a dotting and synchronization word sequence. Each word has error correction/detection bits that are included so that the data content can be verified and possibly corrected if received in error.

Reverse Control Channel

On the reverse control channel, words follow a dotting and synchronization word sequence. Because the reverse channel is randomly accessed by mobile telephones, the dotting sequence in the reverse direction is typically longer than in the forward direction. Each reverse channel word has error detection and correction bits. Messages are sent on the reverse channel in random order and typically coordinated using the busy/idle status from a forward control channel.

Radio Voice Channels

After a mobile telephone is assigned a voice channel, voice and control information must share the same radio channel. Brief control messages that are sent on the voice channel include the following:

1. *Handoff messages* instruct the mobile telephone to tune to a new channel.
2. *Alert* messages tell the mobile telephone to ring when a call is to be received.
3. *Maintenance* command messages monitor the status of the mobile telephone.
4. *Flashes* request a special service from the system (such as 3 way calling).

The analog voice channel typically transfers voice information between the mobile telephone and the base station. Signaling information must also be sent to allow base station control of the mobile telephone. Signaling on the voice channel can be divided into in-band and out-of-band signaling. In-band signaling occurs when audio signals between 300--3000 Hz either replace or occur simultaneously with voice information. Out-of-band signals are above or below the 300--3000 Hz range, and may be transferred without altering voice information. Signals sent on the voice channel include a pilot or supervisory audio tone (SAT), signaling tone (ST), dual tone multi-frequency (DTMF), and blank and burst FSK digital messages.

The supervisory tone provides a reliable transmission path between the mobile telephone and base station, and is transmitted along with the voice to indicate a closed loop. The tone functions are much like the current/voltage functions used in landline telephone systems to indicate that a phone is off the hook[9]. The supervisory tone may be one of the several frequencies (around 6 kHz for AMPS/TACS and 4 kHz for NMT), and this tone is different for nearby cell sites. If the supervisory tone is interrupted for longer than about 5 seconds, the call is terminated. In some systems such as NAMPS or NTACS, the SAT tone is replaced with a digital supervisory signal, which is sent out of band on a sub-band digital signaling channel. Figure 2.19 shows how a supervisory tone is transponded back to the base station.

The use of different supervisory tone frequencies in adjacent cell sites is also used to mute the audio when co-channel interference occurs. Interfering signals have a different supervisory frequency than the one designated by the system for

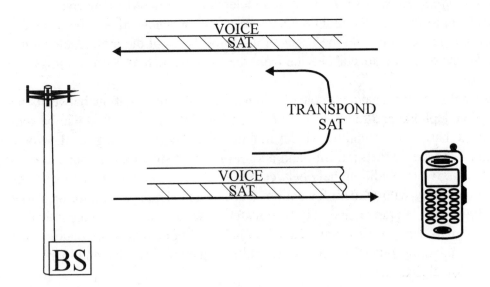

Figure 2.19. Transponding SAT.

the call in progress. The incorrect supervisory tone alerts the mobile telephone to mute the audio from the interfering signal.

Retransmission of the supervisory tone can also be used to locate the mobile telephone's position. An approximate propagation time can be calculated by comparing the phase relationship between the transmitted and received supervisory tones. This propagation time is correlated to the distance from the base station. However, multipath propagation (radio signal reflections) makes this location feature inaccurate and only marginally useful [10]. Only the retransmission of the supervisory tone as a pilot tone is critical to operation.

A signaling tone (ST) is used in some systems to indicate a call status change. It confirms messages sent from the base station and is similar to a landline phone status change of going on or off hook [11]. Similar to the digital supervisory signal, in some systems such as NAMPS or NTACS, the signaling tone is replaced with a digital signaling tone, which is sent out of band on a sub-band digital signaling channel.

Touch-Tone·(registered trademark of AT&T) signals may be sent over the voice channel. DTMF signals are used to retrieve answering machine messages, direct automated PBX systems to extensions, and a variety of other control functions. Bellcore specifies frequency, amplitude, and minimum tone duration for recognition of DTMF tones [12]. The voice channel can transmit DTMF tones, but varying channel conditions can alter the expected results. In poor radio conditions and a fading environment, the radio path may be briefly interrupted, sometimes sending a multiple of digits when a key was depressed only once.

Blank-and-Burst Messages

When signaling data is about to be sent on the voice channel, audio FM signals are inhibited and replaced with digital messages. This interruption of the voice signal is normally so short (less than 1/4 second) that the mobile telephone user

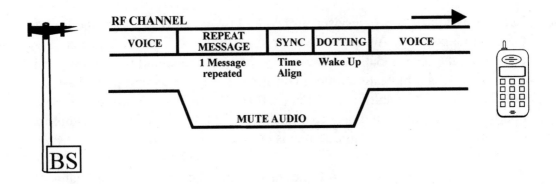

Figure 2.20. In Band Voice Channel Message.

often does not notice it. Like control channel messages, these messages are typically repeated a multiple of times and a majority vote is taken to see which messages will be used.

To inform the receiver that a digital signaling message is coming, a bit dotting sequence is sent preceding the message. After the dotting sequence gets the attention of the receiver, a synchronization word follows that identifies the exact start of the message. Figure 2.20 shows how a voice channel message is sent.

Blank-and-burst signaling differs on the forward and reverse voice channels. On the forward voice channel, messages are repeated more times to ensure control information is reliable even in poor radio conditions. It is likely that messages will be sent in poor radio conditions as handoffs.

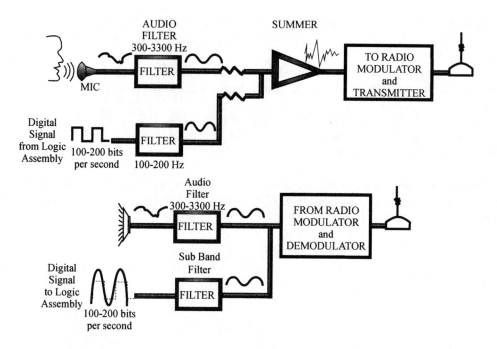

Figure 2.21. Sub-Band Signaling.

Sub-Band Digital Audio Signaling

A unique signaling feature used by some cellular radio systems is the sub-band digital audio signaling. In most analog cellular phones, an audio bandpass filter blocks the audio channel's lower range, but in mobile telephones that have sub-band digital signaling capability, a low-speed digital signal replaces the lower audio range (below 300 Hz) with digital information. Figure 2.21 shows how sub-band digital and audio signals are combined with standard audio.

References

1. Balston, D.M., "Cellular Radio Systems," Artech House, MA, 1993, p. 135.
2. Mehrotra, Asha, "Cellular Radio, Analog and Digital Systems," Artech House, MA, 1994, p. 177.

3. Balston, D.M., "Cellular Radio Systems," Artech House, MA, 1993, p. 113.

4. Lee, William, "Mobile Cellular Telecommunications Systems," McGraw-Hill, NY, 1989, p. 2.

5. Harte, Lawrence, "Dual Mode Cellular," P.T. Steiner Publishing, PA 1991, p. 7-3.

6. FCC Regulations, Part 22, Subpart K, "Domestic Public Cellular Radio Telecommunications Service," 22.903, (June 1981).

7. Balston, D.M., "Cellular Radio Systems," Artech House, MA, 1993, p. 89.

8. *The Bell System Technical Journal*, January 1979, Vol. 58, No. 1, American Telephone and Telegraph Company, Murray Hill, New Jersey.

9. Ibid, p. 47.

10. Bohaychuk, Ron, personal interview, Ericsson Radio Systems, October 7, 1990.

11. *The Bell System Technical Journal*, p. 47, January 1979, Vol. 58, No. 1, American Telephone and Telegraph Company, Murray Hill, New Jersey.

Chapter 3

Digital Cellular Radio Technology

Digital cellular technology involves the combination of digital signal processing with cellular radio technology. Digital cellular radio technology was developed to allow more customers to be served by a reduced number of towers and to allow the addition of advanced features.

Some of the key technologies associated with digital radio include the access technologies used to coordinate multiple users in the network, digital signal processing, expanded cellular applications and different types of services.

Access technologies allow multiple telephones to access the wireless systems. Mobile telephones compete for the services of a wireless system, and the access technologies coordinate the access and assign a portion of the system resources. Different types of access technologies include FDMA, TDMA, CDMA, and SDMA. The core digital signal processing technologies used by digital radio systems include voice digitization, speech compression, control and data channel coding, phase modulation, radio signal amplification, and signaling control.

Technology applications that are key to 3rd generation wireless communication include variable rate speech coding, high-speed packet data, different classes of service, simultaneous multimedia services, shared transfer of calls between cell

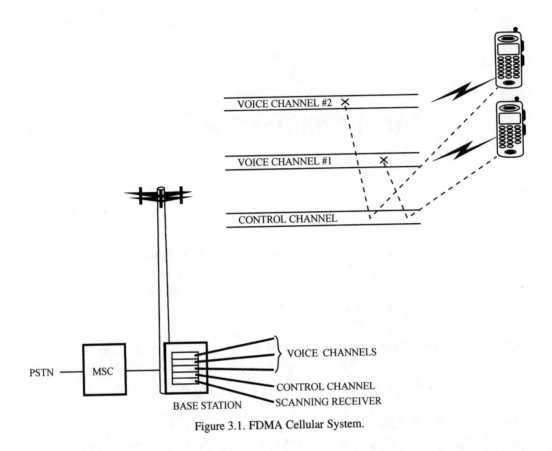

VOICE CHANNEL #2 ✕

VOICE CHANNEL #1 ✕

CONTROL CHANNEL

VOICE CHANNELS

CONTROL CHANNEL

SCANNING RECEIVER

PSTN — MSC

BASE STATION

Figure 3.1. FDMA Cellular System.

sites (soft handover), diversity reception, coordinated RF power control, and sleep modes to extend the battery life. The different classes of services include conversation, streaming, interactive, and background.

Radio Access Technology Basics

There are four basic types of cellular radio access technology: frequency division multiple access (FDMA), time division multiple access (TDMA), code division multiple access (CDMA), and spatial division multiple access (SDMA). Digital cellular systems fall into these categories, and many systems use a combination of these technologies. There are also variations in the way radio technologies allow duplex operation, called frequency division duplex (FDD), and time division duplex (TDD).

Frequency Division Multiple Access (FDMA)

FDMA systems divide a wide frequency band into smaller frequency bands that are assigned to specific users. All cellular systems use FDMA technology (inherent FDMA). Analog cellular systems use FDMA to allow for a single mobile telephone to call on a radio channel at a specific time, while digital systems allow multiple users to share a single radio channel.

Typically, analog FDMA systems use analog FM radio modulation. Figure 3.1 illustrates that FDMA systems typically have two types of radio channels: a control channel that coordinates radio channel assignment and a voice channel to allow voice communication. After the mobile telephone coordinates its access on the control channel, the cellular system assigns it to a voice channel; however, each voice channel can communicate with only one mobile telephone at a time.

It is possible to increase the number of communication channels that can be placed in a cell site by reducing the radio channel bandwidth. This allows more communication channels to be installed in a single cell site (narrow band channels). The limitation of using channels with a narrow bandwidth is their reduced limitation to interference. The degree to which radio channels change (deviate) or shift their radio frequency in relation to the information signal they are transmitting (called modulation) determines their resistance to electrical noise, fading, and interference from nearby radio channels. The modulation allowed for very narrow radio channels is more susceptible to co-channel interference and noise.

To overcome some of the limitations of narrowband modulation, some analog cellular systems to improve their quality by using radio signal interference reporting by the mobile telephone to quickly detect when interfering signals exist and request a change to another radio channel that has less interference. This overcomes some of the effects of decreased modulation levels.

FDMA mobile telephones are less complex than digital mobile telephones. They are relatively simple to design (in comparison to digital telephones), and when large quantities are produced, the cost is usually less than their digital counterparts. However, with the continued integration of digital circuits, the cost to produce FDMA mobile telephones may eventually be equal to or even more expensive than digital mobile telephones.

Time Division Multiple Access (TDMA)

TDMA systems allow several mobile telephones to communicate simultaneously on a single radio carrier frequency by dividing their signals into short time slots. Some TDMA systems assign time slots used by each mobile telephone in sequence or they may be dynamically assigned.

Cellular TDMA systems divide the radio spectrum into radio carrier frequencies typically spaced 30 kHz to 200 kHz wide. TDMA systems typically have narrowband radio voice or traffic channels but can have wideband radio signals. For example, the digital enhanced cordless telephone (DECT) system is a wideband TDMA system with 1.7 MHz wide radio channels.

In TDMA systems, each radio channel (called carrier) is subdivided into several communications channels. Each communication channel on a TDMA system only uses part of the radio carrier channel. Many documents that refer only to analog or FDMA systems (and unfortunately also for some TDMA or CDMA systems as well) use the word "channel" without distinguishing between the two. The reader must be aware that the meaning of the word "channel" may refer to either the radio carrier channel or an individual communication channel that is part of a radio carrier channel.

The key distinguishing feature of TDMA systems is that they employ digital techniques at the base station and in the motile telephone to subdivide the time on each channel into time slots. Each time slot can be assigned to a different mobile telephone. Voice sounds and access control information messages are converted to digital signals that are sent and received during the time slots (may be only part of a single time slot).

When a time slot is transmitted, it sends a burst of information. These bursts of digital information can be encoded, transmitted, and decoded in a fraction of the time required to produce the sound. The result is that only a fraction of the transmission time is used by one communication channel, and other subscribers can use the remaining time on the radio channel.

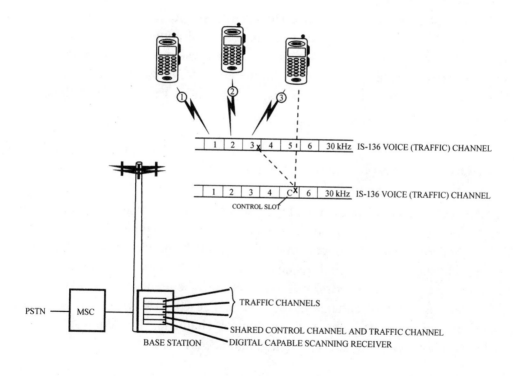

Figure 3.2. TDMA Cellular System.

Most TDMA mobile telephones access a cellular system by communicating on a dedicated control channel time slot as compared to a dedicated RF carrier channel that is used by FDMA systems. Some TDMA systems (such as the IS-136 system) can use the existing analog control channel to assign a mobile telephone to a digital traffic channel. Figure 3.2 illustrates the basic structure of a TDMA cellular system.

Digital mobile telephones are much more complex than FDMA mobile telephones. When implemented in a digital signal processing system (DSP), a typical analog mobile telephone has signal processing capability of half a million instructions per second (MIPS) while TDMA mobile telephones have over 50 MIPS processing capability. This added complexity, limited demand, and lower production numbers of digital phones would have normally resulted in higher costs for digital mobile telephones. However, a single digital signal processing system used in a mobile telephone replaces several analog circuits resulting in lower cost for digital mobile telephones. Digital systems allow more customers to simultaneously use radio channels in the cell site, reducing the total number of required cell sites and radio channels, and ultimately reducing the cellular system infrastructure cost.

Code Division Multiple Access (CDMA)

CDMA technology differs from TDMA technology in that it divides the radio spectrum into wideband digital radio signals with each signal waveform carrying several different coded channels. Each coded channel is identified by a unique channel code. Digital receivers separate the channels by correlating (matching) signals with the proper channel code sequence and enhancing the correlated one without enhancing the others. The CDMA RF signal waveform uses some of its coded channels as control channels. The control channels include a pilot, synchronization, paging, and access channel.

Figure 3.3 illustrates a CDMA system and reveals several changes from an analog system. The base station uses a wide CDMA RF signal waveform that provides for many different coded channels. Some of these coded channels are used for control and access coordination, and others are used for voice communications. The CDMA mobile telephone accesses the system either through an analog control channel or coded channel on the CDMA RF signal waveform.

When the mobile telephone obtains access on the CDMA system, the CDMA control channel responds by assigning the CDMA mobile telephone to a new coded channel. This is typically on the same RF carrier frequency. It is possible to use the same RF carrier frequency in all cells of a CDMA by differentiating channels by codes. Because neighboring cell sites can use the exact same frequency but different codes, this allows CDMA mobile telephones to simultane-

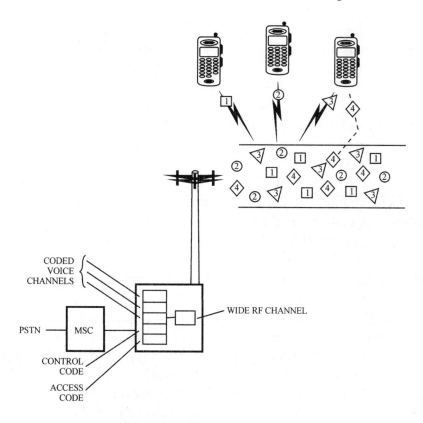

Figure 3.3. CDMA Cellular Stystem.

ously connect with two (or more) cell sites. This allows for more reliable reception as radio distortions that occur on one radio channel (such as signal fading) may not occur on a radio channel that the mobile telephone has with another cell site.

CDMA mobile telephones are similar to TDMA phones in complexity because a CDMA system uses similar digital signal processing techniques.

Spatial Division Multiple Access (SDMA)

Spatial division multiple access (SDMA) is a system access technology that allows a single transmitter location to provide multiple communication channels by dividing the radio coverage into focused radio beams that reuse the same frequency. To allow multiple access, each mobile radio is assigned to a focused radio beam. These radio beams may dynamically change with the location of the mobile radio. SDMA technology has been successfully used in satellite communications for several years.

SDMA systems can dramatically increase the capacity of a wireless system. The ability to focus a radio beam to a very narrow area allows many customers to serve in the same cell site on the same frequency. In addition to the increase in system capacity, the system focusing energy into a narrow beam is increased transmission gain. This gain can be used to extend the maximum distance to communicate from the cell site to the mobile telephone.

Figure 3.4 shows an example of an SDMA system. Diagram (a) shows the conventional sectored method for communicating from a cell site to a mobile telephone. This system transmits a specific frequency to a defined (sectorized) geographic area. Diagram (b) shows a top view of a cell site that uses SDMA technology that is communicating with multiple mobile telephones operating within the same geographic area on a single frequency. In the SDMA system,

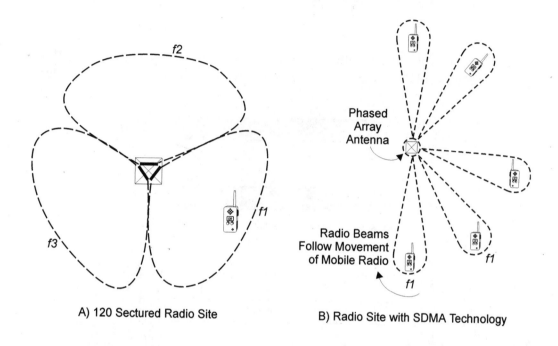

Phased
Array
Antenna

Radio Beams
Follow Movement
of Mobile Radio

f1

f1

f2

f1

f3

A) 120 Sectured Radio Site

B) Radio Site with SDMA Technology

Figure 3.4. SDMA Cellular System.

multiple directional antennas or a phased array antenna system directs independent radio beams to different directions. As the mobile telephone moves within the sector, the system either switches to an alternate beam (for a multibeam system) or adjusts the beam to the new direction (in an adaptive system).

Duplex Operation

To allow apparently simultaneous transmitting and receiving (no need to push to talk), a mobile telephone uses frequency division duplex (FDD) or time division duplex (TDD) systems.

FDD systems allow a transmitter and receiver to work simultaneously at different frequencies. FDD systems must separate the transmitter energy from over-

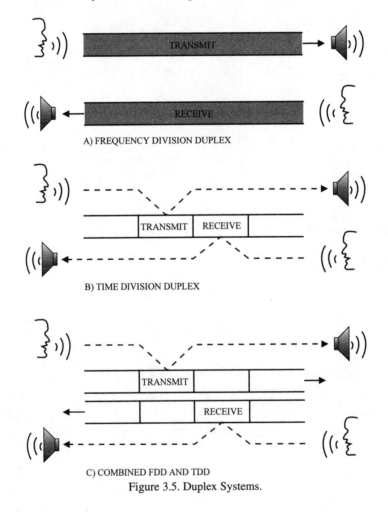

A) FREQUENCY DIVISION DUPLEX

B) TIME DIVISION DUPLEX

C) COMBINED FDD AND TDD

Figure 3.5. Duplex Systems.

powering the receiver. This is made possible by either using two antennas separated by a distance and/or having a filter connected to the receiver and transmitter to block the transmitter frequencies from being connected to the receiver.

TDD uses separate transmit and receive time slots that do not overlap. When the transmitter is operating, the receiver is off. TDD systems may be designed to use the same radio frequency in both directions (such as the CT2 system) This simplifies the design and reduces the number of components in the radio transceiver. It also permits the base unit to use a sophisticated and complex adaptive equalizer to optimize the performance of radio transmission in both directions, without the need to put a similar capability into the mobile set. The disadvantage of using the same frequency for transmit and receive is the coordination of time slot periods. If the TDD system allows the mobile telephone to transmit directly after it has received a time slot, the time delay could cause an overlap with other time slots. The time delay for short-range systems (such as cordless telephones) is not a challenge. However, in systems with large cell sizes (e.g., above 2 to 3 km), the time delay could cause slots to interfere with each other. One method used to address this problem is to design the mobile telephone to have an adjustable transmit timing advance for radio burst transmission. Short-range TDD systems do not normally have this capability.

Most of the long-range TDMA cellular technologies combine FDD and TDD operation. This keeps a similar frequency allocation (dual frequency) that is used for analog cellular systems. Figure 3.5 shows the different types of duplex systems.

Digital Technology Attributes

Most of the new cellular technologies use digital voice technology to achieve the goals of the next generation cellular technologies. Digital technology increases system efficiency by voice digitization, speech compression (coding), channel coding, and use of spectrally efficient modulation.

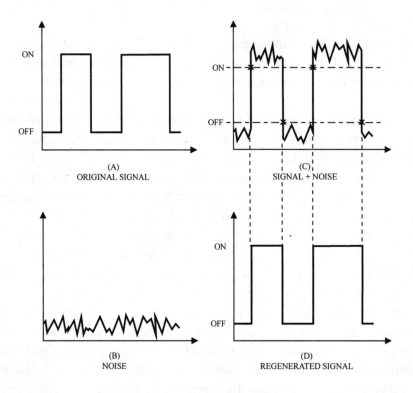

Figure 3.6. Digital Signal Regeneration.

Digital Signal Regeneration

As a radio signal passes through the air, distortion and noise enter the signal. A digital signal can be processed to enhance its resistance to distortion in three ways: signal regeneration, error detection, and error correction. Digital signal regeneration removes the added distortion and noise by creating a new signal without noise from a noisy one. Error detection determines if the channel impairments have exceeded distortion tolerances. Error correction uses extra bits provided with the original signal to recreate correct bits from incorrect ones.

Figure 3.6 shows how noise (b) is added to a digital signal time waveform (a). By using ON/OFF threshold detection and conversion (c), the original signal can be regenerated (d). Provided that the signal is sufficiently stronger than the noise, it can be received almost error-free despite the presence of noise.

Signal Digitization

Figure 3.7 illustrates the conversion from an analog signal to a digital one. Speech into the microphnne creates an analog signal. An audio bandpass filter is used to remove high and low frequencies that can interfere with the digitization process. The filtered signal is then sampled 8,000 times per second. This sample rate is standard in the telephone industry. For each sample, an 8-bit digital value is created. The resulting 64,000 bits per second (64 kbps) represent the voice.

About 64 kbps of data are required to reasonably digitize an analog voice waveform. Because transmitting a digital signal via radio requires about 1 Hz of radio bandwidth for each bit per second (bps), an uncompressed digital voice signal would require more than 64 kHz of radio bandwidth. Without compression, this bandwidth would make digital transmission less efficient than analog FM cellular, which uses only 25--30 kHz. Therefore, very high speech compression is necessary to increase cellular system capacity. Speech compression removes redundancy in the digital signal and attempts to ignore data patterns that are not

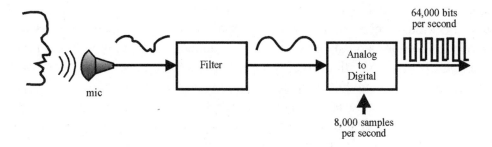

Figure 3.7. Voice Digitization.

characteristic of the human voice. The result is a digital signal that represents the voice audio frequency spectrum content, not a waveform.

Low bit-rate speech coders analyze the 64 kbps digitized speech signal and characterizes the signal into spectrum, pitch, volume, and other parameters. Figure 3.8 illustrates the basic speech compression process. The speech coder examines 10--20 millisecond time windows of the speech signal. Mathematical analysis of this sample of the waveform (which contains many cycles of the speech waveform) produces several numbers called the prediction coefficients. These numbers are used in a mathematical process called predictive coding. When a pulse (in digital numerical representation form) is put into this predictive coder as input, the resulting output is a waveform (also represented in digital form) that has a similar audio frequency spectrum to the original speech. As the speech coder characterizes the input signal, it looks up codes in a code book table that represent various pulse patterns (rather than just a single pulse) to chose the pattern that comes closest to matching the output of the predictive coder to the original time window voice signal. The coding process requires a large number of mathematical calculations because the predictive coder output must be recalculated many times at a rate faster than real time in order to find the best match. The coder system then sends the coefficients used in the predictive coder and the entry from the code book table to a decoder at the other end of the radio link. The compression process may be fixed or variable. When variable, the compression may vary from 4:1 to 64:1 depending on speech activity.

High bit-rate speech coders [(small amount of compression, such as 32 kbps adaptive differential pulse code modulation (ADPCM)] typically convert the waveform into a representative digital signal. Low bit-rate speech coders [high amount of compression such as VSELP or Qualcom code-excited linear prediction (QCELP)] analyze the waveform for key characteristics. In essence, low bit-rate speech coders model the source of the waveform while high bit-rate ones characterize the actual waveform. This process makes low bit-rate speech coders more susceptible to distortion from background noise and bit errors, poorer voice quality from a poor coding process model, and echoes from the speech coder processing time.

When there is a significant amount of background noise, distortion in the coding process occurs. Because the speech coder attempts to characterize the waveform

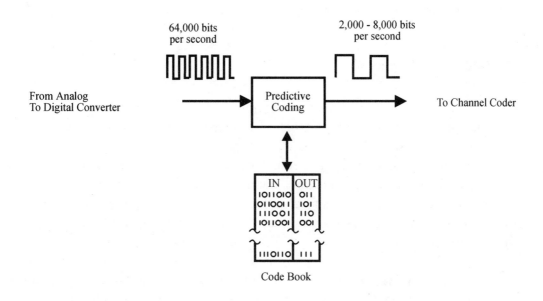

Figure 3.8. Speech Coding.

as a human voice, the background noise is not in its code book. The speech coder will find the code that comes closest to the sound that matches the combined background noise and the human voice. The result is usually distortion.

As a general rule, with the same amount of speech coding analysis, the fewer bits used to characterize the waveform, the lower the quality the speech-signal. If the complexity (signal processing) of the speech coder can be increased, it is possible to get improved voice quality with fewer bits. The speech coders used in the digital cellular phones typically require 8 MIPS to process the voice signal. It has been estimated that it will take four times the amount of processing to reduce the number of bits by additional factor of two.

Voice digitization and speech coding take processing time. Typically, speech frames are digitized every 10--20 msec and input to the speech coder. The digital sampling, signal compression process, time alignment with the radio channel, and decompression process at the receiving, can add about 50--100 msec of delay to the transmitted voice signal.

Digital Radio Channel Coding

Once the digital speech information is compressed, control information bits must be added along with extra bits to protect from errors that will be introduced during radio transmission. Three types of error protection coding are used in wireless systems: block coding, cyclic redundancy check (CRC) codes, and convolutional (continuous) coding. Channel coding also combines control messages (such as power control) with speech information. Control messages are either time multiplexed (simultaneous) or they replace (blank and burst) the speech information.

Block coding and CRC append extra bits to the end of a data block of information. These bits allow the receiver to determine if all the information has been received correctly. Convolutional coding produces a new and longer string of bits by combining the data with another predetermined string of bits in a process analogous to numerical multiplication.

Convolutional coders are described by the relationship between the number of bits entering and leaving the coder. For example, a 1/2 rate convolutional coder generates two bits for every one that enters. The larger the relationship, the more redundancy and better error protection. A 1/4 rate convolutional coder has much more error protection capability than a 1/2 rate coder.

CRC parity generation divides a given binary data value by a predefined binary number. The remainder resulting from this division is appended to the data to allow comparison when received. The division-like process is repeated on the data at the receiver and the quotient is compared. If the quotients do not match, one can infer that an error has occurred, and certain limited patterns of error can be corrected. Figure 3.9 shows a block error detection and convolutional coding system.

Control signals must be either sent along side of voice signals or replace portions of voice information to command the phone's communications with the base station. There are two basic types of control signaling, fast and slow. Slow signaling typically sends continuous channel quality measurements such as signal strength and a report stating the number of bits received in error in the last few frames. Fast signaling primarily sends channel assignment messages that must be acted on quickly. Fast messages replace the speech information for brief periods. Slow messages are transmitted slowly at a low bit rate and are multiplexed into the bit pattern of the speech frames. Figure 3.10 shows the process of fast and slow message signaling.

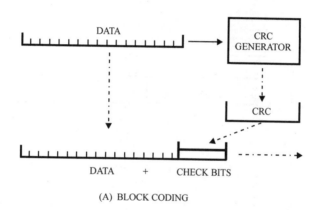

(A) BLOCK CODING

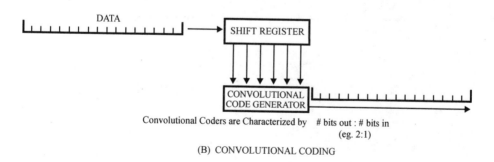

(B) CONVOLUTIONAL CODING

Figure 3.9. Block Error Detection and Convolutional.

Modulation

Modulation is the process of using an information signal (e.g., voice or data signal) to change the amplitude, frequency, or phase of a radio frequency carrier signal (a carrier). Analog cellular typically uses frequency modulation (FM), and digital technologies often use a form of phase modulation (PM). Frequency modulation is a process of shifting the radio frequency in proportion to the amplitude (voltage) of the input signal. Phase modulation is a result of time advancing or

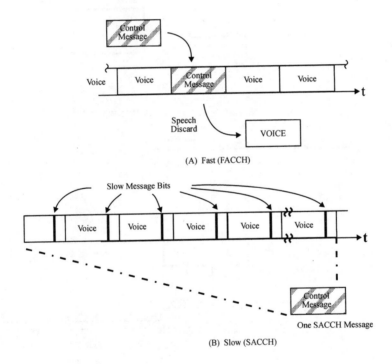

Figure 3.10. Fast and Slow Message Signaling.

retarding the carrier frequency waveform to introduce phase changes at specific points in time.

Figure 3.11 displays a basic digital modulation circuit. The digital signal is supplied to a pulse shaper. The pulse shaper adjusts (smoothes) the edges so the abrupt changes of the digital pulses do not force the modulator to produce energy outside the allowable bandwidth. The modulator converts these pulses to a low-level RF frequency that changes in phase which represent one or more digital pulses.

RF Amplification

The RF amplifier increases (boosts) the low-level RF signal from the modulator to a high power RF signal ready for transmission through the antenna. It is acceptable for analog cellular technologies to use a very efficient RF amplifier of a type called Class C, which may add some signal distortion to the amplification process. Unfortunately, most digital cellular technologies cannot accept this type of distortion, and therefore they use a more linear amplifier. The battery-to RF energy conversion efficiency for linear amplifiers is 30--40% compared with 40--55% RF amplifiers in most analog cellular phones. Linear amplifiers require

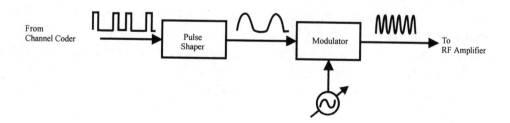

Figure 3.11. Radio Channel Modulation.

more battery power to produce the same RF energy output during transmission. Digital technologies overcome this limitation by either transmitting for shorter periods, or precisely controlling power to transmit at lower average output power.

Signaling

Signaling is the physical process of transferring control information to and from the mobile telephone. Control signals may be sent alongside user information in separate logical or physical channels, by blank-and-burst or dim-and-burst signaling.

Control Channels

A control channel in a wireless system is a radio channel or portion of a radio channel that is dedicated to the sending and/or receiving of controlling messages between the base station and mobile telephones. The control messages may include paging (alerting), access control (channel assignment) and system broadcast information (access parameters and system identification). Control channels may be a separate physical or logical channel.

Physical channels are created by dividing a wireless system resource (e.g., radio spectrum) into separate frequencies or digital codes that are specifically structured to exchange information between base stations and mobile telephones. A logical channel is portion of a physical communications channel that is used for a particular (logical) communications purpose. Third generation systems use both dedicated physical control channels and logical channels to exchange control messages.

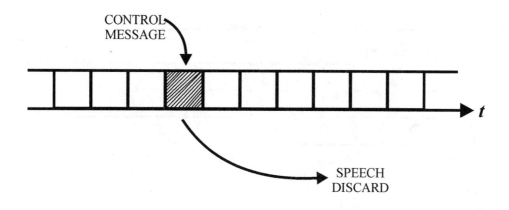

Figure 3.12. Blank-and-Burst Signaling.

Blank and Burst

Blank-and-burst signaling replaces speech data with signal messages. For historical reasons, this is called "in-band signaling." Blank-and-burst message transmissions degrade speech quality because they replace speech frames with signaling information. When blank-and-burst signaling is used, the speech will repeat the sound generated by the previous good frame of digitally coded voice if the current frame quality degradation for only one isolated replacement is almost imperceptible. Figure 3.12 illustrates blank-and-burst signaling.

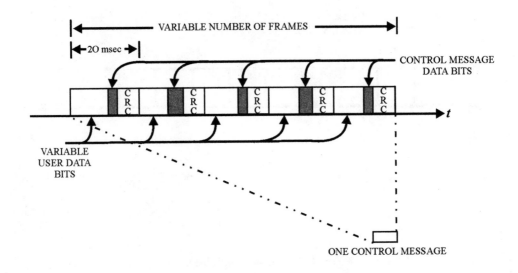

Figure 3.13. Dim-and-Burst Signaling.

Dim and Burst

Dim-and-burst inserts control messages when speech activity is low. It is possible to reduce the digital speech coder rate so that some of the unused bits can be re-assigned for control messages. Because all of the speech bits are not available for the control message, it may take several frames to send a single message. However, with careful timing of sending of dim-and burst messages (e.g. during low speech activity periods), the degrading effect of dim-and-burst messages on speech is almost imperceptible. Figure 3.13 illustrates a dim-and-burst message.

Third Generation Digital Technologies

The key improvements in 3G that are different than 2G cellular technologies include better packet data control, high-speed data transmission (up to 2 Mbps), multiple radio channel bandwidths (narrow 2G and wide 3G), and multiple channel data rates (higher-speed data transmission when radio channel quality is good).

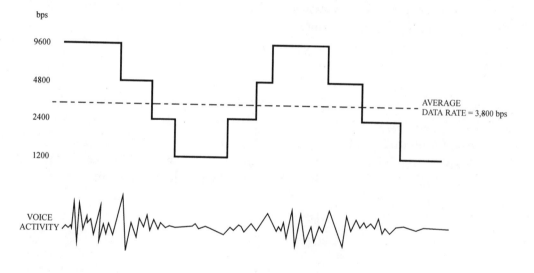

Figure 3.14. Variable Rate Speech Coding.

Variable Rate Speech Coding

Because 3rd generation systems are able to dynamically change data transfer rates, it is possible to take advantage of variable rate speech coding. The name for the speech coding process in 3rd generation systems is called adaptive multirate (AMR) coding. AMR coding is a variable-rate speech-coding process that dynamically changes its speech data compression process based on voice activity detection (VAD), background noise level, and generation of comfort noise.

The variable rate coding process begins with an analog-to-digital converter digitizing the user's voice at a fixed sample rate of 8,000 samples per second or 64 kbps. The digitized voice is supplied to a speech coder, which encodes the speech by characterizing it into voice parameters. When voice activity is low, the variable-rate speech coder represents speech by a digital signal with fewer bits. This added coding efficiency may more than double the wireless system capacity based on the ratio of silence to sound intervals in the speech (approximately 50%).

Figure 3.14 shows how the speech coder compression rate varies with speech activity. The analog speech signal is sampled in short 10--20 msec intervals. The speech coder produces data rates in the range of approximately 8 kbps to 1 kbps. As the speech activity decreases, the bit rate decreases (speech compression increases). The speech coder bit rate is controlled by commands received by the wireless network.

Packet Data

Packet data transmission is the sending of data through a network in small packets (typically under 100 bytes of information). A packet data system divides large quantities of data into small packets for transmission through a switching network that uses the addresses of the packets to dynamically route these packets through a switching network to their ultimate destination. When a data block is divided, the packets are given sequence numbers so that a packet assembler/disassembler (PAD) device can recombine the packets to the original data block after they have been transmitted through the network. Third generation systems use new packet data control channels that allow for rapid and efficient packet channel access.

High-Speed Data Transmission

High-speed data transmission is required to provide multimedia types of services. Third generation systems can dynamically group multiple physical logical channels to achieve data rates of more than 2 Mbps.

Soft Handover

Soft handoff allows the mobile telephone to communicate simultaneously with two or more cell sites to continuously select the best signal quality until handoff is complete. In analog cellular systems, handoff occurs when the base station detects a deterioration in signal strength from the mobile telephone. As analog mobile telephones approach hand-off, signal strength may vary abruptly, and the voice is muted for at least 200 milliseconds in order to send control messages and complete the handoff. In contrast, 3rd generation systems use "soft handover," which is nearly undetectable and loses few if any information frames.

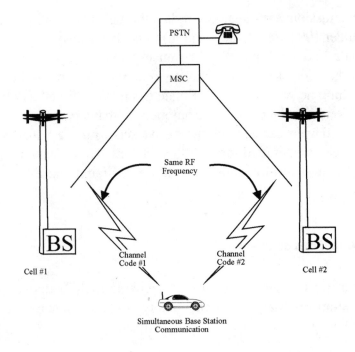

Figure 3.15. Soft Handover.

To allow the soft handover process, 3rd generation mobile telephones measure the signal strength from adjacent cells and transmit the measurements to the serving base station. When an adjacent base station's channel signal is strong enough, the mobile telephone requests the adjacent cell to transmit the call in progress. The serving base station also continues to transmit as well. Thus, prior to complete handoff, the mobile telephone is communicating with both base stations simultaneously. Using two base stations with the same frequency simultaneously during handoff maintains a much higher average signal strength throughout the process. During soft handover, the base station receivers choose the best frames of digitally coded speech from either base station. Figure 3.15 shows how CDMA systems use two base stations simultaneously during handoff.

Diversity Reception (Rake Reception)

Diversity reception is a method of processing whereby two signals are used in the reception process. Traditionally, diversity reception is performed through the

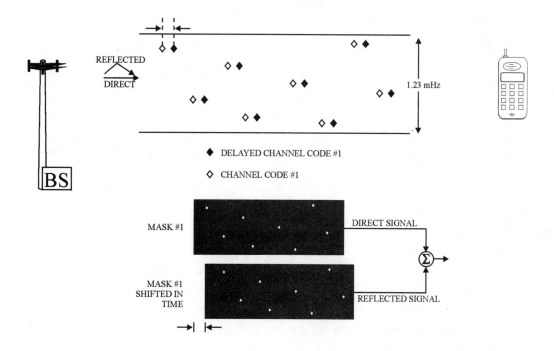

Figure 3.16. Diversity (Rake) Reception.

use of two antennas. In the 3rd generation system, space (multiple transmitter sites) and time (multiple signal path) diversity methods are used.

Diversity reception is primarily used to minimize the effects of radio signal fading. As one of the received radio signals experiences a radio signal fade or interference, the other received signal(s) may be of higher signal strength or better quality. The diversity reception system either combines the signals from the two signal sources or selects the strongest received signal.

When multiple reflected (multipath) signals are received at slightly different times, 3rd generation systems can combine multipath signals, adding several weak multipath signals to construct a stronger one.. The gains from this process are similar to those obtained from antenna diversity. This process is called rake reception. The result is better voice quality and fewer dropped calls than would otherwise be available.

Figure 3.16 shows how a multipath signal can be added to the direct signal. The radio channel shows two code sequences. The shaded codes are time delayed because the original signal was reflected and received a few microseconds later. The original signal is decoded by mask #1. The mask is shifted in time until it matches the delayed signal. The output of each decoded channel is combined to produce a better quality signal.

RF Power Control

Mobile telephones adjust their transmitter output as a result of commands they receive from the wireless network. For most wireless systems, the output power is adjusted by a combination of the received signal strength (called open loop) and fine adjustment messages from the cell site (called closed loop). Figure 3.17 shows that the RF power amplifier can vary its output power as it moves toward and away from the cell site.

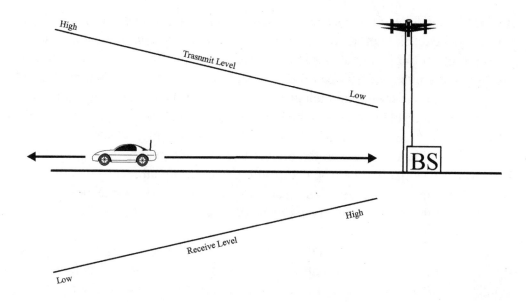

Figure 3.17. Open Loop RF Power Control.

To effectively separate the coded channels on CDMA systems, the received signals at the base station from all mobile telephones must be at almost the same level. If one received signal were much more powerful than the others, the receiver could not effectively decode the weaker ones, making it much less sensitive to weaker channels. To accommodate this requirement for uniform signal levels, the CDMA system precisely controls mobile telephone power. The power control system performs two simultaneous operations: open loop control and closed loop control. The open loop control is a coarse adjustment, and the closed loop control is a fine adjustment.

A CDMA mobile telephone's coarse (open loop) RF amplifier adjustment is controlled by feedback from its receiver section. The mobile telephone continuously measures the radio signal strength received from the base station to estimate the signal strength loss between the base station and mobile telephone. Figure 3.17 shows that as the mobile telephone moves away from the base station, the received signal level decreases. When the received signal is stronger, the mobile telephone reduces its own RF signal output; conversely, when the mobile received signal level is weaker, the mobile telephone increases the amplification of its own RF signal output. The end result is that the signal received at the base station from the mobile telephone remains at about at the same power level regardless of the mobile telephone's distance.

Because the open loop power adjustment does not adequately control received signal level by itself, the base station also fine-adjusts the mobile telephone's RF amplifier gain by sending power level control commands to the mobile telephone during short intervals (666 msec for WCDMA and 1.25 msec for CDMA2000). The commands are determined by the base station's received signal strength. The power control bit communicates the relative change from the previous transmit level, commanding the mobile telephone to increase or decrease power from the previous level.

Figure 3.18 illustrates closed loop power control. As the received signal power sensed by the base station increases or decreases, the base station sends a power control command that signals the mobile telephone to increase or reduce its transmit power level. The combined open and closed loop adjustments precisely control the received signal power at the base station.

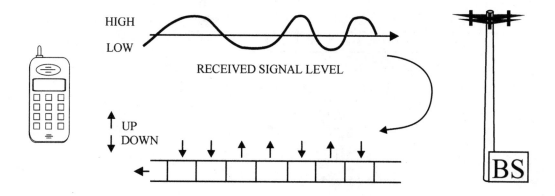

Figure 3.18. Closed Loop RF Power Control.

Discontinuous Reception

Discontinuous reception (DRX) enables mobile telephones to extend the battery life (standby time) by powering off nonessential circuitry during brief periods (sleep) when pages will not expected to be received. To provide for this sleep mode, the paging channel is divided into paging subchannel groups.

Figure 3.19 shows the DRX (sleep mode) process. When the mobile telephone registers on a wireless network, it informs the system of its sleep mode capability. The system responds by assigning the mobile telephone to a paging group.

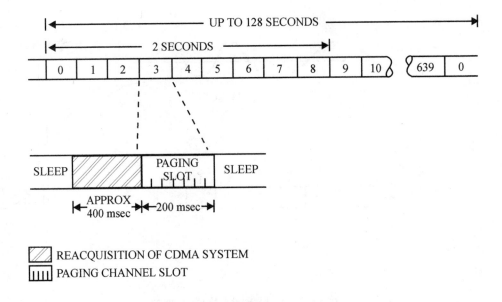

Figure 3.19. Discontinuous Reception (Sleep Mode).

Paging groups are brief periods (typically 20--200 msec) that a mobile telephone must be awake to mointor for its paging messages. There are usually 10 or more paging groups that allow the mobile telephone to sleep for up to 90% of the time.

The system can dynamically assign paging groups and may allow a maximum sleep period of several minutes for nonvoice devices (e.g., pagers). For normal operation, about 10 groups can be used for a maximum delay of about 2 seconds. Shortly before the end of a sleep period (approximately 100--400 msec), the mobile telephone wakes up to allow reacquisition with the control channel.

Soft Capacity

A cellular system is in a condition of over-capacity when more subscribers attempt to access the system than its radio interface can support at a desired quality level. Third generation CDMA technology allows the system to operate in a condition of over-capacity by accepting a higher-than-average bit error rate, or reduced speech coding rate. As the number of subscribers increases beyond a threshold, voice quality begins to deteriorate, but subscribers can still gain access to the system.

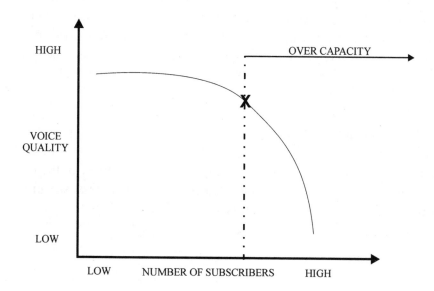

Figure 3.20. Soft Capacity Limit.

Figure 3.20 shows that as more users are added to the system, voice quality deteriorates. When voice quality falls below the allowable minimum (usually determined by an acceptable bit error rate), the system is over capacity. Allowing more subscribers on the system by trading off voice quality (or the subscribers data rate) creates a soft capacity limit.

Third Generation Services

Customers do not desire to purchase mobile telephones or data devices. They desire to purchase the benefits and services these devices should provide. Third generation services can be divided into different groups that have different characteristics. These characteristics include maximum delay, tolerance to errors, changing data transmission rates, and two-way interactivity. There may be other criteria that define the quality of service (QoS) within each of these classes of services.

Third generation digital access technology provides for many more types of services than are possible in first and second generation wireless systems. The ability to offer these advanced services will likely capture more and more of the market over time. These services can be divided into conversational class, streaming class, interactive class, and background class.

Conversational Class

Conversational class service is a circuit-switched (continuous) bearer service. It is primarily used for voice and video conferencing (real-time) communications. The key characteristics for conversational class include a low transmission delay, symmetric or nearly symmetric service. The maximum end-to-end delay for voice signals is 300--400 msec.

The same data transfer rates in each transmit direction (symetric) are commonly used in conversation class. Special attention is given to the maximum transmission delay. Just the speech compression and decompression time in the 3rd generation system contributes approximately 50--100 msec. If a call is completed through several systems (one wireless network customer calling a different wireless network customer), there may be two (or more) compression and decompression steps. Third generation systems address this challenge with a faster speech coding system and tandem free operation (TFO).

Streaming Class

Streaming class of information involves the continuous transferring of information. Streaming class is primarily used in multimedia syrtems for the delivery of real-time or near real-time audio and video. Some of the key characteristics for streaming class include variable data rate, high peak data rates, and time relation of media. Some delay of data is acceptable in the streaming class, and some errors may be tolerated.

High data rates are required for digital video because additional data bandwidth is required when images change (e.g., an action scene). The time relation of the media (sequencing and time relation) is also required. This time relation may be a time stamp or a relative time stamp that is included with the transmitted data packet.

Interactive Class

Interactive class involves two-way communications between the network and the end user. Typical interactive services include product database browsing, gaming, and information services management. This means interactive class service needs to have minimal round trip delay. Delay up to a few seconds may be acceptable. It also requires interactive class to have high reliability of data transmission (data files error free).

Background Class

Background services do not require immediate actions by the customer. Background class is used for email downloads or software updates that may occur during voice conversation. Background class is tolerant to delays of several seconds or even longer, and low data transfer rates may be acceptable.

Chapter 4

GPRS and EDGE (2.5 Generation)

To meet the growing needs for efficient new wireless services without the upgrading of systems to 3rd generation technology, two new standards were created: general packet radio service (GPRS) and enhanced data for global evolution (EDGE). GPRS and EDGE use enhanced GSM technology to provide for higher data transfer rates than are normally available in GSM systems. The combination of GPRS and EDGE is referred to as enhanced GPRS (EGPRS). EGPRS comprises the 43 series of specifications managed by the 3rd generation partnership project (3GPP) [1]

EDGE and GPRS technologies are commonly called 2.5G because they offer capabilities that are above the present day 2G digital cellular systems (greater than 14 kbps) but do not achieve the performance of 3G systems (less than 2 Mbps). Subscriber data transfer rates possible in 2.5G GPRS can achieve over 170 kbps and EDGE technology may exceed 384 kbps if the quality of the radio transmission link is good.

Two-and-a-half generation technology was developed partly to fill what some industry people see as a hole in the price-performance range of the overall 3G plan. For various reasons, some observers of the industry believe that the two most prominent service offerings of this 2.5G strategy may meet the price-performance needs of most subscribers sufficiently well that 2.5 G may effectively compete with 3G systems.

GPRS and EDGE systems are compatible with GSM networks. Mobile telephones that are that have GPRS or EDGE capability can easily provide GSM voice service. To upgrade GSM systems to offer GPRS and EDGE service, packet-switching hardware is added to an existing GSM network. On the radio side, little or no hardware changes are needed. Of course, new mobile telephones (or upgraded models) that are capable of GPRS or EDGE data service are also required for the subscribers that want to use GPRS or EDGE services.

In a cell with a base station that supports both GSM voice and GPRS and/or EDGE, a subscriber with a suitable multimode mobile telephone can simultaneously engage in a GSM voice conversation while transferring data packets via GPRS and/or EDGE. This is called dual transmission mode (DTM).

History

GPRS and EDGE evolved from the GSM and IS-136 TDMA technology. The GPRS system uses the same radio channel structure as the GSM system while the EDGE system enhances the GSM radio channel with improved radio channel modulation technology. EDGE systems are sometimes called GSM384 to indicate that the EDGE system is capable of the UMTS outdoor transmission requirement of 384 kbps.

GPRS belongs to the phase 2+ of the GSM standard. Phase 2+ features (pronounced "two plus") are enhancements to the second phase of GSM technology. GPRS was developed to provide high-speed packet data access for the GSM network. EDGE evolved from contributions of the universal wireless consortium 136 (UWC-136) for more efficient outdoor systems (wide area mobility). As a result, the standards for GPRS and EDGE are substantially the same as the UWC-136-HS-Outdoor standard for data evolution of IS-136 [2]

Figure 4.1 shows the evolution of GPRS and EDGE standards. This diagram shows that the GSM system that was originally developed in Europe has evolved from basic digital voice services (phase 1), through enhanced digital services such as data transmission and short messaging (phase 2), and progressed to offer GPRS packet transmission service (phase 2+). A competing TDMA digital radio system that was originally developed in North America has also evolved from basic digital voice services (IS-54), to enhanced digital services such as short messaging (IS-136), to a new high-speed data transmission system. The combination of GSM radio channel structure (200 kHz), packet switching offered by GPRS, and efficient phase modulation (8QPSK) has been combined to produce the EDGE system.

GPRS and EDGE can coexist on a standard GSM system. Both GPRS and EDGE provide packet data transmission across the radio link between base station and mobile telephone and also via packet switching infrastructure within the network facilities. GPRS and EDGE permit the mobile subscriber to communi-

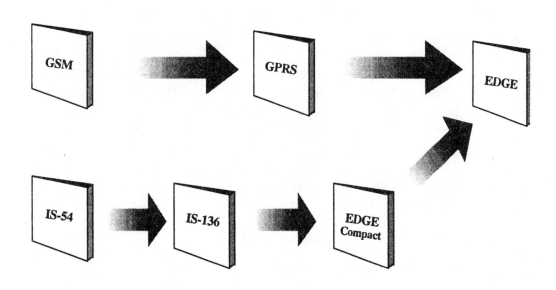

Figure 4.1. Evolution of GPRS and EDGE Standards.

cate with IP networks (or X.25 networks) in their respective "native" packet data formats. This permits the subscriber to have mobile access to the Internet and all its services such as electronic mail, data downloads, graphics, electronic commerce, voice over IP protocol, and so forth.

Global System for Mobile Communication (GSM)

Global system for mobile communication (GSM) is a digital cellular communications system that primarily provides voice, low-speed data, and short messaging services (SMS). GSM technology involves communication between a mobile phone, using a radio interface, to the various parts of the GSM network. GSM technology allows for a wide range of services that are similar and compatible with different types of fixed networks including the public analog and public data telephone networks (such as the Internet).

One of the key attributes of the GSM technology is a standardized digital radio carrier channel that allows multiple users to simultaneously share the channel. In historical analog radio and cellular systems, one radio carrier frequency carries one conversation. Therefore, a channel for a conversation in an analog system is synonymous with and corresponds one-to-one to a carrier frequency. However, in a digital radio system, it is possible to carry more than one conversation, or a conversation and other types of digital information, by means of various types of multiplexing. GSM uses time division multiplexing (TDM) to share one modulated carrier frequency radio waveform among 8 to 16 conversations. Therefore, documents related to GSM are careful to distinguish between a radio carrier and a communication channel.

System Overview

The GSM system includes many of the same basic subsystems as other cellular systems, including a switching network, base stations (BS), and mobile telephones. The GSM system separates the base station controlling function from the base station and moves it into a base station controller (BSC). A single BSC can serve several GSM base stations. GSM systems can serve mobile telephones of two basic types: full rate and half rate. Figure 4.2 shows an overview of a GSM radio system.

System Attributes

The GSM system is created from physical and logical channels. The physical channel is divided into time slots, which are grouped into frames. The physical channel is divided into many logical channels for control messaging and data transmission.

Physical Channels

The GSM system uses a single type of digital radio channel. This radio channel has a fixed bandwidth of 200 kHz and each radio carrier channel is paired with

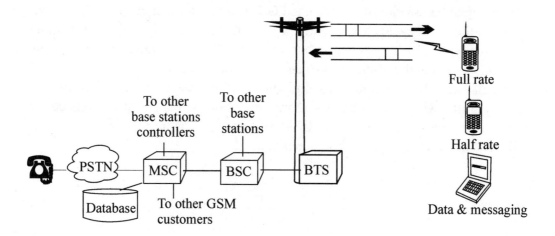

Figure 4.2. Global System for Mobile Communications (GSM).

another frequency to allow duplex operation. GSM radio channels have excellent interference rejection to allow for frequency reuse in nearby cell sites. Radio channels are assigned channel and time slot numbers to identify each communication channel. The data transfer rate of approximately 270 kb/s and the smallest time division of a radio channel are the time slot. Time slots are grouped into frames, which are grouped into multiframes to allow the proper synchronization and creation of many scheduled logical channels for control and user data transmission.

Typically, each cell site has several radio carrier frequencies. On one of these radio carrier frequencies, each cell site has a single time slot dedicated as a control channel. This carrier frequency is called the Beacon frequency. In some cases, where there is a large amount of call setup or short message activity, other time slots in that same carrier frequency signal are also used for these types of setup activity in addition to the first dedicated channel. In GSM documents, the first time slot is labeled with the number 0 (zero).

Radio Channel Bandwidth and Frequency Spacing

The nominal bandwidth of a modulated GSM carrier frequency is 200 kHz (two hundred thousand cycles per second). All modulated radio signals produce some frequency spectrum power emissions outside of their designated bands. This normally restricts the ability to use adjacent radio channel frequencies in adjacent cell sites. To overcome this limitation, GSM uses a special form of frequency shift keying (FSK) that has a low amount of adjacent frequency spectrum power emission. Consequently, in GSM systems there is no restriction on using adjacent carrier frequencies in adjacent cells.

Duplex Channels

Although a GSM mobile station does not transmit and receive at the same time, the radio channel structure is frequency division duplex (FDD). Using the FDD channel division (transmit on one frequency and receive on a different frequency), the mobile telephone receives and transmits at different times. With this time separation, a simple radio switch can be used to connect the antenna to the transmitter and receiver sections in hand portables. The radio frequency separation of forward (downlink) and reverse (uplink) frequencies on the 900 MHz band is 45 MHz (80 MHz for PCS-1900). The transmit band for the base station is 935--960 MHz on the 900 MHz band (1805-1880 MHz for UK DCS-1800). The transmit band for the mobile telephone is 890-915 MHz (1710-1785 MHz for DCS 1800). For the North American PCS-1900 system, the downlink base transmitter uses one of the six licensed sub-bands of the 1930-1990 MHz frequency range, and the uplink uses the corresponding sub-band in the frequency range from 1850-1910 MHz. GSM, PCS-1900 and DCS-1800 use the same 200 kHz carrier waveform bandwidth. Figure 4.3 shows the duplex radio channel structure.

Modulation and Data Rate

GSM uses a particular type of two-level digital FM modulation called Gaussian minimum shift keying (GMSK) to produce a gross data transmission rate of approximately 270 kbps. This modulation was specifically invented for GSM by members of the Council on Science and Technology (COST). The objective of design for GMSK modulation was the optimum or near optimum combination of several desirable properties, which include small susceptibility to radio noise and interference, small bandwidth and constant power level. The minimum susceptibility to radio noise and interference allows for increased frequency reuse in the system (higher channel capacity) and lower distortion (higher voice quality). A small bandwidth allows for the division of large or small amounts of radio spectrum into multiple radio channel carriers (design flexibility) and higher data transfer rates (higher data transfer capacity). A constant power level ("constant envelope") allows for the use of more power-efficient RF amplifiers (resulting in longer battery life). Such an amplifier is called Class C in radio jargon. Most of these criteria pull the radio system designer in opposite directions. The result was a balance between modulation properties and system design.

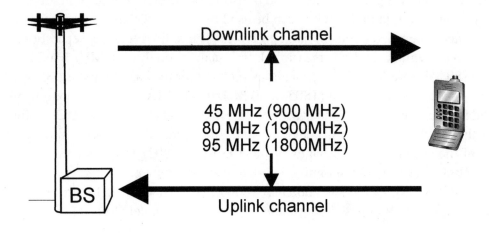

Figure 4.3. GSM Duplex Radio Channels.

The total 270 kbps data transfer rate is shared by multiple users on a single radio carrier channel. For a full rate system, up to eight different users share a single channel. After all the noninformation bits are subtracted from this channel bit rate, the actual assigned bit rate that the subscriber gets to use in each time slot is only 24.8 kbps. Not all of this is used for true "information" bits. Because of fading and other problems on the radio channel, a portion of this gross delivered bit rate is devoted to data bits used to detect (and in some cases correct) erroneous data bit values in other data bits. These extra error protection bits do not carry independent information. Their binary values are computed from the binary bit values of the "real" data. For digitally coded speech using the original GSM digital speech coder, only 13 kbps of this 24.8 kbps is "real" data in the original full rate speech coder.

TDMA Slot Structure

Time slots are the smallest individual time period available to each mobile station when operating on a GSM radio carrier channel. The time period for a single time slot is 577 microsec.

Each time slot normally contains 148 bits of information. Of the 148 bits, some are used to carry data, others are dedicated as control, and still others are used for synchronization. Depending on the use of the time slot (data or control), the purpose and structure (fields) of data bits contained in the time slot varies. The structure of the time slot can also vary dependent if the time slot is on the uplink or downlink radio channel.

When mobile stations transmit during a time slot, this is called a radio burst. There are four types of RF bursts used in the GSM system. Three of these types are in a category called "full duration," and the fourth is a shortened burst in time duration. The three full duration subtypes are: normal, frequency correction, and synchronization bursts. Both the base station and the mobile station use the normal type. The remaining two subtypes, frequency correction and synchronization bursts, are used only by the base transmitter, and when used, they only occur in the first time slot (labeled slot zero) of a particular designated frequency in each cell. That frequency is called the "beacon frequency." Only the mobile transmitter uses the short burst, called the random access burst.

Figure 4.4 shows that the transmit and receive time slots are offset by three time slots. This eliminates the requirement for the mobile station to transmit and receive at the same time. If the mobile station were required to simultaneously transmit and receive, this would require more expensive and bulky radio parts (duplex radio filter).

Normal Burst

The normal burst is used for "normal" communication between the base and mobile stations. The normal burst typically transfers user data (such as digitized speech information). A GSM mobile station normally transmits a burst during one time slot out of eight in the TDMA time frame. In certain special cases, such as a special mobile station transmitting high-bit-rate subscriber data, a mobile station may transmit during more than one of the eight time slots. The standards provide for a half-rate version of the speech coder that only requires the mobile station to transmit during one out of 16 consecutive time slots (one transmit burst out of two consecutive TDMA frames).

The bits transmitted during a normal burst are grouped into logical functions (called bit fields). These functional bit fields include initial tail bits (ramp time), training sequence, flag bits, user data bits, final tail bits, and guard time.

The first three bits of the time slot are dedicated to the gradual increase of transmitter power level. This is called a tail bit field, and during this first tail bit period, the mobile transmitter is gradually increasing its transmitter power level (ramp-up interval). They are called the tail bits because of the method used for

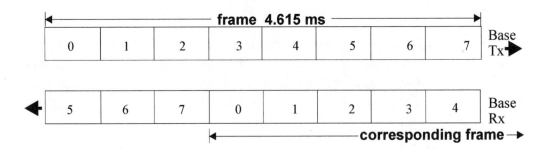

Figure 4.4. Radio Channel Time Slot Offset.

channel coding. The convolutional coder requires several bits to start its error protection coding process. These first 3 bits are all set to binary 1.

After the initial tail bits (ramp time), a group of data bits follows. Normally, these data bits are used for user data (such as digitized voice). However, on occasion these bits can be replaced with signaling information. The indication that these bits are signaling bits (control, or more specifically forward access control channel bits), is determined by the flag bits that follow the data field. The flag and information bits taken together are sometimes called the encrypted bits (because they are normally encrypted to give the subscriber privacy of communication).

In the center of the burst, training bits are included which are used as a relative timing reference and adaptive equalizer training pattern. There are eight different bit patterns used in the GSM system. Each pattern is 26 bits long, and the same synchronization pattern is used in all eight time-slots. The reason for using eight different training bit patterns is this: Other nearby, but not adjacent, cells in a GSM system installation intentionally reuse the same radio carrier frequencies as the cell under consideration.

There is always a potential problem if the receivers in this cell inadvertently pick up signals from another cell having the same carrier frequency. To help ensure that the mobile telephone does not obey radio commands intended for another mobile telephone in another cell, the system assigns different synchronization patterns to other radio channels of the same frequency that are operating in nearby cells. This allows an interfering signal to be distinguished from the desired signal when the receiver discovers that it contains the wrong synchronization pattern. A separate synchronization method (explained later) is used to allow the mobile to identify individual time slots and to determine the beginning and end of an eight slot frame.

At the end of the transmitted burst, three more tail bits are dedicated to the gradual reduction of the RF transmitter signal level in a similar way as the ramp up time period. These bits are called the final tail bits or the ramp bits.

At the end of the burst is a guard period. A guard period is included to allow a buffer time period to ensure transmitted bursts do not overlap as perceived at the base receiver with radio bursts received from other mobile stations due to their distance from the base station (guard periods). During the guard period, the mobile telephone transmitter is off. Figure 4.5 shows the normal burst field structure.

Most of the radio transmission bursts used in GPRS and EDGE involve a normal burst. The 8.25 symbol "silent" time interval is known as the guard period, since it helps to prevents time overlap (and thus mutual interference) of received signals from two different mobile transmitters operating in consecutive time slots when their radio signals arrive at the base receiver. When two mobile transmitters using two consecutive time slots are very different in their distance from the base station, the radio burst from the more distant transmitter will arrive at the base receiver later than the radio burst from the nearby transmitter. This is due to the delay of approximately 3 microseconds per km (5 microsec per mile) from travel of the radio wave through space. GSM, GMSK, and EDGE mobile radios can be commanded by the base station to advance the time of a transmitted radio burst. In this way, the signal from a distant mobile transmitter is properly time aligned to fall in the correct time slot at the base receiver. The 8.25 symbol guard time allows for minor inaccuracies in the advance timing adjustment, or for the presence of some delayed radio power that reflects off of objects in the cell (multipath transmission) and thus arrives later than the expected delay time.

The numbering identification of the eight time slots, from 0 to 7, used for purposes of assignment of particular time slots to particular mobile subscribers during an individual communication, is the same in GPRS and EDGE as for GSM voice or circuit-switched data systems. The numbering identification is assigned to the base and mobile transmitter time slots with a physical difference of three time slots. A particular time slot interval is labeled time slot 4 at the base transmitter, and the same time interval is labeled time slot 1 at the mobile transmitter. In this way, the mobile telephone assigned to use time slot 1 does not physically transmit and receive at the same time. This also permits simplification of the

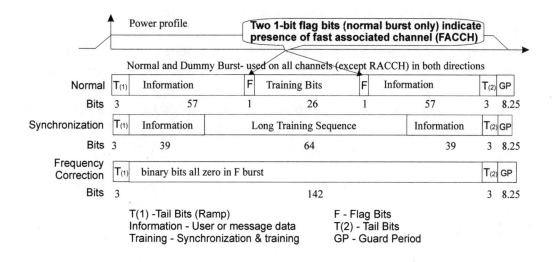

Figure 4.5. Normal Burst Bit Field Structures.

design and structure of the mobile telephone , since there is no need for a frequency filter to prevent the transmit signal from "leaking" back into the receiver.

Random Access (Shortened Burst)

Random access bursts are used when a mobile station attempts to access the cellular system. Because the distance from a base station radio tower is not known when a mobile telephone requests access, the radio transmission travel time from the mobile telephone to the base station can be excessive. This causes normal bursts to overlap in time with bursts that are received from other nearby mobile telephones. To overcome this challenge, initial bursts from mobile telephones are shorter than normal bursts. A shortened burst (access burst) is only 88 bits in duration. Most of these bits are used for preset binary synchronizing and training bit patterns. The primary purpose of the access burst is to get the attention of the base system to indicate an mobile telephone is requesting service. After the

88 bits are transmitted, the mobile telephone does not transmit any radio power until it received further messages from the base transmitter.

In addition to its use for the initial access from the mobile telephone to the base station, a shortened burst may also be used optionally immediately after a handover during a conversation. In theory, a handover may occur in a location where the distance between the mobile telephone and the target base station is not known, and therefore the shortened burst is transmitted once or more during the first (or first few) conversation time slot(s) just after handover. The base station measures the timing relationship of the shortened burst compared to the proper timing for the base receiver time slot, and immediately sends a message to the mobile telephone causing it to make an appropriate timing advance. Then the base station and mobile telephone return to transmitting the digitally coded speech for the conversation using normal bursts in both directions.

Basic Frame Structure

The basic GSM frame is composed of eight 577 microsec time slots to form a frame of a duration of 4.615 msec. The time slots within a frame are labeled from 0 to 7. A typical GSM service assigns a user to one time slot per frame. This same numbered time slot is used in consecutive frames to allow continuous communication. The frame structure for the uplink and downlink radio channels is the same. However, the slot numbers are intentionally offset by three slots to eliminate the requirement of the mobile telephone from having to transmit and receive at the same time. In one GSM system installation (typically a single city), the slot, the frame, and all the other longer frame intervals such as the multiframe, superframe, and hyperframe time occurrences are synchronized at all the base stations.

Figure 4.6 shows the basic frame structure. In this diagram, a single user is assigned to time slot 1. Notice in this diagram that there is a continuous stream of slots on the uplink and downlink direction. The bit stream is shown conceptually as a helix. The data bits in one time specific time slot are shown in the part of the helix which is at the front (closest to the reader) in each turn of the helix.

26 Frame Multiframe Structures

Groups of frames are combined in the GSM system to form multiframes. Multiframes are used to establish schedules for the predetermined use of the time slots in various frames for specific purposes such as traffic (subscriber digitally coded speech) in contrast to certain call processing information (such as the slow associated control channel - SACCH - which is used primarily to provide hand-off-related information). GSM has several multiframe structures. The most basic multiframe in the GSM system is the 26-frame multiframe, and all other multi-frame time intervals are referenced to it. This time interval corresponds to 120 msec, which is exactly the time needed for six blocks of digital speech coder data.

The designers of the GSM system recognized early in their efforts that they wanted to transmit mainly the digital output of the speech coder (now called the

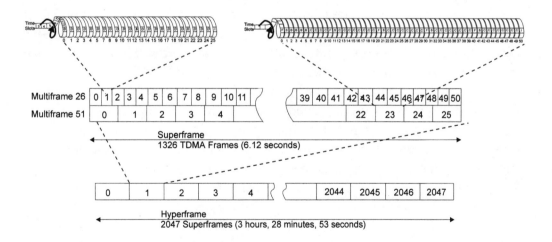

Figure 4.6. GSM Basic Frame Structure.

Traffic Channel – TCH) but also needed to continuously transmit a separate continuous low-bit-rate digital message control signal. This control signal (now called SACCH) is used primarily for the mobile telephone to report signal conditions measured on other channels in preparation for possible handover. When the data rate of each of these sources was considered, the designers found that the ratio of the gross bit rate for the speech coder was about 24 times as big as the data rate for the SACCH information (including the error protection coding). Initially, that would suggest that a 25-frame sequence could be used, with 24 of the frames used for TCH and one used for SACCH. However, they also planned on a future half-rate speech coder. This resulted in one of the frames having an idle period.

Another benefit of the superframe's idle period is that during that period, the mobile telephone has the ability to scan other beacon frequencies in nearby cells to help determine the best target handoff cell. While the mobile telephone can scan some other time slots when it is communicating speech information with the base station, it cannot scan other channels during the time slots for which it is currently transmitting or receiving. The only time slot that is guaranteed to be transmitting in each and every frame is time slot zero of a beacon frequency. This is not a problem if the mobile telephone is involved in a conversation in which the physical time slot is not slot zero, since it then has time slot zero free for these other monitoring uses. But what about the case where the mobile telephone is using time slot zero on a nonbeacon frequency for traffic? One way to ensure that even such an mobile telephone has an occasional opportunity to receive during time slot 0 is to set up the schedule of operations so that there is an occasional "idle" time frame when the mobile telephone does not need to transmit or receive. Then it can use this idle time slot to examine the transmissions on time slot 0 from other cells. The final design of the 26-frame multi-frame structure allows the mobile telephone to do all these things.

51-Frame Multiframe Structures

A 51-frame multiframe structure is used for the control channels (on the beacon frequency). Control channels ALWAYS occur on the beacon frequency in time slot 0 and may also occur at the option of the GSM system administration on slots 2, 4, or 6 of the beacon frequency as well. They also follow a pattern of scheduled use based on a 51-frame multiframe sequence. The 51-frame multiframe is subdivided into prescheduled logical channels. These logical channels include the frequency correction burst, the synchronization burst, the broadcast channel (BCH), the paging and access grant channel (PACCH), and the standalone dedicated control channel (SDCCH) used for call setup and SMS messages. The SDCCH channel is also called the TCH/8 (1/8 rate traffic channel) in some documents.

Superframe

A superframe is composed of 51 of 26 multiframes (6.12 seconds). It is required for an mobile telephone using slot 0 only once per 26-frame interval to eventually scan all the different time frame types of a 51-frame multiframe once. Of course, the mobile telephone cannot see every consecutive slot 0 transmission from the neighboring base station Beacon frequency. But it will see one of them (for example, let us say the 51-frame idle slot to be specific), and then it will be busy for 25 frames, and then it will see another slot, namely the zero time slot, and so on. This pattern of actions will continue until, after 51 intervals of 26 frames each, it is again looking at the same type of slot 0 data (the idle slot in this example) as it was in the previous sentence. Aside from its physical significance as the interval needed to scan over the entire scope of 51 different kinds of slot zero beacon frequency transmission, the superframe is also a time interval which is used to define the hyperframe.

Hyperframe

The hyperframe is the largest time interval in the GSM system, and is composed of 2048 superframes (approximately 3 1/2 hours). During a hyperframe period, every time slot has a unique sequential number composed of frame number and time slot number.

The hyperframe counter is used to synchronize several internal operations in the GSM system, including the sequential transmission of different types of prescheduled information at certain times, and the frequency hopping sequence (which is an optional feature) pattern, and the synchronization of the encryption process for privacy of subscribers' conversations.

The hyperframe is a convenient, long-time interval that permits the proper synchronization of the base system and the mobile stations operating in that system. The hyperframe time counter is used for ensuring proper operation of encryption, frequency hopping, and some other functions. It is defined as 2048 Superframes. The decimal number 2048 is just 2 to the 11th power, which makes it a convenient number to count using an 11-bit binary counter device. The time interval corresponding to the complete cycle of a hyperframe is over three hours, which is much longer than the typical telephone connection. Thus, the encryption process, which uses this counter, will not likely repeat itself during a call of reasonable duration, and privacy will not be compromised.

Once a mobile telephone receives broadcast channel transmissions from a base station, and also a particular scheduled transmission called the synchronizing burst message, it can synchronize its own internal hyperframe counter with the base system's hyperframe counter. Then all the equipment, both base and mobile, in the system is synchronized. It is not necessary that different systems in different cities synchronize their various hyperframe counters.

Other Multiframe Structures

Some logical channels in the GSM system use different multiple frame structures or they use no frame schedule at all. An example of a logical channel, which strictly speaking, has no schedule, is the random access channel (RACH). This is the name for the uplink timeslot zero on the beacon frequency. It is reserved at all times during each and every frame for an mobile telephone to transmit a shortened access burst for the purpose of starting a communication between the mobile telephone and base station. Another nonscheduled logical channel is the FACCH.

Logical Channels

A logical channel is a portion of a physical communications channel that is used to for a particular (logical) communications purpose. The physical channel (radio or wired) may be divided in time, frequency or digital coding to provide for these logical channels.

The two main logical channels for the GSM system are the traffic channel (transfers voice or user data information) and the control channels (signaling). The GSM system subdivides (via time division) these two basic types of channels into many logical channels.

Traffic Channel or Digital Traffic Channel (TCH or DTC)

A traffic channel is the combination of voice and data signals existing within a communication channel. There are three basic types of traffic channels: full rate, half rate, and eighth rate. Variants of these channels also exist.

A full rate traffic channel (TCH/F) dedicates one slot per frame for a communication channel between a user and the cellular system. A half-rate traffic channel (TCH/H) dedicates one slot per every two frames for a communication channel between a user and the cellular system. The eighth rate traffic channel (TCH/8) is used only on the SDCCH for exchange of call setup and/or short message service, to provide limited data transmission rates.

Broadcast Channels (BCH)

The broadcast channel contains several logical channels that are multiplexed onto one communications channel that is continuously broadcast from a cell site. The broadcast channel typically provides the mobile phone with system information, lists of neighboring radio channels and other system configuration information. A cell broadcast channel (CBCH) transfers short messages.

Each cell has a broadcast channel. By examining the signal strength of each nearby broadcast channel, and using the error detecting codes which are incorporated into the digital transmission from that base station, the GSM mobile telephones that are not engaged in a conversation can measure the quality of nearby cell sites' radio channels. This is done to determine which is the optimal control channel to select. Once the mobile telephone has found the best broadcast channel, it continues to receive that frequency and time slot until there is a reason to choose another. The reasons to choose another include movement of the mobile telephone into another cell, which will cause the mobile telephone to move away from the old base station, so the signal strength will decrease and the bit error rate will increase. In that case, the mobile telephone again scans for the best broadcast channel all over again.

One of the most important parameters is the information about the sleep and wake paging cycle. In order to conserve battery power, the base system schedules paging messages (which occur when someone else originates a call to a mobile telephone) so that the mobile telephone does not need to keep its receiver on all the time. The mobile telephone can "go to sleep" (turn off all its internal electronic circuits except the hyperframe counter) most of the time, and "wake up" (turn on its receiver circuits) only periodically when it knows that pages destined for it (if any) will occur.

The FCCH channel is a logical channel that provides a mobile radio with a frequency reference for the telephone system, and also allows the mobile telephone to find the Beacon frequency. For the GSM system, the FCCH only contain a frequency correction burst.

Common Control Channel (CCCH)

The common control channel (CCCH) is the collective name in GSM documentation for a group of logical control channels that support the establishment and maintenance of communication links between mobile telephones and base stations. There are three types of CCCH used in the GSM system: paging channel (PCH), random access channel (RACH), and access grant channel (AGCH).

The paging channel (PCH) is used to transfer call setup pages to a mobile telephone. The paging channel typically sends a page message that contains a temporary mobile telephone identity (TMSI) to alert a mobile telephone that a call is to be received. The TMSI was previously assigned to the mobile telephone by the base GSM system. When the mobile telephone detects a match of the TMSI sent by the system to the TMSI stored in its memory, it will alert the user that an incoming call is to be received. If the user decides to answer the call (typically by pressing the SEND or TALK key), the mobile telephones ends an access request message to the system indicating it is responding to a page message. The PCH is usually present at prescheduled times on the downlink in time slot 0 of the beacon frequency, although additional channels in other frequencies may be assigned if heavy paging traffic is expected.

The random access channel carries random access bursts from mobile telephones so they can transmit their request for service to the base station when they begin to set up a call. The RACH is a shared channel that is acknowledged through shared control feedback (SCF). The RACH is usually in time slot 0 of the uplink beacon frequency, although additional channels can be assigned by the system administration on other frequencies in a GSM system that expects a high number of RACH messages. The successful response to a random access service request is an acknowledgment message on the access grant channel (AGCH). If the base GSM system does not detect the random access request, it will not respond to the mobile telephone and the mobile telephone will automatically wait for a randomly chosen time interval and then re-transmit a new request for service.

The access grant channel is used to assign a mobile phone to a channel (SDCCH) where it can begin to communicate with the system. An access grant channel message is a base GSM system response after a random access channel (RACH) service request message has been sent from the mobile telephone to the base system. The AGCH is usually present at prescheduled times on the downlink in time slot 0 of the beacon frequency, although additional channels in other frequencies may be assigned if heavy call setup and short message traffic is expected.

Stand Alone Dedicated Control Channel (SDCCH)

Stand alone dedicated control channel (SDCCH) transfers control information between the mobile telephone and the base station after the paging, access grant and other starting processes, but before the TCH (voice or customer data channel) is used. The messages on the SDCCH channel may also include short messages. The SDCCH is usually present on a time slot, such as 2, 4, or 6, on the beacon frequency, although certain additional time slots and frequencies may also be assigned in a system that expects to have heavy call setup and/or SMS traffic. The assigned SDCCH channel may be shared by as many as 8 mobile telephones during the process of call setup or SMS data transfer. The logical channel types, which are carried on the SDCCH, include the 1/8 rate traffic channel (TCH/8) and SACCH.

Slow Associated Control Channel (SACCH)

The slow associated control channel (SACCH) is a continuous dedicated stream of signaling data sent at prescheduled times to allow the regular transfer of control information between the mobile telephone and the BS. The SACCH information is sent on frame 12 of the 26-frame multiframe. A SACCH channel is also used on the SDCCH channel but the details are not shown here. Because the SACCH data does not replace speech data, the SACCH channel is called "out-of-band" signaling.

The SACCH channel is primarily used to transfer radio channel signal quality information measured by the mobile telephone back to the BS to assist in the handover process. Because the SACCH channel dedicates a portion of the available data transfer rate to signaling, a balance was maintained to allow the maximum number of bits to be devoted to speech, and to allocate a minimum number of bits to continuous signaling. Figure 4.7 illustrates the SACCH signaling process.

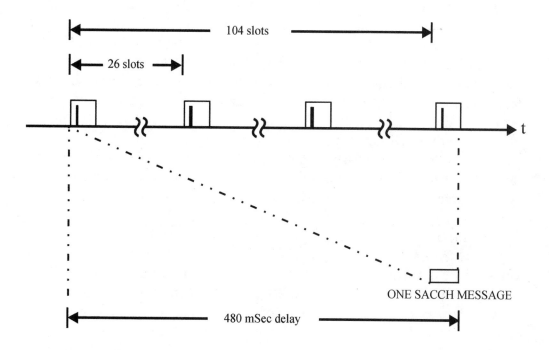

Figure 4.7. SACCH Full Rate Signaling.

Fast Associated Control Channel (FACCH)

The fast associated control channel (FACCH) is used to send urgent (unscheduled) signaling control messages (such as a handoff or power control message). FACCH message signaling is required because the data transmission rate for SACCH messages is very low. A single SACCH message can take seconds to transfer. For rapid message delivery, messages are sent via the FACCH channel instead of the SACCH channel. The FACCH channel sends messages by replacing speech data with signaling data for short periods of time. FACCH messaging is called "in band" signaling.

As many as one out of six speech frames may be stolen for FACCH messages, by replacing speech frame(s) with signaling information, so FACCH messages degrade speech quality slightly. When a frame of coded speech is lost due to replacement by FACCH data (or due to serious radio channel errors), the GSM speech coder can repeat the last good received frame of speech coder data. Under these circumstances, listeners in GSM systems hear a brief persistence of a speech sound (for 20 milliseconds) rather than a silence, "click," or other gross disturbance of speech. FACCH messages result in nonlinear degradation of speech quality as the number of stolen frames increases. Because data is bitinterleaved for radio transmission over eight consecutive channel bursts, the data bits for a FACCH message are transmitted piece by piece over eight sequential channel bursts (57 bits per channel burst). Figure 4.8 illustrates the FACCH signaling process.

Because the FACCH messages replace user information (voice or data), the receiver of the FACCH message must be capable of determining the difference between user data and a FACCH message. This is done by the use of two flag bits in each time slot burst. Normally, these bits are set to 0 for user data. When FACCH data replaces user data, the appropriate flag bits are changed to 1. Because the user data and FACCH information are interleaved, it is possible that only half the bits in one time slot may be is used for FACCH data. This requires the use of two flag bits.

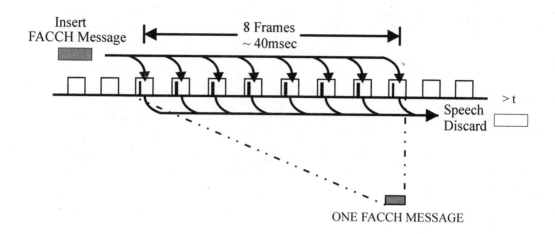

Figure 4.8. FACCH Signaling.

To avoid complications with stealing control time slots during the 26 frame multiframe, the interleaving process for TCH and FACCH "skips over" the SACCH (frame 12) and the idle (frame 25) time frames in the 26-frame multi-frame. FACCH data never is sent during a SACCH or idle slot. Figure 4.9 shows the basic logical channels used in the GSM system.

Basic Operation

There are many other processes a mobile telephone must perform to operate in a GSM network. The basic call processing operation of a mobile telephone includes initialization, call origination, call reception (paging), handover, and ending a call.

Mobile Telephone Initialization

When a GSM mobile telephone is first turned on, before it can make any type of connection to a base station, it must initialize its processes with information from the system it intends to use for obtaining service. It initializes by first scanning

Channel Name	Where it is Used	Comments
AGCH- Access Grant Channel	Downlink Beacon frequency in specified frames of 51-frame schedule.	Tells MS which SDCCH channel to use next.
BCCH or BCH- Broadcast Channel	Downlink Beacon frequency in specified frames of 51-frame schedule.	Broadcasts general information about the system and this particular cell.
CCCH- Common Control Channel	Downlink Beacon frequency in specified frames of 51-frame schedule.	A convenient name for the frames which are time scheduled for PCH or AGCH.
FACCH- Fast Associated Control Channel	Uses same physical channels as TCH, when indicated by flag bits. Up and down link.	Used for occasional unpredictable messages in the midst of a voice, fax or data connection.
FCCH- Frequency Correction Channel	Only on slot zero downlink of the Beacon frequency in each cell.	Allows MS to find the Beacon frequency and provides standard frequency signal.
PCH- Paging Channel	Downlink Beacon frequency in specified frames of 51-frame schedule.	Transmits the TMSI of a particular MS to indicate that a call has arrived for that MS.
RACH- Random Access Channel	Uplink time slot zero of Beacon Frequency †	Other schedules on other frequencies are also permitted.
SACCH- Slow Associated Control Channel	Uses same physical channels as TCH or SDCCH, according to prearranged schedule. Up and down link.	Sends continual low bit-rate data, mostly related to mobile assisted handover (MAHO), by taking pre-arranged bursts from the same physical channel as TCH or SDCCH.
SDCCH or DCCH- Standalone Dedicated Control Channel	Up and Downlink using, e.g., slot 2 of the Beacon Frequency. †	In general, other time slots and other frequencies may be used as well.
SCH- Synchronizing Channel	Only on slot zero downlink of the Beacon frequency in each cell.	Provides most of the bits so MS can synchronize its hyper-frame counter to the base system.
TCH or DTC- Traffic Channel or Digital Traffic Channel	Uses 26-frame multi-frame schedule on almost any channel, Up and downlink.	Carries digitally coded voice, or fax or data, during 24 bursts of the 26-frame schedule (full rate).

Figure 4.9. Logical Channels Used in GSM Systems.

the various base station carrier frequencies for the purpose of identifying certain properties of the base system. The mobile telephone stores this information in its subscriber identity module (SIM). When the SIM is installed and the handset is powered up for the first time, the set will "initialize" itself.

One aspect of this initialization process is to scan all the carrier frequencies in the operating band(s) in which the mobile telephone is capable of operating. There may be 75 or more carrier frequencies used in a system, but typically only 25 or less are used in a single cell. In general, the system operator has configured (at least) one carrier frequency in each cell/sector as the "beacon frequency" for that cell or that sector. The beacon frequency uses its "first" time slot (described as time slot zero) for special purposes. To simplify the call processing steps for the mobile telephone, time slot zero on the beacon frequency is never used for a voice, data, or packet channel. However, other time slots on the beacon frequency may be used for voice, data, or packet channels.

When seeking a radio carrier signal with strong signal strength, it will typically find several qualified (acceptable signal strength) frequencies. Having scanned for radio carrier channels, the mobile telephone then goes back and examines each frequency beginning with the strongest signals. It is seeking a radio carrier channel that contains a control channel. After it has found a control channel, the mobile telephone begins to receive and store certain system broadcast information. This broadcast information includes data that identifies the system and contains access control information (such as initial transmit power level) that allows the mobile telephone to access to the system.

Figure 4.10 shows the basic information that is continuously sent by the system. This information includes system identification, the initial access power level at which the mobile telephones should transmit when requesting service, locations of paging and messaging channels, and other information that coordinates access to the GSM network.

Every installed GSM base service area has a unique mobile network code (MNC), a number that it broadcasts periodically and which identifies it distinctly from other system operators in the same city or anywhere else in the world. The mobile telephone also has the MNC of its own home system stored in its

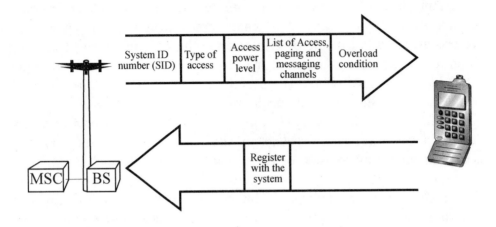

Figure 4.10. System Broadcast Information.

subscriber identity module (SIM) chip. Using the list of qualified beacon channels (sufficient signal strength) and preferred system MNC code (home MNC usually preferred), the mobile telephone chooses the "best" beacon frequency and sends an identifying (system registration) message.

Mobile Call Origination

When a customer initiates a call from a mobile telephone, this is referred to as call origination. This is usually accomplished when a subscriber enters a telephone number via the number buttons, and pressing the SEND button. When this occurs, the mobile telephone attempts access to the system.

A mobile telephone attempts to gain service from the cellular system by transmitting a request after listening to the control channel to determine if the system is not busy. If the system is not busy, it attempts access by transmitting an access burst on the RACH channel. The access burst contains a 5-bit random number that temporarily identifies the mobile telephone that is attempting the access. The access burst also contains a 3-bit code that identifies the type of access requested, such as page response, call origination, or reconnection of an accidentally disconnected call (due to poor quality radio signals). If the system successfully receives the access request message, it sends back the same random number in the immediate assignment message, directing the subscriber unit to tune to a specific radio channel and time slot. After the mobile telephone tunes to its assigned channel, the system typically requests authentication. If the system authorizes service, conversation can begin.

Figure 4.11 shows a functional diagram of how a mobile telephone initiates a call to a GSM network. In step 1, the mobile telephones ends the dialed digits along with the telephone's identification information to a nearby base station. After the dialed digits have been received and the mobile telephone has been authorized for service, the MSC will seize an outside line (trunk) and dial the indicated number (step 2). The GSM network will then command the mobile telephone to tune to a specified radio carrier frequency and time slot for which the call will be connected (step 3). The mobile telephone tunes to the new channel (step 4) and conversation may begin (step 5). During the conversation, the base transceiver station (BTS) is continually measuring the signal strength of the received radio waves from the mobile transmitter to determine if a call handover is required.

Call Handover

Call handover is the process of transferring a call between base stations. (Handover is typically called "handoff" in North America.) Handover is necessary because mobile telephones often move out of range of one base station and into the radio coverage area of another base station.

Because the GSM network is digital and divided in time, the received radio signal strength and channel quality can be continually measured for multiple radio carrier channels. This allows the continual seeking of a better radio frequency and time slot related to an adjacent cell. This is determined necessary when there is either excessive bit error rate (BER) and/or received signal strength below what is known to be adequate for this particular cell. This process of seeking a better target channel is the beginning of a handover.

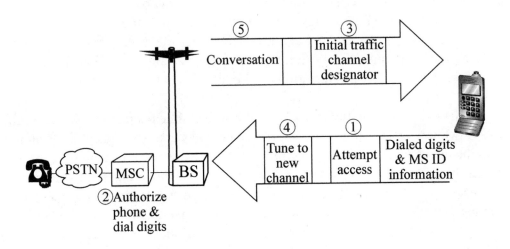

Figure 4.11. Mobile Call Origination.

In the GSM network, there are several additional items of information, which are not available in older analog cellular systems. Because the mobile telephone operates on a carrier frequency in a TDMA operating sequence during a conversation, it only transmits for 1/8 of the total time, and receives a signal from the base station during another 1/8 of the time. During the remaining 6/8 (or 2/3) of the total time, the mobile receiver is idle and can be used to monitor the signal strength and quality from the beacon frequencies in adjacent radio cells. Keep in mind that the mobile telephone receiver can be quickly re-tuned to other radio carrier frequencies during each such time slot, and then tuned back to the frequency needed to communicate with the current base station in adequate time to keep up proper communication for support of the conversation. To facilitate this, a control message is initially sent to each mobile telephone when it begins a conversation in a particular cell. That message contains a command to scan the beacon frequencies of adjacent cells and then their frequency numbers are explicitly listed. The mobile scans the listed frequencies during the otherwise idle mobile receiver time slots, and measures and reports the signal strength and BER of each nearby cell. These reports are transmitted back to the base station periodically in a special scheduled manner that does not interfere with the transmission of digitally coded speech signals. This process of using reports from the mobile telephone to assist in handover is called mobile assisted handover (MAHO).

The base station is then in possession of a dynamically generated list showing the signal strength and BER of signals from all adjacent cells, as measured by the mobile telephone at its present location. The base system also knows which adjacent cells have idle radio channels available as a handover target, and which do not. The control computer in the BSC (or in the MSC, as the case may be) selects the set of adjacent cells that have idle available channels, and from this set it selects that cell that has the best combination of signal strength and BER. A suitable channel (carrier frequency and time slot) is assigned in that cell as the target, and the mobile telephone is commanded to retune to use that channel. At the same time, the base or land portion of the conversation is simultaneously switched over to that assigned target channel in the adjacent cell. When this is done properly, the retuning of the radio occurs during the previously mentioned idle time slots, so the mobile telephone is still in communication with the base stations on the regular schedule of one in eight for both transmit and receive. There is no lost information, and no gap in the speech from the voice codec. This is called a "seamless" TDMA handover.

Figure 4.12 shows the basic call handover process. In this diagram, a mobile telephone is communicating with base station #1. Base station #1 provides the mobile telephone with a list of radio carrier channels to measure of nearby base stations (step 1). After the mobile telephone measures the quality of the radio carrier channels, it returns this information to the serving base station (step 2). Using this information and information from neighboring base stations, the serving base station sends a handover message (step 3), which instructs the mobile telephone to tune to a new radio carrier channel of the adjacent base station #2. The mobile telephone begins transmission on the new channel by sending a short burst (step 4). The new base station uses this information to send a command to adjust the relative timing of the mobile telephone (step 5). After the mobile telephone has adjusted, the voice channel from the MSC is switched from base station #1 to base station #2 and voice conversation can continue (step 6).

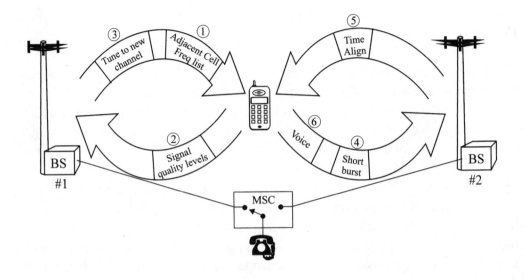

Figure 4.12. Call Handover.

Ending a Call

Eventually, one of the two people involved in the telephone conversation hangs up the telephone (on the land end) or presses the END button on the mobile telephone end. This causes an exchange of messages over the radio link that requests the call to be disconnected along with an acknowledgment message for an intentional disconnection. The system design is very paranoid in this situation, requiring repeated confirming messages in order to prevent an accidental disconnection. After the call is disconnected, the mobile telephones starts scanning again to find the best beacon frequency and be ready for another call. The base station marks the previous channel as free and ready for another use by another conversation.

Receiving a Call on a Mobile Telephone

Receiving a call on a mobile telephone is called call termination. A mobile terminated call is essentially similar to the mobile originated call just described, except for the beginning steps which involve alerting the mobile telephone of an incoming call (called paging). The paging process begins when another caller dials the telephone number of the mobile telephone. When the call is received at the home system, an inquiry message is sent to the customer database to determine the present location of the mobile telephone. The customer database responds with the identification number of last registered location of the mobile telephone. If the mobile telephone is operating in a another (a visited) system, the customer database response includes the system identification and routing information of the visited system. The visited system uses the mobile telephone's identification information to send a page message to the mobile telephone. The page message is sent to the mobile telephone on a radio carrier channel of the base station where it was last located.

The mobile telephone's identification information is called the international mobile subscriber identity (IMSI). Because the IMSI is composed of many digits, systems typically use an abbreviated form of the paging message. The temporary identification number is assigned to the mobile phone when it first registers in a system (typically during initialization). This is called a temporary mobile subscriber identity (TMSI). The TMSI is much shorter than an IMSI.

Figure 4.13 shows the basic process for receiving a call on the GSM network. In the first step, the mobile telephone receives the channel number of the paging channel to monitor. The mobile telephone will listen to this channel until it hears its identification number (step 2). The mobile telephone will then request service from the GSM network indicating in its request that it is responding to a page message (step 3). After the system validates the mobile telephone's identification information, it will assign it to a radio carrier channel (step 4).

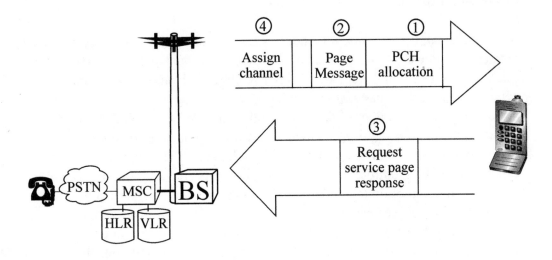

Figure 4.13. Receiving a Call on a Mobile.

General Packet Radio Service (GPRS)

General packet radio service provides high-speed packet data service on a GSM network. GPRS is part of the phase 2+ specifications for GSM, now under control of the 3rd generation partnership project (3GPP). The GPRS system dynamically assigns time slots on a GSM radio channels to allow quick and efficient transfer small packets of data. GPRS allows point-to-point and point-to-multipoint packet data transmission. GPRS provides a maximum data transmission capacity of 171.2 kbps.

System Overview

To use the radio link most effectively for bursty data transmission, the GPRS system dynamically assigns a particular time slot on a particular carrier frequency to a particular user who has packets to transmit in the appropriate direction.

When that user finishes sending packets, the GPRS system can immediately assign the channel to another packet user. This overall process is much more efficient than a circuit switched connection that "wastes" the channel capacity by leaving it assigned to the subscriber even when there is no data to transmit at certain times.

Figure 4.14 shows some of the key GPRS network elements that include a gateway GPRS support node (GGSN), a serving GPRS support node (SGSN) and a GPRS backbone network. The SGSN registers and maintains a list of active packet data radios in its network and coordinates the packet transfer between the mobile radios, local GPRS network, and the GPRS (may be a mobile data device).

The GPRS system is packet based as packets can be randomly sent without the need for continuous assignment of a particular time slot within a frame period. GPRS uses the radio interface that is based on the same time division schedule, originally established for GSM voice and circuit-switched data services. In fact, a single carrier frequency can be used to support a mixture of GSM voice (or circuit switched data) service on some of the eight time slots, while simultaneously supporting GPRS on other time slots.

Some of the key capabilities of the GPRS system include point-to-point data transfer, Internet compatibility, quick SMS transfer, and X.25 interworking. The GPRS system is expected to progress to point-to-multipoint (PTM), multicast and group call capability.

GPRS uses standard communication protocol structures such as the point-to-point protocol (PPP) used in the Internet. Packet-switching points in the GPRS network are called service nodes. The key function of the service node is to switch the.packets it receives toward their destination point. Switching nodes are intelligent switching points and the routes packets may take during a communications session (e.g. file transfer) can dynamically change. This is different than traditional dedicated connections ("circuits") through a MSC for voice calls.

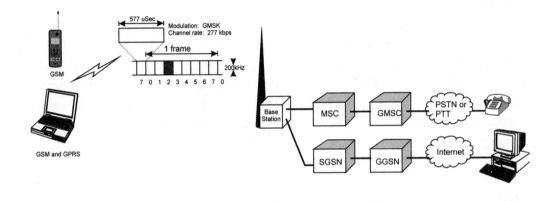

Figure 4.14. General Packet Radio Service (GPRS) System.

The packet radio transmission resources (radio transmitters and time slot assignments) are managed by the serving GPRS service node (SGSN). The SGSN maintains the current communications status with the mobile telephone in a similar process as a serving MSC manages communications with a mobile telephone. The SGSN receives and processes registration requests, and maintains the status of the mobile telephone that is operating within its territory (e.g., idle or ready to receive data) in a temporary database.

The GGSN maintains the location information (anchor location) of the mobile telephone that is using GPRS services. This allows the mobile telephone to migrate to different SGSNs as it travels throughout the GPRS system. The GGSN is also the gateway between the GPRS system and external data networks such as the Internet. The GGSN maintains a tunnel (protected virtual path) between the SGSN and the data network to which it is connected. The GGSN is also the primary gatekeeper for billing information from usage that is passed between the mobile telephone and the data network throughout its session.

A border gateway interconnects the SGSN and GGSN nodes. This is called the GPRS backbone network. The backbone network can be any circuit or packet-connection-based network that is able to route packets based on Internet Protocol (IP). IP only routes packets based on their destination address. An upper layer (monitoring) protocol oversees the sequencing and delivery of packets between the sender and the receiver. The protocols used in the GPRS system to connect between SGSNs and GGSNs include transmission control protocol (TCP), user datagram protocol (UDP), and GPRS tunneling protocol (GTP). TCP involves two-way confirmation of packets sent between two points. While TCP adds confirmation to packet transmission, it also adds delay and overhead information. UDP adds a limited amount of overhead (e.g., sequence numbers for the packets) but does not provide delivery confirmation. GTP sits on top of the TCP/UDP protocols to manage connections and to add security for the tunneling between the SGSN and GGSN.

To communicate between the SGSN and GGSN, a virtual path tunnel is created. The SGSN and GGSN have their own unique address for the tunnel. As the mobile telephone moves throughout the system, alternative SGSNs may be assigned. This means the path is changed so the new SGSN will communicate with the GGSN. The addresses of the SGSN and GGSN are independent of the addresses of the packets sent between the mobile telephone and the data network (e.g., Internet). When the mobile telephone sends an IP packet, it includes the destination address for the packet. This packet, along with the destination address, is encapsulated in a transmission packet that is routed between the SGSN and the GGSN.

Figure 4.15 shows how the encapsulation process works. As the IP packet is sent from the data device (e.g., portable computer) into the wireless device, packets are individually addressed with their destination address (the web site host). When the packet is received at the SGSN, the packet is forwarded to the destination GGSN on the virtual path (tunnel). The forwarding process involves encapsulating the original IP data packet into a packet that is routed to the

GGSN. Both the SGSN and GGSN have their own IP address. The data packets that are sent and received between the computer A and the laptop computer B are simply carried (encapsulated) in packets that are routed between the GGSN and SGSN.

The communication between the base station and the SGSN is based on frame relay. For frame relation connections, virtual circuits (logical channels) can be used to multiplex data from several mobile telephones into larger frame relay packets. A specific protocol, base station subsystem GPRS protocol (BSSGP), was developed to allow the efficient transfer of data and paging messages between the base station and the SGSN. BSSGP protocol messages are only transported by the frame relay connection.

The SGSN can interact with standard network databases including the HLR, VLR, AuC, and EIR using SS7 messages. However, these databases are not required for routing data. They are only necessary to coordinate operation between GPRS and other networks (e.g., short message transfer by GPRS rather than by a GSM or an IS-136 system.

System Attributes

The GPRS system allows dynamic assignment of time slots to users while using the same modulation and radio channel structure as the GSM system. Some of the field structures and new logical channels have been created for the GPRS system.

Modulation and Bit Rate

The GPRS system uses the same GMSK modulation that is used in the GSM system. Because there is a change in the slot structure, there is a slight change in the gross data transmission rate. GPRS does not use the two flag bits per radio burst that are unique to GSM voice and circuit-switched services. It has 116 bits of gross payload per radio burst, and the overall payload-related bit rate of GPRS is thus 25.2 kbps for one time slot, or 201.1 kbps if all eight slots on the same carrier frequency are counted. In the GPRS design, some of the time frames are reserved for other purposes than subscriber data, so no individual subscriber realizes that full gross bit rate. Figure 4.16 shows the GPRS burst slot structure.

Time Slot Interleaving

The packet data bits transmitted for one connection are transmitted in the four frames of a block, and the data bits are time interleaved by means of a rearrangement of bits among the four frames composing a block (called T frames). Four-frame interleaving is used to rapidly transfer packets of data. This is different than the 8-frame interleaving used for full-rate GSM voice service. Interleaving

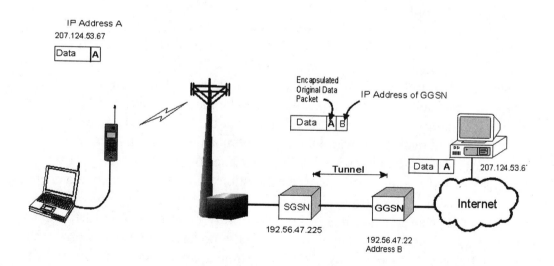

Figure 4.15. IP Datagram Encapsulation.

distributes the bits of data over several time slots to improve the performance of the error protection coding because radio links are more likely to have burst errors that destroy a single time slot as opposed to random errors over several time slots.

Because it is not always possible (or desirable) to interleave bits (e.g., for a single data access), packets not always interleaved. When interleaving is not performed, special types of error protection codes are used (called the I frames.)

Timing Adjustment of Packet Data

Timing adjustment information is needed to ensure that the normal transmit burst from a mobile telephone is received by the base receiver in the "middle" of the time slot assigned to it. As the mobile telephone moves farther away from the base station, the radio wave experiences more time delay before reaching the base receiver. This one-way delay is approximately 3 microsec per km (or 5 microsec per mile). If the radio burst arrives too late, it can overlap with the radio burst in the successive time slot and cause errors in the last few bits of the delayed time slot data and in the first few bits of data in that successive time slot.

When a mobile transmitter is transmitting normal radio bursts almost continuously in a particular time slot, adjustments can be made from time to time based on the measured arrival time of the radio burst at the base station. This situation occurs in traditional GSM when the mobile transmits during its assigned time slot in nearly every frame, or when a long sequence of packet data transmissions occur as part of a transmission to one of the time slots in the packet data channel. To adjust the mobile transmitter burst timing advance, the base receiver first continuously measures the time of arrival of every radio burst from the mobile transmitter. When the radio burst arrives slightly too late at the base receiver, the base station measures the delay and sends a timing control signal to the mobile telephone commanding the mobile transmitter to advance the burst timing to a particular advance value that compensates for the measured delay or lateness. As

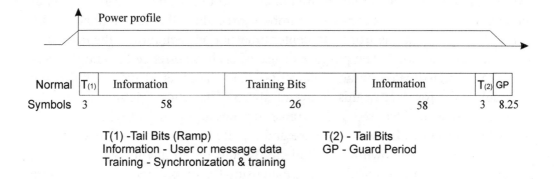

Figure 4.16. GPRS Radio Burst Slot Structure.

the mobile telephone moves farther and farther away from the base station, the base station sends such timing correction signals from time to time, thus keeping the radio burst, as it is perceived at the base receiver, centered in the appropriate time slot.

Packet Data Control Channels

A time slot that is assigned by the base system as a packet data channel (PDCH) uses a 52-frame schedule called a multiframe. Figure 4.17 illustrates the sequence of both frames and time slots on a GPRS radio channel by displaying the sequence of transmitted data as a ribbon that are wound into a helix. The ribbon is marked off into time slots, and at the left end of the upper helix, we see some consecutive time slots numbered 3, 4, 5, 6, 7, 8, and then 0, 1, 2. The helix may be viewed as though the ribbon is wound around a cylinder of the proper diameter so that one turn of the helix corresponds to one frame (eight time slots).

The duration of each time frame is 4.615 msec and the time duration of the entire 52-frame multiframe is thus 240 msec.

Although time slot number labels are not used throughout the diagram, the reader can see from the sequence of numbers preceding the first alphabetically labeled time slot that the front-and-center time slot on each turn of the helix corresponds to time slot 4. The purpose or use of each occurrence of time slot 3 in each frame is indicated by an alphabetic label. The letter D indicates that the schedule calls for data in this frame of slot 3. The letter T indicates that the PTCCH signals will be used in this frame, for measuring (uplink) the time delay (related to distance) between the base and mobile telephones, and sending timing advance signals (downlink). The letter I indicates an intentionally idle time frame for time slot 3, set aside to facilitate using the mobile receiver to measure signal strength and quality from other base stations in nearby cells to facilitate MAHO.

The 52-frame multiframe schedule comprises twelve blocks, and each block consists of four consecutive frames. The 12 blocks are labeled B0 through B11. The digital contents of these data blocks are used for the packet data traffic channels (PDTCHs). In the case where messages are exchanged prior to connection setup, certain blocks are designated to carry other types of system packet data, namely the packet broadcast control channel (PBCCH), the packet common control channels (PCCCH), and the packet dedicated control channels (PDCCH).

Logical Channels

The GPRS system uses new logical channels to coordinate, assign, and transfer data on a GSM radio channel. The logical channels have similar functions to the broadcast, common control, and dedicated traffic channels used by the GSM system.

A packet broadcast control channel (PBCCH) provides system information to GPRS capable mobile telephones (used for initialization and access control). A

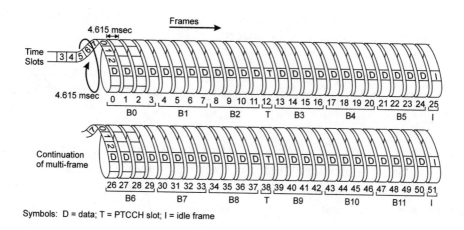

Figure 4.17. 52-Frame Multiframe.

packet random access channel (PRACH) is used by the mobile telephone to request access to the GPRS system for data transfer. The packet paging channel (PPCH) is used by the GPRS system to inform the mobile telephone there is data to be received. The packet access grant channel (PAGCH) is used by the system to assign a packet traffic channel to specific mobile telephones. The packet notification channel (PNCH) informs groups of mobile telephones that multicast transmissions are about to occur.

A mobile telephone transmits data on the packet data traffic channel (PDTCH). Specific control commands (e.g., signaling messages) are exchanged with the specific mobile telephone during a data session through a packet associated control channel (PACCH).

The GPRS system defines many new logical channels, separate from their traditional GSM counterparts, are set aside for packet transactions. Packet data channel (PDCH) is a "category" term used in GPRS for physical channels that may carry various more specific types of packet data. The names of the types of packet data channels that occur as subcategories of PDCH are

Packet broadcast control channel (PBCCH). This broadcasts information about the cell, similar to the cell and system information used in the traditional GSM BCCH.

Packet common control channel (PCCCH). Like its counterpart the CCCH, it is a category name for a channel that may carry any one of several subcategories. This channel type is shared by messages addressed to particular users and broadcast type messages. These subcategories are:

Packet access grant channel (PACCH) (downlink only). This carries access grant messages from the base to a mobile telephone following a request on the PRACH channel.

Packet paging channel (PPCH) (downlink only). Alerts the mobile telephone that data is ready to be received.

PRACH (uplink only). Carries a shortened burst from mobile telephone to the base station when mobile telephone desires access to the base station.

Packet notification channel (PNCH) (downlink only). This is used to notify a specific group of mobile telephones that a broadcast or point-to-multpoint transmission follows. It has no exact counterpart in traditional GSM that does not support broadcast messages for voice or subscriber circuit-switched data.

Packet dedicated control channel (PDCCH) is used to transfer call processing data to a specific mobile telephone (not for subscriber data). Its subtypes have several counterpart(s) in traditional GSM. It can be viewed as comprised of three distinct logical sub-types:

Packet associated control channel (PACCH). Although logically associated with the PDCCH in documentation, it shares physical channel (time slot) resources with the PDTCH. It is the counterpart of the traditional GSM FACCH or SACCH.

Packet timing advance control channel/uplink (PTCCH/U) (uplink only). It is used by a test transmission from the mobile telephone to the base intended partly for estimation of proper timing advance setting. The uplink PTCCH channel does not have a single unique logical channel counterpart in traditional GSM, since packets are transmitted intermittently in GPRS or EDGE, so a test transmission must be sent occasionally in the X time frame of the 52-frame schedule for the purpose of testing the timing delay. When a mobile telephone is engaged in continual transmission of uplink data via one of the other logical channels, it is not necesssary to use the PTCCH/U separately since timing delay is measurable from those other uplink transmissions. In traditional GSM, radio bursts are transmitted continually, so no special channel is needed to determine the present timing delay.

Packet timing advance control channel/downlink (PTCCH/D) (downlink only). This is used to transmit a timing advance setting to one or more mobile telephones. Typically one PTCCH/D channel is paired with several PTCCH/U channels. A sample of each distinct mobile telephone transmission is needed to measure the delay time from that mobile, but a single downlink message can contain data intended for several mobile telephone receivers at different locations in the cell. The downlink message may be sent during the X time frame of the 52-frame schedule, but it may also be sent via other frames when the mobile telephone is engaged in receiving the appropriate physical channel. The downlink PTCCH channels have various counterparts in traditional GSM, since timing advance setting messages in traditional GSM can be sent via various different logical channels.

Packet data traffic channel (PDTCH) carries subscriber packet data and is analogous to the TCH in GSM voice or circuit-switched data service.

Logical Channel Division

The fact that there are so many different logical channel types of GPRS does not imply that an equally large number of separate and distinct physical channels are used. All of these logical channels may share the very same physical channel (a particular carrier frequency and time slot) at the option of the system operator. In some cases certain different types of packet messages pass back and forth on the same physical channel during certain scheduled time intervals. Because of this, we describe these messages as being sent in different logical channels.

Note that the system operator has the option of using either all, or only a part, of these logical channel types in a specific physical PDCH (that is, a specific time slot on a specific carrier frequency). One of the following three combinations is permitted in a specific instance:

PDCH = PBCCH + PCCCH + PDTCH + PACCH + PTCCH
PDCH =   PCCCH + PDTCH + PACCH + PTCCH
PDCH =   PDTCH + PACCH + PTCCH

The fact that all of these different types of logical channels can be accommodated on one physical time slot in one carrier frequency is good news to a system operator who is just starting to offer GPRS or EDGE services on a legacy GSM voice system. It is not necessary to set aside separate physical channels for the PBCCH or PCCCH when there is very little overall packet traffic and very few packet data subscribers. Thus, there is little initial reduction in the number of channels needed to support traditional GSM voice service, which is the source of most of the system operators income at the beginning of packet data service offerings.

Variable Error Protection Coding Formats

The GPRS system uses different error protection coding formats dependent on the quality of the radio channel and data transmission needs of the subscriber. If the radio channel quality is good (high signal strength and little interference from other cells), less error protection is required and high data transmission rates can be achieved. For non-real-time data transmission (e.g., Internet web browsing), retransmission of data can be performed reducing the need for high levels of error protection. For real-time data transmission (e.g., internet telephony or interactive communication), retransmission may not be possible and high levels of error protection may be required. Error protection can be in the form of added bits that are transmitted between the mobile telephone and the system and/or through the coordination and reduction of interference sources (e.g., inhibiting transmissions from neighboring cells).

Different types of data packets are protected from interference to different degrees according to their relative importance. Those packets that would cause system-wide problems if they were received incorrectly are transmitted at times when all other co-carrier transmissions from nearby cells are prevented. Other packets that are not of such global importance are transmitted without suppressing all co-carrier interference. Even in this latter case, the ratio of the underlying data to the total amount of bits transmitted can be dynamically modified (as explained below) according to the prevailing level of interference and fading. When radio channel errors are not occurring, the system can dispense with error protection codes and use almost the total available bit rate for unprotected data. This would occur when the mobile telephone is stationary and is very close to the base station. Conversely, when the radio channel conditions are very severe, the strongest level of error protection coding will automatically be put into effect. These bad channel conditions would occur when the mobile telephone is moving rapidly so that fading is apparent and is near the outer boundary of the cell, so that radio signal strength is low. This flexibility in the use of different error protection codes will improve the probability of being able to receive the data contained in each packet on the first try. Of course, a higher amount of error protection bits reduces the portion of each transmission used for the net payload. And any packet that is not received correctly can be retransmitted, more than once if necessary, until a correct and consistent message is received.

The capability of retransmitting a packet that was not received correctly on its first transmission is not new—many other packet data systems do this aside from

GPRS. However, GPRS cleverly uses so-called punctured error protection coding to increase the amount of error correcting information available at the receiver after each additional retransmission. The result of this method is that the number of retransmissions typically required is minimized, even under very bad interference and fading conditions.

GPRS systems have different data protection coding schemes to allow higher data transmission rates when the radio channel transmission quality is good. The system may chose from among four coding schemes, with coding rates ranging from 1/2 (1 bit of data for every 2 bits transmitted) to a high of 1 (no error protection). Figure 4.18 shows the different coding scheme formats. Coding scheme one (CS1) allows for 9.05 kbps for each frame time slot. Coding schemes CS2 and CS3 use punctured 1/2 rate convolution codes. Coding scheme three (CS3) has no error protection that allows a maximum data transmission rate of 21.4 kbps for each frame's time slot. If all eight time slots within a frame are used for GPRS and a very good radio channel connection is maintained (which is a rare condition), the maximum data transmission rate is 171.2 kbps.

Error protection codes in general use a method (an algorithm) to produce redundant data from the original net payload data bits. The overall set of bits thus generated are transmitted over a communication channel that may be subject to errors. At the receiving end of this channel, the overall set of bits thus produced can be tested for internal consistency by means of a testing algorithm. When an inconsistency is detected, this indicates that one or more bit errors have occurred during transmission. In certain cases, the nature of the inconsistency points to specific bit error(s) in specific place(s) in the string of bits. When this is so, we can correct the indicated error(s) by reversing the value of the indicated erroneous binary bits (that is, replace a binary 1 by a 0, and vice versa). In this case, the code is called an error-correcting code.

The type error protection code used in GPRS is convolutional coding with optional puncturing. Convolutional coding is a process that generates multiple output bits for each input data bit. The value of the output bits is calculated by combining selected previous input bits over a time window of several consecutive bits.

Coding	Data Rate (kbps)	Error Protection
CS1	9.05	½ rate convolutional
CS2	13.4	½ rate punctured
CS3	15.6	½ rate punctured
CS4	21.4	None

Figure 4.18. GPRS Channel Coding Schemes.

Packet Medium Access Control (MAC)

One of the important differences of call processing for GPRS and EDGE as compared to GSM is the message exchanges are all in the form of packets. Because of this, all the channels used for both call setup messages and exchange of subscriber packet data are not assigned to one subscriber exclusively (except for special cases and for brief time intervals). Instead they use packet media access control (MAC) algorithms that are more efficient because individual logical channels are assigned based on present needs for data rate instead of using a fixed, long-term allocation. There are three packet medium access control (MAC) modes used in the GPRS system: dynamic, extended dynamic, and fixed allocation.

For short random burst, dynamic allocation mode is used to assign time slots on an as needed basis. The base system can assign up to eight active mobile telephones for each time slot. A bit field in every downlink packet transmission seen by that mobile telephone contains a 3 bit code called the uplink status flag (USF). When a mobile telephone sees that the downlink USF is equal to its own internal USF value (assigned to that mobile telephone by the prior packet uplink assignment message), it then has permission to transmit in that PDCH channel.

When the transmission of data involves longer segments or high-bit rates of data, extended dynamic allocation mode may be used that allows the mobile telephone to transmit on multiple time slots. In this mode, the base station first assigns to the mobile telephone a set of time slots on the present carrier frequency. For example, the base station may assign time slots 2, 3, and 7 to that particular mobile telephone for use in extended dynamic allocation. In time slot 2 that mobile telephone also uses USF code value, for example 5, (binary 101). When the mobile telephone sees USF code 101 in time slot 2 in a particular block, it knows that it can also transmit more packet data in time slots 3 and 7 as well, without the need to first examine the packets in downlink time slots 3 and 7. For high-data-transmission rates, this process is faster and simpler to use than dynamic allocation as less overhead management information is required.

When a consistent data transmission rate is required or reduced delay variation in packet transmission is necessary, fixed allocation mode can be used to assign repetitive time slots in advance. For fixed allocation mode, the base station assigns a particular mobile telephone a particular set of PDCHs for a fixed time interval (e.g., every 1400 msec). Multiple time slots may be assigned to the same mobile telephone. When fixed allocation mode is used, the mobile telephone does not need to monitor the uplink since it is the only mobile telephone with permission to transmit on that PDCH during that particular time interval. This is useful when data must be transmitted rapidly and simply.

When a mobile telephone attempts access to the system, the request for service may occur at the same time another mobile telephone is accessing the system. If the mobile telephone is so unfortunate as to transmit its packet channel request at the same time as another mobile telephone, and cause a "collision" preventing correct reception of the radio signal, there will be no response from the base station. In that case, the mobile telephone will wait a short but randomly chosen time interval and try again, providing that the base receiver status is idle. Again, eventually the mobile telephone should succeed and act on a successful packet uplink assignment.

Frequency Hopping

Frequency hopping is a radio transmission process where a message or voice communications is sent on a radio channel that regularly changes frequency (hops) according to a predetermined code sequence. The receiver of the message or voice information must also receive on the same set of frequencies using the same frequency hopping sequence.

Frequency hopping offers a significant benefit of interference averaging. Traditional cellular systems are designed for worst-case interference as frequencies that are assigned to nearby cells are calculated and tested to have acceptable signal to interference levels at their boundaries. Many of the mobile telephones that are operating inside the cell's radio boundaries experience low levels of interference. For those mobile telephones, frequencies could be used more often, increasing the system capacity. Frequency hopping allows for more aggressive frequency reuse as interference is averaged over multiple time slots. If high levels of interference occur, other slots will make up for the lost data.

There are typically only six cells that produce most of the radio interference experienced by each data session or conversation. These cells are located near to the cell that is providing the service and are assigned the same carrier frequency. Other cells in the system also have the same carrier frequencies assigned but are so far away that they are over the horizon and thus are shielded by the earth from the cell of interest.

The system operator has the option of frequency hopping for GSM and GPRS, and use of this option effectively increases the number of statistically independent random interference sources, without increasing the average amount of interference! Frequency hopping thus effectively reduces the amount of fluctuation in the interference level. Then the system performs almost as though the interference had been reduced uniformly by a factor of 1/2 (for the case of 50% average transmitter on time).

Frequency hopping also provides for frequency diversity that reduces the effects of fast radio signal fading. Fast fading is the result of multipath radio transmission. In a cluttered environment where multipath radio transmission occurs, a portion of the radio power goes directly in a straight line from the transmitter to the receiver. This is called a direct ray. Other portions of the power initially go off from the transmitting antenna in other directions and then reflect off of intermediate objects. These reflected rays eventually reach the receiving antenna at a later time than the direct ray. Due to their longer zig-zag path, they are delayed in time compared to the directly received waveform. Therefore, the delayed ray could, in the worst case, partially or even completely cancel out the directly received signal.

This worst case occurs only when there is one direct ray and just one delayed ray, and the delayed ray has exactly the same power as the directly ray, and is also exactly one-half cycle (180°) out of phase (or any odd number of half-cycles). In most realistic cases, there are many delayed rays, and the delayed ray(s) has/have lower power than the directly received waveform, so the sum of all the various component rays is reduced in total power, but it is not reduced to zero. However, it can typically be reduced by a ratio as low as 1/10 or 1/100 (reduced by 10 or 20 dB) compared to the directly received waveform acting alone. Some of the names that define fast fading include "Rayleigh distribution" and "Ricean distribution "

Basic Operation

The basic states of a GPRS mobile telephone are initialization with the system information (idle), prepared to send and receive data (standby), and willing to send and receive data (ready).

Initially, the mobile telephone must capture information from a broadcast channel. The broadcast channel may also contain a message indicating to any GPRS mobile telephones where (carrier frequency and time slot) to find a channel that handles packet data. Even when this message is not present, the GPRS mobile receiver can scan all the carrier frequencies and time slots and eventually find which one(s) are carrying packet data.

To accomplish dynamic time slot assignment, a number of different GPRS users are assigned to share a particular channel and time slot at a particular time. The base station may transmit packet data to any one of a pre-designated group of eight of these users during each frame interval. Other mobile telephone receivers assigned to this channel may also receive this data, but they will ignore it upon examination of the addressing information. When a particular mobile receiver finds that a particular packet is not addressed to itself, that receiver will ignore the data. Furthermore, the "wrong" mobile receiver(s) cannot "comprehend" packets intended for other users, because of the user-specific encryption that is applied to payload data bits.

With regard to the uplink transmission of data, any one of the specified eight subscribers who are currently in a designated user group may be assigned by the base station to be the next mobile unit to transmit in that particular time slot. The command code user status flag (USF), indicates which of the eight mobile units should transmit next. The particular uplink time slot is contained in a particular data field in the downlink and is more heavily protected with error correction code than any of the payload data or other control data.

Some GPRS users may be assigned to multiple time slots (more than one time slot per frame) of the same carrier frequency, when their requirements for bit rate are greater than what can be accommodated by a single time slot. It is permissible to assign different quantity of time slots to the same mobile in the uplink and downlink direction for GPRS. For example, for Internet browsing applications that involve receiving more download information (e.g., picture download), five downlink and 1 uplink time slot can be assigned to the same mobile telephone.

Idle

In the idle mode, the mobile telephone initializes itself with the system information. The mobile telephone initializes with the system by finding the beacon frequency and receiving broadcast information. Time slot-0 on the beacon frequency broadcasts certain information in the downlink direction according to a schedule. This schedule repeats in a time interval of 51 TDMA time frames numbered consecutively from 0 through 50. This time interval is known as a 51-frame multiframe.

The schedule requires certain types of signals to be transmitted at certain times. The precise details or data values of these types of signals may vary from time to time, but only a particular type can be transmitted in a particular scheduled time frame. All the base stations in a GSM and GPRS system are synchronized, using time slot zero for all the carrier frequencies on all the base stations in this particular system (or city).

Beacon Channel Selection

When a mobile telephone has identified several candidate base station beacon frequencies that have comparable signal strength as perceived at the mobile receiver, the information regarding the requested mobile transmit level can be used to refine the choice of the best beacon frequency to use. The broadcast messages requesting the smallest mobile transmit power may indicate the best cell (beacon frequency) to use because the mobile must be close to the center of a small cell. This implies the mobile would use the lowest transmit power to communicate with that base station. Any other beacon frequency most likely comes from another larger cell, and it is likely that the mobile telephone is farther away from the base antenna of that larger cell. However, an alternative beacon channel may be selected if the identification information of the base station is preferred. For example, the more distant cell (lower beacon signal strength) is the home system, and the closer cell (stronger beacon signal) is from a competing carrier.

Once the appropriate mobile telephone has obtained a suitable beacon frequency, and also has its internal hyperframe counter properly synchronized to the base system, it can continue as is appropriate for its capabilities (e.g., voice, data, or data and voice). If the mobile telephone only (or primarily) supports GSM voice or circuit-switched data services, it will continue using traditional GSM processes. For a GPRS mobile telephone that is ready for packet data transmission, the preliminary operations can be done using packet messages as packet data control channels. The GPRS mobile telephone can find the PBCCH channel via a search, or find it faster aided by information broadcast in the traditional BCCH channel.

Another special signal is transmitted by the base station on the beacon frequency during time slot 0 in time frames 1, 11, 21, 31, and 41. This is a digitally modulated signal called the synchronizing signal. The synchronizing signal an invariable binary pattern of 1s and 0s that is used to help synchronize the mobile telephone with the base station vis-à-vis time slot timing. The synchronizing channel also contains a binary number indicating the present value of the internal system clock called the hyperframe counter.

Many events that occur according to a schedule in the GSM and GPRS systems are based on the value of the system hyperframe counter, so it is important for all the mobile telephones that are powered up in the cells of the system to know its present value. These things include the multiframe schedule itself, the frequency hopping schedule, the synchronization of the radio link encryption, scheduled paging messages, and other scheduled processes. The hyperframe counter counts frames, from a starting value of zero up to 2,715,647 and then starts again. Since each frame is 4.6 msec in duration, a time interval of 3 hours, 28 minutes, 53 seconds and 760 msec is consumed to cycle the hyperframe counter through its complete counting range.

Initial Registration

At some point, before it can make or receive a call or start packet service, a "new" mobile telephone, not previously present with its power on in this particular cellular system, must perform a "location update" process. This involves an exchange of messages with the base station so that the base system knows that this particular mobile telephone is present in this cell.

First the mobile telephone will "get the attention" of the base station, by transmitting a radio burst to the base receiver on time slot zero of the beacon uplink frequency. This channel is called the random access channel (RACH). Because the mobile telephone does not know in advance of this transmission what the precise distance is between itself (the mobile telephone) and the base station, it uses a shortened burst. This transmitted burst contains data that temporarily identifies mobile telephone and indicates that the reason for transmitting this burst is to perform a location update. Another bit field in the burst contains a temporary identifier in the form of a 5-bit binary number that the mobile telephone selected by means of a software random number generator. There are 32 specific choices for this 5-bit binary code (that is, $2^5 = 32$).

Also, the first time that a "new" mobile telephone does a location update in a system, that system determines if it is an authentic mobile telephone authorized to get service (in contrast to a fraudulent mobile telephone presenting false identification). When a mobile telephone is roaming (requesting service from a system other than its home system) and performs its first location update procedure in a visited system, it also triggers terrestrial system messages via the transmission links between the home and visited systems. These messages are used to support identification and authentication of the mobile telephone, using data stored in the HLR (home location register) data base associated with that mobile telephone's home system. One result of the identification and authentication processes is that appropriate information is stored in the VLR database associated with the visited system.

Standby

In the standby mode, the mobile telephone continuously accesses the system to maintain its location and registration information with the system as it moves between radio coverage areas (cells).

Regular Location Updates

After a mobile telephone has recognized that the MNC of the base station is different from the MNC of the last base station it was receiving, the mobile telephone must perform a location update. The mobile telephone will continuously perform location updates as it moves throughout different parts of the network.

Monitoring the Paging Channel

Once a mobile telephone is registered with the network, it watches the PPCH for information that is specific to its operation (incoming page alert or broadcast message.) In most installations, the base system establishes a paging schedule, based on the last few digits of the TMSI or some other designated identifying number for the mobile telephone. The mobile telephone engages in a "wake and sleep" cycle, only awakening during the scheduled time intervals when a paging message may be scheduled for this mobile telephone and others having the same few last digits in their numbers. When a packet paging message does occur comprising the TMSI of this particular mobile telephone, it responds with a packet channel request message. The paging message may occur on several different carrier frequencies in several cells, but the mobile telephone will respond on only one. This packet channel request message contains a parameter indicating that it is a paging response in contrast to the mobile telephone initiating the packet channel request.

Ready

In the ready mode, the mobile telephone attaches itself to the system. To allow the mobile telephone to transfer data, the system creates a virtual connection between the SGSN and the GGSN. The GGSN adapts and routes the data to the external data network (e.g., the Internet).

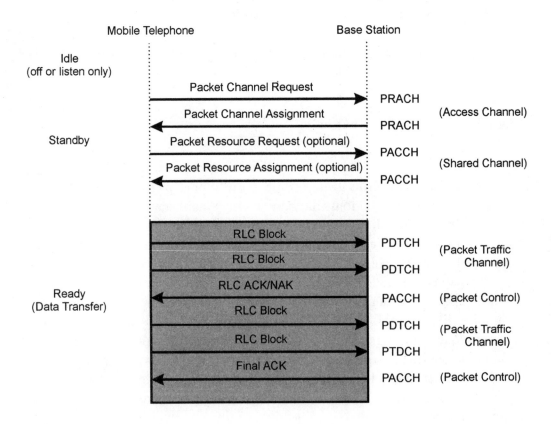

Figure 4.19. GPRS Radio Channel Assignment.

Figure 4.19 shows the process used for GPRS radio channel assignment. This diagram shows that when the mobile telephone first turns on, it senses that the system has GPRS capability. The mobile telephone then retrieves system identification and access information. After it has initialized, it may register with the system as it moves between different radio coverage areas (cells). The system responds to the registration by authenticating the mobile telephone (checking with the home location register) and assigning a temporary system identification code called a tempoary logic link identifier (TLLI). The SGSN maintains a record of which cell the mobile telephone is operating within its system. When the mobile telephone has data to send, it enters the ready mode

Establishing a Logical Connection

Merely being "attached" to the network does not imply that the mobile telephone is engaged in a voice call quite yet, nor does it imply that a packet mobile telephone is ready for—or wants to—exchange packet data. The next step is the result of the subscriber establishing a logical connection such as an Internet access to a web page, or a request to get the subscriber's e-mail, using a portable data terminal. When the mobile packet data station needs to transmit to the base station, it already is continually receiving whatever the base station transmits on the packet paging channel (PPCH). The mobile telephone may be engaged in a sleep--wake cycle of alternately receiving and then "sleeping" to conserve battery power. The mobile may also use the PTCCH from time to time to send a shortened burst and have its timing advance corrected, so it is always prepared to make a normal burst transmission without concern that the normal burst will arrive too early or too late at the base receiver.

When the subscriber makes the action that starts this process, the mobile telephone will prepare to attempt to transmit a Packet Channel Request. This is done using the PRACH uplink channel. Of course, the mobile must do this when there is no other mobile telephone attempting simultaneous uplink transmission on this channel. Every packet downlink transmission in the PCCCH channel (and the PDCH channel in general) contains a status data bit field (SB) indicating the status of the base receiver. This indicates whether it is presently busy receiving a packet, or whether it is idle and ready to receive a mobile transmitted packet. When the mobile determines from this bit field that the receiver is idle, it transmits a packet channel request message. This message can specify several things about the desired packet transmission: the desired data rate throughput, the radio link control mode (RLC), whether the packet(s) are to be acknowledged by a particular ARQ protocol, and a priority code.

If the base receiver is not already in the midst of receiving packets from eight different mobile telephones on every available PDCH, it will generally send a packet uplink assignment message on the PAGCH/D channel. This message will tell the mobile the physical channel to use as the PDCH. This is for the case where the system operator has configured the system so that the PAGCH is in a separate physical channel than the PDCH. The message will also tell the mobile telephone what mode of RLC control is to be used. One of the modes allows up to 8 mobile telephones to share the uplink PDCH. To facilitate this, a 3-bit binary code called the USF is assigned to this particular mobile telephone. Each of other mobile telephone (7 or fewer) has other binary values for their own USF. In another mode, called fixed allocation mode, the mobile will be assigned a fixed set of time slots that it uses until the entire amount of data "uploaded." The fixed allocation mode is assigned usually when many packets are to be sent.

The packet uplink assignment message only assigns an uplink channel. If the mobile telephone needs a downlink channel to receive packet data, a separate assignment will be performed for the downlink channel. The two channels may or may not use the same numbered time slot. One of the two, uplink or downlink, may be assigned multiple time slots, or in general a different quantity of time slots than its opposite direction.

Data Transmission

To transmit data, the mobile telephone starts transmitting uplink packets as controlled by one of the media access control methods. Unless the mobile telephone is operating in unacknowledged mode, each block of transmitted data will be acknowledged by the base station. Acknowledgment may occur as a part of other packets containing downlink data, or the base may send downlink packets for the sole purpose of acknowledging. The acknowledgments may be on the same or on another physical time slot. Access control methods described above relate only to uplink (mobile transmit) situations where there is a potential conflict if multiple mobile telephones transmit simultaneously. In the downlink there is only one base transmitter. Therefore, no corresponding downlink control is needed to prevent multiple simultaneous transmissions.

In some cases, the base receiver is not ready. In that case, it may send back one of the following messages:

1. *Packet access reject.* In this case the mobile telephone may wait an indefinite time interval and try again using the same PCCCH. The mobile telephone may follow the same strategy if there is no response of any kind from the base station. In some cases the mobile telephone may try to scan and find another cell signal having another PCCCH so it can try again there.
2. *Packet queuing notification.* The base receiver is expected to be available soon, so the mobile telephone waits on that same PCCCH (or the PAGCH/D to be more specific) for further instructions.

Responding to a Voice Call During a Data Transfer

A GPRS or EDGE mobile telephone may receive a voice call while already engaged in a data transfer session. The MSC-SGSN "knows" that this mobile telephone is engaged in the data transfer process. Therefore, unlike the traditional cellular paging and call setup, the MSC-SGSN sends a packet call alert message directly to this mobile telephone on the data channel. If the mobile telephone is capable of both voice and data transmission on the same radio carrier, the customer may be informed of an incoming call (the phone may ring or screen may display a message.)

The same information (parameters) that would be exchanged in a traditional GSM call setup are transmitted in packet format, mixed in with the other ongoing packet exchanges involving this particular mobile telephone. The handset will ring or otherwise alert the subscriber. Caller ID information will appear on the display panel of the handset. The subscriber can answer by pressing the SEND or TALK button, and the conversation begins. From the subscriber's point of view, the call begins and continues exactly like other voice calls. The result of this exchange of messages is that a GSM voice connection is established using another time slot on the same carrier frequency as the time slot(s) used for packet data transfers. A packet data session using all eight time slots would preclude a voice conversation.

The voice conversation and the packet transactions can then continue, apparently simultaneously from the subscriber's point of view. Either the packet session or the voice conversation may be ended independently without affecting the other process. When a handover occurs, both processes hand over simultaneously.

Initiating Data Calls When on a Voice Call

The somewhat similar process of setting up a packet session when the subscriber is already engaged in a voice conversation is also permitted for the appropriate mobile telephone classes. In this case, the FACCH channel is used to send a message to the mobile telephone, causing it to open up another time slot on the same carrier frequency for packet exchange (PDCH) use or to utilize an previously established PDCH channel on the same carrier frequency. If necessary, the mobile telephone voice conversation can be handed over (without the subscriber perceiving it!) to another carrier frequency in the cell that already has an underutilized PDCH channel and a free time slot for voice conversation use on it.

Alerting of Voice and Data calls from a Different System

It is possible to transfer voice and data calls between different types of systems (e.g., GPRS and IS-136). When a mobile telephone is in communication with one type of system and an alternate communication process is requested, the communication link may be transferred. However, if the subscriber answers or a data session begins on another session, the previous session (e.g., voice or packet session) must be either suspended or released via a packet TBF release message. The radio portion of a B136 handset cannot simultaneously handle the 30 kHz IS-136 voice channel and the 200 kHz EDGE channel on a separate carrier frequency.

Detaching from the Network

Ultimately, the session ends because the subscriber no longer wants to "surf the net" or get any more e-mail. The subscriber may end the process by closing a window on the portable computer, and as a result the mobile telephone will send a packet temporary block flow release message, which is acknowledged. The USF previously assigned to this mobile telephone is no longer meaningful for it, and may in fact be assigned later to another mobile telephone. The mobile telephone is effectively "disconnected" with regard to this particular session. It is still attached to the GPRS or EDGE base system, and separate messages may be needed to detach it. The portable computer may automatically engage in a detach process when all the programs on that computer that use GPRS or EDGE data communication are shut down.

Enhanced Data for Global Evolution (EDGE)

EDGE is an evolved version of the global system for mobile (GSM) radio channels that uses new phase modulation and packet transmission to provide for advanced high-speed data services. The EDGE system uses eight level phase shift keying (8PSK) to allow one symbol change to represent 3 bits of information. This is three times the amount of information that is transferred by a standard two level GMSK signal used by first generation GSM systems. This results in a gross radio channel data transmission rate of 604.8 kbps and a net maximum delivered data transmission rate of approximately 474 kbps. The GPRS advanced packet transmission control system allows for constantly varying data transmission rates in either direction between mobile radios.

System Overview

The key changes to allow EDGE system operation are mobile telephones and base station transceivers that are capable of transmitting and receiving using the new 8PSK modulation. The EDGE system allows for mixing both types of modulation on a single radio channel. This means one time slot may use 8PSK modulation, and another time slot can use GMSK modulation. This mixing of technologies allows for existing GSM mobile telephones (non-EDGE compatible) to access the system. Although it is possible that single-mode EDGE mobile telephones may be built, most EDGE mobile telephones are capable of both GSM and EDGE transmission.

The highest EDGE data rates are permitted only when the radio channel conditions are optimum. Optimum radio channel performance usually occurs when the subscriber is close to the base station and is either stationary or moving only very slowly. Close proximity to the base station implies a strong desired radio signal from that base station, and weak interfering radio signal strength from the other cells in the system. Low or zero velocity of movement implies that degradation of channel quality due to variations in received signal strength from multipath fading will be minimal as well. When the radio channel is less than optimum, the subscriber will still obtain service, but the available data rate will be less than the respective maximum figure just stated.

EDGE technology can be used for both voice (circuit-switched) and packet data service. GPRS (packet data) is, in a sense, a subset of EDGE. Almost all base stations that have GPRS upgrade(s) installed as a first packet data service are expected ultimately to be further upgraded to support EDGE in the near future as well. Such EDGE base stations will thus ultimately support both EDGE and GPRS data rates. In the calendar plan for introduction of 2.5 G data services, it is important to provide some packet data service to subscribers as soon as possible, even if it does not immediately support the highest feasible data rate and all the elegant features of EDGE. Thus, GPRS is implemented first.

Because EDGE radios have both GMSK and 8QPSK modulation capability, base stations will be able to continue the support of existing GSM and GPRS mobile telephones. If a particular subscriber experiences a truly horrible channel (due, for example, to a combination of rapid movement of the mobile telephone and/or high radio interference), this user will be given a data rate far lower than the maximum data rate. If this particular horrible channel can only support the lowest net channel data rate (about 10 kbps), that is what this particular subscriber will get, regardless of whether that subscriber is using a GPRS mobile telephone or a EDGE mobile telephone. This is an illustration of the fact that the lowest data rates provided by EDGE data service are similar to the data rates provided by GPRS.

Figure 4.20 shows an EDGE system. This diagram shows that EDGE uses the same GPRS packet-switching technology and a standard GSM radio channel that is modified to use a new modulation technology. The 8-level quadrature phase shift keying (8QPSK) modulation using EDGE modulation can be inserted on a slot-by-slot basis on the GSM channel. Existing GSM mobile telephones will ignore the EDGE 8QPSK time slots because they cannot demodulate and decode them.

System Attributes

Some of the key system attributes of the EDGE system include new phase modulation, mixed GSM and EDGE transmission, variable coding rates, and new classes of mobile telephones.

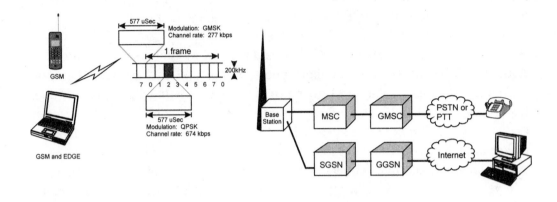

Figure 4.20. Enhanced Data rates for Global Evolution (EDGE) System.

Modulation and Bit Rate

The 8PSK modulation used in EDGE is differential phase modulation that has a pre-defined phase angle change occurs in the carrier for each symbol. Each symbol has eight possible phase decision points. As a result, each symbol can represent a three-bit binary value ($2^3 = 8$). This results in a payload bit rate for EDGE that is approximately three times as large as the corresponding bit rates for GSM and GPRS.

The permitted phase angle changes are all multiples of 45 degrees. Figure 4.21 shows that in addition to the phase changes shown in the figure, the phase is changed by an angle of 22.5 degrees from one symbol to the next, to get continual phase changes from symbol to symbol. The permitted phase changes are specifically designed to prevent a 180 degree phase change between consecutive

8PSK Constellation

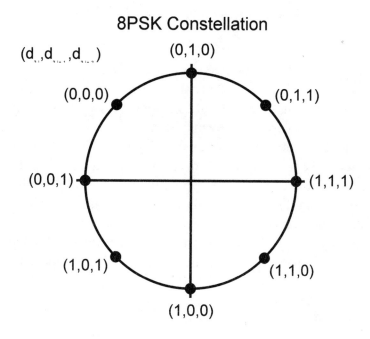

Figure 4.21. 8QPSK Differential Modulation.

symbols. A phase change of 180 degrees produces an almost instantaneous reversal of the carrier waveform voltage, which is very undesirable because a waveform that has a voltage jump produced by an instantaneous phase reversal inherently produces a large amount of transmitter power outside the intended band width of the normally modulated carrier. This type of excess momentary bandwidth is called spurious emission.

The symbol rate is sometimes stated using the unit name "baud" (Bd) rather than the equivalent term "symbols/second." The name baud commemorates Emile Baudot, the 19th century French inventor of an early kind of teletypewriter. For any coding method having 2 bits per symbol, such as GMSK, the bit rate and baud rate are the same, namely 270 kbps for GSM and GMSK. For any coding method having more than 2 bits per symbol, the bit rate will be larger than the baud rate.

Both GMSK and 8PSK are so-called constant envelope modulation methods. This term describes the fact that the instantaneous power level of the transmitted radio signal does not change by design during the transition from one symbol to the next. Constant envelope waveforms are advantageous because they can be amplified without waveform distortion by so-called Class C radio frequency power amplifiers. The term "Class C" describes a category of amplifier designs. Class C amplifiers are very efficient: typically from 60 to 80% efficient in converting dc power from the power supply into radio frequency power. Their high efficiency occurs because they draw electric current from the dc power supply for only a small fraction of each carrier frequency cycle. But they can only amplify without waveform distortion using a constant envelope sine wave.

Time Slot Structure

Although the time slot for EDGE is the same as GSM and GPRS, the higher data transmission rate results in a larger payload per time slot. Time slots carry different payloads dependent on the modulation and grouping of blocks.

Figure 4.22 summarizes, for GPRS and for EDGE, the number of gross payload bits per time slot and per block of four time slots (each time slot located in the same relative slot position, for example, slot 3, but each in a different frame of the block). The purpose of the various modulation and coding schemes described later is to produce a block of data bits incorporating both appropriate heading information and error protection coding along with the net payload data bits.

Mixing GSM and EDGE Transmissions

It is possible to mix GSM, GPRS, and EDGE radio channel formats on the same radio carrier. These three formats allow for GSM voice or circuit-switched data,

Parameter	Using GPRS GMSK modulation	Using EDGE 8PSK modulation
Gross payload bits per time slot	116	464
Gross payload bits per block (4 time slots)	348	1392

Figure 4.22. GPRS and EDGE Slot Payloads.

GPRS packet data, and high-speed EDGE data transmission. The type of traffic carried on a particular time slot may be reassigned dynamically on an entirely flexible basis. This capability of the system design, to mix the three different types of traffic in a flexible way, is economically very important. This flexibility produces what is called high "trunking efficiency."

It is also possible to support both voice and packet data users in a system that is IS-136 mixed with an EDGE compact. This would allow the system operator to migrate toward a completely flexible system by offering IS-136 voice, GSM voice, high-speed EDGE and/or GPRS data services.

8PSK modulation is more sensitive to interference than GMSK modulation. In EDGE systems, 8PSK modulation is used only when channel conditions are good. When radio channel conditions are bad, EDGE systems automatically change back to GMSK modulation.

Use of 8PSK modulation in EDGE data service does not increase the radio bandwidth compared to GSM GMSK modulation. It does increase the bit rate by increasing the number of different specific bit choices that can be transmitted in each symbol–in other words, we get more bits per second per unit of radio bandwidth. (The unit of radio bandwidth is the cycle per second, or Hertz.) This increase in bit rate without increasing the bandwidth of the radio signal is sometimes described as increasing the "spectral efficiency" of the radio signal. The bandwidth of an EDGE signal is still 200 kHz on a modulated carrier, but the data bit rate is three times as great as that of GPRS or GSM. However, this comes at a price! An 8PSK signal is far more sensitive to noise and interference than a GMSK signal of the same power level. For example, under typical fading conditions, a GMSK radio signal can operate when the energy received from interference signals (e.g., from nearby cell sites that are operating on the same frequency) is approximately 10% of its received power level. This means the GMSK can tolerate a carrier to noise plus interference ratio (C / (I + n) ratio) of about 10 dB (the C / (I + n) ratio is 10 to 1) and achieve about 1% gross BER most of the time.

The QPSK modulation used in EDGE can only tolerate approximately interference of only 0.5% of its received power level to achieve a 1% gross BER. As a result, 8PSK signal may require 23 dB gross C / (I + n) (a power ratio of 200 to 1) to achieve the same gross 1% BER. This implies that we need to exercise great care in the geographic planning of a cellular system using 8PSK modulation. This may result in an increased distance requirement between cells that use the same frequency (reduced frequency reuse).

Variable Error Protection Coding Formats

EDGE can use the best coding rate for the present level of errors occurring on the channel. Different error protection code formats are assigned based on the radio channel quality. The radio channel quality is estimated using present physical channel bit error rate derived from counting the appearance of detectable or correctable errors in the received data.

The EDGE system design allows eight different distinct amounts of error correction code, corresponding to error correction code ratios ranging from a low of approximately 1/3 to a high of 1. A channel code rate of 1 implies that no error protection coding is used and the payload bit stream is 100% net data. Figure 4.23 shows the different channel coding formats used in the EDGE system.

Mobile Telephone Classes for EDGE and GPRS

The radio channel access and modulation capability of the mobile telephone determines its potential classes of operation. The different classes of operation are based on the ability of a mobile telephone to transmit and receive at the same time (full duplex compared to half duplex) and types of transmission modes ("multimode") capability (e.g., GSM, GPRS, EDGE, and IS-136).

Code Rate	Scheme	Modulation	Data Rate kb/s
1.0	MCS-9	8PSK	59.2
0.92	MCS-8	8PSK	59.4
0.76	MCS-7	8PSK	44.8
0.49	MCS-6	8PSK	29.6
			27.2
0.37	MCS-5	8PSK	22.4
1.0	MCS-4	GMSK	17.6
0.80	MCS-3	GMSK	14.8
			13.6
0.66	MCS-2	GMSK	11.2
0.53	MCS-1	GMSK	8.8

Figure 4.23. EDGE Channel Coding Schemes.

Although all mobile telephones are capable of transmitting and receiving, some mobile telephones cannot do this simultaneously and this restricts their ability to simultaneously send and receive data. This may restrict the number of multiple slots that can be assigned to a customer for each frame (highest data-rate transmission).

Each frame within a GSM or GPRS radio carrier channel is composed of eight time slots, and each communication channel is composed of two radio carriers; one frequency for a downlink (base to mobile telephone) and one frequency for an uplink channel (mobile telephone to base). When multiple time slots (four or more), are assigned to the same mobile telephone, it must transmit and receive simultaneously. Although is it possible for the system to simultaneously transmit and receive, the mobile telephone must be physically designed to accommodate this. To do this, a frequency filter using passive electrical components (capacitors, inductors, and the like) can be used to isolate the transmitter and receiver sections by strongly attenuating the mobile transmitter signal from entering the receiver section. A filter used for this purpose is called a duplexer or diplexer.

Assigning multiple time slots to a single user is also limited by the capability of the mobile telephone's digital signal processing section and the need to measure other radio channels for handover operations. During communications, the mobile telephone performs many system functions such as decoding received signals and encoding signals to be transmitted. In traditional operation, the mobile telephone has idle time within each frame to encode and decode information. If the mobile telephone is required to simultaneously decode and encode data, this increases the digital signal processing requirements of the mobile telephone.

The mobile telephone must also periodically measure other radio carrier channels when operating on a call or during data transfer to assist in handover decisions. Mobile assisted hand over (MAHO) requires the receiver to periodically measure radio signal strength and signal quality from time slot 0 of beacon frequencies on nearby base stations, and report that information to its own base station periodically. If the mobile receiver is busy with communication from its own base station during every time slot of every time frame, then it cannot also make the measurements needed for MAHO. To ensure that all mobile receivers have an opportunity to measure signals for MAHO purposes, the schedule used for GPRS includes some intentional "idle" time frames. Thanks to these intentionally idle time frames, each mobile telephone can scan other radio carrier channels to acquire the needed MAHO data. It is possible to do this even when all eight time slots of that mobile telephone are involved in communication with its own base station. The multiframe schedule allows the mobile telephone to perform MAHO scanning at least twice during each 52 frames.

Some mobile telephones have multiple transmission mode capability (e.g., GSM, EDGE, and IS-136) and others do not. When the mobile telephone is capable of multiple modes, it must be capable of receiving and processing messages for each of the modes. This means messages may be received from one system indicating service is required from a different technology. For example, if the mobile telephone is connected to the Internet on a data call via the EDGE system, a message may be received indicating a voice call is waiting on an IS-136 channel. The mobile telephone must then be capable of either terminating or suspending the data call and responding (answering) the IS-136 voice call.

A mobile telephone may also be capable of both voice and data transmission capability on the same radio system (e.g., GSM voice and GPRS data). This would allow a subscriber to browse the web (Internet) while on a voice call. Because of the different situations that are anticipated as GPRS and EDGE are introduced into various existing networks, the following four types of mobile telephones are identified in the standards documents, in addition to voice handsets served only by GSM or only by IS-136 base stations. Figure 4.24 shows the different classes of mobile telephones for GPRS and EDGE.

Radio Link Block Formats

Packets on the radio link are grouped into block formats. In most cases the end user is sending and receiving TCP/IP or UDP/IP packets over the Internet. These Internet packets are usually much longer than one radio link packet payload, so

Class	Capability	Comments
A	Simultaneous GSM voice with GPRS or EDGE.	Used in base systems supporting GSM with GPRS or EDGE. Talk while you download an Internet file! Such a mobile station would typically use two (or more) time slots on the same carrier frequency, one for voice and the other(s) for packet data.
B	Non-simultaneous GSM voice or GPRS or EDGE.	Voice at some times, data at other times.
B136	Non-simultaneous IS-136 voice or EDGE Compact.	Voice at some times via IS-136, data at other times via EDGE Compact.
C	GPRS or EDGE data services only. No voice.	Example: Via a PCMCIA card in a portable computer.

Figure 4.24. Mobile Telephone Classes.

it is necessary to chop up an end-user packet or message (or some kinds of EDGE or GPRS system messages as well) into "chunks" that will fit conveniently into the various payload sizes. To make this cutting and slicing choice simpler, the system allows only five sizes of "chunks" (actually, one of the five choices is a repeat of one of the other four with some dummy padding bits appended in each chunk). The chunks are either 22, 28, 34, or 37 octets (bytes) in size. It is also permitted to make up a 37-octet chunk directly from a piece of the data to be encoded and transmitted, or to use a 34 byte chunk and pad it by appending three dummy octets.

There are nine different modulation and coding (MCS) schemes for transmitting packet data over the radio link in EDGE. Each one has a designation number, written as MCS-n, where n ranges from 1 to 9. The 9 choices used in EDGE allow different degrees of error protection (coding rate) and net data throughput bit rate (bits per second). The system adaptively tries different MCS choices from time to time so that it is always obtaining the highest throughput with accurate resulting data reception. The user does not need to do anything to get the system to continually adjust itself to the optimum MCS choice, since that happens automatically as a result of the system design. Figure 4.25 summarizes the choices and the details of the different EDGE channel coding formats.

These nine MCS choices are also described as being members of three "families" named A, B, and C. Family B comprises MCS-2, MCS-5 and MCS-7. If a radio block is transmitted using MCS-7 and is not acknowledged, it is also possible to break up the data chunks in it and send them again, but this time as two MCS-5 blocks, or four MCS-2 blocks. A similar relationship exists between the members of family C, namely MCS-1 and MCS-4. Family A comprises MCS-3, MCS-6, MCS-8, and MCS-9. Note that if an MCS-8 radio block is transmitted and not acknowledged, it is also possible to pad out the 34 octet chunks into 37

MCS Choice	Modu-lation	Net data bits per radio block	"Chunks" carried: nxL where L is length in octets	Net data rate using one time slot, in kbit/s.
MCS-1	GMSK	176 bits (= 22 octets or bytes)	1x22	8.8
MCS-2	GMSK	592 bits (= 74 bytes)	3x28	11.2
MCS-3	GMSK	296 bits (= 37 octets)	1x37	14.8 [13.6] Note 1
MCS-4	GMSK	352 bits (= 44 octets)	2x22	17.6
MCS-5	8PSK	448 bits (= 56 octets)	2x28	22.4
MCS-6	8PSK	592 bits (= 74 octets)	2x37	29.6 [27.2] Note 1.
MCS-7	8PSK	896 bits (112 octets)	4x28	44.8
MCS-8	8PSK	1088 bits (136 octets)	4x34	54.4
MCS-9	8PSK	1184 bits (148 octets)	4x37	59.2 [54.4] Note 1

Note 1: One type of 37 octet chunk is made up of 34 data octets and 3 filler octets. In this case, the actual data throughput is lower than for true 37 octet chunks. The lower bit rate is given in square brackets [].

Figure 4.25. Radio Link Block Formats.

octet chunks, and then transmit the data as two MCS-6 blocks. However, note that changing to another MCS choice is not the only way to handle retransmission when the first transmission is not acknowledged. The other way is repeated retransmission using incremental redundancy.

Basic Operation

The basic operation of EDGE is almost identical to GPRS. The key difference is the use of new modulation technology that increases the data transmission rate.

Figure 4.26 shows how EDGE systems assign a radio channel. This diagram shows that the EDGE compatible mobile telephone looks for an EDGE channel

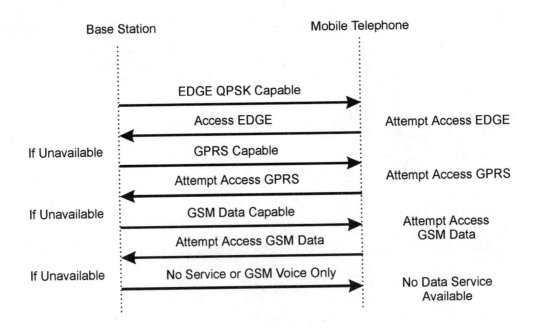

Figure 4.26. EDGE Radio Channel Assignment.

first. If available, the mobile telephone will use EDGE 8QPSK modulation when accessing the system. If EDGE is not available, the mobile telephone will use standard GMSK modulation to access the system using GPRS technology. If GPRS is not available (no packet data channel), it will access the system using standard GSM data transmission technology (slow speed data).

EDGE Compact

EDGE compact is a version of EDGE that allows the close packing of GSM radio channel frequencies (frequency reuse of three) to allow an overlay of GSM technology into other systems (such as IS-136 TDMA) with a minimum loss of existing channel frequencies. Because EDGE compact reuses frequencies in nearby cells, the average interference level for each time slot is higher. Although it is acceptable to discard data packets that experience high levels of interference, discarding packets that contain control messages (such as handoff or packet data paging messages) is unacceptable. To help ensure most control messages reach their destination, EDGE compact reduces interference to control packets by inhibiting the transmission of messages on the same frequency and time slot in nearby cell sites.

EDGE compact systems are expected to be converted back to use standard EDGE technology (unscheduled channels) as more channels are made available for EDGE/GPRS/GSM transmission. This is expected to occur when customers are converted from the other system (e.g., IS-136 TDMA) to EDGE/GPRS/GSM. As the existing IS-136 radio channels become lightly loaded, they can be removed from service and replaced with EDGE transceivers. This allows the gradual conversion from one technology to compatible GSM/GPRS/EDGE technology. The plan for integration of EDGE into existing IS-136 networks is sometimes named "EDGE compact."

In a cell without GSM voice support, but one that supports IS-136 voice together with EDGE compact, a subscriber with a suitable dual-mode, voice-data handset can engage in a voice call and receive notification (similar to call waiting) that there is data waiting for the subscriber in EDGE mode. Similarly, if the subscriber is engaged in data communication via the EDGE mode, the subscriber can receive notification (via ringing) that a voice call is waiting. In either of these cases, the subscriber has the option of ending the first communication mode and immediately starting a second communication in the second mode.

System Overview

The key aspects of the EDGE compact system include coordinated radio transmission for tighter frequency reuse and adaptation of GSM infrastructure for operation with IS-41 infrastructure (primarily used in the Americas).

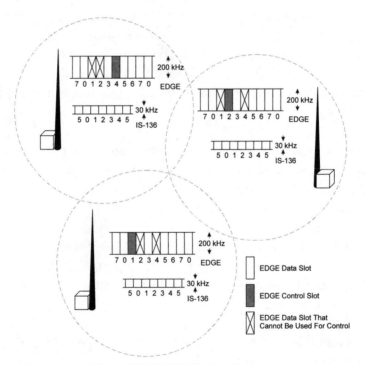

Figure 4.27. EDGE Compact System.

The EDGE compact system uses the same basic network structure as the standard EDGE system. Because EDGE compact can be used with other systems (e.g., IS-136, the EDGE network infrastructure (MAP SS7 signaling) is adapted to IS-136 network infrastructure (IS-41 signaling). Figure 4.27 shows an EDGE compact system. This diagram shows that the key concept of EDGE compact is the coordination of control messages between nearby base stations. Standard EDGE radio transceivers and EDGE capable mobile telephones are used in the system. The primary change coordination is the inhibiting of transmission on control time slots in nearby (alternate) cells.

System Attributes

Some of the key system attributes for the EDGE compact system include scheduled transmissions for interference reduction and compatibility of EDGE and IS-136 network infrastructure.

Scheduled Transmissions for Interference Reduction

For EDGE compact, certain radio transmissions are scheduled to avoid co-carrier interference at the same time. The standards group recognized that the smallest practical frequency plan for use with EDGE cells is $n = 4$. A frequency plan characterized by $n = 3$ uses 1/3 of the allocated EDGE carrier frequencies in each cell—possibly just one carrier frequency at first in each cell, supporting several EDGE users on its various time slots. This particular example, with one carrier frequency per cell, would only require that 600 kHz of spectrum be assigned to EDGE in the early installations. However, using a three-cell frequency plan for EDGE presents a serious problem in configuration of a working system since the $c / (i + n)$ ratio will be smaller than is desired. In the future, a more desirable frequency plan for EDGE would use four or possibly seven cells. This is likely to be used only after the amount of EDGE (and likely also GSM voice) traffic in the system is very substantial so that the amount of radio spectrum devoted to EDGE is no longer an issue.

The initial use of a frequency reuse of $n = 3$ will produce more errors in all data, but particularly for call-processing-related messages such as packet paging, packet access grant, and the like, and thus slow down the system operation. Therefore, some further system design steps are used in this type of installation, called EDGE compact, to minimize the effects of strong co-carrier interference arising from $n = 3$ cell clusters. The most significant measures are scheduled transmissions to minimize co-carrier interference for highly important system call processing messages.

To achieve this scheduling, EDGE compact systems establish typically four time groups. Cells in the $n = 3$ frequency plan that would be the closest ones to other co-carrier cells are intentionally assigned to different and distinct time groups. Figure 4.28 shows that the different time groups transmit and receive certain call processing packets at distinct, scheduled times. This figure uses the conventional representation of each cell as a hexagon. This example shows omni-directional cells, but the method illustrated can also be used for sectored cells as well even though that alternative is not illustrated. This figure shows that any group of three cells that meet at a common point have three different carrier frequency groups assigned. At the first installation of EDGE compact, there may be just one EDGE carrier frequency in each cell, but later the symbol F1 may actually represent two or more carrier frequencies. For example, carrier frequencies 1, 4, 7, etc., may all be used in a cell labeled F1, while carrier frequencies 2, 5, 8, etc., may be used in a cell labeled F2, and so on.

Further examination of Figure 4.28 will disclose that each cell in a group of four clustered adjacent cells is labeled with one of the four time group numbers. You can visualize this cluster geometrically in various ways, but one view is that Time Group 1 is the label at the top center of a cluster, Time Group 2 is at the left, Time Group 3 at the right, and Time Group 4 at the bottom center. Since 12 is the least common multiple of 3 and 4, we can also identify a group of 12 cells that have no internal repetition of the same frequency plan code and time group code in any one cell. Such a group of 12 cells is outlined with a dark line in the figure. The combination of the frequency plan and time group plan contained in

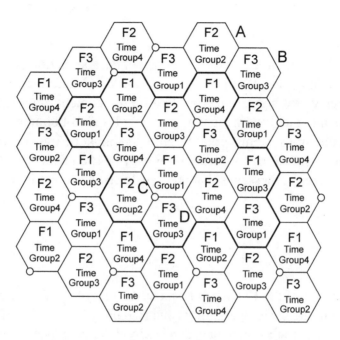

Figure 4.28. EDGE Compact Frequency Planning.

this 12-cell group can be used as the basic building block to make other similar 12-cell groups throughout the EDGE compact system. For example, the two cells at the upper right corner of the figure, labeled A and B, can be seen to be a small part of a another geographical installation of the 12-cell group pattern. They match up with the two cells labeled D and C in the lower left boundary of the original 12-cell group.

Compatible EDGE Compact and IS-136 Networks

It is possible to mix EDGE compact and IS-136 networks. This allows a customer who is receiving a data transmission on an EDGE channel to be notified that a call is incoming on an IS-136 channel. Unfortunately, because the infrastructure is not directly compatible, some network changes had to occur to allow this to happen.

EDGE is a GSM technology that relies on mobile application part (MAP) for intersystem signaling, and IS-136 TDMA networks rely on interim standard 41 (IS-41) for intersystem signaling. Although the fundamental information transfer is the same, the intersystem signaling protocols are not compatible. To allow compatibility, the intersystem signaling protocols must be translated. To simplify network interconnection, a separate HLR may be used for GPRS/EDGE technology to minimize the messages that are transferred between the EDGE and IS-136 system.

Basic Operation

The basic operation of the EDGE compact system involves adding channel time slot scheduling to the basic operation of the EDGE system. Scheduling can be a little complicated as logical channels can be divided into subchannels (e.g., paging and broadcast channels can be divided) and this involves different scheduling times.) The basic operation of EDGE compact also involves the sharing of network resources between EDGE (GSM MAP SS7 signaling) and IS-136 (IS-41 signaling). This allows voice and data calls to be exchanged between the different types of systems.

The system operator has the option of using a PDCH channel for all types of packet messages, or alternatively the operator can separate the PBCCH and PCCCH logical channels from the PDTCH and its associated logical channels (PACCH and PTCCH). The PCCCH carries call processing messages (such as are in the PRACH/U messages) from mobile telephones that want attention from the base station, or PAGCH/D messages from the base to a mobile telephone assigning a mobile telephone to a particular PDTCH for subscriber data transfers. We place these PCCCH channels in particular time slots and schedule them in four different time schedules so that there are no simultaneous transmissions from other cells on the same co-channel time slots. This time slot transmission coordination is primarily to protect call processing messages of the type that are logically PBCCH or PCCCH.

For example, when cells in Time Group 1 use time slot 1 for call processing messages, all other time groups are idle during time slot 1. When time group 2 uses, for example, time slot 3 for call processing messages, all other time groups are idle during time slot 3, and so forth. To allow mobile telephones to make MAHO related measurements on the signals from other cells, we also "rotate" the time groups through a cycle of four choices of time slots for call processing messages for each 4 52-frame multiframes (208 frames).

The standard method is to use odd-numbered time slots in the following way. For example, Time Group 1, time slot 1, is used for control messages during the first 52-frame multiframe. Time slot 7 is then used for call processing messages during the next multiframe. This is followed by time slot 5 is used during the next multiframe, and then time slot 3 is used during the fourth multiframe. After this sequence is complete, the rotation cycle begins again.

The identification of the four multiframes (actually numbered 0, 1, 2, 3 as is usual in these standards documents) is established with reference to the remainder produced by dividing the hyperframe counter count of 52-frame multiframes by the constant 4. The three other time groups use other odd-numbered time slots to avoid both time groups using the same time slot in the same multiframe for call processing messages. Figure 4.29 shows the packet data channel transmission on the 52-frame multiframe.

This may sound complicated on paper, but its implementation is simple in the system, merely requiring the use of some software or hardware counters. A similar type of process is already used in GSM frequency hopping, for example. When EDGE compact data traffic increases, the system operator will allocate more radio spectrum bandwidth to EDGE, install multiple carrier frequencies in each cell, and introduce frequency hopping. Frequency hopping can only be implemented when there are three or more carrier frequencies installed in a cell. When enough spectrum is devoted to EDGE, the frequency hopping can continue to be used, but the overall cell frequency plan can be modified to use $n = 4$ or $n = 7$ cell clusters. At this point, it is no longer necessary to use the scheduled idle time slots as is the practice in establishing time groups. In typical cases, there is a net gain in traffic capacity at this point. Remember that the overall throughput capacity of a system with time groups is somewhat reduced by requiring some of the time slots to be idle part of the time to avoid interference. In comparison, the use of an $n = 4$ frequency plan does not allow placing as many carrier frequencies in each cell as $n = 3$, but for $n = 4$, all time slots can transmit at all times without the need to enforce scheduled idleness on some time slots at some times.

Upgrading to GPRS and EDGE

Beginning from an existing GSM circuit-switched voice base system network, there are two hardware upgrades in the base system for GPRS and EDGE. The first is a modification of the air (or Um) interface to support packet switching instead of circuit switching. In GPRS this is essentially just a protocol change, since the hardware aspects related to modulation are the same as GSM. Both GSM and GPRS use the same GMSK modulation. EDGE may require limited hardware changes in the base transceiver (depending on the specific internal hardware design), since the type of modulation is changed from GMSK to 8PSK.

The second upgrade is a packet-network-switching capability in the system infrastructure. This packet-switching capability extends end-to-end from the packet oriented mobile telephone, via the base station in the cell with the mobile data station, via the SGSN, through a suitable TCP/IP network, to the other participant in the packet communication. The SGSN switch for packet data is analogous to the MSC switch for voice. A packet-oriented mobile telephone may be a personal computer with a PCMCIA radio card, or a personal computer connected via a short data cable to a radio handset.

Various different configurations are permitted to install a gateway packet switch (GGSN). In theory, a GGSN could be designed and used so that it only handles

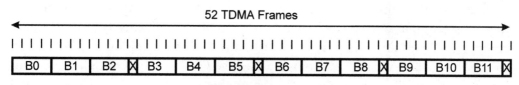

Figure 4.29. Packet Data Channel Transmission on 52-Frame Multiframe.

packet traffic. For most installations, it is more likely that an existing MSC will be upgraded to handle both circuit-switched voice traffic and packet traffic. This may require the addition of one or more printed wiring cards in an existing MSC switch to provide packet switching, in addition to the circuit switching already provided for GSM voice service.

To upgrade a base station, new packet-switching hardware may be required within the base station controller (BSC) or radio network controller (RNC), depending on the original design. GPRS and EDGE networks can handle both IP and X.25 packets, although the IP packet format is clearly more popular today.

For each installation of a GPRS or EDGE system, one or more specific GSGN packet switch(es) in the backbone (the "private" network of GSGN switches) is used to provide an "anchor" public Internet network IP address for each mobile telephone. The gateway (GPSN) may be directly connected to radio base stations, or it may be interfaced to another service node (SGSN). The SGSN, serves as an infrastructure network intermediate or transit switch node, located in between the land Internet and the "mobile service" network of GSGN switches.

It is hypothetically possible to construct a data network using only the component devices to support only GPRS and EDGE. An example of this application is the addition of a high-speed packet data network to an independent or incompatible system. In this type of system, a mobile telephone is typically connected to a data terminal device, such as a laptop computer or other type of portable computer. A portable computer with a built-in mobile telephone radio (in the form of a PCMCIA card, for example) uses the GPRS or EDGE radio link (Um interface) to transfer packet data information between the mobile telephone and the base station system (BSS).

The BSS comprises a base station controller (BSC) and, typically, multiple base transceiver systems (BTSs). In general, multiple BSS devices are connected via wire links to a central packet data switch, called a serving GPRS support node (SGSN). The SGSN in turn may be linked to other SGSNs to form a private data network, called a "backbone." The use of the word "private" only indicates that some of the network addresses used for routing packets may be assigned without concern that they duplicate the same number values already used somewhere in the public Internet network. Subscribers who are members of the public are not prevented from using this private network. This backbone packet data network operates much like the public Internet. One or more of these SGSN switches is/are equipped as a gateway GGSN to connect to the backbone network via some of its connection ports and also to the public Internet via other ports. In practical networks, implementers are expected to take advantage of the high level of commonality and backward compatibility between GPRS/EDGE and GSM voice network hardware.

A typical system structure based on GSM hardware is shown in Figure 4.30. This structure will support both voice and data services. Two representative mobile telephone users are shown. One is using voice service, and another is using data service. For certain classes of mobile telephones (described below), a subscriber may engage in a voice conversation while his or her computer is simultaneously engaged in packet data transfers via the same radio handset. Of course, on a time scale of milliseconds, the radio is not transferring digitally coded speech and packet data simultaneously, but the two processes are interleaved via TDMA technology so that the user perceives continuous voice and substantially continuous data service simultaneously. The base station system (BSS) supports both GSM voice and GPRS/EDGE packet data service, sometimes by assigning different time slots of the same carrier frequency to the two services. One of the previously noted advantages of GPRS and EDGE is the ease of using the same base radio transceivers for all these types of radio signals. The MSC-SGSN-GGSN is a single switch that contains both circuit switching and packet switching hardware. In addition, it also acts as the gateway to the Internet in this figure, as well as connecting voice conversations to the PSTN. Of course, in a system with multiple MSC-SGSN switches, they can be linked together to provide the private packet data network mentioned above, and typically one of the multiple MSC-SGSN switches will also act as the GGSN gateway.

We have not shown explicitly the structure of an EDGE Compact system. It is typically built on a legacy IS-136 base system. In one base station there will be distinct base station transceivers for the EDGE radio signals, in addition to the preexisting IS-136 base transceivers. However, these distinct base transceivers will typically connect to the same base station antennas. They will typically use the same base station controller, and will also share a single MSC-SGSN switch. This switch will connect to the PSTN for voice service, and to other packet data switches as well. Voice and packet data connections will typically use distinct wire ports on the switch. When there are multiple MSC-SGSN switches connected via packet data links to make up a private packet data network, one of them will be designated as the GGSN. In a smaller network installation, a single switch may serve as the MSC-SGSN-GGSN, as in Figure 4.30 for the simple GSM-based system.

Eventually, an all-digital packet data network could be used for both data and packet voice transmission. With advances in voice over Internet protocol (VoIP) systems, a simple gateway could be added to allow packetized voice transmission over the GPRS or EDGE network. However, packet voice transmission requires very short transmission delays, and VoIP packets are typically short (10 msec) and often have excessive overhead for addressing and control messages. This will likely require enhancements to the EDGE system to allow for efficient compression technology and new quality of service (QoS) levels that allow rapid packet delivery for packetized voice (real-time) systems.

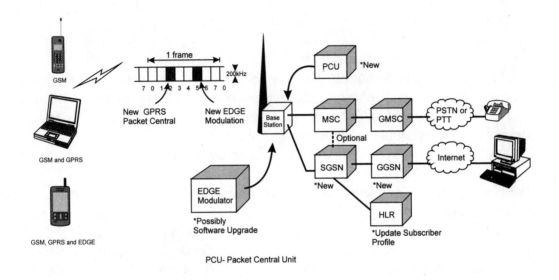

Figure 4.30. Integrating GSM with GPRS and EDGE.

References:

1. Digital Cellular Telecommunications System (Phase 2+) General Packet Radio Service (GPRS), 3GPP TS 43.064 V4.0.0, January 2001, www.3GPP.org.
2. "Enhanced Data-rates for Global Evolution (EDGE): An Overview," Universal Wireless Communications Consortium (UWCC), March 2001, www.uwcc.org.

Chapter 5

Code Division Multiple Access 2000 (CDMA2000)

The code division multiple access 2000 (CDMA2000) system is a 3rd generation (3G) wireless specification that is based on the IS-95 industry specification developed in the United States. CDMA2000 radio transmission technology (RTT) combines new wideband (up to 15 MHz) digital spread spectrum CDMA channels with narrowband (1.25 MHz) IS-95 CDMA channels. The CDMA2000 specification is backward compatible with IS-95 as any type of CDMA channel can be used in 3G frequency or the standard cellular and PCS/PCN frequency bands.

CDMA systems differ from FDMA (analog) and TDMA systems through the use of coded radio channels. In a CDMA system, users can operate on the same radio channel simultaneously by using different coded sequences.

History

Spread spectrum radio technology has been used for many years in military applications. CDMA is a particular form of spread spectrum radio technology. In 1989 CDMA spread spectrum technology was presented to the Telecommunications Industry Association (TIA) in the United States as a proposal for the 2nd generation of mobile communications system. Unfortunately, it did not meet with immediate approval by the standards committee since it had just resolved a two-year debate between TDMA and FDMA and was not eager to consider another access technology. To prove the advantages of CDMA technology, CDMA cellular service began testing in the United States in San Diego, California, during 1991. As a result of continued persistence of CDMA proponents, in 1995, IS-95 CDMA commercial service began in Hong Kong, and a 1.9 -GHz all-digital system started service in the United States in October 1996.

The development of CDMA was partially inspired by an attempt to satisfy the goals of the Cellular Telecommunications Industry Association (CTIA) user performance requirements (UPR) objectives for the next generation of cellular technology, particularly the goal of increasing capacity to 10 times that of analog cellular technology. In response to these objectives, radio specifications were created that CDMA proponents claimed would satisfy the requirements. A proprietary specification was presented by Qualcomm to the Telecommunications Industry Association (TIA) which modified and accepted it as the IS-95 CDMA specification.

The CDMA2000 system was standardized by the Third Generation Partnership Project 2 (3GPP2). The 3GPP2 group was formed to develop the necessary extensions to the IS-95 CDMA standard to satisfy the IMT-2000 system requirements. A key factor for the development of CDMA2000 system was to allow the upgrade of existing IS-95 CDMA systems and to use the IS-41 intersystem signaling system (developed for the Americas). It is expected that the CDMA system will also be compatible with the global system for mobile (GSM) communications system's mobile applications part (MAP) infrastructure. In October 2000, the first commercial third generation wireless system was started by SK Telecom in Korea [1].

In 2001, IS-95 CDMA had over 11.8% global market share with more than 84.6 million subscribers [2]. This market share was achieved despite the late entry of the CDMA system into the marketplace. IS-95 CDMA systems rapidly gained market share through the key benefits of spread spectrum technology. Information about the history and standards for WCDMA can be found at www.3GPP2.org.

Figure 5.1 shows the development of the CDMA2000 standard. This diagram shows that the CDMA2000 wireless standard was influenced by a variety of standards including Advanced Mobile Phone System (AMPS), IS-54 TDMA, IS-136 TDMA, and GSM. The IS-95 CDMA standard also evolved through revisions A and B. Revision B provides for higher data transmission rates. The CDMA2000 standard is divided into two phases. Phase 1 enhances the 1.25 MHz radio channel (called 1XRTT) to provide for higher data rates. Phase 2

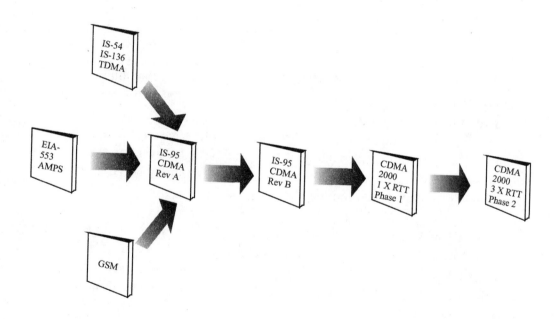

Figure 5.1. Development of CDMA2000 Standard.

allows for multiples of 1.25 MHz to provide for higher data transmission rates and options of multicarrier transmission or direct sequence spreading.

CDMA2000 System Overview

The CDMA2000 system is an enhancement of the IS-95 CDMA mobile communications system. The CDMA2000 system allows for voice or data communications on either a standard 1.25 MHz IS-95 CDMA radio channel or CDMA2000 channels that are multiples of the 1.25 MHz CDMA radio channel bandwidth. These multiples are 3, 6, 9 or 12 times (up to 15 MHz wide). The use of wider radio channels allows for user data transmission rates to reach over 2 Mbps.

IS-95 CDMA Core System

The IS-95 system defines a 1.25-MHz digital radio channel that allows multiple mobile telephones to communicate on the same frequency at the same time by special coding of their radio signals. This type of digital radio channel modulation is called direct sequence code division multiple access (DS-CDMA). The IS-95 CDMA system includes many of the same basic subsystems as other cellular systems, including a switching network, base stations (BS), and mobile telephones (officially called mobile stations).

The IS-95 CDMA system was developed with dual mode capability. It allows for both CDMA mobile radios and AMPS to access the system. When AMPS mobile telephone telephones access the system, they conform to the TIA/EIA-553 standard. Hand off from IS-95 CDMA to AMPS channels is supported in the IS-95 CDMA system.

Figure 5.2 shows a basic IS-95 CDMA system. This diagram shows that there are several types of devices that can be used in the CDMA system. These include IS-95 CDMA single-mode telephones, AMPS mobile telephones, and dual-mode IS-95 CDMA and AMPS mobile telephones. The IS-95 CDMA cellular system can have three basic types of physical radio channels: 1.25 MHz IS-95 CDMA RF channels, 30 kHz AMPS control channels, and 30 kHz AMPS voice channels. The single type of CDMA radio channel provides for both control and user information transfer. In many CDMA systems, analog channels are not used.

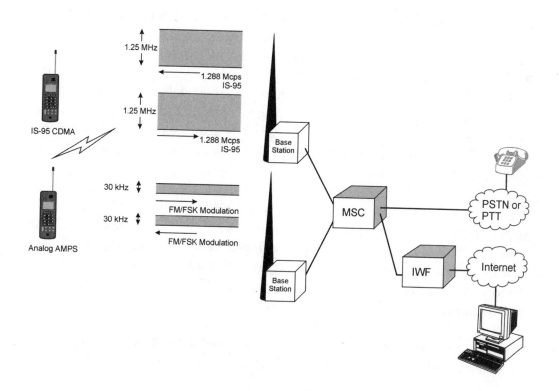

Figure 5.2. IS-95 CDMA Radio System.

FDD/CDMA2000

The FDD/CDMA2000 (usually referred to as CDMA2000) system uses paired multiples of 1.25 MHz radio channels: one for the downlink (base to mobile telephone) and one for the uplink (mobile telephone to the base). These radio channels are composed of multiple physical carriers, each having a unique code (spreading sequence). Each of the physical radio channels are divided into 5 to 20 msec frames and each frame is divided into 1.25 msec time slots. During a voice conversation with the mobile telephone, the mobile telephone usually transmits and receives simultaneously on each of the time slots in both directions. The mobile telephone can simultaneously decode other physical channels on the same frequency by using their unique channel codes.

The FDD/CDMA 2000 system is unique as it can use variable spreading codes and combine multiple channels to produce a user-available data rate of up to 307.2 kbps for each 1.25-MHz downlink channel and up to 1036.8 kbps for three combined channels in a 5-MHz bandwidth. It is also possible to allow several physical (data traffic) channels to coexist on the same frequencies using Walsh code multiplication.

Figure 5.3 shows an overview of a CDMA2000 radio system. This diagram shows that there are several types of devices that can be used in the CDMA2000 system. These include CDMA2000 multiple bandwidth radios and IS-95 CDMA-compatible mobile telephones. The CDMA2000 mobile telephone devices are usually capable of operating as IS-95 CDMA and CDMA2000 mobile radios.

CDMA2000 radio channels carry control, voice, and data functionality by dividing a single traffic channel (TCH) into different subchannels. Each of these chan-

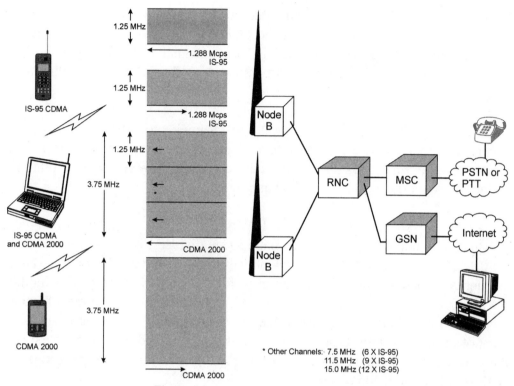

Figure 5.3. CDMA2000 Radio System.

nels is identified by a unique code. When operating on a CDMA radio channel, each user is assigned to a different code for transmission and reception. Some codes in the TCH transfer control channel information, and some transfer voice channel information.

TDD/CDMA2000

A time division duplex (TDD) version of the CDMA2000 system was proposed to the ITU in June 1998 to allow a single 5-MHz physical radio channel to allow two-way communications on systems that do not have two available frequency bands [3]. Many of the attributes of the FDD/CDMA2000 system were maintained including the 1.25-MHz multiple radio channel width and base 1.228-Mcps chip rate to easily allow inter-operation with the FDD/CDMA2000 system.

The TDD/CDMA system divides the radio channel into 20 msec or 5 msec frames, and each frame is divided into 1.25-msec time slots. The time slots are assigned at different times for transmit and receive to allow two-way communications between the mobile telephone and the system.

Figure 5.4 shows how the TDD/CDMA2000 system operates. TDD/CDMA2000 full duplex radio channels are divided by code sequences and time periods. TDD/CDMA mobile telephones transmit and receive on one same frequency. Separate time slots are assigned for transmit and receive, and multiple time slots may be assigned to allow different data transmission rates for the downlink and uplink. During usual operation, the mobile telephone receives a burst of data, waits until its assigned transmit time slot, and transmits a burst on the same frequency. This process is continually repeated, allowing data to steadily flow in both directions.

A key challenge for TDD operation is the added requirement of guard times to ensure bursts of data do not overlap. For mobile telephones that are used close to the base station, the amount (percentage) of guard time allocated to transmission bursts is small. However, as the distance from the cell site becomes larger, the amount of required guard time for each time slot becomes larger. This limits the use of TDD to operation of within 7 km of the base station [4].

IS-95 CDMA System

Code division multiple access is a form of spread spectrum communications which allows multiple users to share the same frequency band by spreading the information signal (audio or data) for each user over a wide frequency bandwidth.

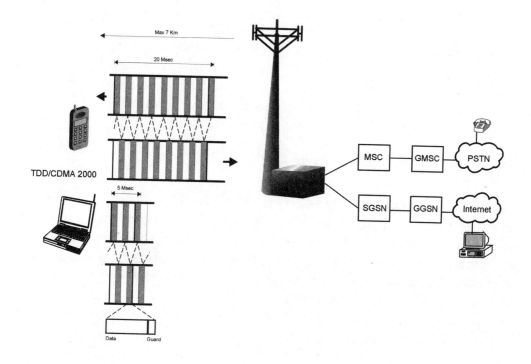

Figure 5.4. Time Division Duplex (TDD) CDMA2000 System.

The IS-95 CDMA (usually referred to as CDMA or IS-95) system uses two radio channels: one for the downlink (base to mobile telephone) and one for the uplink (mobile telephone to base). Each of the radio channels is divided into 20 msec frames, and each frame is divided into 15 time slots (1.25 msec each).

Although the IS-95 CDMA system uses a single type of digital radio carrier, there are several types of CDMA (coded) channels. These include a reference channel identifier (pilot), timing reference (synchronization), an alerting channel (paging), channel assignment coordination (access) and channels that transfer user data such as voice (traffic channels).

Key system attributes for the IS-95 CDMA system include increased frequency reuse, efficient variable rate speech compression, enhanced RF power control, lower average transmit power, ability to simultaneously receive and combine several signals to increase service reliability, seamless handoff, extended battery life (power saving), and advanced information service features.

Spreading (Walsh) Codes in IS-95 CDMA

The spread spectrum encoding system in IS-95 CDMA systems use orthogonal codes, also referred to as a Walsh code (WC). Orthogonal coding is a system of spreading codes that have no relationship to each other. The system also combines these orthogonal codes with two pseudorandom noise (PN) sequences for each communication channel. There are different codes used for different types of channels. The overhead channels (control channels) have designated codes to be used while traffic channels codes are selected at the time the transmission or when a call is originated.

The IS-95 CDMA system uses fixed length orthogonal codes (Walsh codes) to uniquely identify each physical channel. This allows a 1.25-MHz CDMA radio channel to have 64 unique physical communication channels. Because each physical channel experiences interference from nearby transmitting cell sites and mobile telephones (called interference limited), not all channels are used. As a result, the combined data throughput for all users cannot usually exceed 192 kbps [5]. To obtain a maximum of 64 communication channels for each CDMA radio channel, the average data rate for each user should approximate 3 kbps. If the average data rate is higher, less than 64 traffic channels can be used. CDMA systems can vary the data rate for each user dependent on voice activity (variable rate speech coding), thereby decreasing the average number of bits per user to about 3.8 kbps [6]. Varying the data rate according to user requirement allows more users to share the radio channel, but with slightly reduced voice quality. This is called soft capacity limit.

There are 64 different Walsh codes used in the IS-95 CDMA system, each having a fixed length of 64 bits. On the forward link, Walsh codes are used to separate the channels. The reverse link channel generation uses the Walsh code for orthogonal modulation, also known as orthogonal signaling. Orthogonal describes the property of the code where the addition of each does not create interference to other codes. However, in a multipath environment, perfect orthogonality is difficult to achieve.

Figure 5.5 shows how CDMA channels share each radio channel. Digital signals are coded to produce multiple chips (radio energy) for each bit of information to be transmitted. A "chip" is a name for one of the bits in the PN bit sequence that is generated at a higher bit rate than the data rate to be coded. The receiver has an internal chip generator that can produce exactly the same PN chip sequence as the one used for encoding at the transmitter. The time delay of this chip generator in the receiver is adjustable to allow for the time that the radio signal requires to travel from the transmitter to the receiver. The receiver shifts the PN chip pattern in time until it matches the coded pattern. The particular chip pattern is illustrated symbolically by a combination of pictures such as circles, squares, and diamonds in Figure 5.5. Chips on the forward link are selected to collide only infrequently with chips from other users. A chip collision occurs when the binary sequence of a chip pattern (such as 011010111000) matches that of another chip pattern for a short interval of time. When two chip-sequence patterns are designed so that there is no complete collision between the two during one data bit interval, this is known as orthogonal coding. The 64 chip or PN patterns used in CDMA are perfectly orthogonal to each other, but each pattern is combined with a pattern that is unique to the mobile telephone used for that channel, and some codes are used in adjacent cells. As a result, chip patterns from many mobile radios may produce short-term collisions on the reverse channel.

Several chips are created for each bit of user information (speech or data), so if some of them encounter interference form of code collisions shown in Figure 5.5, most of the remaining chips will still be received successfully. CDMA chan-

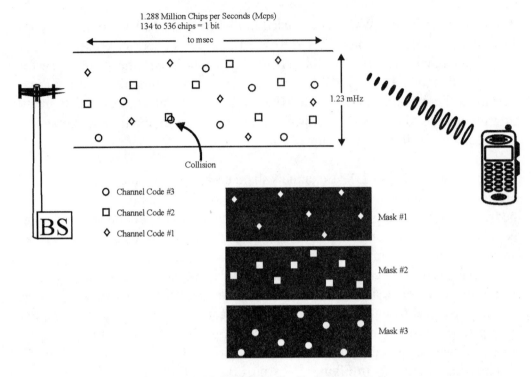

Figure 5.5. IS-95 CDMA Radio Channel Codes.

nels are designed using error-protection codes so that they can operate with some limited amount of interference among users (chip collisions), so CDMA radio channels can tolerate a limited amount of interference without significantly reducing voice quality.

Each IS-95 CDMA physical radio channel can be divided into many logical (Walsh coded) channels. A few of these channels are used for control, and the remaining channels carry voice information and data.

The CDMA system uses two types of PN code sequences: long and short sequences. The PN codes help the mobile telephone to time-synchronize with the base station and uniquely identify the mobile telephone and base station channels. The process of time shifting the PN codes is referred to as masking.

The short code is 32,768 bits long and is used for quadrature spreading on both the forward and reverse links. On the forward link, the short code is masked to identify the cell or sector in addition to the quadrature spreading. This is masking of the short code is referred to as a pilot offset or PN offset.

The long code sequence is 4,400 billion bits long and is used for separating reverse link channels and data scrambling on the forward link. The long code is masked by the electronic serial number (ESN) of the mobile telephone or a unique cell address.

Channel Coding and Modulation

There are different types of channel coding and modulation on the forward and reverse channels. Channel coding involves speech data compression, error protection coding, and the addition of channel codes.

Forward Link Channel Coding

Figure 5.6 shows a basic block diagram of a forward link (base station to mobile telephone) voice channel modulation process. This diagram shows that an audio signal is digitized to 64 kbps. This is supplied to the voice coder (Vocoder). Error protection bits and repetition bits (discussed later) are then added. These bits are then interleaved (alternated in time) to avoid the effects of group errors due to radio signal distortion. The bits are then randomized by the PN code, primarily for voice privacy. The error protection coded data signal is then spread (multiplied) by the orthogonal codes to create a high speed data signal of 1.228 million information bits per second. This information signal is spread again by the long PN code. Finally, the data is sent to the modulator where it modulates the RF carrier for radio transmission.

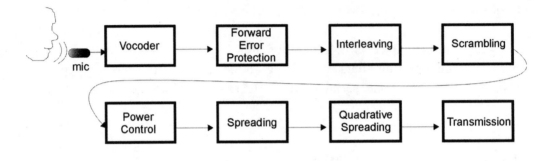

Figure 5.6. IS-95 CDMA Forward Link Voice Channel Coding and Modulation.

Voice Encoder/Decoder (Speech Coder or Vocoder): Speech coding compresses the voice data samples into a 20-msec variable rate frames. The data rate is based on speech activity.

Forward Error Correction (FEC) and repetition: FEC builds redundancy into the data signal to reduce the errors at the receiver. The data from the FEC block is referred to as symbols, and the data rate becomes 19.2 ksps (kilosymbols per second). The symbols are repeated to maintain a constant symbol rate through the remainder of the channel modulation. The amount of repetition depends on the vocoder at lower energy output.

Interleaving: Interleaving distributes (resequences) bits throughout the 20-msec frame of data in a predetermine manner. Because radio transmission is more subject to burst errors, this prevents the loss of consecutive data bits.

Scrambling: Applies a pseudorandom noise (PN) code randomizing the data and providing for voice privacy.

Spreading: Spreads each symbol using orthogonal Walsh codes. This code separates the data from other signals in the same cell. The spreading increases the data rate by a factor of 64 (for IS-95 CDMA) and 128 (for CDMA2000). The data from the spreading block is referred to as chips. The data rate is multiples 1.2288 Mcps (million-chips per second).

Quadrature Spreading: Applies a pseudorandom noise (PN) code, making the signal appear like radio noise and identifying the signal from each cell. This spreading process does not increase the data rate.

Forward Link Modulation: The CDMA system uses efficient quadrature phase shift modulation. The use of quadrature phase shift modulation allows each transmitted symbol (phase shift) to represent 2 bits of information. The base station modulator combines all the different coded digital signals into one radio channel carrier. There may be several radio channel carriers per cell site or sector within a cell site. Up to 64 coded channels can be transmitted in a single 1.25-MHz wideband signal.

RF Transmission: The modulated RF signal is supplied to a linear RF amplifier. The amount of amplification a mobile radio provides is determined by the received signal level and commands received from the base station. The RF power levels of each communication channel within a base station transmitted signal is usually equally set.

Reverse Link Channel Coding

Figure 5.7 shows a basic block diagram of a reverse link (mobile radio to base) voice channel coding and modulation. This diagram shows that an audio signal is digitized to 64 kbps. This is supplied to the voice coder (vocoder). Error protection bits are then added. These bits are then interleaved (alternated in time) to avoid the effects of group errors due to radio signal distortion. The bits are then randomized by the PN code, primarily for voice privacy. The error protection coded data signal is then spread (multiplied) by the orthogonal codes to create a high speed data signal of 1.228 million information bits per second. This information signal is spread again by the long PN code. A burst randomizer is used to repeat specific groups of data (discussed later). Finally, the data is sent to the modulator where it modulates the RF carrier for radio transmission.

Voice Encoder/Decoder (Vocoder): Speech coding compresses the voice data samples into a 20-msec variable rate frames. The data rate is based on speech activity.

Forward Error Correction (FEC) and Repetition: FEC builds redundancy into the data signal to reduce the errors at the receiver. The data from the FEC block is referred to as symbols and the data rate is now 28.8 ksps (kilo-symbols per second). The symbols are repeated to maintain a constant symbol rate through the remainder of the modulation. The amount of repetition depends on the output of the speech coder.

Interleaving: Repositions the sequence bits over the 20 msec of data in a predetermined manner to prevent the loss of consecutive data symbols.

Orthogonal Signaling: Selects one of 64 orthogonal codes to be transmitted in place of six symbols of user data. The orthogonal signaling block increases the data rate by a factor of about 11. The data from the orthogonal signaling block is referred to as a modulation symbol (Walsh chip), and the data rate is 307.2 kcps.

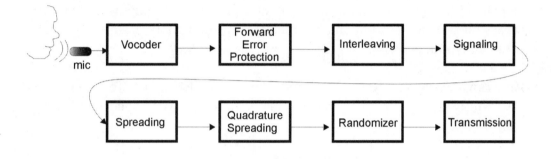

Figure 5.7. CDMA Reverse Link Voice Channel Coding and Modulation.

Spreading: Spreads each digit of user data with four digits of a pseudorandom noise (PN) code. This code separates the signal from other signals in the reverse link. The spreading increases the data rate by a factor of 4. The data from the spreading block is referred to as chips.

Quadrature Spreading: Applies a pseudorandom noise (PN) code making the signal noise-like. This spreading process does not increase the data rate.

Burst Randomizer: Randomly selects which group of the repeated symbols will be transmitted.

Reverse Link Modulation: The CDMA system uses a different type of modulation for the reverse link compared to the forward link. The reverse channel uses offset quadrature phase shift keying (O-QPSK). O-QPSK differs from QPSK in that it does not require the transmitter to pass the signal through the 0 signal level when both the I and Q phase shifted signals are at zero levels. This allows the mobile telephone's RF amplifier to operate more efficiently with O-QPSK because it does not need to amplify the signal as linearly (precisely) as it must with QPSK modulation.

RF Transmission: Converts the digital signal into a RF signal. Transmission is a 1.25-msec burst. The burst transmission is on a 1.25-MHz wideband RF signal.

CDMA Coded Channels

There are four types of coded channels originating from the cell site: pilot, sync, paging, and traffic. There are two types of coded channels originating from the MS: access and traffic. Figure 5.8 illustrates the code channels and the associated links. The pilot, sync, paging, and access channels carry the necessary control data while the traffic channels carry digital voice and same control data.

Pilot Channel (PC)

The pilot channel (PC) is an unmodulated spread spectrum signal that provides the mobile telephone timing and phase reference information for coherent detection. The pilot channels also acts as a beacon signal that is used to measure the received signal strength and provide for power control functions. The pilot channel is the strongest signal transmitted from the cell and always uses Walsh code 0. The mobile telephone first acquires the pilot channel. The pilot channel contains no message only the PN short code, which is time-shifted for cell identification.

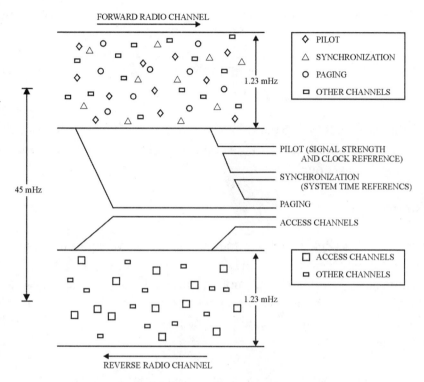

Figure 5.8. Types of IS-95 CDMA Coded Channels.

Sync Channel (SC)

The sync channel (SC) provides the mobile telephone with critical time synchronization data. The message on the SC contains information necessary for the mobile telephone to align its timing with the system's timing. The SC also contains information about the network air interface revision, system data, and paging channel data rate.

The mobile telephone uses the sync channel for time alignment. Once the MS timing is aligned, it will not reuse the SC until after completion of a call or it powers on again. The sync channel message is broken into frames and transmitted at 1200 bps. The frame is the length of the PN short code, and is time-aligned with the start of the pilot PN sequence.

The sync channel sends Walsh code 32 and the mobile telephone has one second to acquire it. Frame alignment with the cell PN allows a mobile telephone to easily receive the sync channel.

Paging Channel (PgC)

The paging channel (PgC) contains messages with parameters that the mobile telephone needs for access and paging. The messages convey system parameters, access parameters, neighbor list, mobile directed paging messages, mobile directed orders, and channel assignment information to the mobile telephone. This channel is used to communicate with the mobile telephone when there is no call in progress.

The PgC is divided into 80 msec slots and grouped into 2048 slots. Each slot is further divided into eight half-frames used to send a mobile telephone directed message, such as pages or service messages. It can be configured for either 4800 or 9600 bps data rate. Each cell may be configured to have from one to seven PgC. WC one is the default, while two through seven are optional. The mobile telephone monitors only one PgC.

Forward traffic Channel (FTC)

The forward traffic channel (FTC) carries user voice and data information along with signaling messages. The base station multiplexes mobile telephone directed messages into the FTC frames.

FTC frames are variable rate frames with the maximum transmit rates of either 9600 bps or 14.4 kbps. The maximum transmission rate for a traffic channel is determined by the rate set (RS). Rate set 1 is a required rate set that allows up to

9600 bps. Rate set 2 (RS2) is an optional rate set that uses a lower level of error protection (1/2 rate convolutional coding instead of 1/3 rate convolutional coding) to achieve higher data rates. The FTC frames are 20 msec long and contain varying rates of data. Because the Walsh coding processes is a fixed amount of spreading, varying rates of data for the IS-95 system are accomplished by either changing the channel coding (reduced error protection or puncturing) or through the use of repetition. For example, to achieve a data rate of 4800 bps, some bits are transmitted two times. The transmitted channel (traffic channel) always maintains the same data transmitted bit rate.

When a FTC is setup the assigned WC will be sent to the mobile telephone using the PgC. The WC is designated for a specific mobile telephone for the duration of the call in that cell. The WC will be used in adjacent cells but the PN offset of the short code will prevent the signals from interfering.

Access Channel (AC)

The access channel (AC) is used to carry mobile telephone responses to paging commands that are received from the base station and for messages that are created for call origination requests. The mobile telephone communicates with the base station when there is no reverse traffic channel (RTC) by using an access channel (AC).

There can be up to 32 ACs for each PgC, and each AC uses a unique time shift of the PN long code. Each mobile telephone is assigned to a PgC but the AC will be randomly selected each time an access attempt is made. AC messages are sent at 4800 bps using a 20-msec frame containing 96 information bits.

Reverse traffic Channel (RTC)

Like the FTC, the reverse traffic channel (RTC) is a variable rate channel capable of carrying voice data, control data, or voice and control data together. The base station multiplexes mobile telephone directed messages into the FTC frames. RTC frames are variable rate frames with the maximum transmit rates of either 9600 bps (RS1) or 14.4 kbps (RS2). The RTC frames are 20 msec long and contain varying rates of data.

Similar to the forward link, to achieve lower data rates when using fixed Walsh codes (fixed spreading), the same bits are setup to be transmitted multiple times. This allows the transmitted channel (traffic channel) to always maintain the same data transmitted bit rate. However, for the reverse link, the mobile telephone may omit duplicate transmissions (shut its transmitter off) during the duplicate transmission to save battery power consumption.

When a RTC is setup, the public mask and the ESN of the mobile telephone number are used to time shift the PN long code. The mobile telephone will use the PN offset for the duration of the call. Private masks can be used in place of the public mask providing an additional measure of privacy and security.

IS-95 CDMA System Attributes and Features

The CDMA system has several key attributes that differentiate it from other multiple accessing schemes. Among these attributes are, a wideband signal to mitigate the affects of fading, variable rate vocoders to reduce the level of interference, dynamic power control to provide the correct amount of power, rake receivers, soft handoff, dim-and-burst signaling, and a paging channel sleep mode. In addition to these unique features built into the modulation scheme there is the ability to employ a frequency reuse of $n = 1$, a higher capacity than other technologies.

Frequency Reuse

Frequency reuse is the ability to reuse the same radio channel frequency at other cell sites within a cellular system. Because the CDMA system uses of orthogonal codes and a PN short code that have limited interference with other coded channels, it is possible for adjacent cells to use the same CDMA radio channel frequency. Figure 5.9 illustrates how the same frequency (f1) is being reused in the adjacent cells, known in the cellular and PCS industry as a frequency plan with $n = 1$. In the shaded area where interference is significant, chip collisions from adjacent cells and other subscribers are more frequent, but this only reduces the number of users that can share the radio channel.

Reusing the same frequency in every cell eliminates the need for frequency planning in a CDMA system. However, pilot PN offset planning must be done in place of the frequency planning. Pilot PN offsets ensure that the received signal from one cell does not correlate with the signal from a nearby cell.

The CDMA standard specifies 512 PN offsets, which are 64 chips apart in time. That delay equates to approximately 10 miles of signal coverage. A PN offset of

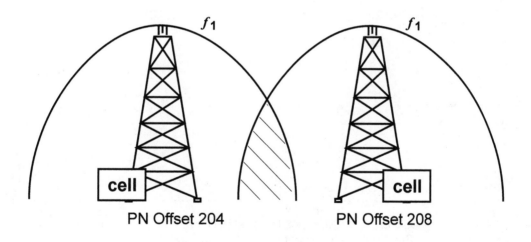

PN Offset 204   PN Offset 208

Figure 5.9. CDMA Frequency Reuse.

3 corresponds to 3 * 64 (chips). PN offset planning is quickly and easily accomplished using a CDMA network-planning tool. Figure 5.10 illustrates the PN offset plan for cells.

Variable Rate Speech Coder (Vocoder)

The IS-95 CDMA system uses a speech coder (vocoder) that compresses the digitized voice signal. The amount of compression varies based on the speech activity. Speech activity can be divided into active (talking) and inactive (silence) periods. In a typical full-duplex two-way voice conversation, the duty cycle (talking compared to silence period) of each voice is about 35 to 40 %. When duty cycle is low, the variable-rate vocoder represents the speech with a lower

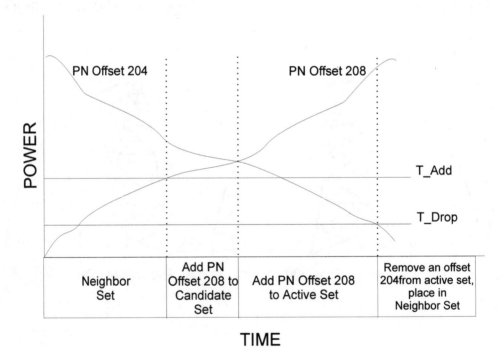

Figure 5.10. PN Offset Planning.

data rate. The vocoder algorithm uses coded excited linear prediction (CELP), and the CDMA specific algorithm is termed QCELP. This added coding efficiency increases CDMA system capacity by a factor related to the ratio of silence to sound intervals in the speech.

In addition to the variable rate encoding process, there is also a dynamic threshold adjustment in the vocoder. When the vocoder detects background noise, such as vehicle traffic or wind blowing, the vocoder raises the threshold for noise encoding only active speech and not the background noise.

The vocoder outputs one voice frame every 20 msec. The data in the frame will be either at the full, half, quarter, or eighth rate. The number of bits for each voice frame rate depends on the vocoder used. The Vocoders used in CDMA have a maximum voice data rate of 8 kbps and 13 kbps. Each 20 msec voice frame will have overhead bits multiplexed into the frame, which increases the transmit rate. The transmit data rates for the 8 kbps vocoder, with overhead bits, are 9600 bps, 4800 bps, 2400 bps, and 1200 bps. Transmit data rates for the 13 kbps vocoder, with overhead bits, are 14.4 kbps, 7.2 kbps, 3.6 kbps, and 1.8 kbps. Due to the variable rate, encoding the average data rate is about 4 kbps and 7 kbps, respectively.

The voice encoding process begins with an analog-to-digital conversion of the user's voice, done at a fixed sample rate of 8,000 samples per second with 8 bits per sample. The resulting data rate is 64 kbps. The vocoder characterizes the speech into parameters that are placed into 20 msec frames.

Figure 5.11 illustrates how the speech coder compression rate varies with speech activity. The speech signal is divided into 20 msec intervals. The bit rate increases and decreases as the speech activity increases and decreases.

At the receiver, the frame quality bits (CRC) will be used to aid in determining the frame rate. This is called blind rate detection as there are no signaling mes-

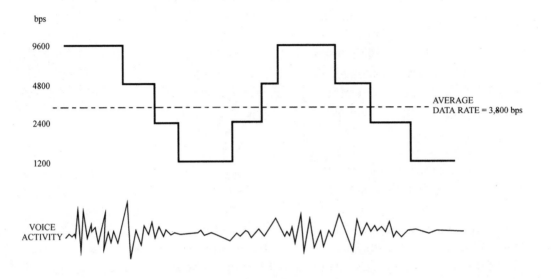

Figure 5.11. Variable Rate Speech Coding.

sages required to change the data transmission rate. If the frame quality bits do not check for one data rate, decoding at another data rate will be attempted until the correct data rate is determined. The receiving vocoder then decodes the received speech packet into voice samples.

Radio Channel

A radio channel is typically characterized by path loss (the signal loss between the mobile telephone and cells) and the amount of signal fading (dips in received levels due to signal cancellation). The physical environment reflects the transmitted signal, causing multiple signals of varying strengths. Each signal will travel a different path to the receiver arriving with a time delay when referenced to an earlier arriving signal. At cellular and PCS frequencies, these time delays may create deep fades that are 200/300 kHz wide. The fading is a function of the mobile telephone's position, speed, and signal bandwidth. Therefore, a small change in the MS's physical location changes the delay associated with all paths. In the 800-MHz cellular band a mobile telephone experiences one fade per second per mile per hour. In the 1900 MHz PCS band, a mobile telephone experiences two fades per second per mile per hour. Fading is very harmful to the communications channel and requires additional power to overcome.

The CDMA radio channel spreads the signal over a relatively wide 1.25-MHz frequency range, making it less susceptible to radio signal fading that occurs only over a specific narrow frequency range. As a result, radio signal fades affect only a portion of the CDMA signal bandwidth, and most of the information gets through successfully. With only a small portion of information corrupted, digital information transmissions over a CDMA radio channel are relatively robust.

Power Control

Power control is the adjustment of the transmitted power level of the mobile telephone or base station transmitter. Power control is very important in CDMA. The system limits both forward link and reverse link traffic channel communication to the minimum transmitter power required for the receiving device to accurately retrieve call data. This reduces the amount of interference that a traffic channel imposes on other channels. Forward link power control is facilitated by the cell site minimizing its transmit power by evaluating signal quality messages from the mobile. Reverse link power control messages are mixed in with the voice data on the traffic channel. They instruct the mobile to either increase or decrease its transmitted power.

The power level of the mobile telephone is continually adjusted. This allows the mobile telephone to overcome the effects of path loss and fading and the power on the FTC, RTC, and AC, and to provide the correct power level needed to obtain the desired signal quality. The objective of the reverse link power control is to normalize all the signals received at the cell regardless of the mobile telephone's position, or propagation loss. Therefore, the signals arrive at the cell with minimum required signal-to-interference ratio. Normalizing this helps to maximize the capacity of the CDMA system, in terms of the number of simultaneous users.

When the signal arrives at the cell with too low a received power level, the bit error rate will be too high for quality communications. When the signal arrives at the cell with too high a received power level, the quality will be good but the interference to other mobile telephones will be too high. The capacity of the system will be degraded when there is too much interference for other mobiles, sharing the same frequency.

To accommodate this requirement for normalized signal levels, IS-95 CDMA systems precisely control mobile telephone power. The power control performs two simultaneous operations: an open loop estimate and a fast closed loop. The open loop estimate is a coarse adjustment and the closed loop is a fine adjustment. The power control system maintains received signals within ±1 dB (33%) of each other. Demonstrations have also shown that a strong interfering signal reduces the number of users per radio channel in a serving cell site. When interference is too great, mobiles are handed off to another cell.

The open loop and fast closed loop power control is designed for the nominal cases. But there will be occasions for exceptions to the nominal case. For example, a small radius cell need not transmit a high power level as a large radius cell. However, when the mobile telephone is a certain distance from a low power cell, it receives a weaker signal than it does from a high power cell. The mobile telephone transmits with a higher power than is necessary for the short range. Because of this, each cell transmits a set of parameters designed to make adjustments to the MS's estimate to meet the characteristics of the cell.

Reverse Open Loop Estimate

Radio signal path loss changes slowly and is considered to be the same for both the forward and reverse link. Therefore an open loop estimate is used whenever the mobile telephone transmits on the AC or RTC. A mobile's open loop estimate is a coarse adjustment of the RF amplifier and is controlled by feedback from its receiver section. The mobile telephone continuously measures the received signal strength from the cell.

The mobile estimates the loss between the mobile telephone and cell. Figure 5.12 shows that as the mobile telephone moves away from the cell, the received signal strength at the MS decreases. When the received signal is strong, the mobile telephone reduces its transmit power; conversely, when the received signal level is weaker, the mobile telephone increases its transmit power. The end result is that the signal received at the cell from the mobile remains at about at the same power level regardless of the mobile's distance.

The open loop power control is based primarily on the received power at the mobile telephone. This is simple but is not very accurate because of the level of

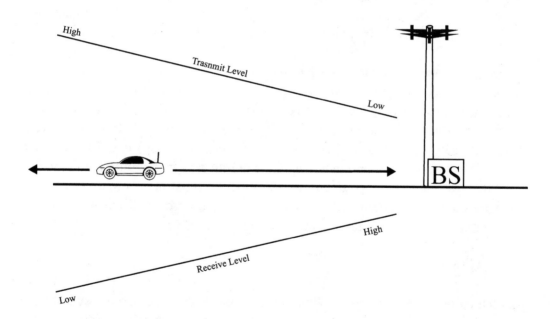

Figure 5.12. CDMA Open Loop RF Power Control.

interference at a mobile. To improve this process, the open loop power control algorithm was modified to consider the strength of the serving pilot.

Fast Closed Loop

Because the forward and reverse link channels fade differently a fast closed loop power control mechanism is employed to help overcome the fades not apparent to the mobile telephone. The base station then fine-tunes the mobile's transmit power by sending power control commands to the mobile telephone during each 1.25-msec time interval. The command is a single bit sent on a power control subchannel on the FTC. The location of the power control bit within each 1.25-mrec time interval is randomly selected using the PN long code. This command adjusts the transmit power of the mobile telephone in 1-dB steps. The adjustment is determined by the received signal strength at the cell. The power control bit communicates the relative change from the previous transmit level, commanding the mobile telephone to increase or decrease power from the previous level.

Figure 5.13 illustrates the closed loop power control. As the received signal strength is too high, the power control bit instructs the mobile telephone to reduce transmit power. When the received signal strength is lower than desired, the power control bit instructs the mobile telephone to increase transmit power. The closed loop adjustment range (relative to the open loop) is ± 24 dB minimum. The mobile telephone must adjust its output power to within 0.3 dB within 500 msec. The combined open and closed loop adjustments precisely control the received signal strength at the cell. The power control mechanism is analog in nature and has a combined dynamic range of 80 dB [7].

Forward Link Power Control

In conjunction with the reverse link power control, there is also a forward link power control. The power for each FTC is dynamically controlled in response to information received from the mobile telephone listening to the FTC. In certain locations, the link from the cell to mobile telephone may be unusually disadvantaged. This requires that the power being transmitted to this mobile telephone be increased or it will have unacceptable signal quality.

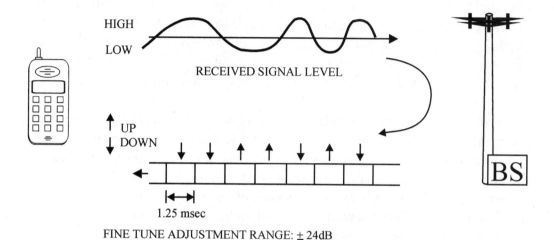

HIGH

LOW

RECEIVED SIGNAL LEVEL

↑ UP
↓ DOWN

1.25 msec

FINE TUNE ADJUSTMENT RANGE: ± 24dB

BS

Figure 5.13. CDMA Closed Loop RF Power Control.

When the cell enables FTC power control, the mobile telephone reports frame error rate (FER) statistics. When the mobile telephone senses an increase in received FER, it reports the increase by sending a message or setting a bit. The message or bit may be sent periodically or when the FER reaches a specified threshold. The cell site responds by adjusting its power level that is dedicated to the mobile telephone on the FTC. The rate of change in transmit power is slower than used for the mobile telephone. The adjustment can be made once every 20 msec.

Discontinuous Transmission (DTx)

CDMA reduces the average power transmitted on FTC by distributing the power allocated to each bit across all the repeated symbols out of the repetition block. On the reverse link, the mobile telephone is able to reduce the average power by employing a burst transmission scheme. The burst transmission reduces the average power over time. To ensure that all mobile stations do not burst at the same moment, each mobile's burst transmission period is randomized.

The use of a variable rate vocoder makes this burst transmission possible. The reverse link is the weaker of the two links and is therefore designed to randomly transmit one of the repeated frames of data but at the full power allocated by the power control loops. This transmission burst is 1.25 msec in duration. This period of time corresponds to the frequency of the fast closed loop power control,enabling the mobile telephone to quickly adjust its transmit power to match the conditions of the radio channel. Figure 5.14 shows how a 4800 bps channel transmits only half of the time.

Rake Receiver

In narrowband radio channels, such as those used for analog systems, the existence of multipath signals causes severe fading. With wideband CDMA signals however, the different paths may be discriminated against in the demodulation process. The ability to discriminate greatly reduces the severity of the multipath fading. In a wideband signal, such as with CDMA, that have a 1-MHz PN chip rate, multipath signals greater than one microsec apart are useful for demodulation. However, multipath signals that are less than one microsec apart will result in a fading behavior.

Both the mobile and cell employ a rake receiver allowing the demodulation of multipath signals. When multipath signals are received at slightly different times, a receiver is assigned to the signal. The receiver demodulates the signal and com-

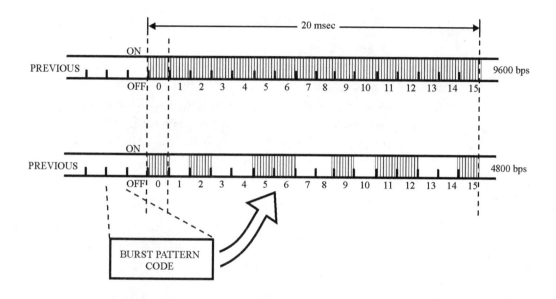

Figure 5.14. CDMA mobile telephone Transmit Power Bursts.

bines it with other weak multipath signals to construct a stronger one. This process is called Rake reception. The result is better voice quality and fewer dropped calls than would otherwise be possible.

Figure 5.15 illustrates how a multipath signal can be added to the direct signal. The radio channel shows two code sequences. The shaded codes are time delayed because the original signal was reflected and received a few microseconds later. The original signal is decoded by mask #1. The code is shifted in time until it matches the delayed signal. The output of each receiver is coherently combined to produce a better quality signal. Because of CDMA's wideband signal, three receivers are used in both the mobile and cells.

Soft Handoff

Because each cell uses the same frequency and codes are used to separate users, the mobile telephone can demodulate two or more FTCs simultaneously, this process is referred to as a soft handoff. A soft handoff provides a more reliable and higher quality signal. This is different than "hard" handoffs in analog systems. In analog cellular systems, a handoff occurs when the cell detects deterioration in signal strength from the mobile telephone.

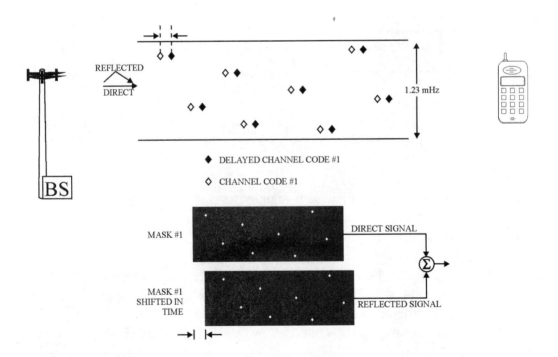

Figure 5.15. CDMA Rake Reception.

As an analog mobile telephone approaches a handoff, signal strength may vary abruptly, and the voice is muted for at least 200 msec in order to send control messages, give the mobile telephone time to change frequencies, and complete the handoff. This is referred to as a "break-before-make" because the mobile telephone must stop transmitting and change to a new frequency. In contrast, CDMA systems use a unique soft handoff while in the traffic state, in which handoff undetectable.

Soft handoff allows the mobile telephone to communicate simultaneously with two or more cells where the best signal quality is selected until the handoff is complete. The standards allow for a soft handoff on up to six FTCs at the same time.

The soft handoff is a mobile assisted process. Figure 5.16 illustrates the process of a mobile assisted handoff. The mobile telephone measures the PC signal strength from surrounding cells. It then transmits the measurements to the serving cell. The serving cell obtains a WC from the cell #2 and sends it to the mobile telephone.

Both the mobile telephone and the new cell begin receiving traffic, while the mobile telephone continues to receive traffic from the original serving cell. Using multiple cells with the same frequency simultaneously during the handoff helps to maintain a much higher average received signal strength at the mobile telephone. During soft handoff, each cell sends a vocoded frame of speech to the vocoder where the best frame is selected for decoding. The mobile telephone uses its rake receiver to optimally combine the cell signals, even if they do not arrive at the mobile telephone synchronized due to varying distances from the two cells.

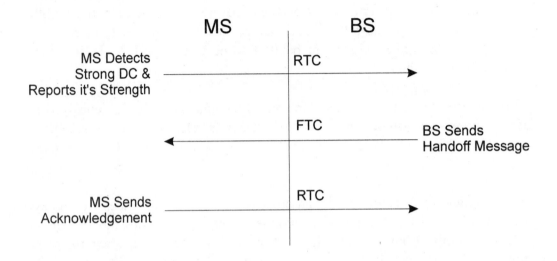

Figure 5.16. Mobile Telephone-Assisted Handoff.

Discontinuous Reception - DRx (Sleep Mode)

The mobile telephone can use a sleep mode when listening to the PgC. The mobile telephone goes to sleep (shuts down unnecessary functions) and wakes up on a periodic basis to check messages and for a page. The PgC messages are distributed throughout the PgC, and mobile-telephone-directed messages will be inserted into slots where the mobile telephone knows to look. Therefore, discontinuous reception (DRx) enables mobile telephones that are not in the traffic state to power-off nonessential circuitry during periods when pages will not be sent. The sleep cycle may be in multiples of 1.28 seconds with the maximum sleep period being 163.84 seconds. Figure 5.17 illustrates the DRx (sleep mode) process. When the mobile telephone registers the base station and mobile telephone select the slot cycle index for the length of the sleep mode.

Signaling

When a mobile telephone is not involved in a call, signaling functions must be provided with the base station. For this purpose, the IS-95 CDMA system uses the sync channel, paging channel, or access channel. Signaling on all channels uses a synchronized bit-oriented protocol. The transmission of the messages is bit synchronized to correspond to the start of the PN short code. The format of

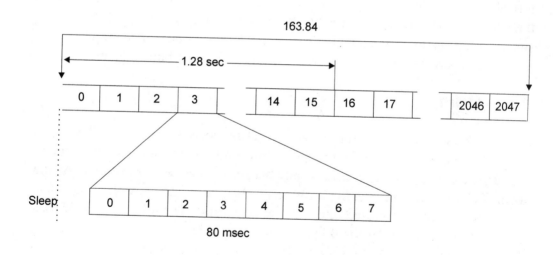

Figure 5.17. Discontinuous Reception - DRx (Sleep Mode).

the message capsule consists of a message and padding. Padding is used on some channels to make the message fit into a frame.

Control messages that are sent on the traffic channel can be transferred by either blank-and-burst or dim-and-burst signaling. Blank-and-burst signaling replaces one or more frames of primary traffic data, typically vocoded voice, with signaling data. Dim-and-burst signaling sends control information in the unused portion of a vocoded frame during periods of low speech activity. Variable rate speech coding varies the coding rate allowing both voice and control messages to be sent during each 20 msec frame, permitting both fast or slow dim-and-burst signaling.

Blank and Burst

Blank-and-burst signaling replaces speech data with signal messages. For historical reasons, this is called "in-band signaling." Blank-and-burst message transmissions degrade speech quality because they replace speech frames with signaling information. The quality degradation for only one isolated replacement is almost imperceptible. Figure 5.18 illustrates blank-and-burst signaling.

Dim and Burst

Dim-and-burst inserts control messages when speech activity is low. The QCELP vocoder is designed to produce a lower bit rate when the voice is silent, between syllables and when there is only background noise, for example. As the vocoder changes the bit rate, the lower voice data rate and a portion of the overhead message are multiplexed into a higher rate frame. The 8-kbps vocoder uses only the full rate frame of 9600 bps to multiplex voice and signaling data. The 13 kbps vocoder can use any vocoder frame for voice and signaling.

The number of required frames for sending the message varies according to speech activity, length, and priority of the message. The dim-and-burst messages have no effect on speech quality, but the message requires somewhat more time to be transmitted.

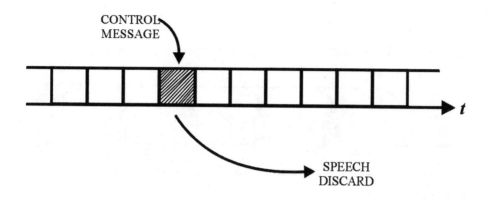

Figure 5.18. CDMA Blank-and-Burst Signaling.

When a vocoded frame has both voice and signaling data a mixed mode bit is set indicating to the receiver there is a mix of voice and signaling data in the frame. Additional flag bits include a traffic type and traffic mode flag for the 8-kbps vocoder. For the 13 kbps vocoder there are additional mixed mode and frame mode flag bits. These bits indicate to the receiver whether the message is being sent via blank-and-burst or dim-and-burst, and give the proportional mix between voice and signaling data. Figure 5.19 illustrates a dim-and-burst message.

Registration

Registration is the process by which a mobile telephone notifies the base station of its location. This allows the base station to more efficiently locate the mobile

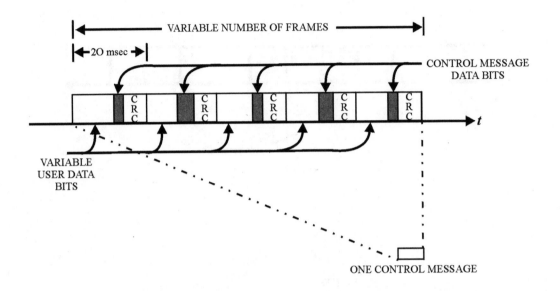

Figure 5.19. CDMA Dim-and-Burst Signaling.

telephone for paging. The mobile telephone uses the registration to notify the base station of its mobile identification number (MIN), PgC slot, Station Class Mark (SCM), and mobile terminated call status.

There is a tradeoff between the rate of registrations and the paging of mobiles. When a mobile telephone does not register, the base station does not know whether the mobile telephone is on, off, or where it is located. Therefore the system must page the entire network, placing a heavy load on the PgC. If frequent registrations are used, then the system will know where the mobile telephone is located with a high degree of accuracy. However, this places a high load on the AC and a moderate load on the PgC, since the system must acknowledge each registration.

The standard defines nine types of registration:

Power-up registration: The mobile telephone registers whenever it powers on, when it switches from using an alternate system, the analog system, or a different frequency band class.

Power-down registration: The mobile telephone registers when powering off if it is registered in the current system.

Timer-based registration: The mobile telephone registers when a timer expires. The mobile telephone timer counts the paging slots to determine time.

Distance-based registration: The mobile telephone will register whenever it moves more than a certain distance from where it last registered. The cells send their latitude and longitude, and a distance threshold. The mobile telephone determines it has moved a certain distance by computing a distance based on the difference in latitude and longitude between the current cell and the cell where it last registered. If the distance measured exceeds the threshold, a registration is sent.

Zone-based registration: The mobile telephone registers when it enters a new zone. A mobile telephone may be registered in more than one zone. However, the base station controls the maximum number of zones in which a mobile telephone may be registered.

Parameter-change registration: The mobile telephone registers when certain stored parameters change, or when it enters a new system. The parameters that will initiate a registration are a change in MIN, band class, slot cycle, operating mode, or call termination indicators.

Ordered registration: The mobile telephone registers when instructed to by the base station.

Implicit registration: The mobile telephone is registered when it makes a call attempt or responds to a message. The base station can infer the MS's location.

Traffic channel registration: When the base station has registration information for a mobile telephone that has been assigned to a traffic channel, the base station notifies the mobile telephone that it is registered.

The first five methods of registration are called autonomous registration and are initiated in response to an event. The base station can enable or disable any of the various types of registration. It is expected that combinations of registration methods will be the most effective.

Data Transfer

Both circuit and packet data transmission can be provided for in the IS-95 CDMA system. To provide for high-speed circuit-switched data, TIA/EIA-95 is designed to satisfy the growing data requirements with an optional medium data rate (MDR). The MDR allows up to eight FTCs to be used together. To allow for simultaneous voice and data communication, there is a fundamental channel and supplemental traffic channels defined. The fundamental channel will be used to carry primary (voice), secondary, and or signaling traffic. Signaling will only occur on the fundamental channel. Supplemental channels may carry voice or secondary data, but not both. The supplemental channel must be the same rate as the fundamental channel and will only operate at the full data rate.

Handoffs

The IS-95 CDMA standard defines three mobile telephone states when a handoff may occur. These states are the idle state, access state, and traffic state.

Idle Handoff

The idle handoff will occur in the idle state and will take place when a mobile telephone has moved from the coverage area of one cell into the coverage area of another cell. When the mobile telephone detects that a PC from a new cell is twice as strong (3 dB) than the current PC, the mobile telephone starts listening to the PgC of the new cell.

Access Handoff

Access handoffs are similar to idle handoffs. All are hard handoffs from one PgC to another. The access handoffs may occur before the mobile telephone begins sending access probes, during access probes, and after receiving an acknowledgment to a probe.

The access entry handoff allows mobile telephone to perform an idle handoff to the best cell. This handoff would occur just after entering the access state but before updating the information from the PgC.

After the mobile telephone begins making access probes, a new and stronger pilot may provide a better chance of service. The mobile telephone can then perform an access probe handoff to prevent the access attempt from failing.

After the mobile telephone has received an acknowledgment to a probe, the access attempt is complete. A handoff to a new and stronger pilot may be possible and necessary to prevent an access failure.

Soft Handoff

A soft handoff is when new cells or a sector of the existing cell communicates on a FTC with the mobile telephone without interrupting the FTC of the old cell or sector. The base station can direct the mobile telephone to perform a soft handoff only when the FTC of the new cell or sector has the same frequency, band classes, and frame offset.

During the soft handoff while in the traffic state, the mobile telephone receives a list of neighboring cells from the PgC. This list of neighboring sites is a list of PN offsets for neighboring cells' pilot channels. These PN offsets are the most likely candidates for handoff. When the PC of new cell has sufficient energy at the mobile telephone for handoff, the mobile telephone requests simultaneous transmission from that channel. The system then assigns the new channel to transmit simultaneously from both the current cell and the new cell. The mobile telephone decodes both channels (different codes on the same frequency) and optimally combining the received information. When the signal strength of the original channel falls below a threshold, the mobile telephone requests release of the original channel ending the communication with the cell. The mobile telephone is capable of simultaneously communicating with two or more cells at the same time.

A soft handoff is initiated when a pilot strength goes above the threshold for adding a pilot (called T_ADD). The pilot will be considered usable until it drops below and stays below a defined drop threshold (T_DROP) for more than a defined amount of time (TT_DROP). The soft handoff is based on the threshold level of the received pilot. Although this is a simple method for determining when to perform a handoff to a new cell it is possible for a mobile telephone to obtain more FTC than would be necessary, thus adding to the level of interference. Therefore dynamic thresholds parameters have been added to the soft handoff process. These dynamic thresholds are used to trigger handoff based on a comparison of pilots to the combined pilot energy. To aid the mobile telephone in the search, parameters and process for sending messages, there are four pilot sets defined.

Active Set: All pilots associated with assigned FTC.
Candidate Set: Pilots with sufficient signal strength to indicate that a FTC could be demodulated but have not been assigned to an FTC.
Neighbor Set: Pilots that are likely candidates for handoff.

Remain Set: The set of all possible pilots in the current system, excluding the pilots in the neighbor set, candidate set, and active set.

Hard Handoff

A CDMA-to-CDMA hard handoff occurs when a base station commands a mobile telephone to transition between disjointed sets of networks, different frequency assignments, different frame offsets, or different band classes.

A CDMA-to-analog hard handoff occurs when the base station commands a mobile telephone to change from a FTC to an 800 MHz analog voice channel. The hard handoff can occur on a IS-95 CDMA system operating in the cellular or PCS bands. A hard handoff from PCS band to cellular band analog mode requires the mobile to support the analog-operating mode. Since IS-95 CDMA is a migration from AMPS the need for AMPS to CDMA hard handoff is not necessary. Because there are no AMPS to CDMA handoffs, the signaling format of the AMPS voice channel is unchanged.

CDMA2000 System

The CDMA2000 cellular system has several key attributes that are different from other FDMA (analog) and 2nd generation (digital) cellular systems. The CDMA2000 system uses wide 5-MHz radio carriers that can be reused in adjacent cell sites. This eliminates the need for frequency planning and the wideband radio channel provides less severe fading, which results in more consistent quality voice transmission under varying radio signal conditions.

Band Class

The CDMA2000 system can be used in existing wireless systems in addition to frequencies assigned to the IMT-2000 system. The CDMA2000 system defines specific channel numbers for use in each specific wireless system. Because

CDMA2000 radio channels are relatively wide compared to 1st and 2nd generation systems, a CDMA2000 mobile telephone may only be able to operate in parts of these bands. Some channels may be restricted for use as transmission of a wideband CDMA radio channel may interfere with radios that are operating in adjacent frequency bands from other systems. In addition, some of these frequency bands are divided into smaller portions that are assigned to specific service providers ("carriers"). As a result, the band class of a CDMA2000 telephone may also include subclass identifiers. Figure 5.20 shows the different types of systems and their approximate frequency range.

Band Class (Subclass)	System	Mobile Transmit Frequency Range (MHz)	Base Transmit Frequency Range (MHz)
0	North American Cellular	824-849	869-894
1	North American PCS	1850-1910	1930-1990
2	Total Access Communications System	872-915	917-960
3	Japan Total Access Communications System (A1)	887-889	832-834
3	Japan Total Access Communications System (A3)	893-898	838-843
3	Japan Total Access Communications System (A2)	898-901	843-846
3	Japan Total Access Communications System (A)	915-925	860-870
4	Korean PCS Band	1750-1780	1840-1870
5(0)	Nordic Mobile Telephone - 450 (A)	452.500-457.475	462.500-467.475
5(1)	Nordic Mobile Telephone - 450 (B)	452.000-456.475	462.000-466.475
5(2)	Nordic Mobile Telephone - 450 (C)	450.000-454.800	460.000-464.800
5(3)	Nordic Mobile Telephone - 450 (D)	411.675-415.850	421.675-425.850
5(4)	Nordic Mobile Telephone - 450 (E)	415.500-419.975	425.500-429.975
5(5)	Nordic Mobile Telephone - 450 (F)	479.000-483.480	489.000-493.480
5(6)	Nordic Mobile Telephone - 450 (G)	455.230-459.990	465.230-469.990
5(7)	Nordic Mobile Telephone - 450 (H)	451.310-455.730	461.310-465.730
6	IMT-2000	1920-1980	2110-2170
7	North American 700	776-794	746-764
8	1800 MHz	1710-1785	1805-1880
9	900 MHz	880-915	925-960

Figure 5.20. CDMA2000 Frequency Band Classes.

CDMA2000 Radio Channels

Each CDMA radio channel is logically divided into several different types of control and voice channels by the use of different channel codes. The CDMA2000 system divides the radio spectrum into multiples of 1.25 MHz digital radio channels, in groups of three. CDMA radio channels differ from other technologies in that it multiplies (and therefore spreads the spectrum bandwidth of) each signal with a unique pseudo-random noise (PN) code that identifies each user within a radio channel. Each CDMA2000 radio channel transmits digitized voice and control signals on the same frequency band. Each CDMA2000 radio channel contains the signals of many ongoing calls (voice channels) together with pilot, synchronization, paging, and access (control) channels. Digital mobile telephones select the signal they are receiving by correlating (matching) the received signal with the proper PN sequence. The correlation enhances the power level of the selected signal and leaves others unenhanced.

The CDMA radio channel is constructed of coded signals on the same frequency, so if adjacent cells use different codes they may reuse the same radio frequency. Interference from neighboring cells appears only as chip collisions when the PN chip codes for the two conversations are not completely orthogonal. The effect of chip collision interference is to reduce system capacity.

Multicarrier (MC) Transmission

Each most basic CDMA2000 radio carrier transmits at a chip rate of 1.228 million chips per second (Mcps). To increase the data transmission capacity of the channel, radio channels with wider bandwidths are used. There are two options for creating wider radio channels: direct sequence spread spectrum modulation on a single radio carrier or the combination of multiple RF channels. When multiple carriers are combined, this is called multicarrier (MC) transmission. In either process, the resulting chip rate is increased by multiplying the 1.228 Mcps rate by the number of combined radio carriers.

Figure 5.21 shows how the 5 MHz RF channel bandwidth has the option to use multicarrier (MC) channels or direct sequence spread spectrum modulation. This diagram shows that either three independent 1.25 MHz downlink channels can be combined to produce 3.684 Mcps or one 3.75 MHz channel can be created.

Spreading Rates (SR)

The CDMA2000 system allows multiples radio channel bandwidth in multiples of three: 1, 3, 6, 9, 12. Phase 1 of the CDMA2000 system uses $n = 1$ (1.25 MHz) channels. Phase 2 allows spreading rates of three (3.75 MHz). Future evolution

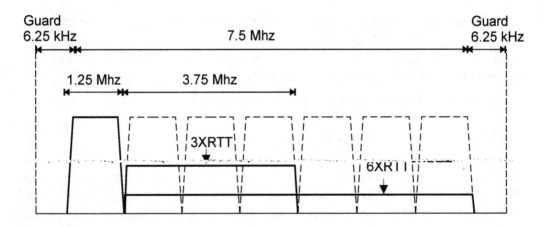

Figure 5.21. Multicarrier (MC) Mode.

of the CDMA2000 system will allow up to 12 1.25-MHz radio channels to be combined (15 MHz).

The CDMA2000 system can have multiples of 1.25 MHz channels, including 1.25 MHz, 3.75 MHz, 7.5 MHz, 11.25 MHz, and 15 MHz. When operated as part of the CDMA2000 system, these channels can be positioned adjacent to each other. When used adjacent to other systems, a guard band of 625 kHz is typically required [8]. Figure 5.22 shows that 1.228 MHz-radio channels can be combined to produce larger channels with higher data transmission rates.

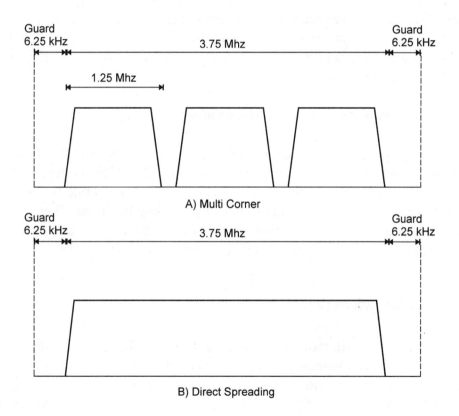

Figure 5.22. Multiple Spreading Rates.

Large Number of Walsh Codes

The CDMA2000 system has a total of 128 orthogonal Walsh codes compared to the IS-95 CDMA system which has a maximum of 64 coded (logical) traffic channels. The increase of the number of available Walsh codes comes from QPSK channel spreading (4 level) as opposed to BPSK channel spreading (2 level) used in IS-95.

Variable Length Walsh Codes

The CDMA2000 system can use Walsh codes of different length to achieve a different amount of spreading. This allows for variable bandwidth. The IS-95 CDMA system achieved variable bandwidth by repeating the data multiple times within each frame.

Quasi-Orthogonal Walsh Code Multiplication

It is possible to increase the number of Walsh codes to increase the number of available channels in single radio channel (beyond 128). If the system is limited by the number of Walsh codes (as opposed by interference limited), it is possible to increase the number of Walsh codes by masking functions. These masked Walsh codes are called quasi-orthogonal functions as they are not completely orthogonal. This can more than double the number of available Walsh codes.

Radio Configurations (RC)

There are presently six radio configurations (RC) for the reverse radio channel and nine radio configurations for the forward radio channel used in the CDMA2000 system. Radio configurations are a mixture of spreading modulation (BPSK compared to QPSK), spreading ratio (1, 3, or more 1.23-MHz channels), and channel coding rates (1/2- to 1/6-rate convolutional coding). Some configurations use punctured channel coding (dual convolutional coding that uses let bits) to increase the data transmission rate by up to 50 percent.

For the forward radio configuration, RC1 is the basic IS-95 radio channel structure. RC2 is the enhanced IS-95 radio channel that uses punctured convolutional coding coding to increase the traffic channel data rates by 50%. RC3-RC9 all use the new QPSK walsh code modulation with various levels of channel coding. RC3-5 use the $n = 1$ fundamental channel bandwidth of 1.23 MHz (1.228 Mcps) while RC6-9 use the wider $n = 3$ channel bandwidth (3.684 Mcps). The data rates are not exactly proportional to the modulation, and spreading ratio and channel coding vary due to the use of puncturing codes and error correction codes. It is not allowed to mix radio configurations 1 or 2 with radio configurations 3 or above on the same radio channel. Figure 5.23 shows the different types of radio configurations for the forward channel.

For the reverse radio configuration, RC1 is the basic IS-95 radio channel structure. RC2 is the enhanced IS-95 radio channel that uses 1/2-rate convolutional coding instead of 1/3-rate convolutional coding to increase the traffic channel

Radio Configuration	Spreading Modulation	Spreading Ratio	Chip Rate (SR)/ Mcps	Channel Coding	Data Rates (kbps)
1	BPSK	1	1.228	1/2	1.2 - 9.6
2	BPSK	1	1.228	1/2 punctured	1.8 - 14.4
3	QPSK	1	1.228	1/4	1.2 - 153.6
4	QPSK	1	1.228	1/2	1.2 - 307.2
5	QPSK	1	1.228	1/4 punctured	1.8 - 230.4
6	QPSK	3	3.684	1/6	1.2 - 307.2
7	QPSK	3	3.684	1/3	1.2 - 614.4
8	QPSK	3	3.684	1/4 or 1/3	1.8 - 460.8
9	QPSK	3	3.684	1/2 or 1/3	1.8 - 1036.8

Figure 5.23. Forward Channel Radio Configurations.

data rates by 50%. RC3-6 all use the new QPSK Walsh code modulation with various levels of channel coding. RC3 and RC4 use the $n = 1$ fundamental channel bandwidth of 1.23 MHz (1.228 Mcps) while RC5-RC6 use the wider $n = 3$ channel bandwidth (3.684 Mcps). The data rates are not exactly proportional to the modulation, and spreading ratio and channel coding vary due to the use of puncturing codes and error correction codes. It is not allowed to mix radio configurations 1 or 2 with radio configurations 3 or above on the same radio channel. Figure 5.24 shows the different types of radio configurations for the reverse channel.

Because the radio channel configurations are different on the forward channel and reverse channel, mobile telephones must be capable of specific pairs of radio channel configurations. If the mobile telephone is capable of receiving the forward channel in configurations 6 or 7, it must be capable of transmitting on the reverse channel in radio configurations 3 or 5. If the mobile telephone is capable

Radio Configuration	Spreading Modulation	Spreading Ratio	Chip Rate (SR)/ Mcps	Channel Coding	Data Rates (kbps)
1	BPSK	1	1.228	1/3	1.2 - 9.6
2	BPSK	1	1.228	1/2	1.8 - 14.4
3	QPSK	1	1.228	1/4 or 1/2	1.2 - 153.6
4	QPSK	1	1.228	1/4 punctured	1.2 - 307.2
5	QPSK	3	3.684	1/3	1.8 - 230.4
6	QPSK	3	3.684	1/2	1.2 - 307.2

Figure 5.24. Reverse Channel Radio Configurations.

of receiving the forward channel in configurations 8 or 9, it must be capable of transmitting on the reverse channel in radio configurations 4 or 6.

Physical Radio Carriers (Channels)

There are different types of physical channels that are used for specific purposes. They are designed so they cycle through a prescheduled sequence of operations, and different types of information are transmitted on each time slot during this cycle. These physical channels include shared and dedicated control channels. In the CDMA2000 system specifications, physical channels are characterized by the use of acronyms using uppercase letters.

Some physical radio channels are exclusively used as control channels, and other data channels share control and user information on the same physical channel. For the dedicated physical control channels, a specific fixed spreading sequence is typically used to uniquely identify each channel. This allows the mobile telephone to more easily discover and decode the control channel.

Forward Pilot Channel (F-PICH)

The CDMA2000 system uses a forward pilot channel (F-PICH) to assist the mobile telephone in demodulating the CDMA carrier and to help the mobile telephone in the initial cell searching (channel scanning) process. The pilot channel provides a known sequence of information that the mobile telephone can easily identify and measure.

The pilot channel is distinguished from other coded channels by a particular PN code. CDMA2000 mobile telephones simultaneously measure the pilot signal strengths of all neighboring base stations in the system.

Forward Paging Channel (F-PCH)

A forward paging channel (F-PCH) carries paging or alert messages to the mobile telephone. The data rate for the F-PCH is either 4.8 kbps or 9.6 kbps with a 20 msec frame size. The paging channel only uses spreading rate 1 (1.228 Mcps). The paging channel is divided into paging channel slots that are 80 msec long.

At least one paging channel is the minimum system configuration. However, multiple paging channels can be allocated based on the paging and control needs of the system.

One of the most important parameters is the information about the sleep and wake paging cycle. In order to conserve battery power, the base system schedules paging messages (which occur when someone else originates a call to a mobile telephone) so that the mobile telephone does not need to keep its receiver on all the time. The mobile telephone can "go to sleep" (turn off all its internal electronic circuits except the hyperframe counter) most of the time, and "wake up" (turn on its receiver circuits) only periodically when it knows that pages destined for it (if any) will occur.

Forward Sync Channel (F-sync)

The synchronization channel is used to allow the mobile telephone to initially synchronize its timing information with the system's timing information. There are type types of F-sync channels used in CDMA2000: shared F-sync and wideband F-sync. The shared F-sync provide service to both IS-95 CDMA and CDMA2000 mobile telephones. The wideband F-Sync is transmitted across the entire wideband channel.

Forward Common Control Channel (F-CCCH)

The forward common control channel (F-CCCH) is a downlink channel that transmits messages that are to be received by a specific mobile telephone that is known to be operating within its coverage area. The frame sizes for the F-CCCH may be set to 5, 10 , or 20 msec which provides for data rates of 9.6, 19.2, and 38.4 kbps respectively.

Forward Common Auxiliary Pilot Channel (F-CAPICH)

The forward common auxiliary pilot channel (F-CAPICH) is a downlink channel that carries pilot reference information that can be used for beam forming applications. This allows the system to use spot beams to localize transmission to specific area (such as to a home using wireless local loop).

Forward Quick Paging Channel (F-QPCH)

A forward quick paging channel (F-QPCH) provides information to the mobile telephone that can be used for slotted reception ("sleep") mode on the paging channel or on the forward control channel. This allows the mobile telephone to sleep between pages and dramatically increase the battery life.

Forward Broadcast Common Channel (F-BCCH)

The forward broadcast common channel (F-BCCH) provides continuous system related information. The F-BCCH uses a fixed Walsh code that is provided to the mobile on the F-Sync channel. The F-BCCH can also be used to transmit broadcast short messages.

Forward Dedicated Auxiliary Pilot Channel (F-DAPICH)

A dedicated auxiliary pilot channel (F-CAPICH) is a downlink channel that can provide pilot reference information that can be used for beam forming applications while the motile telephone is communicating with the system. This allows the system to use spot beams to localize transmission to specific area (such as used through a smart antenna system) where the mobile telephone is located and assist in the redirecting of the beam as the mobile telephone changes location.

Forward Dedicated Common Control Channel (F-DCCH)

The forward dedicated control channel (F-DCCH) transfers control information between the system and the mobile telephone.

Forward Fundamental Traffic Channel (F-FCH)

The forward fundamental traffic channel (F-FCH) is a dedicated physical data channel that transfers user data on the downlink channel. The fundamental channel uses a fixed amount of spreading. Variable data rates are achieved by repeating the data symbols. Figure 5.25 shows the reverse fundamental channel data rates.

Radio Configuration	Spreading	Data Transmission Rates	Frame Size	Channel Coding
1	1.228 Mcps	9600, 4,800, 2400, 1200	20 msec	1/2
2	1.228 Mcps	14400, 7200, 3600, 1800	20 msec	1/2
3	1.228 Mcps	9600	5 msec	1/4
3	1.228 Mcps	9600, 4,800, 2400, 1200	20 msec	1/4
4	1.228 Mcps	9600	5 msec	1/2
4	1.228 Mcps	14400, 7200, 3600, 1800	20 msec	1/2
5	1.228 Mcps	9600	5 msec	1/4
5	1.228 Mcps	9600, 4,800, 2400, 1200	20 msec	1/4
6	3.684 Mcps	9600	5 msec	1/6
6	3.684 Mcps	14400, 7200, 3600, 1800	20 msec	1/6

Figure 5.25. Reverse Fundamental Channel Data Rates.

Forward Supplementary Coded Channel (F-SCH)

A forward supplementary coded traffic channel (F-SCH) can carry voice or data information. Up to seven supplemental channels can be used with a fundamental channel. The supplementary coded traffic channel is only used in radio configurations 1 and 2 (BPSK for Walsh code spreading and 1.228 Mcps). The relative timing of the supplementary channel compared to the fundamental channel can be offset by 1.25 msec (time slots). Figure 5.26 shows supplementary coded channel code rates.

Forward Supplemental Channel

The forward supplemental channel provides user data rates that vary from 1200 bps to 1,036,800 bps. The supplemental channel uses variable length Walsh codes to provide for variable data rates.

Radio Configuration	Spreading	Data Transmission Rates	Frame Size
1	1.228 Mcps	9600	20 msec
2	1.228 Mcps	14400	20 msec

Figure 5.26. CDMA2000 Supplementary Coded Channel Data Rates.

The forward supplemental channel applies only to radio configurations that use quadrature spreading (RC3-9). Up to two supplemental channels can be used with a fundamental channel. The supplemental channel frames can be 20, 40, or 80 msec in duration. The longer the frames, the lower the user data transmission rates. Figure 5.27 shows the forward supplemental channel code rates for the 20-msec frame size.

Reverse Access Channel (R-ACH)

The reverse random access channel (R-ACH) is an uplink channel that allows a mobile telephone to randomly transmit access requests (bursts) when a mobile telephone attempts to access the cellular system. Because these service access

Radio Configuration	Spreading	Data Transmission Rates	Frame Size
3	1.228 Mcps	153600, 76800, 38400, 19200, 9600, 4800, 2700, 1500	20 msec
4	1.228 Mcps	307200, 153600, 76800, 38400, 19200, 9600, 4800, 2700, 1500	20 msec
5	1.228 Mcps	230400, 115200, 57600, 28800, 14400, 7200, 3600, 1800	20 msec
6	3.684 Mcps	307200, 153600, 76800, 38400, 19200, 9600, 4800, 2700, 1500	20 msec
7	3.684 Mcps	614400, 307200, 153600, 76800, 38400, 19200, 9600, 4800, 2700, 1500	20 msec
8	3.684 Mcps	460800, 230400, 115200, 57600, 28800, 14400, 7200, 3600, 1800	20 msec
9	3.684 Mcps	1036800, 460800, 230400, 115200, 57600, 28800, 14400, 7200, 3600, 1800	20 msec

Figure 5.27. Forward Supplemental Channel Data Rates (20 msec frames).

requests are randomly received by the system, to help the base station to discover and decode the service request messages, random access attempts are performed during specific time periods (slots).

Each CDMA2000 radio channel can have up to 32 separate (coded) access channels. Each access channel is associated with a single paging channel. Access channel messages are grouped into 20-msec frames of 88 information bits. The gross channel rate for the access channel is 9600 bps. Access channel messages are repeated twice, reducing the effective channel rate to 4800 bps.

Reverse Enhanced Access Channel

The enhanced access channel allows mobile telephones to randomly request access and transmit small amounts of data the base station. The enhanced access channel can have frame sizes of 5 , 10 and 20 msec. This provides data transmission rates of 9.6, 19.2 and 38.4 kbps. respectively.

Reverse Common Control Channel (R-CCCH)

The reverse common control channel (R-CCCH) is a mobile access channel (MAC) that offers extended packet access to the CDMA2000 system. The R-CCCH provides faster access (reduced latency) for packet access. In addition to the 20-msec, 9.6-kbps channel (identical to the R-ACH channel), the R-CCCH channel has the option to use new 5-msec and 10-msec frames that offer data transmission rates of 19.2 and 38.4 kbps. The reverse common control channel can be used in reservation access or designated access mode. There is at least one reverse common control channel for each forward common control channel.

Reverse Pilot Channel (R-PICH)

A reverse pilot channel (R-PICH) provides a fixed reference value that can be used to assist initial system acquisition and channel recovery. The R-PICH channel also includes power control information (power control subchannel) that can be used to adjust the transmission power of the forward link.

Reverse Dedicated Control Channel (R-DCCH)

The reverse dedicated control channel (R-DCCH) transfers control information between the system and the mobile telephone. When the R-DCCH channel is present (the R-DCCH may not be included at all times), it is mixed with the reverse pilot channel (that is always used).

Reverse Fundamental Channel (R-FCH)

The reverse fundamental channel (R-FCH) is a dedicated physical data channel transfers user data on the uplink channel. The R-FCH allows for 5-msec and 20-msec frame periods. The smaller frame sizes allow for lower data transmission

Radio Configuration	Spreading	Data Transmission Rates	Frame Size	Channel Coding
1	1.228 Mcps	9600, 4,800, 2400, 1200	20 msec	1/2
2	1.228 Mcps	14400, 7200, 3600, 1800	20 msec	1/2
3	1.228 Mcps	9600	5 msec	1/4
3	1.228 Mcps	9600, 4,800, 2400, 1200	20 msec	1/4
4	1.228 Mcps	9600	5 msec	1/2
4	1.228 Mcps	14400, 7200, 3600, 1800	20 msec	1/2
5	1.228 Mcps	9600	5 msec	1/4
5	1.228 Mcps	9600, 4,800, 2400, 1200	20 msec	1/4
6	3.684 Mcps	9600	5 msec	1/6
6	3.684 Mcps	14400, 7200, 3600, 1800	20 msec	1/6

Figure 5.28. Reverse Fundamental Channel Data Rates.

rates without the need for repeated transmissions. Figure 5.28 shows the reverse fundamental channel data rates in their associated radio configurations.

Reverse Supplementary Code Channel (R-SCH)

A forward supplementary coded traffic channel (R-SCH) can carry voice or data information. Up to seven supplemental channels can be used with a fundamental channel. The supplementary coded traffic channel is only used in radio configurations 1 and 2 (BPSK for Walsh code and 1.228 Mcps). The relative timing of the supplementary channel compared to the fundamental channel can be offset by 1.25 msec (time slots). Figure 5.29 shows supplementary coded channel code rates.

Radio Configuration	Spreading	Data Transmission Rates	Frame Size
1	1.228 Mcps	9600	20 msec
2	1.228 Mcps	14400	20 msec

Figure 5.29. CDMA2000 Supplementary Coded Channel Data Rates.

Reverse Supplemental Channel

The reverse supplemental channel provides user data rates that vary from 1200 bps to 1,036,800 bps. The supplemental channel uses variable length Walsh codes to provide for variable data rates.

The reverse supplemental channel applies only to radio configurations that use quadrature spreading (RC3-RC6). Up to two supplemental channels can be used with a fundamental channel. The supplemental channel frames can be 20, 40, or 80 msec in duration. The longer the frames, the lower the user data transmission rates. Figure 5.30 shows the reverse supplemental channel code rates for the 20-msec frame size.

Radio Configuration	Spreading	Data Transmission Rates	Frame Size
3	1.228 Mcps	307200, 153600, 76800, 38400, 19200, 9600, 4800, 2700, 1500	20 msec
4	1.228 Mcps	460800, 230400, 115200, 57600, 28800, 14400, 7200, 3600, 1800	20 msec
5	3.684 Mcps	614400, 307200, 153600, 76800, 38400, 19200, 9600, 4800, 2700, 1500	20 msec
6	3.684 Mcps	1036800, 460800, 230400, 115200, 57600, 28800, 14400, 7200, 3600, 1800	20 msec

Figure 5.30. Reverse Supplemental Channel Data Rates (20 msec frames).

Physical Downlink Shared Channel (PDSCH)

The physical downlink shared channel provides (shares) control information to mobile telephones operating within its coverage area. The PDSCH is always associated with a downlink dedicated channel (DCH).

Acquisition Indication Channel (AICH)

The AICH channel is used to assign a mobile telephone to a data channel (DCH) where it can begin to communicate with the system. A channel assignment message is a system response after a random access channel (RACH) service request message has been sent from the mobile telephone to the base system.

Page Indication Channel (PICH)

The page indicator channel (PICH) is used to coordinate the mobile telephone's receiver sleep modes. The PICH works with the paging channel (PCH) to assign the mobile telephone to a paging repetition ratio that determines how often a mobile telephone must "wakeup" to receive its paging messages.

Logical Channels

CDMA2000 uses a single type of radio carrier frequency waveform to transfer data between the base station and mobile telephone. The data on this radio channel is divided into transport (logical) channels that perform specific functions. These transport ("logical") channels carry control and user data information. Control channels transfer broadcast, paging, and access control. Data channels transfer voice and data (e.g., fax) information. These logical channels are assigned to one or more physical (coded) channels.

Dedicated Traffic Channel (DTCH)

The dedicated traffic channel (DTCH) is a bidirectional channel that is used to transfer user data. It is a point-to-point channel.

Common Traffic Channel (CTCH)

A common traffic channel (ctch) is a shared access channel that can carry short messages that are designated to specific mobile telephones known to be operating within the cell site's radio coverage area.

Forward and Reverse Dedicated MAC Channel (DMCH)

The dedicated MAC channel (DMCH) is a control channel that coordinates medium access control (channel access and assignment) to information between the system and a specific mobile telephone during communication. The DMCH carries messages to a specific mobile telephone.

Reverse Common MAC Channel (R-CMCH)

A reverse common MAC channel (R-CMCH) is a reverse control channel that is shared by groups of users (active mobile telephones) when they want to obtain access to the system.

Forward Common MAC Channel (F-CMCH)

The forward common MAC channel (F-CMCH) is a control channel that is used to transfer medium access control messages to groups of mobile telephones that are unregistered or idle in the system.

Common Signaling Channel (CSCH)

The common signaling channel (CSCH) transfers signaling messages with groups of mobile telephones.

Dedicated Signaling Channel (DSCH)

The dedicated signaling channel (DSCH) transfers signaling control messages with a mobile telephone during conversation.

Channel Structure

The different transport (logical) channels are assigned (mapped) to physical channels. Some transport channels can be assigned to several different physical channels dependent on the system. This is called physical layer-dependent convergence function (PLDCF). Other logical channels provide data transport without being dependent on the underlying physical layer. This is called physical layer-independent convergence function (PLICF).

Forward Link Channel Structure

Figure 5.31 shows the channel structure for the forward channel. This diagram shows that forward link channel structure includes pilot channels, system information channels, paging and common control channels, and various traffic channels that are used to transfer user data.

In addition to the forward pilot channel, other pilot channels can be used to assist in the demodulation of forward link channels. Multiple auxiliary pilot channels can be used to assist in helping mobile telephones find localized coverage areas ("beam forming"). System information channels include a sync channel for timing information and broadcast channels for system identification and access control information. Paging and common control channels are used to provide paging alert messages and to send data messages to specific mobile telephones operating within the cell's radio coverage area. The different types of traffic channels include a dedicated control channel (for control messages), fundamental channel (primarily for voice), supplemental code channel (slow speed-data), and supplementary channel (high-speed data). For radio configurations RC1 and RC2, the system can include up to seven supplemental code channels for each fundamental channel. Up to two supplemental channels can be used with a fundamental

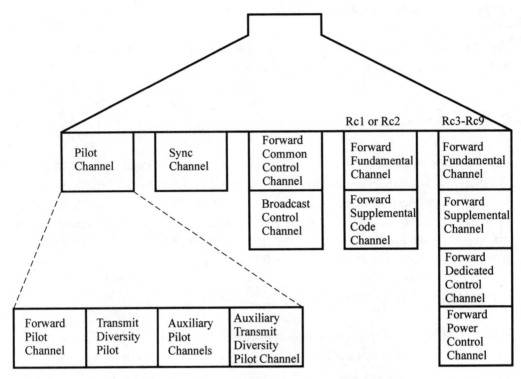

Figure 5.31. Forward Link Channel Structure.

channel when operating in RC3 and above. Figure 5.32 shows the different types of forward channels that are used in the CDMA2000 system.

Reverse Link Channel Structure

Figure 5.33 shows the channel structure for the reverse channel. This diagram shows that there are two types of access channel, standard access and enhanced access. The enhanced access allows for packet data and includes a pilot channel to allow the base station to more easily detect and decode its messages.

Channel Type	Channel Use
Forward pilot channel	Demodulation reference and beacon for signal strength estimation
Transmit diversity pilot channel	Provides a reference for multiple transmission sources
Auxiliary pilot channel	Used for focused beam patterns for smart antenna systems
Auxiliary transmit diversity pilot channel	Used during communication for adaptive antenna systems
Synchronization channel	Provides system timing information to mobile telephones
Paging channel	Alerts a mobile telephone of an incoming call or service
Broadcast control channel	Provides system identification and access parameter information to mobile telephones
Quick paging channel	Enable extended battery life by enabling sleep mode
Forward common control channel	Provides paging or data messages to a specific mobile telephone.
Forward dedicated control channel	Used to send signaling messages to the mobile telephone during communication
Forward fundamental channel	Basic communications channel for voice communications (max 14.4 kbps)
Forward supplemental code channel (RC1 and RC2)	Additional communication channel(s) for voice of data communication (max 14.4 kbps). Up to 7 channels can be combined with a fundamental channel
Forward supplemental channel (RC3-RC9)	Additional communication channel(s) for voice or data communication (max 1036.8 kbps). Up to 2 channels can be used with a fundamental channel

Figure 5.32. CDMA2000 Forward Channel Types.

The CDMA2000 reverse traffic channel includes a pilot channel to allow the base station to more accurately decode the reverse channel. It also includes a dedicated control channel to allow control messaging to be transmitting from the mobile telephone and the base station while the mobile telephone is in conversation mode. There are two types of user data transmission channels on the reverse traffic channel: fundamental channel (primarily for low-speed voice) and supplemental channels (primarily for high-speed data). Up to two supplemental channels can be used with a fundamental channel. Figure 5.34 shows a summary of the different types of reverse channels that are used in the CDMA2000 system.

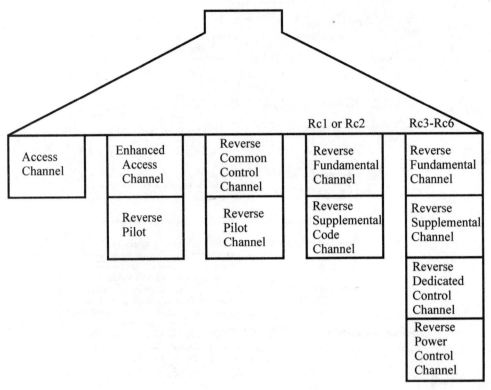

Figure 5.33. Reverse Link Channel Structure.

Speech Coding

The CDMA2000 system is able to use a new type of speech coder called a selectable mode vocoder (SMV). SMV is a relatively new technology that provides quality gains while reducing the average data transmission rate (increased speech compression) below 4 kbps on IS-95 and CDMA2000 systems while achieving excellent voice quality. The 3GPP2, with support from the CDG, developed the SMV algorithm. The SMV algorithm allows the continual adjustment of encoding rates based on speech characteristics. This helps to ensure the quality of sound to remain high, even in dynamically changing bandwidth conditions. The use of SMV allows carriers to trade off small quality losses in speech quality to gain increased system capacity. Wireless operators may gain up to 75% increase

Transmit diversity pilot channel	Provides a reference for multiple transmission sources
Access channel	Standard IS-95 CDMA access channel
Enhanced access channel	Enhanced access channel that allows fast access for packet data
Reverse common control channel	Coordinates extended packet access and data transmission
Reverse dedicated control channel	Used to send signaling messages to the base station during communication
Reverse fundamental channel	Basic communications channel for voice communications (max 14.4 kbps)
Reverse supplemental coded channel (RC1 and RC2)	Additional communication channel(s) for voice of data communication (max 14.4 kbps). Up to 7 channels can be used with a fundamental channel
Forward supplemental channel (RC3-RC6)	Additional communication channel(s) for voice or data communication (max 10xx.xx kbps). Up to 2 channels can be used with a fundamental channel

Figure 5.34. CDMA2000 Reverse Channel Types.

in system capacity by using the lower encoding rates of SMV [9]. The SMV operational mode can be controlled by the operator or on a dynamic basis. The SMV standardization process was started at the beginning of 1999 by the 3GPP2. It was completed in February 2001.

Soft Capacity

A cellular system is in a condition of overcapacity when more subscribers attempt to access the system than its radio interface can support at a desired quality level. CDMA2000 technology allows the system to operate in a condition of over capacity (allowing more mobile telephones to communicate with the system) by accepting a higher-than-average bit error rate, or reduced speech-coding rate. As the number of subscribers increases beyond a threshold, voice quality begins to deteriorate, but subscribers can still gain access to and use the system.

Figure 5.35 shows that as more users are added to the system, voice quality deteriorates. When voice quality falls below the allowable minimum (usually determined by an acceptable bit error rate), the system is over capacity. Allowing more subscribers on the system by trading off voice quality (or the subscriber's data rate) creates a soft capacity limit.

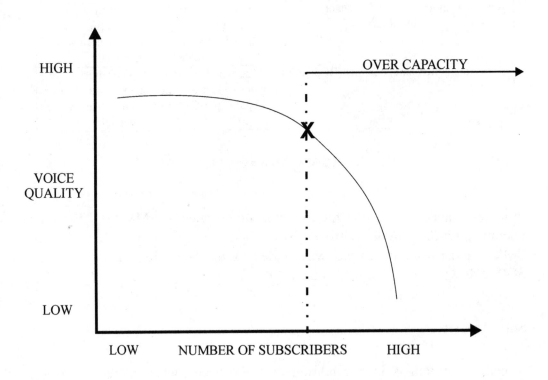

Figure 5.35. CDMA2000 Soft Capacity Limit.

Beam Forming

The CDMA2000 system has been preplanned to allow for smart antenna systems. New auxiliary pilot channels have been created to allow mobile telephones to distinguish between common system control channels and control and traffic channels that are associated with a specific beam pattern. By using multiple beam patterns, the CDMA2000 system can reuse the same code and/or frequency within the system more often. This offers a dramatic increase in the capacity of the system.

Figure 5.36 shows that a single cell site can have multiple pilot channels. The primary pilot channel is used by the mobile telephone to first acquire the system. The auxiliary pilot channel is then used to synchronize the mobile telephone to a specific radio beam pattern. There may be several auxiliary channels within a single cell.

Basic Operation

When a CDMA2000 mobile telephone is first powered on, it initializes by scanning for pilot channels, synchronization channel, and broadcast channel. After initially finding more than one pilot channel, it usually tunes to the channel with the strongest or best quality signal. It will then initialize with the system.

During initialization, it acquires all of the system information needed to monitor for paging messages and information about how to access the system. After the mobile telephone has initialized with the system, it will register its presence with the system. This allows the serving cell site to inform the system of its location so incoming calls and messages can be redirected to that particular cell. The mobile telephone will then continually register with the system as it moves and detects that it has entered into a new cell site's radio coverage area.

After the mobile telephone has initialized and registered with the system, it enters an idle mode and waits either to be paged for an incoming call (page alert)

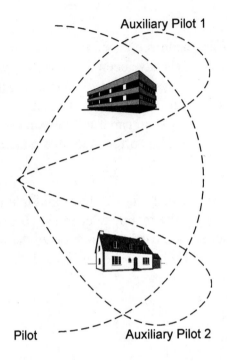

Figure 5.36. Beam Forming using Auxiliary Pilot Channels.

or for the user to place a call (call origination). When a call is to be received or placed, the mobile telephone enters system access mode to try to access the system via the access channel (regular), enhanced access channel, or common (packet data) control channel.

When access is granted, the control channel commands the mobile telephone to tune to a fundamental channel where further call setup messages are transmitted back and forth, and then ultimately conversation can begin.

During the conversation, the mobile telephone may move throughout the system and require the transfer (handoff) of the radio link from one cell (going out of radio coverage range) to another cell (going into radio coverage range).

Eventually, the conversation or data communications session is ended by either party or sending a call termination message. The other device (or system) confirms the disconnection with an acknowledgment message.

Access

A CDMA2000 mobile telephone attempts to gain service from the cellular system by transmitting a request on an access channel. If the system is not busy, the mobile telephone attempts access by transmitting access bursts on the access channel. The access bursts are coordinated into specific access time slots.

There are three channels that can be used when accessing the CDMA2000 system: standard access channel, enhanced access channel, and common control channel. The standard access channel is the IS-95 CDMA access channel. The enhanced access channel allows for access control and some packet data transmission. The common control channel is used to send signaling messages and user data to the base station when reverse traffic channels are not in use.

The access request burst will initially start at a low power level and gradually increase to a maximum allowable level. If the system does not respond to the access request within a specific period of time, the mobile telephone will stop transmitting and will wait a random amount of time before attempting access again.

When the system has acknowledged the service request, the system sends a command message on the forward control channel to the mobile telephone that commands it to tune to a specific radio frequency and channel code and conversation can begin. Figure 5.37 illustrates the system access process.

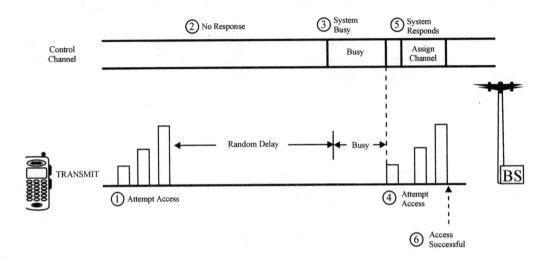

Figure 5.37. CDMA2000 System Access.

For enhanced access, there are three modes; basic access, power controlled access, and reservation access. The basic access procedure includes transmitting an enhanced access preamble prior to the enhanced access data transmission. The power controlled access and reservation access procedures include an enhanced access header message. The reverse pilot channel is transmitted when the enhanced access channel is sending header or access data information.

Paging

Paging is the process of sending a page message to the mobile telephone to indicate that a call is to be received. Paging and other messages can be sent to the mobile telephone on the paging channel or forward control channel.

CDMA2000 paging channels and forward control channels can send paging messages in groups (called "slotted mode") to allow the mobile telephone to sleep between specific paging groups. The paging channel uses spreading rate 1 (1.228 Mcps) only [10]. The primary paging channel is paging channel number 1.

Because the CDMA mobile telephone can simultaneously decode more than one coded channel, it can monitor multiple paging channels. When the mobile telephone determines that a neighboring cell site has a higher quality paging channel, it initiates handoff (registers) to the new paging channel.

The basic paging process involves the mobile telephone receiving a paging message from the system on the paging channel or forward control channel. The mobile telephone then transmits an access request message on the access channel along with an indication the access request is in response to a paging (or other types of alert) message. When the system responds, it assigns the mobile telephone to a specific data channel and conversation may begin.

Handoff (Handover)

Handoff (called handover in other sytsems) is the process of transferring a call between cell sites. The CDMA2000 system enhances the handoff process by allowing the mobile telephone to transfer calls to different types of systems including IS-95 CDMA. The CDMA2000 system can perform soft handoff (same frequency and system) and hard handoff.

Soft handoff requires the simultaneous reception of communication with two cell sites (two communication channels). Hard handoff is the process transferring a call between other frequencies or systems where simultaneous transmission (multiple channels) is not possible.

The soft handoff process is usually undetectable and loses few, if any, information frames. Soft handoff allows the mobile telephone to communicate simultaneously with two or more cell sites to continuously select the best signal quality until handoff is complete.

During soft handoff, the CDMA mobile telephone measures the pilot channel signal strength from adjacent cells and transmits the measurements to the serving base station. When an adjacent base station's pilot channel signal is strong enough, the mobile telephone requests the adjacent cell to transmit the call in progress. The serving base station also continues to transmit as well. Thus, prior to complete handoff, the mobile telephone is communicating with both base stations simultaneously. Using two base stations with the same frequency and the same PN chip code simultaneously during handoff maintains a much higher average signal strength throughout the process. During soft handoff, the base receivers choose the best frames of digitally coded speech from either base station by sending both frames to the MSC via digital links and having the MSC evaluate the errors disclosed via the error protection coding used with the digitally coded speech. The mobile telephone uses its RAKE receiver (multiple channel decoder) to add or optimally combine the two base transmitter signals, even if they do not arrive at the mobile telephone in synchronism due to different distances from the two base stations. As a result, soft handoff produces almost no perceptible interruption in voice communications, and does not lose any data bits for modems, credit card machines, and other services transferring digital data.

Figure 5.38 illustrates CDMA2000 system handoff. Before handoff, the mobile telephone has received a list of neighboring cells' pilot channels that are candidates for handoff from the serving cell (#1, time 1). The mobile telephone continuously measures the signal strength of the candidate radio channels (time 2). When the pilot channel of a neighboring cell #2 is sufficient for handoff, the mobile telephone requests simultaneous transmission from that channel (time 3). The system then assigns the new channel for the mobile telephone to transmit simultaneously from cell #1 and cell #2 (time 4). The mobile telephone continues to decode both channels (different codes on the same frequency) using the channel with the best signal quality level. When the signal strength of the original channel falls below a threshold, the mobile telephone requests release of the original channel (time 5) and voice transmissions from cell #1 ends (time 6). The illustration shows the mobile telephone simultaneously communicating with only two base stations, but simultaneous communication with more than two base stations is possible.

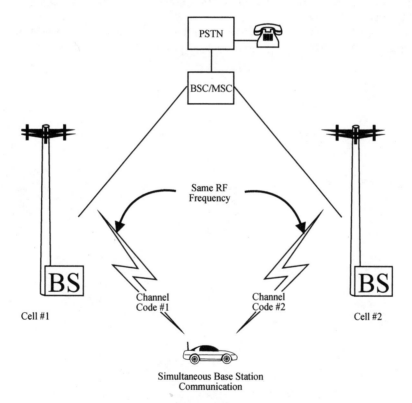

Figure 5.38. CDMA2000 Soft Handoff.

References:

1. www.cdg.org, 14 May 2001.
2. www.GSMmobile.com, 31 Dec 2000.
3. Telecommunications Industry Association (TIA), "The CDMA2000 ITU-R RTT Candidate Submission," TR.45.5.4/98.06.15.04, 1998, pp. 154-175.
4. Telecommunications Industry Association (TIA), "The CDMA2000 ITU-R RTT Candidate Submission," TR.45.5.4/98.06.15.04, 1998, pp. 154.
5. CDMA maximum data rate for RF channel
6. CDMA average speech coding data rate
7. ANSI J-STD-008; par. 2.1.2.3.1
8. Vijay K. Garg, "IS-95 CDMA and CDMA2000," Prentice Hall, NJ, 2000, pp. 387.
9. www.cdg.org, 14 May 2001.
10. 3rd Generation Partnership Project 2, "Physical Layer Standard for cdma2000 spread spectrum systems," 3GPP2 C.S0002-0-2, version 1.13, April 24, 2001, pp. 3-111.

Chapter 6

Wideband CDMA (WCDMA)

Wideband CDMA is system is 3rd generation digital radio system that uses a combination of code division multiple access (CDMA) and time division multiple access (TDMA) technology to provide for multimedia data services and cost-effective voice services. WCDMA emerged from a group of companies that desired to develop a global standard for the 3rd generation mobile communication system.

History

WCDMA is a digital cellular specification that was initially created to provide a single global cellular system. WCDMA began development in 1996, and the first commercial WCDMA digital cellular system was activated in 2001 in Japan. Because the specification was created by representatives from many countries, it is accepted as the next generation digital standard by more than 75 countries.

In 2001, GSM was the world leader in digital cellular systems with global market share of over 60% [1]. This market share dominance was achieved despite the GSM system having limited advanced features and less efficient use of radio spectrum when compared to other digital wireless systems. The GSM systems gained worldwide market domination through detailed standardization, cooperation between multiple manufacturers, and aggressive (low-cost) pricing of systems and mobile telephones. Information about the history and standards for WCDMA can be found at www.3GPP.org.

Figure 6.1 shows the development of the WCDMA standard. This diagram shows that the 3rd· generation wireless standard was influenced from a variety of standards, including nontraditional standards such as paging, land mobile radio, and cordless telephone technology.

System Overview

The WCDMA cellular system allows over 100 mobile telephones (voice) and many more data devices to simultaneously share a single 5-MHz bandwidth radio carrier channel for voice or data communications. The WCDMA radio

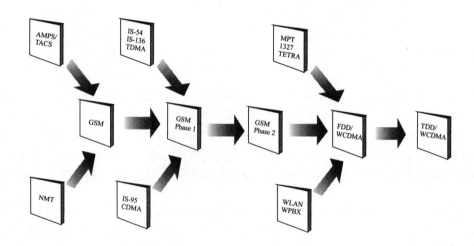

Figure 6.1. Development of WCDMA Standard.

channel structure allows multiple mobile telephones to communicate on the same frequency by using different codes on the radio channel.

The WCDMA system includes many of the same basic subsystems as 2nd generation wireless systems. However, some of the network parts have been renamed and a few of the functions (switching) have been enhanced. There are three basic parts to the WCDMA system: user equipment (UE), UMTS terrestrial access network (UTRAN), and the core system network.

The WCDMA network includes mobile telephones (sometimes called mobile stations), radio base stations (called Node B), radio network controllers, circuit- and packet-switching systems, gateways that adapt the WCDMA system to public voice and data networks, and a variety of databases and protocols that connect the network elements together. The WCDMA system separates the base station controlling function and moves it into a radio network controller (RNC). A single RNC can serve several WCDMA base stations. WCDMA systems can serve mobile telephones with a variety of data rates and services.

Figure 6.2 shows the basic functions of the WCDMA radio system. This diagram shows user equipment (UE) communicates with the UTRAN network. The UTRAN network is interconnected by the core network (CN). This diagram shows that the UTRAN network provides for WCDMA and GSM operation.

A WCDMA system uses a single type of radio channel to transfer for voice, data, and control information. This radio channel is divided into overlapping physical and logical (transport) channels. The physical channels are uniquely defined by spreading codes, and the logical (functional) channels (e.g., control, voice, and data) are composed of groups of bits (frames and fields). The basic physical channel is organized into 10-msec frames that have 15 time-slot bursts of 666 usec each. From each frame, each user may be assigned to one or more time slots burst for reception, and a particular corresponding burst for transmission. Some slots in the data transport channel may be temporarily assigned for control information, and some for voice channel information.

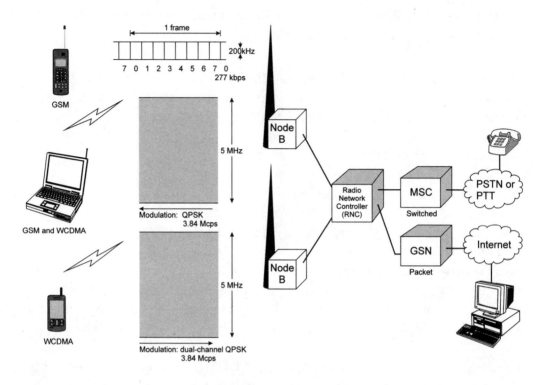

Figure 6.2. Basic WCDMA System.

WCDMA voice communications are usually conducted on two 5-MHz carrier frequency waveforms, a downlink or forward carrier (from the cell site to the mobile telephone), and an uplink or reverse carrier (from the mobile telephone to the cell site). The time slots between downlink/forward and uplink/reverse channels are related so that the mobile telephone does not simultaneously transmit and receive. This simplifies the design of the mobile telephone.

The WCDMA system has several types of control channels that are used in conjunction with the digital traffic channel. Each carrier frequency that is used in each cell or sector carries control channels. These digital control channels carry system and paging information, and coordinates access like the control channels on analog systems. The WCDMA digital control channels have many more capabilities than GSM control channels such as the coordination of multimedia, high-speed packet data, broadcast messaging, and fast power control. Because the WCDMA control channels can use different spreading codes, they coexist on the same carrier frequency with traffic channels that are used for voice and data communication.

WCDMA systems allow several users to share each radio channel carrier frequency by dedicating a specific spreading code sequence from individual users. Voice channels can be either full rate or half rate. Full rate WCDMA systems assign one time slot per frame to each user, allowing up to 100 users to simultaneously share a radio channel. WCDMA is designed so that it can easily accommodate a variable bit rate and lower bit rate speech coder. The variable bit-rate speech coder is called adaptive multirate (AMR) speech coding. Lower bit-rate speech coders may also be used (approximately 6.5 kbps for each user), allowing up to 200 users to simultaneously share a radio channel.

There are two types of WCDMA systems: frequency division duplex (FDD) wideband code division multiple access (FDD/WCDMA) and time division duplex (TDD) wideband code division multiple access (TDD/WCDMA). FDD/WCDMA uses two frequencies to allow for separate transmission and reception on two different frequencies. TDD/WCDMA allows for duplex transmission on the same frequency by assigning different time slots in a single frame for transmission and reception.

FDD/WCDMA

The FDD/WCDMA system uses two 5-MHz radio channels; one for the downlink (base to mobile telephone) and one for the uplink (mobile telephone to the base). Each of the radio channels are divided into 10-msec frames, and each frame is divided into 15 time slots. During a voice conversation at the mobile telephone, one or more time slots are dedicated for transmitting, one or more for receiving, and several remain idle. The mobile telephone uses the idle time slots to measure the signal strength of surrounding cell carrier channels. These measurements assist in channel selection and handoff.

Variable spreading codes and time-slot sharing results in a user-available data rate of up to 960 kbps for each downlink channel and up to 480 kbps for each uplink transmission (assumes each channel uses half-rate convolutional coding for error protection). Several physical (data traffic) channels (four to six) can coexist on the same frequencies using different spreading codes and may be combined to provide user data rates in excess of 2 Mbps.

Subscribers talk and listen at the same time, so the mobile telephone must function as if it is simultaneously sending and receiving (called full duplex). When in conversation mode (called dedicated mode), WCDMA mobile telephones do not normally transmit and receive simultaneously when examined on a detailed time scale, but only appear to do so. Speech data bursts alternate between transmitting and receiving, and when received, the compressed speech bursts are expanded in time to create a continuous audio signal.

Figure 6.3 shows how FDD/WCDMA full duplex radio channels are divided using two frequencies, code sequences, and time periods. WCDMA mobile telephones transmit on one frequency and receive on another frequency that is 190 MHz higher. When it transmits and receives, it uses a code sequence that is uniquely identifiable so that other mobile telephones and base stations do not receive the information. During usual operation, the mobile telephone transmits a burst of data on one frequency in a specific time slot (or time slots), then receives a burst on another frequency and time slot (or time slots), and is briefly idle before repeating the process.

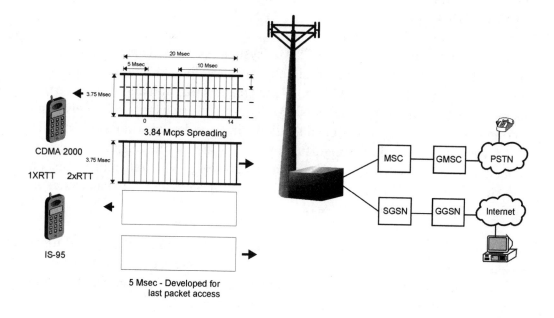

Figure 6.3. Frequency Division Duplex (FDD) WCDMA - FDD/WCDMA System.

TDD/WCDMA

The TDD/WCDMA system allows a single 5-MHz physical radio channel to serve users. Each radio channel is divided into 10-msec frame, and each frame is divided into 15 time slots (666 usec). The time slots are assigned at different times for transmit and receive to allow two-way communications between the mobile telephone and the system.

The TDD/WCDMA system was created to allow two way communications on systems that do not have two available frequency bands. Many of the attributes of the FDD/WCDMA system were maintained, including the 5-MHz radio channel width, frame size, and time-slot size to allow interoperation with the FDD/WCDMA system.

Figure 6.4 shows how the TDD/WCDMA system operates. This diagram shows how TDD/WCDMA full duplex radio channels are divided by code sequences, and time periods. TDD/WCDMA mobile telephones transmit and receive on one same frequency. Separate time slots are assigned for transmit and receive and multiple time slots may be assigned to allow different data transmission rates for the downlink and uplink. During usual operation, the mobile telephone receives a burst of data, waits until its assigned transmit time slot and transmits a burst on the same frequency. This process is continually repeated allowing data to steadily flow in both directions.

A key disadvantage of TDD operation is the added requirement of guard times to ensure bursts of data do not overlap. For near distances, the amount (percentage) of guard time is small. However, as the distance from the cell site becomes larger, the percentage of guard time becomes excessive limiting the use of TDD to use in smaller areas (e.g., inside office buildings).

System Attributes

The key attributes of a WCDMA system include a wide bandwidth CDMA radio channel, the coexistence of multiple physical channels on the same frequency, many logical (transport) channels, multiple signaling methods, increased frequency reuse, multiple speech coding technologies, improved paging methods, mulisystem operation, and other advanced operational features.

Radio Channel Spreading, Scrambling and Modulation

The WCDMA radio carrier frequency bandwidth is relatively wide when compared to first and second generation wireless systems. The 5-MHz wide radio

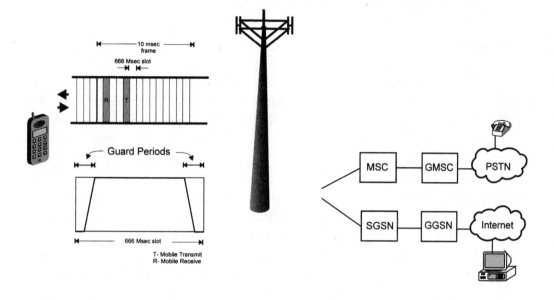

Figure 6.4. Time Division Duplex (TDD) WCDMA - TDD/WCDMA System.

carrier bandwidth allows for reduced signal fading and has the potential for much higher data rates than are possible in earlier systems. The WCDMA system includes a new set of control channels and features that allow the wireless telephone to perform advanced functions such as packet data that had been unavailable or inefficiently performed by earlier wireless systems.

The WCDMA system uses direct sequence code division multiple access technology that represents user data in the form of many bits of coded signal. To produce a high bit-rate digital signal, this digital signal is uniquely coded (called spreading) to identify it from other sequences that are operating on the system, and this digital signal is imposed on a radio carrier by modulating (changing) the characteristics (phase and amplitude) of the radio wave.

Modulation

The radio carrier in the WCDMA system is modulated differently on the downlink and uplink. The downlink modulation uses quadrature phase shift keying (QPSK) modulation for all transport channels. The uplink uses dual channel modulation, one channel for the data channel and one for the control channel. The downlink is continuous, while the uplink slow-speed data channel may be cycled on during discontinuous transmission. Uplink modulation uses two transmission channels: one for data and the other for control. Two separate physical channels are used so the cycling of the transmitter on and of during time slots does not cause substantial audible interference. Audible interference due to pulsed RF transmission results was discovered during the introduction of second generation mobile systems (e.g., GSM, IS-95 CDMA, and IS-136 TDMA). Although the RF power level will be reduced when DTX operation is off, a low level continuous RF signal of control information (pilot signal and power control) remains on.

Figure 6.5 shows dual channel quadrature phase shift keying (QPSK) modulation that is used in the uplink. This diagram shows that the user data is channel coded and applied to the I channel of the DQPSK modulator, and the control data is channel coded (different code) and applied to the Q channel of the modulator.

Radio Channel Spreading and Scrambling

The digital information (data) from the user (digital voice or data) is multipled (spread) by a code to produce a long sequence for each digital bit of information. The result is several chips of transmitted signal for each a single bit of informa-

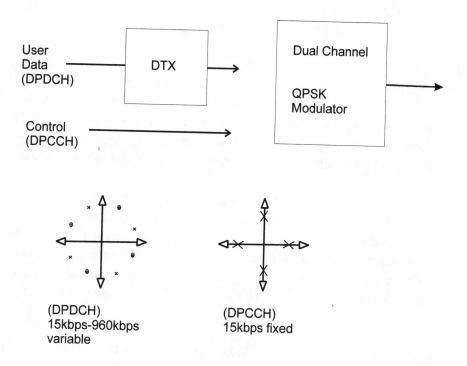

Figure 6.5. Dual Channel Quadrature Phase Shift Keying (QPSK) Modulation.

tion. Because each bit of data is represented by several chips of information, if a few of the chips are lost due to collisions with other signals, a majority will get through and the correct user data can be recreated.

The higher the spreading factor, the more protection from interference (less susceptibility) a transmitted signal has. But using higher amounts of spreading results in a lower data-transmission rate. Thus, spread spectrum communications is a fairly robust communications method.

To achieve bandwidth on demand (BoD), the number of chips representing each bit of information is changed. Each physical communication channel on the

WCDMA system is identified by a unique spreading sequence. By changing the amount of spreading, the amount of data represented can change.

Figure 6.6 shows the downlink radio channel spreading and scrambling process. This diagram shows that user data is multiplied (spread) by a combination of a channelization code and a scrambling code. The channelization code spreads the channel, producing a wide radio carrier from a lower data-rate signal. This high-speed wide channel is then modified by a scrambling code that uniquely identifies the signal from other users that are operating on the same frequency.

The downlink channel uses QPSK modulation that is transmitted at a symbol rate of 3.84 million symbols per second. Each symbol represents 2 bits of information (four levels). Using the minimum spreading factor of 4, this provides a gross (unprotected) channel data rate of 1920 kbps. Adding error protection (half rate convolution coding) and some overhead signaling information (data and control share the same downlink channel), this results in a maximum net data rate of 936 kbps.

To achieve the higher data rates required by IMT-2000, up to three downlink physical channels can be combined on the same cell and frequency. Using a spreading factor of 4, this provides a maximum gross data transmission rate of 5760 kbps and a net data transmission rate of 2300 kbps. The addition of multiple physical channels on the same cell and frequency increases the interference level and reduces the effective cell size.

The uplink channel uses dual channel modulation where each symbol equals 1 bit of information. Transmitting at a symbol rate of 3.84 million symbols per second, and using a minimum spreading factor of 4, this provides a gross (unprotected) channel data rate of 960 kbps. Adding error protection (half rate convolution coding) this results in a maximum net data rate of 480 kbps. For the uplink channel, control and data information are sent on separate channels.

Spreading factor	Channel data rate (kbps)	Net data rate (kbps) (with 1/2 rate convolutional coding + overhead)
4 (minimum spreading)	1920	936
8	960	456
16	480	215
32	240	105
64	120	45
128	60	12
256	30	6
512	15	3

Note 1: Up to 6 traffic channels can be combined with a spreading factor of 4 to provide a maximum gross data transmission rate of 5760 kbps and a net data transmission rate of 2880 kbps.

Figure 6.6. Downlink Radio Channel Spreading.

Up to six uplink physical channels can be combined on the same cell and frequency. Using a spreading factor of 4, this provides a maximum gross data transmission rate of 5760 kbps and a net data transmission rate of 2880 kbps. See Figure 6.7.

Channelization Code Trees

Each communication channel is uniquely identified by a channelization code. The channelization codes selected for each channel are part of a special set (called orthogonal codes) that do not interfere with each other during transmission. Grouping the orthogonal codes into sets allows multiple spreading codes to

Spreading factor	Channel data rate (kbps)	Net data rate (kbps) (with 1/2 rate convolutional coding)
4 (minimum spreading)	960	480
8	480	240
16	240	120
32	120	60
64	60	30
128	30	15
256	15	7.5

Note 1: Up to 6 traffic channels can be combined with a spreading factor of 4 to provide a maximum gross data transmission rate of 5760 kbps and a net data transmission rate of 2880 kbps. Figure 6.x shows the uplink radio channel spreading.

Figure 6.7. Uplink Radio Channel Spreading.

be used on the same RF channel without interfering with each other. This is called orthogonal variable spreading factor (OVSF).

The channelization codes do not change the amount of spreading. They only modify the signal that has been spread to uniquely identify it among other channels that have different channelization codes that are operating on the same frequency.

The channelization codes have a hierarchical structure where low-level code spreading factors are subsets of higher-level codes. The higher-level codes relate to higher data-transfer rates. When a higher-level code is used, lower-level codes cannot be used. Figure 6.8 shows the channelization code process and the sample code tree. This diagram shows the channel is first composed by the channel scrambling code and modified by the channelization code. Once a high-level code is used (small amount of spreading factor), lower-level codes that are derivatives of that code cannot be used. Figure 6.8 shows that the code tree extends all the way down to the largest spreading factors, 512 for the downlink and 256 for the uplink.

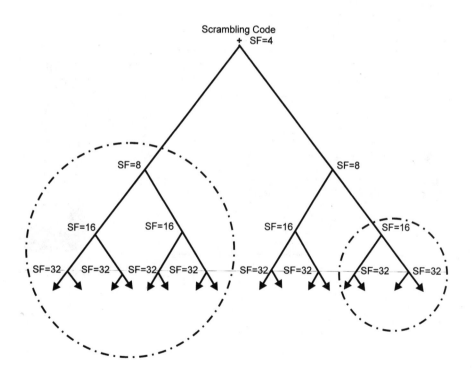

Figure 6.8. Channel Code Tree.

Frame and Slot Structure

Figure 6.9 shows the uplink dedicated channel structure. This diagram shows that the the physical channel is divided into 10-msec frames and each frame has 15 time slots of 666 usec each. Each time slot contains groups of bits called fields. Fields serve a specific purpose such as to hold control messages or user data. There are several slot structures dependent on the physical and logical channels. The number of bits contained within a time slot depends on the channel data rate (determined by the spreading factor). A message that is transferred on a logical channel may extend over several time slots.

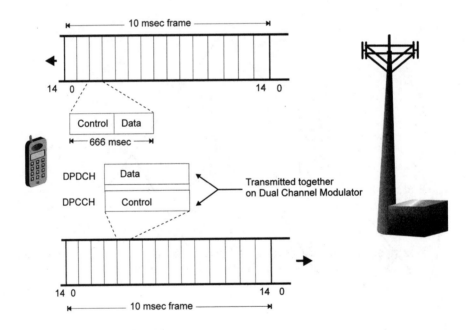

Figure 6.9. Frame and Slot Structure.

The channel chip rate of 3.84 Mcps and the number of bits per time slot depend on the amount of channel spreading. This diagram shows two different time slots for the uplink. This is because the dual channel modulation has two simultaneous channels. The control time slot contains a pilot signal, transport format combination identifier (TFCI), feedback information (FBI), and transmission power control (TPC). The dedicated channel uses different spreading codes, and the control channels typically use fixed spreading amounts. The diagram shows that the downlink channel time slots are divided into control and data.

Multisystem Operation

Although the WCDMA system uses a single type of wideband digital-only channel, the system was designed to be backward-compatible with other established cellular systems. This allows the gradual transition between legacy systems such as GSM and the advanced WCDMA system.

Physical Radio Carriers (Channels)

WCDMA radio carriers use a complex radio waveform that is divided into coded signals where many frequency elements called "chips" are used to identify data that is intended for a specific wireless telephone or groups of wireless telephones. Wireless telephones constantly decode (correlate) the code sequences that are assigned for its operation.

Each WCDMA radio carrier is divided into several different types of control and voice channels by the use of different codes and time slots. On an analog cellular system, there is one carrier frequency for each voice channel, so the two terms are used synonymously. In a TDMA system such as GSM, the standard terminology established in the GSM standards documents distinguishes clearly between a carrier frequency waveform and the time-divided channels that compose it. For the GSM system, voice and control signals can share the same channel, but they are divided into different time periods. For the WCDMA system, different channels can use different code sequences but they are also assigned to specific time slots.

WCDMA control channels continually provide information to mobile telephones that are operating in the system but not engaged in a conversation, and coordinate their access to the system. Each WCDMA carrier has a dedicated transport (logical) system broadcast control channel.

The WCDMA radio system multiplexes several users onto a single radio carrier waveform through the use of code sequences and assignment to time slots. A WCDMA carrier transmits at a chip rate of 3.84 Mcps. However, based on the spreading sequence (4-512 chips per bit), number of assigned time slots (1-15), and error protection coding (1 to 1/4-rate convolutional coding), the data rate for each user can vary from under 1 kbps to 1920 kbps (downlink) and 960 kbps (uplink). Multiple physical channels can be combined to produce much higher data rates. Up to three parallel channels can be combined on the downlink, and up to six physical channels can be combined on the uplink.

Figure 6.10 shows how one 5-MHz RF channel can be shared by multiple physical channels. Because each RF channel has a unique scrambled spreading sequence. This diagram shows that while each of these channels can cause some interference to the other physical channels, it is minimal.

Some physical radio channels are exclusively used as control channels, and other data channels share control and user information on the same physical channel. For the dedicated physical control channels, a specific fixed spreading sequence is typically used to uniquely identify each channel. This allows the mobile telephone to more easily discover and decode the control channel.

There are different types of physical channels used for specific purposes. They are designed so they cycle through a prescheduled sequence of operations, and different types of information are transmitted on each time slot during this cycle. These physical channels include shared and dedicated control channels.

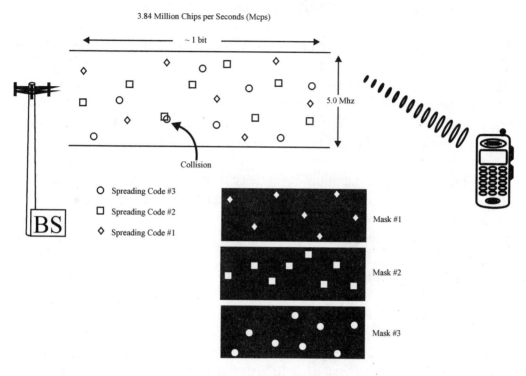

Figure 6.10. Multiple Physical Channels on the Same Frequency.

Primary Common Control Physical Channel (PCCPCH)

The primary common control physical channel is a downlink channel that continuously transmits (broadcasts) the system's identification and access control information. Its spreading code is permanently allocated to 256 to provide a gross data transmission rate of 30 kbps. To protect the critical broadcast information, half rate convolutional coding is used, and interleaving is performed over two consecutive frames (20 msec interleaving).

Secondary Common Control Physical Channel (SCCPCH)

The secondary common control physical channel is a downlink channel that carries forward access channel (FACH) information (control) along with paging channel (PACH) messages for mobile telephones that have registered with the system. The spreading factor is fixed according to the mobile telephone reception capabilities. The spreading code is changed to allow the maximum (fastest) data transmission rate that the mobile telephone can process.

Minimum system configuration is at least one secondary control channel. However, multiple secondary control channels can be allocated based on the paging and control needs of the system and the capability of mobile telephones that are operating within the system.

Physical Random Access Channel (PRACH)

The physical random access channel is an uplink channel that allows a mobile telephone to randomly transmit access requests (bursts) when a mobile telephone attempts to access the cellular system. Because these service access requests are randomly received by the system, to help the base station to discover and decode the service request messages, a fixed spreading factor is used. The basic data transmission rate on the RACH channel is 16 kbps.

Dedicated Physical Data Channel (DPDCH)

The dedicated physical data channel transfers user data on the uplink and downlink channels. Because the uplink and downlink channels use different modulations, the amount of spreading that the dedicated physical channel can use differs between the uplink and downlink channel. The DPDCH uses a spreading factor that can range from 4 to 256 for the downlink and from 4 to 512 for the uplink. The spreading for the data channel can change on a frame-by-frame basis.

The dedicated physical data channel for the uplink uses dual channel I/Q (phase) modulation. This allows each symbol (phase change) to represent bits from two different data sources. One of the data sources in the dual channel modulation is from user data, and the other is the control signal. This allows the simultaneous sending of data and control information. Figure 6.11 shows the slot structure for the two communication channels.

Dedicated Physical Control Channel (DPCCH)

The dedicated downlink physical control channel (DPCCH) transfers control information between the system and the mobile telephone. Both the uplink and downlink DPCCH carry pilot bits and the transport format combination identifi-

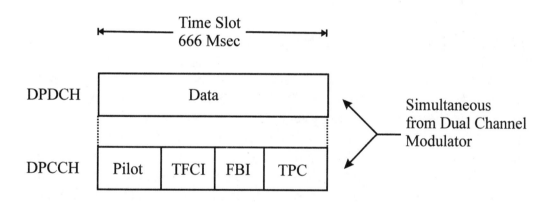

TFCI- Transport Format Combination Indicator
FBI- Feedback Information
TPC- Transmitter Power Control

Figure 6.11. Uplink Physical Data Channel Slot Structure.

er (TFCI). The pilot bits help the recovery of the control and data channel, and the TFCI determines if multiple physical channels are combined. The downlink control channel must also include transmission power control (TPC) and feedback information (FBI) bits.

Figure 6.12 shows the downlink physical data channel slot structure. Unlike the dual channel signals used in the uplink data channel, the downlink channel is subdivided into logical data and control channels by time slots. The control portion of the slot includes pilot bits, the TFCI, and TPC.

Physical Downlink Shared Channel (PDSCH)

The physical downlink shared channel provides (shares) control information to mobile telephones operating within its coverage area. The PDSCH is always associated with a downlink dedicated channel (DCH). The spreading factor of the PDSCH is allowed to vary from 4 to 256.

Physical Common Packet Channel (PCPCH)

The physical common packet channel (PCPCH) is specifically designed to carry packet data. The operation of the PCPCH channel is similar to the RACH channel. To gain the attention of the system, the mobile telephone monitors the system to see if it is not busy, transmits brief access request bursts, and gradually increases the power of each burst until the system responds to its request. Unlike the RACH channel, the PCPCH channel continues to transmit data on the common channel after the system acknowledges the transmission of the mobile telephone.

Synchronization Channel (SCH)

The synchronization channel (SCH) assists in the cell searching process and is divided into primary and secondary channels. The primary channel uses a 256

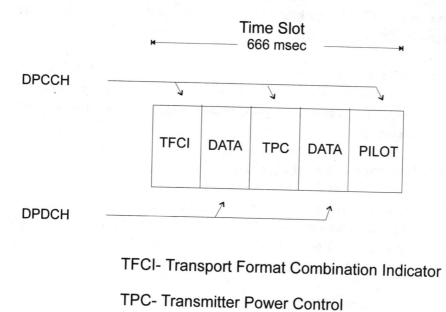

TFCI- Transport Format Combination Indicator

TPC- Transmitter Power Control

Figure 6.12. Downlink Physical Data Channel Slot Structure.

sequence that is identical in every cell. The secondary channel provides frame and time-slot synchronization timing reference for that particular cell.

Common Pilot Channel (CPICH)

Each WCDMA cell site transceiver transmits a pilot signal for reference timing signal for demodulating the signal. The pilot channel can be also used to estimate the received signal strength to indicate which cell site can best communicate with the mobile telephone. The CPICH uses a spreading factor of 256 that produces a data transmission rate of 30 kbps.

The pilot channel is distinguished from other coded channels by a particular scrambling code. WCDMA mobile telephones simultaneously measure the pilot signal strengths of all neighboring base stations in the system.

There are two types of pilot channels: primary and secondary. There is only one primary channel code for each cell (or sector). The secondary pilot channel may have other codes. The secondary pilot channel may assist with directional (smart) antenna systems.

Acquisition Indication Channel (AICH)

The AICH channel is used to assign a mobile telephone to a data channel (DCH) where it can begin to communicate with the system. A channel assignment message is a system response after a random access channel (RACH) service request message has been sent from the mobile telephone to the base system.

Page Indication Channel (PICH)

The page indicator channel (PICH) is used to coordinate the mobile telephone's receiver sleep modes. The PICH works with the paging channel (PCH) to assign the mobile telephone to a paging repetition ratio that determines how often a mobile telephone must "wake up" to receive its paging messages.

Transport (Logical) Channels

WCDMA uses a single type of radio carrier frequency waveform to transfer data between the base station and mobile telephone. The data on this radio channel is divided into transport (logical) channels that perform specific functions. The transport channels carry control and user data information. Control channels transfer broadcast, paging, and access control. Data channels transfer voice and data (e.g., fax) information. These logical channels are assigned to physical (coded) channels.

Broadcast Channel (BCH)

The broadcast channel (BCH) is a downlink channel that transmits information that is specific to that system and cell that can be used to identify and assist mobile telephones that are operating with their system. The broadcast channel typically provides the mobile phone with system information, lists of neighboring radio channels, and other system configuration information. The broadcast channel identifies the available random access channels and their scrambling codes.

Each cell has a broadcast channel. By examining the signal strength of each nearby broadcast channel, and using the error detecting codes that are incorporated into the digital transmission from that base station, the WCDMA mobile telephones that are not engaged in a conversation can measure the quality of nearby cell sites' radio channels. This is done to determine which is the optimal control channel to select. Once the mobile telephone has found the best broadcast channel, it continues to receive that code and time slot until there is a reason to choose another.

Forward Access Channel (FACH)

The forward access channel (FACH) is a downlink channel that carries control information to terminals that have registered with the system. The FACH channel may also carry packet data, and there can be more than one FACH in a cell. However, at least one FACH channel must have a low data-transmission rate to allow all mobiles to be able to receive FACH messages. If multiple FACH channels are used in the cell, the additional FACH messages can have a higher data-transmission rate.

Paging Channel (PCH)

The paging channel (PCH) is a downlink channel that carries messages that alert mobile telephones of an impending event, often a call page. The paging channel is also used to alert a mobile telephone of a short message, data session, or required maintenance service (e.g., location registration).

One of the most important parameters is the information about the sleep and wake paging cycle. In order to conserve battery power, the base system schedules paging messages (which occur when someone else originates a call to a mobile telephone) so that the mobile telephone does not need to keep its receiver on all the time. The mobile telephone can "go to sleep" (turn off all its internal electronic circuits except the hyperframe counter) most of the time, and "wake up" (turn on its receiver circuits) only periodically when it knows that pages destined for it (if any) will occur.

Random Access Channel (RACH)

The random access channel (RACH) is an uplink channel that carries requests for service from mobile telephones to the base stations when they begin to set up a call. The RACH is a shared channel that is acknowledged through acquisition indicator channel (AICH) channel.

An advanced feature of the RACH channel for WCDMA is the ability of the mobile telephone to send small amounts of data with the RACH message. This is an efficient packet data-transmission system because the mobile telephone will not have to be assigned to a dedicated data channel when it only needs to send small amounts of data.

Uplink Common Packet Channel (CPCH)

Uplink channel that expands the capability of the RACH to allow for packet services. When the mobile telephone has small amounts of data to transmit, and if the system supports the CPCH channel, the mobile telephone can access the system using the CPCH channel. The key difference between the RACH and CPCH channel is that the mobile telephone continues transmitting data on the CPCH after it attempts access. It is also possible for the system to control the power level of the CPCH channel.

Downlink Shared Channel (DSCH)

The downlink shared channel allows multiple users to share the same physical channel code sequence by time sharing. To use the radio link most effectively for bursty data transmission, the UMTS packet scheduling system dynamically assigns a particular time slot on a particular carrier frequency and code to a particular user who has packets to transmit in the appropriate direction. When that user finishes sending packets, the packet scheduling system can immediately assign the channel to another packet user.

Mapping Transport Channels onto Physical Channels

The different transport (logical) channels are assigned (mapped) to physical channels. Some transport channels can be assigned to several different physical channels dependent on the system needs, and several transport channels are specifically assigned to their own type of physical channels. Figure 6.13 shows the logical channels and the physical channels they can be mapped to.

Frequency Reuse (Code Planning)

Capacity expansion in the WCDMA system is primarily a result of allowing several users to simultaneously share a single radio carrier frequency through the use of multiple coded channels. A secondary improvement in capacity arises from the ability of WCDMA to reuse frequencies in every cell ($n = 1$). The ability to reuse frequencies in every cell is due to the coordinated use of spreading codes that average the interference of other radio channels operating on the same frequency that use different spreading codes.

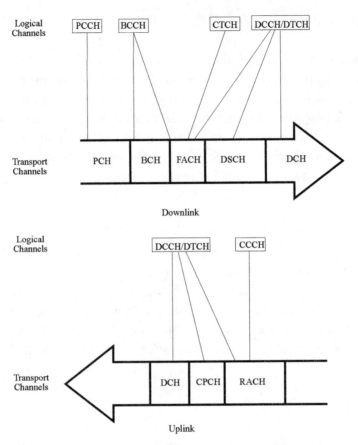

Figure 6.13. Mapping of Transport (Logical) Channels to Physical Channels.

WCDMA uses a wider bandwidth radio carrier waveform than its first and second generation cellular predecessors. It uses digital error protection coding and modulation to better reject interfering radio signals. These factors allow the radio channel frequencies to be reused in all cells within the system.

Packet Data

Packet transmission in the WCDMA is controlled by the packet scheduler (PS). The PS divides the air interface capacity between multiple users, decides which transport channel is to be used for each user's packet data, and monitors and coordinates the packet data allocations on the system.

Packet data on the WCDMA system improves on the general packet radio service (GPRS) that is used by GSM systems. It improves this service by allowing packet data to be sent on common channels in addition to dedicated channels.

The packet scheduler can assign different codes and/or different time slots dependent on the needs of the users. Packet data users may share the same code and/or time slots as other users, or they may be assigned a dedicated resource (code channel or time slots).

The packet scheduler is usually located on the RNC. This allows packet data transmission to be coordinated among several cells. There are three types of transport channels used for packet data: common, dedicated, and shared transport.

The common channels are the RACH (for the uplink) and the FACH (for the downlink). The channels normally carry signaling data; however, they are also able to carry small amounts of packet data. Unfortunately, common channels do not have the ability to offer feedback for packet data transmission.

Packet and circuit-switched data can be sent on the dedicated channels. Although sending data on dedicated channels does involve additional setup time, it does have the capability for high-speed data transmission and soft handovers.

Shared channels are well suited to transfer short data packets of data. For shared channels, a single orthogonal code may be assigned to many packet data users. When this occurs, each user must share the channel by time division (time slots).

The common packet channel (CPCH) is similar to a shared channel. Several users can share this channel by time division. There can be several CPCHs per cell, and each can have different bit rates.

Speech Coding

To allow many users to share a single 5-MHz wide radio carrier, voice signals are digitally coded and compressed (speech coding) before transmission. Because the medium of transmission is digital and many different data transmission rates can be allowed, different types of speech coding processes can be used. The lower the data transmission rate is (higher speech compression), the higher the system capacity can be (more users can simultaneously share each radio channel).

The speech coding in the WCDMA system can use multiple source rates. These include the standard 12.2-kbps GSM enhanced full rate (EFR), 10.2-kbps, 7.95-kbps, 7.4-kbps interim standard 641 (IS-641), 6.7-kbps Pacific digital cellular (PDC) EFR, 5.9-kbps, 5.15-kbps, and 4.75-kbps. Other types of speech coders may be added as advances in speech coding technology are improved.

The selection of the speech coder is determined by the system. The combination of these different data rates is called adaptive multirate (AMR) speech coding. By using adaptive speech coding technology, the data transmission rate for each user can be reduced when necessary, thus increasing the capacity of the system or extending the boundaries of the cell size.

The adaptive multirate speech coding that is used in the UMTS system is based on the multirate algebraic code excited linear predictive coding (MR-ACELP). The maximum coding rate is specified by the system and is not dependent on speech activity. The speech coding rate can be switched every 20 msec.

The UMTS system protects speech-coding bits according to their level of importance. There are three classes of bits: A, B, and C. Class A bits are the most important, as errors that occur in class A bits results in dramatic changes in the sound. Thus, class A bits receive a higher level of error protection than B class, and the B class receives more error protection than the C class of bits.

In the case of several frames that are lost due to errors, previous speech frames can be repeated or muted. This is called error concealment. The AMR speech codec can tolerate about 1% frame error rate (FER) [2] without any degradation of speech quality.

The speech-coding process can be combined with a voice activity detector (VAD) to allow discontinuous transmission (DTX). When there is no speech activity (e.g., when a user temporarily stops talking to listen to the other user), the speech compression may be temporarily suspended and the transmitter may be shut off. When this occurs, the talker would not hear any sound from the user and may become concerned that the connection is lost ("are you still there?"). To overcome this challenge, a silence descriptor (SID) frame is periodically sent to allow for the realistic creation of comfort noise (background noise) at the receiving end when no voice activity is present.

Discontinuous Reception (Sleep Mode)

To increase the time until battery recharge of a WCDMA mobile telephone, the system was designed to allow the mobile telephone to power off nonessential circuitry (sleep) during periods when paging messages will not be received. This is known as discontinuous reception (DRX). To provide for DRX capability, the paging channel is divided into paging subchannel groups. The number of the paging sub-channel is determined by the system assigning the mobile telephone to a paging group.

The paging indicator channel (PICH) is divided into 10-msec frames. Each 10-msec paging indicator channel (PICH) slot is composed of 300 bits (288 bits for the paging data, and 12 bits are idle). At the beginning of the paging channel frame is a paging indicator (PI) that identifies the paging group. The system assigns the mobile telephone to specific paging indicators that are scheduled for repetition. The repetition ratios can be set to a cycle of 18, 36, 72, or 144. Figure 6.14 shows the DRX (sleep mode) process. Mobile telephones can sleep during

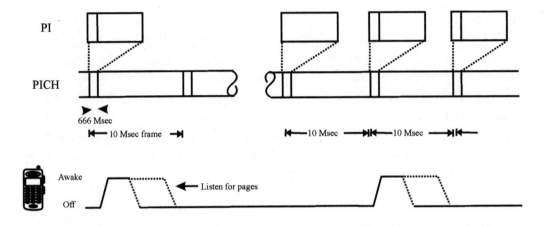

Figure 6.14. Discontinuous Reception (Sleep Mode).

paging groups that are not part of its paging indicator. In the sleep mode, only a simple electronic timer is operating in the mobile telephone set, and the receiver and transmitter circuits are off and are not using power.

Intersystem Handover

The WCDMA system has the capability to handover to the GSM system. This allows WCDMA mobile telephones to have access to established GSM systems while the WCDMA systems are being constructed.

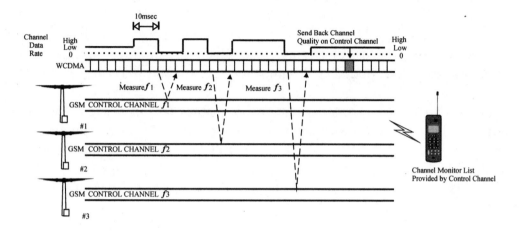

Figure 6.15. Compressed Mode and Inter-System Handover.

Performing the handover of calls between the 5-MHz WCDMA RF channel to a 200-kHz TDMA channel has unique challenges. These include different frequency, and particular time-slot periods. The WCDMA system usually continuously transmits a data signal. This would normally not allow the WCDMA telephone to tune to another RF channel while communicating with the WCDMA system. To allow the WCDMA telephone to monitor GSM channels, a special compressed transmission mode was created. This compressed mode allows the mobile telephone to adapt its transmission rate to allow for brief pauses in data transmission so the mobile telephone can monitor the transmission and transfer to GSM (and possibly other types) radio channels.

In the compressed mode (also called the slotted mode), transmission and reception of the WCDMA signal is stopped for a few milliseconds to allow the WCDMA system to perform measurements of other radio channels. These small time periods are called transmission gap lengths (TGLs). These TGLs are created by either lowering the data rate (e.g. changing the speech coder rate), reducing the spreading factor (increasing the channel data rate), or puncturing the error protection code (reducing the amount of error protection).

Figure 6.15 shows how compressed mode enables the intersystem handover process. This diagram shows that during a conversation, the speech compression process is accelerated to allow gaps in data transmission. These gaps allow the mobile telephone to scan and retune to the radio channels of other systems (e.g., GSM). This information can be used by the UMTS system to determine if handoff to the other system is necessary.

RF Power Control

The WCDMA uses RF power control on both he base station and mobile telephone. Mobile telephones and base stations require only enough radio energy to maintain a quality radio link to the nearest base station. Minimizing the transmitted energy allows the same radio frequencies and codes to be reused in nearby cell sites with less interference. The advantages of RF power control include:

-It minimizes changes in base receiver RF signal strength from slot to slot
-It minimizes interference to nearby cell sites operating on the same radio channel
-It increases the time interval until battery recharge for portable mobile telephones
-It reduces out-of-band radiation.

RF power control in the WCDMA system is a combination of open-loop and closed-loop power control. Open-loop power control is based on the mobile telephone determining its transmitted power level from various sources of informa-

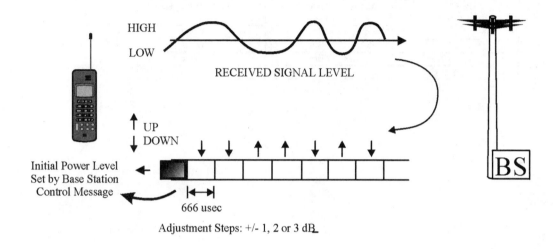

Figure 6.16. Open and Closed Loop WCDMA RF Power Control.

tion. Closed-loop power control involves continually adjusting the power level of the mobile telephone using messages that are received from the base station.

Open-loop power control can result from a maximum transmitter power level setting that the mobile telephone has discovered from the broadcast channel in that cell. It can also be estimated based on the received signal level from the base station transmitter.

The WCDMA system also uses closed-loop power control where the base station command-react cycle occurs at 1,500 times per second. When in closed loop operation, the mobile telephone is able to change its output power in 1, 2, or 3

UE Class	Maximum Power Level (dB)	Maximum Power Level Watts
1	+33 dBm	2.0 Watts
2	+27 dBm	0.5 Watts
3	+24 dBm	0.25 Watts
4	+21 dBm	0.125 Watts

Figure 6.17. Mobile Telephone User Equipment (UE) Power Classification.

dB steps, and its power level is controlled by the base station. When closed loop power control is used, the power level can be adjusted 1500 times per second (every 666 usec time slot). Figure 6.16 shows that both open-loop power control and closed-loop power control is used in the WCDMA system.

Mobile telephones in the WCDMA system are grouped into user equipment (UE) power classes. The maximum power level allowed for mobile telephones depends on the type of device. For example, mobile telephones mounted in cars may have a higher maximum power level than portable mobile telephones. Different types of mobile telephones are grouped into maximum power classes 1-4. Figure 6.17 shows the different power levels associated with each type of mobile telephone.

Combining Channel Codes

The UMTS is capable of combining multiple physical channels to provide for higher data-transmission rates. The combining of multiple channel codes (inverse multiplexing) allows for data rates that are higher than 2 Mbps. To combine multiple channels, the system coordinates the data supplied to each physical channel and transmits a control message that identifies how the independent physical channels and their associated logical channels are combined or divided.

Figure 6.18 shows how the WCDMA system combines multiple physical channels to provide high-speed data bandwidth on demand (BoD) services. This diagram shows that the 5-MHz channel can share its space with several RF carriers. Each RF carrier is differentiated by a different scrambling code. These physical channels are given a transport format combination indicator (TFCI) code. The TFCI is decoded to provide a transport format indicator (TFI) for each transport (logical channel).

Basic Operation

When a WCDMA mobile telephone is first powered on, it initializes by scanning for pilot frequencies, synchronisation channel (SCH), and broadcast channels (BCH). After initially finding more than one broadcast channel, it usually tunes to the channel with the strongest or best quality signal. The mobile telephone may tune to an alternate broadcast channel if the signal quality is acceptable and the broadcast channel is from a preferred system (e.g., home system as compared to a visited system). It will then initialize with the system.

During initialization, it acquires all of the system information it needs to monitor for paging messages and information about how to access the system. After the mobile telephone has initialized with the system, it will register its presence with the system. This allows the serving cell site to inform the system of its location so incoming calls and messages can be redirected to that particular cell. The

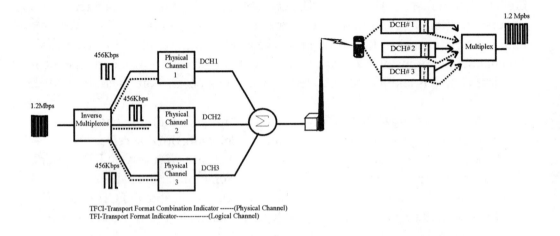

TFCI-Transport Format Combination Indicator ------(Physical Channel)
TFI-Transport Format Indicator-------------(Logical Channel)

Figure 6.18. Combining Coded Channels.

mobile telephone will continually register with the system as it detects it has entered into a new cell site radio coverage area.

After the mobile telephone has initialized and registered with the system, it enters an idle mode and waits either to be paged for an incoming call or for the user to place a call (access). When a call is to be received or placed, the mobile telephone enters system access mode to try to access the system via the RACH (regular) or CPCH (packet) control channel.

When access is granted, the control channel commands the mobile telephone to tune to a dedicated data channel where further call setup messages are transmitted back and forth, and then ultimately conversation can begin.

During the conversation, the mobile telephone may move throughout the system and require the transfer (handover) of the radio link from one cell (going out of radio coverage range) to another cell (going into radio coverage range). There are three options for handover: soft handover, softer handover and hard handover.

Eventually, the conversation or data communications session is ended by either party or sending a call termination message. The other device (or system) confirms the disconnection with an acknowledgment message.

Access

A mobile telephone attempts to gain service from the cellular system by transmitting a request on the random access channel (RACH). If the system is not busy, the mobile telephone attempts access by transmitting access bursts on the RACH channel. The access bursts are coordinated into specific access time slots.

The access burst will initially start at a low power level and gradually increase to a maximum allowable level. If the system does not respond to the access request within a specific period of time, the mobile telephone will stop transmitting and will wait a random amount of time before attempting access again. The access burst contains a short identification number that temporarily identifies the mobile telephone attempting the access. If the system detects the access request message, it will acknowledge by sending a confirmation message on the acquisition indicator channel (AICH).

When the system has acknowledged the service request, the mobile telephone will then continue to transmit its request for service (and a small data packet it may have) on the RACH channel. The access request will contain a code that identifies the type of access requested, such as page response, call origination, or reconnection of an accidentally disconnected call (due to poor quality radio signals). If the system successfully receives the access request message, it sends a command message on the control channel to the mobile telephone that commands it to tune to a specific radio frequency and channel code and conversation can begin. Figure 6.19 illustrates the system access process.

Paging

Paging is the process of sending a page message to the mobile telephone to indicate that a call is to be received. Page messages are sent on the paging channel (PCH) in specific paging group that are identified by a paging indicator (PI) code. After the mobile telephone has discovered it has been paged, it attempts access to the system with an indication that the access attempt is the result of a paging request.

The basic paging process involves the mobile telephone receiving a paging message from the system on the PCH. The mobile telephone then transmits an access request message on the RACH channel along with an indication that the access request is in response to a paging (or other types of alert) message. When the system responds, it assigns the mobile telephone to a specific data channel and conversation may begin.

Packet Access

Packet access involves the sending packets of data between the mobile telephone and the UMTS network. Mobile telephones can send packets of data to the system through the RACH or CPCH channel. When the amount of data to be transmitted is very small, the mobile telephone can send the data directly through the RACH channel. When the data packets are a little larger, it can send them through the CPCH channel. If the amount of data is very large, the mobile telephone can request channel assignment through the RACH channel and transmit the data on the dedicated data channel (DCH).

To send packets on the CPCH channel, the mobile telephone attempts access on the CPCH in a similar method to accessing on the RACH channel. If the system

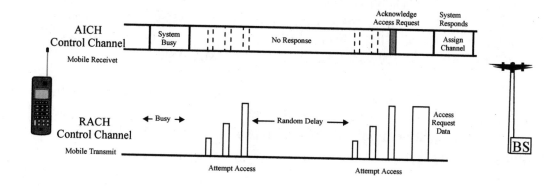

Figure 6.19. System Access.

is not busy, the mobile telephone attempts access by transmitting access bursts on the CPCH channel. The access bursts are coordinated into specific access time slots.

The access request bursts start at a low power level and gradually increase to a maximum allowable level. If the system does not respond to the access request within a specific period of time, the mobile telephone will stop transmitting and will wait a random amount of time before attempting access again. The access attempt message contains a short identification number that temporarily identifies the mobile telephone attempting the access. If the system detects the access request message, it will acknowledge by sending a confirmation message on the CPCH AP-AICH.

After the mobile telephone has determined the system has noticed its presence, it will continue to transmit additional information that is necessary to set up the packet data transmission session. This continued transmission is confirmed and coordinated by CD/CA-ICH channel. The CD/CA-ICH channel helps to coordinate the shared packet access channel of the WCDMA system.

When the system has acknowledged the service request, the mobile telephone will then continue to transmit packet data on the CPCH. For extended packet data transmission, the mobile telephone transmission power level may be controlled by the system.

Figure 6.20 shows the basic options for mobile telephone to send data through the WCDMA system on the CPCH. In this diagram, the mobile telephone attempts access to the system on the CPCH. This request is acknowledged on the AP-AICH and the mobile telephone continues to transmit packet data access request information. The CD/CA-ICH channel coordinates the access, and the mobile telephone continues to send data on the CPCH channel. As the mobile telephone transmits data, its power is adjusted up and down by commands received from the system.

Handover

Handover (sometimes called handoff) is the process of transferring a call between cell sites. First generation analog systems rely entirely upon receivers in the base stations to measure the signal strength of mobiles and determine when a handover is required. Second generation systems use information collected by the mobile telephone to assist in the handover process. The 3rd generation WCDMA system enhances the handover process by allowing the mobile telephone to transfer calls to different types of systems.

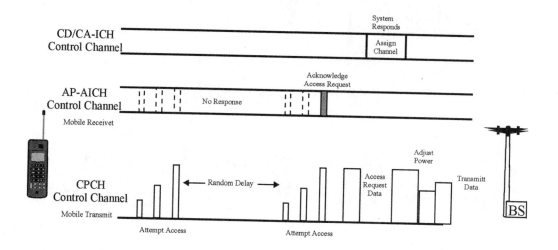

Figure 6.20. Packet Access.

The WCDMA system has three basic types of handover: soft handover, softer handover, and hard handover. Soft handover requires the simultaneous reception of communication with two cell sites (two communication channels). Softer handover involves the coordination of handover between two sites, but only one of the radio links has power control. Hard handover is the process of call transfer between other frequencies or systems where simultaneous transmission (multiple channels) is not possible.

A radio communication is handed over when the RNC determines that channel quality has fallen below a desired level, and another better radio channel is available. The RNC continuously receives radio channel quality information from the base station and the mobile telephone. The RNC also can receive continuous

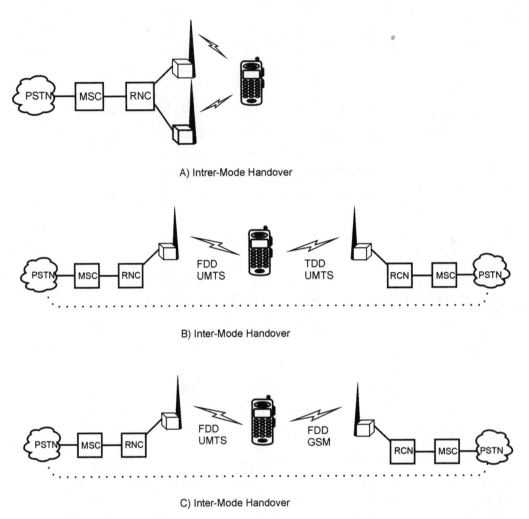

A) Intrer-Mode Handover

B) Inter-Mode Handover

C) Inter-Mode Handover

Figure 6.21. Handover in the WCDMA System.

channel quality information from the mobile telephone during the handover process. The mobile telephone measures the received signal code power (RSCP) and received signal strength indicator (RSSI) and returns this to the system on the uplink control channel.

If a hard handover is required, the RNC will command the mobile telephone to enter into the compressed mode to allow short timing gaps. During these gaps, the mobile telephone can measure the channel quality of other radio channels.

Figure 6.21 illustrates the different types of handover that are possible in the WCDMA system. Figure 6.21 (a) shows the soft handover process where two sites are simultaneously communicating with the mobile telephone. Figure 6.21 (b) shows softer handover where only one of the radio links has power control. Figure 6.21 (c) shows that call being transferred to different systems. When transferring to another system, the mobile telephone will enter into the compressed mode to allow measurement of other radio channel frequencies.

References:

1. www.GSMmobile.com, 31 Dec 2000.
2. Harri Holma and Antti Toskala, "WCDMA for UMTS," John Wiley, 2000, pg. 13.

Chapter 7

Wireless Telephones

Wireless telephones connect the end user (or communication device) with the pubic telephone or data network. Mobile telephone design and product performance requirements will change dramatically over the next five years as the industry evolves to its third generation (3G) multimedia content and entertainment driven future.

Third generation wireless will present the broadest offering of wireless handset terminal/device diversity, interface methods (input/output) — large color displays, various keyboards, including pen-based input, touch screen, and speech recognition technologies. It is expected that various consumer electronic and computing companies will also enter the field. Each of these manufacturers will bring in their ideas to the many shapes that the future of handsets and devices may take. Second generation mobile devices are optimized for voice (cellular phones), organization (personal digital assistants, -or PDAs) and portable computing functionality. These will be fundamentally redesigned to meet the evolving information, communication and entertainment needs of 3G wireless users. The user interface design of 3G terminals will be key to the handling of data and multimedia files in a technology-efficient, cost-effective and user-friendly way. This interface will center on the ability to meet users' needs for applications access, be it fun, security, messaging, database access, or plain old connectivity.

Wireless telephones may be mobile radios mounted in motor vehicles, transportable radios (mobile radios configured with batteries for out-of-the-car use), or self-contained portable units. Whether mobiles, transportables, or portables, their functions are almost identical. Because all wireless telephone equipment provides benefits to the subscriber of the service, we refer to all types of wireless telephones by the same name, as wireless telephones, called user equipment (UE) in the 3rd generation system.

Wireless telephones can be divided into the following parts: user interface, radio section, signal-processing section, power supply, and accessories. The user interface, sometimes called a man machine interface (MMI), allows the user to originate and respond to calls and messages. The radio frequency (RF) assembly converts the baseband signal (analog or digitally coded voice) into RF signals for transfer between the base station and the wireless telephone. The signal-processor section conditions the voice (audio and digital compression) and controls the internal operations of the wireless telephone (logic). The power supply provides the energy to operate the mobile telephone.

In addition to the key assemblies contained in a wireless telephone, accessories are often connected to adapt the wireless telephone to perform an optional feature such as hands free operation. The user interface, radio section, signal processing, power supply, and any attached accessories must work together as a system. For example, when a portable wireless telephone is connected to a hands-free accessory, the wireless telephone must sense the accessory is connected, disable its microphone and speaker, and route the hands-free accessory (microphone and speaker) to the signal-processing section.

CDMA systems basically use a single type of digital radio channel to provide many types of radio services. Optionally, UMTS wireless telephones may access 2nd generation (and possibly 1st generation) systems using other forms of radio channels if UMTS channels are not available.

There are several different frequencies used by 3rd generation wireless telephones. Second generation systems operate on different frequency bands than 3G systems. To provide for universal availability of service, some UMTS wireless telephones have the capability to operate as dual mode (multiple technologies) and dual frequencies (900 MHz and 2000 MHz).

User Interface

Customers control and receive status information from their mobile phone via the user interface. This interface consists of audio input (microphone) and output (speaker), display device, keypad, and an accessory connector to allow optional devices to be connected to the mobile phone. The mobile phone's software coordinates all these assemblies.

Audio Interface

The audio interface assembly consists of a speaker and microphone that allow customers to talk and listen on their wireless telephones. While the audio assemblies are located in a handset, they can be temporarily disabled and replaced by a hands-free accessory.

The microphone in small portable telephones is very sensitive. It allows the mobile phone to detect normal conversation even when the microphone is not placed directly in front of the speaker's mouth. This is especially important for the microportable phones that have a length smaller that the distance between a customer's ear and mouth.

Because of their small size, portable units have microphone systems with a substantial amount of gain. This allows the microphone to still pick up normal conversation even when it is not placed directly in front of the speaker's mouth. This is especially important for the smaller portable units that have a length smaller that the distance between a person's ear and mouth. Similar to the public telephone system, a sidetone is generated to allow users the capability to hear what they are saying into the microphone. Figure 7.1 shows an audio interface block diagram.

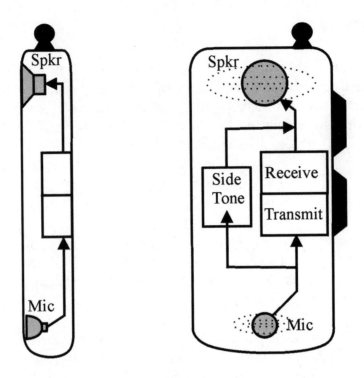

Figure 7.1. Audio Interface.

Display

Traditional wireless telephones have a display assembly that allows the customer to see their dialed digits, status information, stored information, messages, and call status information such as radio signal strength. For UMTS mobile phones, dialed digits are displayed and can be changed before the call is initiated. This is known as preorigination dialing.

The display allows the customer to decide if they want to change the dialed digits before the call is initiated. The user is also provided with a symbol (e.g., IN

USE or TRANSMIT) that is displayed when a call is initiated or received, indicating that RF power is being transmitted. Other common display information includes a received signal strength indicator (RSSI), call timer, or other services. In recent years, the display has been used to implement advanced service features, which include calling number identification (caller ID or calling line ID, known as CLID), name and number storage, and selecting preferences for the mobile telephone operation.

Most wireless telephones have the capability to store and manipulate small amounts of information in an electronic phonebook. In addition to storing phone numbers, some models allow the storage of a name tag along with the number. Because most displays are small and can only display 8 to 12 characters across, name tags are typically limited to only a few letters.

The UMTS system is capable of sending text messages to wireless telephones. There are several creative approaches to displaying these alphanumeric messages. Some phones show messages in "pages" one screen at a time. Other phones use a technique known as marquee scrolling, in which a message is stepped across the screen. To display lengthy messages to the customer, the mobile phone can display only a few characters per line.

There are two basic types of displays used in wireless telephones:liquid crystal display (LCD) and light emitting diode (LED). LCD require a minimal amount of power to operate and can be masked to create custom icons. However, LCD do not operate as well as LEDs in the cold, and require a backlight for use in dimly lit situations. Unfortunately, LED have a moderate amount of power consumption and are thus required to be turned off when they are not in use.

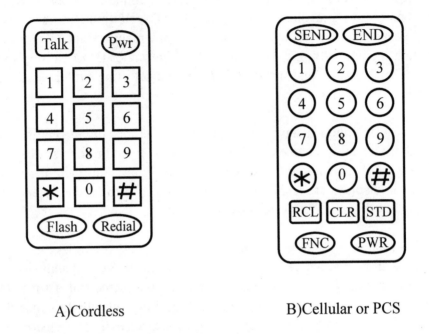

A)Cordless   B)Cellular or PCS

Figure 7.2. Typical Keypad Assembly.

Keypad

The keypad allows the customer to dial phone numbers, answer incoming calls, enter name tags into the phone's memory or, in some cases, use the phone as a remote control device via the cellular system. While a keypad is typically used in mobile phones, the keypad may sometimes be replaced by an automatic dialer (autosecurity) or a voice recognition unit.

The layout and design of keypads vary greatly among different types of wireless telephones. This is because of differences in ways a customer controls the telephone. Cordless telephones usually allow the customer to dial a phone number

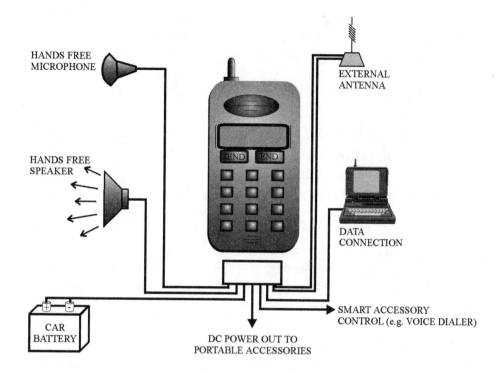

Figure 7.3. Typical Accessory Connection.

without confirming the dialed digits. Mobile (cellular and PCS) telephones require the customer to initiate the call by pressing a SEND button and disconnect the call by pressing the END button. A typical wireless keypad will contain keys for the numbers 0 to 9, the * and # keys (used to activate many subscriber services in the network), volume keys, and a few other keys to control the user functions.

Because portable wireless telephones can be very small, this limits the maximum number of available keys. As a result, some keys may have more than one function. For example, to turn the power on, the customer may press and hold the END button. There also may be several keypad assemblies mounted on a wireless telephone. Alternative keypad locations include side-mounted buttons and secondary (hidden) keypads. Figure 7.2 shows how a keypad varies for a UMTS telephone that may provide for home cordless and wide area mobile operation.

Accessory Interface

Accessories for mobile telephones can be attached via an optional electrical connector (plug), infrared or other wireless interface. The accessory interface connector typically provides control lines (for dialing and display information), data signals (for connection to computers), audio lines (for hands free), antenna connection (for an external antenna), and power lines (in and out) to connect to and from accessory devices. No standard accessory interface connection exists for wireless telephones. Each manufacturer, and often each model, will have a unique accessory interface. The accessory connector is normally on the bottom or end of the wireless telephone. Figure 7.3 shows a sample accessory connection diagram.

A popular new accessory interface is a short-range wireless connection called "Bluetooth." If the wireless telephone has Bluetooth capability, it allows the telephone to connect to accessory devices without wires. These devices include printers, external keyboards, personal digital assistants, and laptop computers.

The types of accessories vary from active devices such as computer modems to passive devices like external antennas. A hands-free kit includes an external microphone and speaker to allow the subscriber to talk on the telephone without using the handset, usually in a vehicle. An external power supply (such as a car battery) may be used to charge the battery. The wireless telephone may provide power from the phone's battery to external devices such as computer modems. An antenna connection allows the use of high-gain, external antennas that may be mounted on a car. When a data device such as a modem is used, it typically requires an audio or digital signal connection (for the data) and a control connection (to dial and automatically set the wireless telephone's features). Other smart accessories (such as a voice dialer) may require audio and control line connection.

Radio Frequency Section

The mobile phone's radio frequency (RF) section consists of a transmitter, receiver, and antenna assemblies. The transmitter converts low-level audio signals to modulated shifts in the RF carrier frequency. The receiver amplifies and demodulates low-level RF signals into their original audio form. The antenna section converts RF energy to and from electromagnetic signals.

Most wireless telephone designs today use the microprocessor and digital signal processors (DSPs) to initialize and control the RF section of the mobile telephone. RF amplifiers vary in their type and conversion efficiency. Analog mobile telephones and some digital units use nonlinear (class C) amplifiers, and most digital mobile telephones use linear (class A or AB) amplifiers. The efficiency of the RF amplifier is the rating of energy conversion (typically from a battery) to RF energy. Because the RF amplifier typically is the largest power consuming section during transmit, the higher the conversion efficiency, the longer the battery recharge life during conversation (transmission). While class C amplifiers add some distortion to the radio signal and may be above 50% efficient, linear amplifiers add very little distortion and are sometimes only 30-40% efficient. The terms class A, B, AB, and C refer to categories of amplifier design widely used in the electronics industry. class A, B and AB amplifiers draw battery current throughout all of the time of each cycle of the RF waveform. Class B or AB amplifiers use two complementary sections, which each amplify a part of the waveform (one section amplifies the positive voltage half-cycles of the waveform, while the other section amplifies the negative half-cycle). Class C amplifiers draw only a single short pulse of current from the battery during each cycle, which is why they are more efficient.

Transmitter

The transmitter section contains a modulator, a frequency synthesizer, and an RF amplifier. The modulator converts audio signals to low-level radio frequency (modulated radio signals) on the assigned channel. A frequency synthesizer creates the specific RF frequency the cellular phone will use to transmit the RF signal. The RF amplifier boosts the signal to a level necessary to be received by the base station.

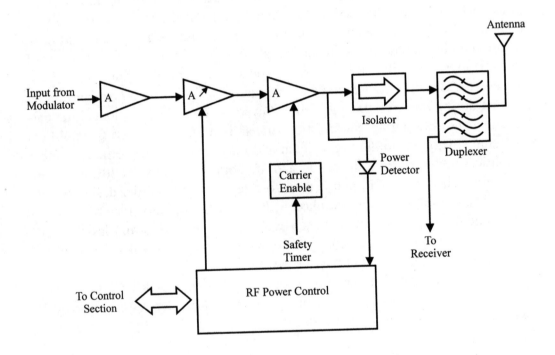

Figure 7.4. Transmitter Section Block Diagram.

The transmitter is capable of adjusting its transmitted power up and down in small steps dependent on its received signal strength (course adjustment) and commands it receives from its serving base station (fine adjustment). This allows the mobile phone to transmit only the necessary power level to be received at the serving base station, and this reduces interference to nearby base stations that may be operating on the same frequency.

The CDMA digital radio channel phase modulation requires the use of linear (precision) amplifiers. The frequency accuracy for CDMA mobile phone transmitters requires the use of more precise frequency control than is used for analog phones. To maintain accurate frequency control, the frequency synthesizer (signal generators) is locked to the incoming radio signal of the base station. If the mobile phone has the capability for dual bands of frequencies, additional filters must be used for the transmitter section to allow for both 900-MHz and 2000- MHz channels.

Figure 7.4 displays a typical transmitter section block diagram. The RF section receives its low-level input signal from the modulator. The RF amplifier is capable of adjusting its output level as a result of commands sent by the base station. To inhibit the RF transmitter from accidental transmission in the event of a failure of the wireless telephone, a safety, or watchdog, timer is used. The timer is periodically reset to allow transmission. If the time expires, in the event of equipment failure, the time will run to its final count value, expire, and inhibit the transmitter. Power level detectors control the transmitted energy to a precise transmission level sample a portion of the output radio energy signal. Some wireless telephones (usually high-power mobile telephones) use an isolator that prevents radio energy from being reflected back into the transmitter in the event that the antenna becomes disconnected. The high-power radio signal is then passed through a duplex filter (duplexer) or transmit/receive (T/R) switch that prevents the transmitter energy from entering into the receiver assembly.

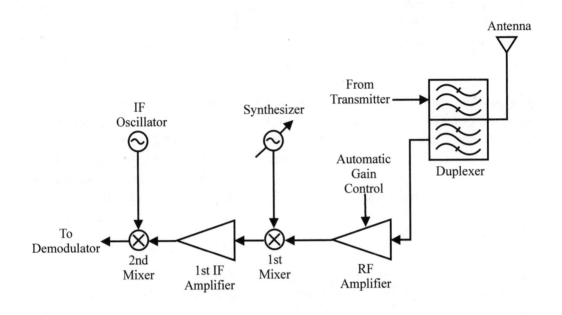

Figure 7.5. Receiver Section Block Diagram.

Receiver

The receiver section processes the low-power level received RF signals into a low-frequency signal that can be demodulated into the original audio signal. The receiver contains a receiver amplifier with automatic gain control (AGC), frequency down-converting RF mixers, intermediate frequency amplifying and frequency-filtering sections, and a local oscillator signal source for the mixers.

The receiver section contains a bandpass filter, low-level RF amplifier, RF mixer, and a demodulator. RF signals, from the antenna, are first filtered to eliminate radio signals that are not in the UMTS or cellular bands (such as television signals). The remaining signals are sent to a low-level RF amplifier and are routed to a RF mixer assembly. The mixer converts the frequency to a lower frequency that is either directly provided to a demodulator or sent to another mixer to convert the frequency even lower (dual-stage converter). The demodulator converts the proportional frequency or phase changes into low level analog or digital signals. If the wireless telephone has the capability for dual bands of frequencies, additional filters and a high frequency mixer must be used to allow for both 900-MHz and 2000-MHz channels.

Figure 7.5 shows that the low-level RF signal is first passed to a filter (part of the duplexer in some cases), which removes unwanted radio signals outside the band of channels designated for the wireless telephone. Radio signals within the desired band of channels are amplified and converted to a lower frequency by the first mixer. A frequency synthesizer (frequency generator) tunes to a frequency that converts the desired radio channel to a fixed intermediate frequency (typically 45 or 70 MHz). The output of the first IF amplifier is passed through a filter so only the desired channel within the allowable band of channels can be supplied to the second frequency mixer. The second frequency mixer is used to convert the first IF frequency to a lower frequency, which allows signal demodulation.

Antenna Section

An antenna section converts electrical energy into electromagnetic energy. Although antennas are passive devices (no signal amplification possible), they can provide a signal gain by focusing the transmission in a desired direction.

The antenna may be an integral part of the mobile phone (in a handheld portable phone) or may be externally mounted (on the top of a car). Antennas can have a gain where energy is focused into a beamwidth area. This focused energy gives the ability to communicate over greater distances, but as the angle of the antenna changes, the direction of the beam also changes, reducing performance. For example, car-mounted antennas that have been tilted to match the style lines of the automobile often result in extremely poor performance.

The antenna section consists of an antenna, cabling, duplexer or TR switch, and possibly a coupling device for antenna connection through glass. The performance of the antenna system can enhance or seriously reduce the performance of the wireless telephone. The antenna may be an integral part of the transceiver section (such as a portable handset) or externally mounted (on the top of a car). Antennas can have a signal gain characteristic that describes the ability of the antenna to focus or concentrate the radiated energy into a particular direction (narrow beam width) area rather than radiate it in all directions indiscriminately. This focused energy gives the wireless telephone the ability to communicate over greater distances. Unfortunately, as the angle of the antenna changes, the direction of the beam also changes, reducing performance. For example, car-mounted antennas that have been tilted to match the style lines of the automobile often result in extremely poor performance.

In early vehicle-mounted wireless telephones, separate antennas were used for transmitters and receivers to prevent the high-power transmitters from overpowering the receiver. A duplexer or a transmit/receive (TR) switch allows a single antenna to serve both the transmitter and receiver. A duplexer consists of two RF filters: one for transmission, one for reception. A duplexer is required for the WCDMA and CDMA2000 transmission system. It is possible to use a simple TR switch for the TD/CDMA system. The TR switch connects either the transmitter or the receiver to the antenna, but never at the same time.

For vehicle-mounted mobile telephones, the cabling connects the transmitter to the external antenna experiences signal attenuation (losses) that reduces the performance of the antenna assembly. This loss ranges from approximately 0.01 to 0.1 dB per foot of cable. High-gain antennas may be used to overcome these losses and possibly allow for a lower power output [1].

Figure 7.6 shows a vehicle-mounted mobile telephone antenna system. The mobile radio transceiver is typically mounted in the trunk of the car or under a seat. An antenna cable is routed to the trunk and up to the rear window where it can be connected to the coupling box of a glass mounted antenna. The coupling box of the glass-mounted antenna operates like a capacitor that allows the signal to pass through the glass to the base of the antenna. The antenna then converts the electrical energy into radio waves that are transmitted to and from the cell site.

Typical antennas are a quarter-wavelength long. Wavelength is the distance a signal travels at the speed of light in on signal cycle. Because the speed of light is 300 million meters per second, a 300-MHz signal has a wavelength of 1 meter. A 2000-MHz signal has a wavelength 15 cm (5.9 inches), and a 900-MHz signal has a wavelength of 33 cm (13 inches). Wireless telephones may have the capa-

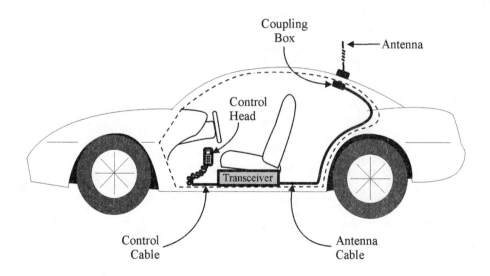

Figure 7.6. Mobile Telephone Antenna System.

bility to operate on dual bands of frequencies, 2000-MHz for UMTS and 900-MHz for 2nd generation systems. Therefore, a quarter-wavelength dual band antenna will be approximately 8 cm tall (3 inches), 4 cm for 2000-MHz and 8 cm for 900-MHz. Figure 7.7 shows an example of a dual-band antenna.

Signal Processing

Signal processing is the manipulation of electrical signals from one form to another. Signal processing can be analog signal processing (e.g., high-frequency filtering) or digital signal processing (e.g., data compression). Once an analog signal is digitized, many of the traditional analog signal processing functions (such as filtering) can be performed by software manipulation. As a result, a majority of the signal processing for UMTS phones is digital.

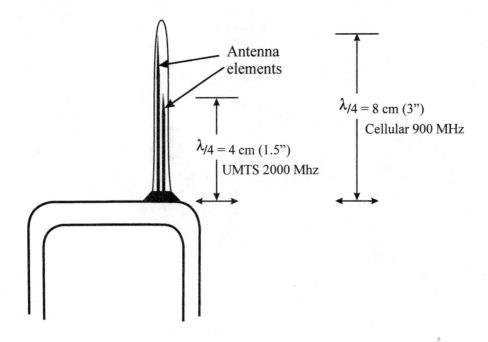

Figure 7.7. Dual Band Antenna.

To process the digital signals, UMTS telephones typically use high-speed digital signal processors (DSPs) or application specific integrated circuits (ASICs). UMTS telephones require over 40-60 MIPS, compared to the less than 1 MIPS system processing required by analog cellular phones.

The power consumption of high-speed digital signal processors (DSPs) are roughly proportional to the operating voltage and processing speed of the DSP. The first DSPs consumed well over 20 to 30 mW per MIP, which was a challenge for extended battery life in portable wireless telephones. The newest commercial DSPs technologies consume less than 5 mW per MIPS.

Speech Coding

Speech coding is the process of analyzing and compressing a digitized audio signal, transmitting that compressed digital signal to another point, and decoding the compressed signal to recreate the original (or approximate of the original) signal. A significant portion of the digital signal processing that is used in UMTS CDMA phones involves digital speech compression and expansion that is called speech coding.

The speech coding process involves the conversion of analog (audio) signals into digital signals (analog to digital conversion). The digitized voice signal is then further processed by a speech-coding program to create a characteristic representation of the original voice signal (key parameters). The UMTS system uses adaptive multirate coding (AMR) that changes the compression ratio dependent on the voice activity and available capacity of the wireless system. This compressed speech signal is then sent to the channel coding process where error protection is added.

When the compressed speech coded signal is received, it is recreated to the original analog signal by decoding the information using a speech-decoding program. The UMTS system can use various types of speech coding to maintain system backward compatibility and at the same time, offering enhanced voice quality to customers.

Channel Coding

Channel coding is the process of adding error protection, detection bits, and multiplexing control signals with the transmitted information. Error protection and detection bits (they may be the same bits) are used to detect and correct errors that occur on the radio channel during transmission. The output of the speech coder is encoded with additional error protection and detection bits, according to the channel coding rules for its particular specification. This extra information allows the receiver to determine if distortion from the radio transmission has caused errors in the received signal. Control signals such as power control, timing advances, and frequency handoff must also be merged into the digital information to be transmitted. The control information may have a more reliable type of error protection and detection process that is different than the speech data. This is because control messages are more important to the operation of the mobile phone than voice signals. The tradeoff for added error protection and detection bits is the reduced amount of data that is available for voice signals or control messages. The ability to detect and correct errors has a big advantage of digital coding formats over analog formats but it does come at the cost of the additional data required.

Audio Processing

In addition to the digital signal processing for speech coding and channel coding, a digital mobile phone can do other audio processing to enhance its overall quality. Audio processing may include detecting speech among background noise, noise cancellation, or echo cancellation.

Echo is a particular problem for audio signals in digital systems. Echo can be introduced by the delay involved in the speech compression algorithm or through normal speakerphone operation. The echo signals can be removed by sampling the audio signal in brief time periods and looking for previous audio signal patterns. If the echo canceller finds a matched signal, it is subtracted, thus removing the echo. While this sounds simple, there may be several sources and levels of echo and they may change over the duration of the call that complicates this process.

Logic Control Section

The logic control section usually contains a simple microprocessor or microprocessor section stored in a portion of an ASIC. The logic section coordinates the overall operation of the transmitter and receiver sections by extracting, processing, and inserting control messages. The logic control section operates from a program that is stored in the mobile phone's memory.

There are various types of memory storage that are used in UMTS telephones. Part of the memory holds the operating software for the logic control section. Most telephones use flash (erasable) memory to allow the upgrading of this operating software to allow software correction or the addition of new features. Typical amounts of memory for UMTS phones are 1-8 megabytes or more. While the operating software is typically loaded into the telephone at the factory, some mobile telephones have the capability to have their memory updated in the field. This is discussed later in the software download section.

Read only memory (ROM) is used to hold information that should not be changed in the phone, such as the startup processing procedures. Random access memory (RAM) is used to hold the temporary information (such as channel number and temporary mobile system identifier or TMSI). Flash memory is typically used to hold the operating program and user information (such as names and stored phone numbers).

Digital wireless telephones typically use DSPs or application specific integrated circuits (ASICs) to process all types of signals. If the wireless telephone has multi-mode capability (such as WCDMA, GSM, or AMPS), the same DSP can be used to process all types of analog and digital signals. DSPs are high performance computing devices that are specifically designed to allow rapid signal processing. Advances in DSP technology allow increased signal processing ability of 40 to 60 MIPS, lower operating battery voltage (3 volts vs 5 volts), and reduced cost. ASICs are custom designed integrated circuits and are typically created to combine several functional assemblies. For example, a single ASIC could contain all the control circuits necessary to connect the display and keypad to the DSP. By replacing several components with one ASIC, cost and size are reduced.

Universal Subscriber Identity Module (USIM)

Each UMTS telephone must contain identification information to provide a unique identification to wireless systems. UMTS telephones have several unique identifying codes to control access for different types of services. Identification and other profile information is stored in a removable universal subscriber identity module (USIM) card.

The USIM contains information specific to a subscriber, such as its telephone number, unique serial number, and home system identification information. The information is used to identify the UMTS telephone user to a base station and mobile switching center (MSC). The unique identification number includes the mobile station international ISDN number (MSISDN) and international mobile subscriber identity (IMSI) number. A new feature for UMTS telephones is the group identification information for dispatch (e.g., trunked radio) type operation. The USIM may store more than one MSISDN telephone number (e.g. business number, residential number, and data number). When operating in a UMTS wireless network, the wireless telephone is also assigned a temporary mobile subscriber identity (TMSI). The TMSI is an abbreviated identifier that is assigned when the mobile telephone registers with the system.

In addition to the identification information that is stored in the USIM (that can be changed), there is also a unique electronic equipment serial number that is assigned to each UMTS wireless telephone. The mobile equipment identifier is an electronic serial number that is contained in the UMTS wireless telephone that cannot be altered. This number allows service providers to decline service to unauthorized, stolen, or defective telephones.

The USIM is programmed with a access priority control classes to allow different types of users to have higher priority levels when accessing the system. There are 15 different access priority classes. Classes 0-9 are assigned for regular customers and classes 10-14 are assigned to high priority customers (such as police or public safety personnel).

In addition to basic customer identification information, the SIM card can store other unique identification and processing information. This includes the preferred features such as speed dialing numbers, stored information (e.g., short messages), and processed information such as privacy encryption codes.

The USIM card holds the preferred languages for the user in order of priority. The user may visit systems that use more than one language. USIMS also hold cipher (encryption) codes and processes that are used to ensure the privacy of digitized voice and packet data.

The USIM also holds a list of preferred and prohibited public land mobile networks (PLMNs) in order of priority and the amount of time allocated to the search of preferred networks. If there are several systems available, the user may prefer to operate on a specific system even if the quality of the received signal is a lower level than others that are available. A prohibited PLMN list ensures the customer will avoid accessing unwanted or high cost systems.

The USIM contains an extensive list of authorized services such as short message service (SMS), advice of charge (AoC), 2nd generation system access capa-

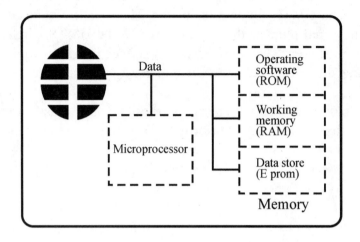

Figure 7.8. UMTS SIM (USIM) Card Functional Diagram.

bility, and image (IMG) transfer. Even though the system may be capable of advanced services, the user may desire not to receive the services or be unable to process the information (e.g., receiving an image file when no image display is available).

The USIM card contains a short message storage area. This allows SMS messages to stay with the customer as the USIM is moved from telephone to telephone. This allows the customer to use another telephone capable of reading the USIM card to receive and send their personal messages.

Other forms of information are regularly stored in the USIM card. The USIM card holds the charging rates (for prepaid and AoC service). Incoming and outgoing call information including the numbers dialed or received along with the call duration is stored on the USIM card. Dialing codes may be stored that include emergency call codes that can be used even with the telephone is locked.

An important function of the USIM card is the authentication procedure. The authentication process uses various sources of information to create responses to identify validation requests (authentication requests). There may be several different authentication procedures stored on a USIM, as different systems may use different authentication procedures.

The USIM is actually an integrated circuit assembly that is called the USIM integrated circuit card (UICC). The card stores information in elementary files (EFs). The UICC cards come in three varieties: 5V, 3V, and 1.8V cards. Voltage is supplied on pin 1, pin 2 is a reset line, clock reference signal is applied to pin 3, and pin 7 is used for data input/output. Figure 7.8 shows a basic block diagram for a USIM card.

Power Supply

All wireless telephones require power to operate. Power may be supplied to the telephone by an internal battery, power line voltage, or other source such as a car battery or cigarette lighter socket. Initially, almost all mobile telephones were wired directly to a car battery. Some car telephones were converted to transportable phones that operated from a battery (usually 12 volts) or were plugged into a cigarette lighter. A majority of wireless telephones today are portable telephones that operate from small rechargeable batteries. The first few portable telephones operated from 7.2 volt batteries, and the trend is towards lower voltage batteries.

There are a variety of power supply options that include batteries, converters and chargers. Several sizes (capacities) of batteries are usually available for each model of wireless telephone made by a manufacturer. The capacity of the battery varies dependent on its size and battery technology. Most mobile phone models also have available a "battery eliminator" that is used to directly connect a mobile phone to a cigarette lighter in the car. When connected to the cigarette lighter, battery eliminators may also be able to charge the battery of the telephone.

There are several types of batteries used in mobile phones: alkaline, nickel cadmium (NiCd), nickel metal hydride (NiMH) and lithium ion (Li-Ion). A new type of battery technology, zinc air, has been introduced that has increased energy storage capacity.

Battery packs are composed of cells. Each battery cell has a specific operating voltage range. To achieve the necessary voltage that is used by the wireless telephone, several cells are connected together in series.

With the introduction of portable cellular phones in the mid-1980s, battery technology became one of the key technologies for users of cellular phones. In the mid-1990s, over 80% of all cellular phones sold were portable or transportable models rather than fixed installation car phones. Battery technology is a key factor in determining portable phones' size, talk time, and standby time.

Batteries are categorized as primary or secondary. Primary batteries must be disposed of once they have been discharged while secondary batteries can be discharged and recharged for several cycles. Primary cells (disposable batteries), which include carbon, alkaline, and lithium have a limited use in wireless telephones.

Batteries

Alkaline batteries are disposable batteries that are rarely used for mobile telephones. This is because, although alkaline batteries are readily available, they must be replaced after several hours of use and are more expensive than the cost of a rechargeable a battery. However, disposable batteries have the advantages of a very long shelf life and no need for a charging system.

Nickel cadmium (NiCd) batteries are rechargeable batteries that are constructed of two metal plates made of nickel and cadmium placed in a chemical solution. A NiCd cell can typically be cycled (charged and discharged) 500 to 1000 times and is capable of providing high power (current) demands required by the radio transmitter sections of portable wireless telephones. While NiCd cells are available in many standard cell sizes such as AAA and AA, the battery packs used in cellular phones are typically uniquely designed for particular models of mobile phones. Early versions of NiCd batteries developed a memory of their charging and discharging cycles and their useful life was considerably shortened if they were correctly discharged. This is known as the "memory effect," where the battery remembers a certain charge level and won't provide more energy even if completely charged. Newer NiCd batteries use different materials and designs that reduce the memory effect.

Nickel metal-hydride (NiMH) batteries are rechargeable batteries that use a hydrogen adsorbing metal electrode instead of the cadmium plate. NiMH batteries can provide up to 30% more capacity than a similarly sized NiCd battery. However, for the same energy and weight performance, NiMH batteries cost about twice as much as NiCd batteries.

Li-Ion batteries are either disposable or rechargeable batteries. Li-Ion is the newest technology that is being used in portable telephones. They provide increased capacity versus weight and size. A typical Li-Ion cell provides 3.6 volts versus 1.2 volts for NiCd and NiMH cells. This means that only one-third the number of cells is needed to provide the same voltage. Figure 7.9 shows the relative capacity of different battery types.

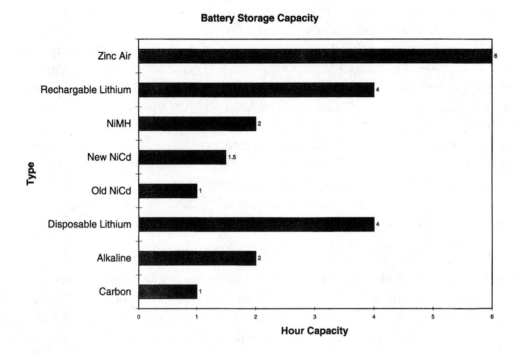

Figure 7.9. Battery Storage Capacity.

Standby and Talk Time

UMTS technology provides unique tools for decreasing the phone power consumption and increasing the standby time of batteries. The grouping of messages on digital control channel into paging groups allows UMTS telephones to sleep when they do not expect to receive the paging information. Since the telephone and system are synchronized together, the phone can power off some of its circuitry while waiting between messages. This means that typically only a few messages of information have to be read on the control channel each second - drastically increasing the battery life from hours to days (or more).

Accessories .

Accessories are optional devices that may be connected to wireless telephones to increase their functionality. Accessory devices include hands-free speaker-phones, smart accessories (modems), voice activation devices, battery chargers, high-gain antennas, and many others.

Hands-Free Speakerphone

Hands-free car kits typically include a microphone and speaker to allow the sub-scriber to listen and talk to the telephone without using the handset. The hands-free speaker is usually located in the cradle assembly, while the microphone is typically installed in a remote location (usually located near the visor). Because digital cellular systems take time to process and convert audio signals, this adds delay to audio signals and multiple delayed echoes caused by hands-free opera-tion can be very annoying to the user. The wireless telephone and/or wireless net-work may contain sophisticated echo cancellers to help reduce the effects of delayed echo. Figure 7.10 shows a hands-free car kit.

Data Transfer Adapters

Subscribers sometimes want to send digital (data) information via their wireless telephones. The wireless telephone can offer optional connections for a facsimi-le, modem, or a standard plain old telephone service (POTS) dial tone to the wireless phone.

Digital wireless transmission allows new possibilities for data transmission. Instead of converting digital bits (pulses) into audio tones that are sent on the radio channel, the digital bits are sent directly into the phase modulator of the wireless telephones digital transmitter. This allows much higher data transmis-sion rates. Unfortunately, when the digital bits are received on the other end at

Figure 7.10. Hands-Free Speakerphone.

Source: Cellport

the base station, they must be converted to a format that can be transmitted through the public switched telephone network (PSTN).

To connect a UMTS wireless telephone to a computer, a data transfer adapter is required. This data transfer adapter plugs into the bottom of a wireless telephone and connects to a personal computer memory card adapter (PCMCIA) slot or serial port on a computer or data device.

Voice Activation

Another optional feature is voice activation which allows calls to be dialed and controlled by voice commands. To improve driving safety, it is recommended that a call should not be dialed by a handset keypad while driving [2]. However, it may be possible to via voice activation without significant distraction.

Two types of speech recognition exist—speaker dependent and speaker independent. Speaker-dependent recognition requires the user to store (program) their voice commands that are to be associated with a particular command. These recorded commands are used to match words spoken during operation. Speaker-independent recognition allows multiple users to control the telephone without the recording of a particular voice. Speaker-independent recognition is generally less accurate than speaker-dependent recognition, and often may require the user to repeat the command if not recognized the first time. To prevent accidental operation of the cellular telephone by words in normal conversation, key words such as "phone start" are used to indicate a voice command.

Battery Chargers

There are two types of battery chargers: trickle and rapid charge. A trickle charger will slowly charge up a battery by only allowing a small amount of current to be sent to the wireless telephone. The battery charger may also be used to keep a charged battery at full capacity if the telephone is regularly connected to an external power source (such as a car's cigarette lighter socket). Rapid chargers allow a large amount of current to be sent to the battery to fully charge it as soon as possible. The limitation on the rate of charging is often the amount of heat generated. That is, the larger the amount of current sent to the battery, the larger the amount of heat.

The charging process is controlled by either the telephone itself or by circuits in the charging device. For some batteries, rapid charging reduces the amount of charge and discharge cycles. A battery charger will supply current for a period of time, until a voltage transient occurs (called a knee voltage). The charging circuit usually checks for temperature of the battery to protect it from overcharging. The full charge is indicated by a couple of different conditions. Either the temperature of the battery has reached a level where the charging must be turned off (the voltage level will reach its peak value for that battery type) or the voltage level will stop increasing. Most chargers will then enter a trickle charge mode to keep the battery fully charged. Some chargers for NiCd batteries discharge the battery before charging to reduce the memory effect. This is called battery reconditioning.

Software Download Transfer Equipment

Some wireless telephones have the capability of reprogramming their operating system memory after leaving the factor (in the field) to allow new or upgraded software to add feature enhancements or to correct software errors. The new operating software is typically downloaded using a service accessory that normally contains an adapter box connected to a portable computer and a software disk. The new software is transferred from the computer through the adapter box to the mobile phone. Optionally, an adapter box can contain a memory chip with the new software that eliminates the need for the portable computer. Changes can be made easily in the field without opening the case of the wireless telephone. Figure 7.11 shows how software downloading can occur from a personal computer to a mobile telephone.

UMTS Telephone

The complexity of a UMTS wireless telephone is much greater than an analog mobile telephone due primarily to the more advanced signal processing that is required. Figure 7.12 shows a basic block diagram for a WCDMA UMTS mobile

Personal Computer

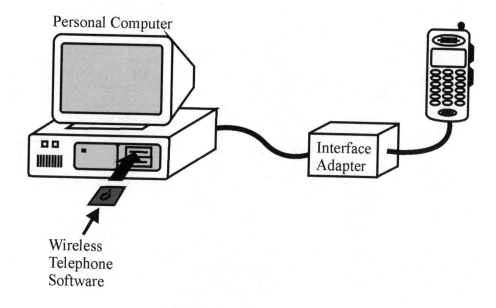

Interface
Adapter

Wireless
Telephone
Software

Figure 7.11. Software Downloading.

telephone. In this diagram, the transmitter audio section samples sound pressure from the mobile phone's microphone into a 64 kbps digital signal. The digital signal is then divided into 10-msec groups that are sent to the speech coder for analysis and compression. The speech coder compresses the 64 kbps signal to a variable data rate of up to 8 kbps. Data compression rate varies with the speech activity. The lower the speech activity (e.g., silence period), the lower the data rate from the speech coder (e.g., 2 kbps compared to 8 kbps). The channel coder then adds error protection to some of the data bits using convolutional coding and control information is added. This combined data signal is multiplied by the channel code (signal spreading), which increases the data transfer rate to the 5-MHz channel. The signal is supplied to the modulator that mixes the digital with the output of the RF synthesizer to produce an RF channel at the desired frequency. The RF amplifier boosts the signal for transmission. When transmitting, the RF amplifier power gain is continuously adjusted by the microprocessor con-

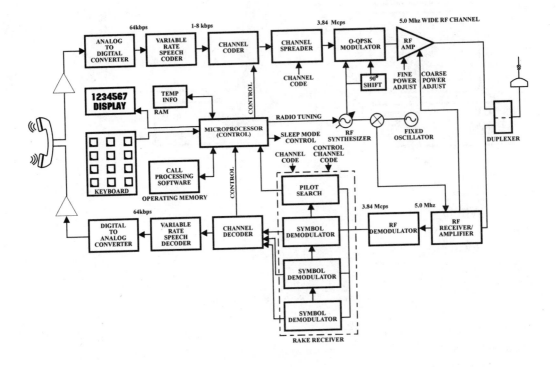

Figure 7.12. WCDMA Mobile Phone Detailed Block Diagram.

trol section in inverse proportion to the received radio signal strength (open loop) and by continuous adjustments received from the base station (closed loop).

A received UMTS radio signal is down-converted and amplified by the RF receiver and amplifier section. Because the incoming radio signal is related to the transmitted signal, a frequency synthesizer (variable frequency) produces the fixed frequency for down-conversion. The down-conversion mixer produces a first intermediate frequency (IF) signal which is either digitized and supplied to a demodulator, or down-converted by a second IF mixer to reduce the frequency even lower. A rake receiver is used to decode delayed signals and combined them with the desired signal. This increases the quality of the received signal.

The channel decoder then extracts the data and control information and supplies the control information to the microprocessor and the speech data to the speech decoder. The speech decoder converts the data slots into 64 kbps PCM signal that is then converted back to its original analog (audio) form.

The microprocessor section controls the overall operation of the mobile phone. It receives commands from a keypad (or other control device), provides status indication to the display (or other alert device); and receives, processes, and transmits control commands to various functional assemblies in the mobile phone.

References:

1. MRT editorial staff, "Why Cellular Mobiles Use 'High-Gain' Antennas," Mobile Radio Technology, pp.44-46, Volume 5, Issue 5, May 1987.
2. CTIA, winter exposition, "Safety," San Diego, 1981.

Chapter 8

Wireless Networks

Wireless networks interconnect wireless telephones with nearby radio towers (base stations) that route calls through switching systems to other wireless telephone to other telephone or data networks. Creating and managing a wireless network involves equipment selection and installation, implementation methods, inter-connection to the public switched telephone network (PTSN) and other networks such as the Internet, and system planning.

Wireless networks consist of cell site radio towers (called "node Bs" in 3G systems), communication links, switching center, network databases, and link to public telephone and data networks.

The main switching system in the universal mobile telephone service (UMTS) wireless network is the mobile switching center (MSC). The MSC coordinates the overall allocation and routing of calls throughout the wireless system. Inter-system connections can link different wireless network systems to allow wireless telephones to move from cell site to cell site and system to system. The UMTS system defines intersystem connections in detail to allow universal and uniform service availability for 3rd generation wireless devices.

Figure 8.1 illustrates the fundamental parts and interconnections in a UMTS network. The user equipment (UE) is a wireless telephone. The UE is the combination of the physical mobile equipment (ME) and the UMTS subscriber identity module (USIM). The network radio parts of the UMTS system is called UMTS terrestrial radio access network (UTRAN). The UTRAN is composed of node Bs and radio network controllers (RNCs). The base stations convert radio signals from wireless telephones to a form suitable for transfer to the telephone or data network.

All of the radio parts are part of the radio network subsystem (RNS). The RNS may be composed of third generation (e.g., WCDMA or CDMA2000) or other technologies (e.g., GSM, IS-95 CDMA, or IS-136 TDMA). The UMTS system uses a radio network controller (a small switch) that manages and switches calls

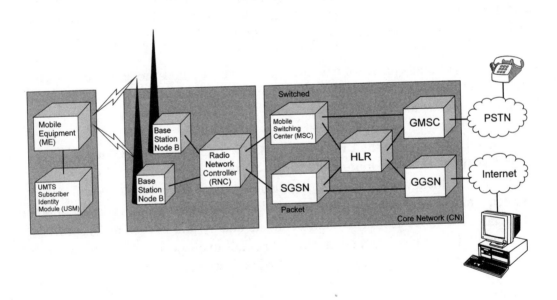

Figure 8.1. 3rd Generation System Network Block Diagram.

between base stations in its area. The RNC controls calls as they are transferred between cells within the system are called handovers (European terminology) or handoffs (America's terminology). When calls are transferred between cell sites in adjacent systems, they are called intersystem handovers.

The core network (CN) is the backbone network that interconnects the UTRAN. The CN consists of mobile switching centers (circuit switches) and general packet radio services switches (packet routers). The MSC coordinates a majority of the voice service processes. Regardless of the type of radio transmission, the MSC routes calls to and from cell sites and the PSTN.

The UMTS system has added a packet switching network as an integrated part of its network. A general packet radio service (GPRS) switch is connected to the RNS. The serving GPRS service node (SGSN) coordinates the active wireless data devices (may be a wireless telephone with data capability) in its area. A gateway GPRS service node routes the packets between the UTRAN and other data networks (such as the Internet). The combination of all the user, radio network and core network forms the public land mobile network (PLMN).

The UMTS system specifically defines the interfaces between network parts. These open interfaces are defined in such detail and precision that network equipment that is produced by different manufacturers can interoperate with each other. Open interfaces are successfully used in the GSM system, and, as a result, there are more manufacturers of network equipment parts and lower equipment costs due to market competition.

Node B (Base Stations)

Node Bs (base stations) may be stand-alone transmission systems or part of a cell site, and is composed of an antenna system (typically a radio tower), a building, and base station radio equipment. Node B radio equipment consists of RF equipment (transceivers and antenna interface equipment), controllers, and power supplies. Node B transceivers have many of the same functional elements as a wireless telephone. However, base station radios are coordinated by the UMTS system's RNC and have many additional functions than a mobile telephone.

The radio transceiver section is divided into transmitter and receiver assemblies. The transmitter section converts a voice signal to RF for transmission to wireless telephones and the receiver section converts RF from the wireless telephone to voice signals routed to the MSC or packet-switching network. The controller section commands insertion and extraction of signaling information.

Unlike the wireless telephone, the transmit, receive, and control sections of a node B are usually grouped into equipment racks. For example, a single equipment rack may contain all of the RF amplifiers or voice channel cards. Unlike analog or early-version digital cellular systems that dedicated one transceiver in each base station for a control channel, the UMTS system combines control channels and voice channels on a single physical radio channel.

The components of a base station include transceiver assemblies, usually mounted in an equipment rack, each containing multiple assemblies or modules, one for each 5-MHz RF channel. Base station components include the voice or data cards (sometimes called line cards), radio transmitters and receivers, power supplies, and antenna assemblies.

Analog base stations are equipped with a radio channel scanning receiver (sometimes called a locating receiver) to measure wireless telephones' signal strength and channel quality during handover. The UMTS handover process has the advantage of using both base station receiver channel monitoring and radio channel quality information provided back to the system by the wireless telephones (radio signal strength and bit error rate) to assist in the handover process. This information greatly improves the RNC's handoff decisions.

Radio Antenna Towers

Wireless base station antenna heights can vary from a few feet to more than 300 feet. Radio towers raise the height of antennas to provide greater area coverage. There may be several different antenna systems mounted on the same radio tower. These other antennas may be used for paging systems, point-to-point microwave communication links, or land mobile radio (LMR) dispatch systems. Shared use of towers by different types of radio systems in this way is very common, due to the economies realized by sharing the cost of the tower and shelter. However, great care must be taken in the installation and testing to avoid mutual radio interference between the various systems.

A typical cell site antenna system has multiple antennas. One antenna is used for transmitting, and two are used for reception for each radio coverage sector. In some cases, where space or other limitations prevent the use of three separate antennas, two antennas may be used, with one of the two serving as both a transmit and receive antenna, and the other as a receive antenna only. Special radio frequency filters are used with the shared antenna to prevent the strong transmit signal from causing deleterious effects on the receiver.

The basic antenna options are monopole-mount, guy-wire, freestanding, or man-made structures such as water towers, office buildings, and church steeples. Monopole heights range from 30-70 feet; freestanding towers range from 20-100 feet; and guy wire towers can exceed 300 feet. Cell site radio antennas can also be disguised to fit in with the surroundings. Figure 8.2 illustrates several antenna systems. Figure 8.2(a) shows a freestanding single pole antenna called a monopole. Figure 8.2(b) is a tower supported by guy wires. Freestanding antenna towers as shown in Figure 8.2(c) are self-supporting structures with three or four legs. Cellular system antennas can also be located on building or disguised inside a building as shown in Figure 8.2(d).

Radio Equipment

A radio transmitter in the base station contains audio processing, modulation, and RF power amplifier assemblies. An audio processing section converts digital audio signals from the communications link to channel-coded and phase-shift modulated signals. The transmitter audio section also inserts control information such as power control messages to the wireless telephone. A modulation section converts the audio signals into proportional phase shifts at the carrier frequency.

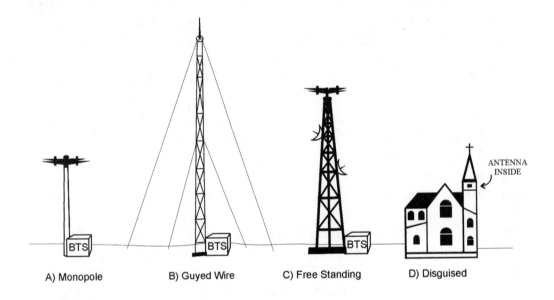

A) Monopole   B) Guyed Wire   C) Free Standing   D) Disguised

Figure 8.2. Cell Site Radio Towers.

The RF power amplifier boosts the signal to much higher power levels. This is typically several watts per RF communication channel compared to the low power of the wireless telephone (typically much less than 1 watt).

In the UMTS system, the transmitter power level for the control channel is usually fixed to define the cell boundaries (e.g., a control channel). The power level of dedicated (individual) channels may dynamically change to the lowest level possible that allows quality communication with the wireless telephone. This reduction in energy level reduces the overall interference to other wireless telephones that are operating in neighboring cells.

Receiver

The base station receiver sections consist of a sensitive low-noise RF amplifier, demodulator, and audio processor. The RF amplifier boosts the low-level signals received from wireless telephones to a level appropriate for input to the demodulator/correlator. The demodulator/correlator section converts the 5-MHz RF signal to its baseband digital signal. This digital signal is processed to extract control information (e.g., power level control and channel assignment) and to forward the digitized voice signal to the speech decoder. In addition to all of these functions, most receivers are also able to select or combine the strongest radio signals that are received on the two different receive antennas or from delayed signals. This process called diversity rake reception.

RF Combiner

The RF combiner has certain similarities to the duplexer in a wireless telephone. Each of a base stations many radio channels are usually served by a dedicated RF amplifier. The RF combiner allows multiple RF amplifiers to share one antenna without their signals interfering with each other. RF combiners are bandpass filters with directional couplers that allow only one specified frequency to pass through. The filtering and directional coupling prohibits signals from one amplifier from leaking into another. A RF filter is a tuned chamber or cavity which is designed to produce a special internal electromagnetic field pattern called a standing wave, with dimensions that allow only a specific range of frequencies (and their corresponding wavelengths) to pass. To change the resonant frequency, the chamber's dimensions can be changed by moving a threaded metal rod inside it either manually by a screw device or automatically changed by a servo motor (for autotune combiners). Turning the rod to extend it further into the cavity produces resonance and a peak bandpass frequency that is lower (and corresponds to a longer wavelength), while shortening the length of the rod inside the cavity raises the resonant frequency (corresponding to a shorter wavelength).

Receiver Multicoupler

To allow one antenna to serve several receivers, a receiver multicoupler must be attached to each receiving antenna. Figure 8.3 illustrates a receiver multicoupler assembly. Because a receiver multicoupler output is provided for each receiver antenna input, the splitting of received signal reduces its total available power to each individual receiver. By increasing the number of receivers, the signal to noise ratio to each receiver section is reduced. Low-noise RF preamplifiers are included with the multicoupler to boost the low-level received signals prior to the RF multicoupler splitter.

Communication Links

Communication links carry both data and voice information between the MSC, GSN, RNCs, and the base stations. Options for the physical connections include wire, microwave, or fiber-optic links. Alternate communication links are sometimes provided to prevent a single communication link failure from disabling communication [1]. Some terrain conditions may prohibit the use of one type of communication link. For example, microwave systems are not usually used in extremely earthquake-prone areas because they require precise line-of-sight connection. Small shifts in the earth can misalign microwave transceivers to break communications.

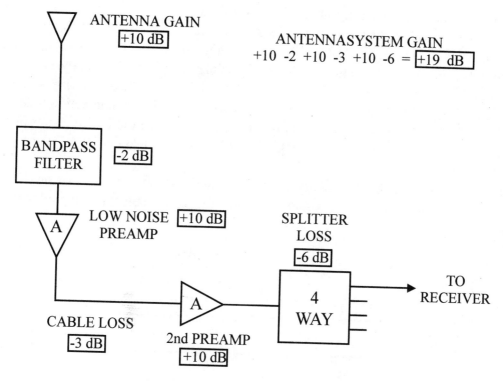

Figure 8.3. Receiver Multicoupler.

Regardless of the physical type of communication link, the channel format is usually the same. Communication links are typically digital time-multiplexed to increase the efficiency of the communication line. The standard format for time-multiplexing communication channels between cell sites in North America is the 24-channel T1 line, or multiple T1 channels. The standard format outside of North America is the 32-channel (30 useable channels) E1 line.

Figure 8.4 illustrates T1 (North American) and E1 (European) standard communication links. The T1 communication link is divided into time frames that contain 24 time slots plus a framing bit. To allow for control signaling in standard telephone systems, the last of the 8 bits are "stolen" from various slots in one out of every six consecutive frames. This has a negligible effect on the quality of speech transmitted. In cellular base station links, signaling is usually accomplished by setting aside one channel for control signaling instead of voice, so the "stolen" or "robbed" bit method need not be used. An E1 communication link is divided into time frames that contain 32 time slots. Two of the E1 time slots are dedicated as synchronization and signaling control slots, leaving 30 for voice.

Each time slot in the communication link contains 8 bits of information. For standard landline voice transmission, each analog voice channel is sampled 8000

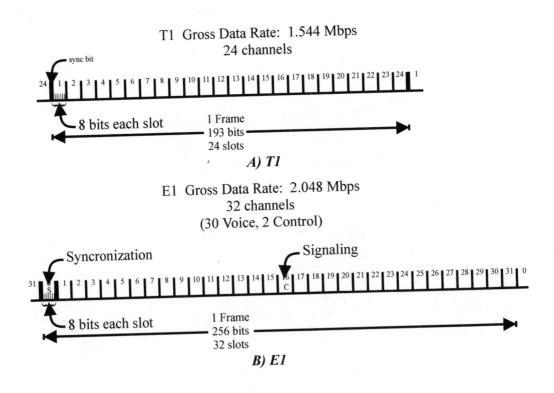

Figure 8.4. T1 and E1 Communication Links.

times per second and converted to an 8-bit PCM digital word. The 8000 samples x 8 bits per sample results in a data rate of 64 kb/s, and it is called a DS0 or PCM (one channel).

For T1 communication lines, 24 DS0's plus a framing bit are time multiplexed onto the high speed T1 channel frame. Therefore, with a frame length of 193 bits, the data rate is 8000 x 193 = 1.544 Mbps. For E1 communication lines, 32 PCM channels are time multiplexed, resulting in a gross data rate of 2.048 Mbps.

Because of the high-speed data transmission capability of the UMTS system, much of the infrastructure equipment is expected to use asynchronous transfer mode (ATM) transmission. ATM is a high-speed packet data transmission and switching system that rapidly transfers information by using fixed length 53-byte cells and high-speed communication links.

The ATM switching system is connection based. When an ATM communication circuit is first established, a path through multiple switches is set up and remains in place until the connection is completed. ATM service was developed to allow one communication medium (high-speed packet data) to provide for voice, data, and video service.

As of the 1990s, ATM has become a standard for high-speed digital backbone networks. ATM networks are widely used by large telecommunications service providers to interconnect their network parts (e.g., RNCs, GMSCs, and GGSN).

The ATM switch rapidly transfers and routes packets to the predesignated destinations. The basic transmission rate for an ATM system is 155 Mbps, and some interconnecting channels may be many multiples of 155 Mbps. These high-speed channels are divided into 53-byte packets (5 bytes for circuit identification and 48 bytes for user data). Fast ATM packet switches interconnect these high-speed transmission lines.

To transfer packets to their destination, each ATM switch maintains a database (called a routing table). The routing table instructs the ATM switch which chan-

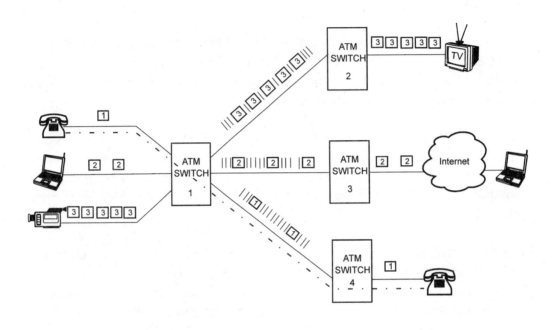

Figure 8.5. ATM Packet Switching.

nel to transfer the incoming packet to and what priority should be given to the packet. The routing table is updated each time a connection is set up or disconnected. This allows the ATM switch to forward packets to the next ATM switch or destination point without spending much processing time.

The ATM switch also may prioritize or discard packets based on network availability (congestion). The ATM switch determines the prioritization and discard options by the type of channels and packets within the channels that are being switched by the ATM switch.

Figure 8.5 shows a functional diagram of an ATM packet switching system. This diagram shows that there are three signal sources going through an ATM network to different destinations. The first signal source (signal 1) is a 64-kbps voice circuit. The data from the voice circuit is divided into short packets and sent to ATM switch 1. ATM switch 1 looks in its routing table and determines the packet is destined for ATM switch 4, and ATM switch 4 adapts (slows down the transmission speed) and routes it to it destination voice circuit. The routing from ATM switch 1 to ATM switch 4 is accomplished by assigning the ATM packet a virtual circuit identifier (VCI) that the ATM switch can understand (the packet routing address). This VCI code remains for the duration of the communication. The second signal source (signal 2) is an 384-kbps Internet session. ATM switch 1 determines that the destination of these packets is ATM switch 3, and ATM switch 3 routes these packets to the Internet data network. The third signal source (signal 3) is a 1 Mbps digital video signal from a digital camera. ATM switch 1 determines this signal is destined for ATM switch 2, and ATM switch 2 routes this signal to a digital television.

Antenna Assembly

When a wide area cellular system is first established, base station antenna assemblies usually employ horizontally omnidirectional antennas [2]. As the system matures, directional (sectored) antennas replace the original antennas to reduce interference. An antenna assembly in each sector usually consists of one transmitting antenna and two receiving antennas.

Separate transmit and receive antennas are used to keep excessive amounts of the transmitter's RF energy from being coupled into receive antennas. The few feet of separation between the antennas provide more than 40 dB of isolation. In some installations, where antenna tower platform space is limited, and three antennas cannot be used, one antenna must also be used for transmitting. In this case, a very deep notch isolation filter is used to prevent the transmit signal from leaking into receivers on the shared antenna.

Two receive antennas may be used to provide spatial diversity reception to minimize the effects of Rayleigh signal fading. Raleigh signal fading is position (distance) sensitive and results when two signals are received from the same source and one of these signals is slightly delayed resulting in signals canceling. Using two receiving antennas enables diversity reception that allows the selection (or signal combining) from the antenna that is receiving the stronger signal. The technique improves power reception up to 6 dB or more, improves the signal to noise ratio (S/N) up to 3 dB or more, and reduces the effects of fading signals.

Scanning or Locating Channel (Receiver)

UMTS systems have a frequency reuse of one that allows existing base station equipment to monitor the signal quality level of wireless telephones that are operating on nearby cell sites. This information is used for the handover process. When the signal strength falls below a level or the bit error rate (BER) increases beyond a specific limit, the base station signals the RNC that a handover will be necessary soon. The RNC then commands one or more adjacent cell sites to monitor the wireless telephone's radio channel code and continually measure and report the signal strength. The RNC (or other base station controller) compares the reported signal strength with other signal levels to decide handoff.

For first generation cellular systems, a scanning or locating receiver is used to measure wireless telephone signal strength for handoff decisions. Because first and second generation systems used different frequencies in adjacent cells, a scanning receiver can tune to any channel and measure the received signal strength, from which it determines a wireless telephone's approximate distance from the base station.

The 3rd generation UMTS system allows for handover decisions to be assisted by information reported by the wireless telephone and by simultaneous transmissions during soft handover. Using signal and interference levels measured by wireless telephones, the UMTS system can better decide when a handovers may be necessary. The information from wireless telephones also reduces the data-communications traffic burden of communications between adjacent base stations while coordinating (passing signal quality information) the handover process.

Power Supplies and Backup Energy Sources

Power supplies convert the base station power source to regulated and filtered AC and DC voltage levels required by the base station electronics assemblies. Batteries and generators are used to power a base station when primary power is interrupted. Backup power is also needed for radio equipment and cooling systems.

Backup power supplies are critical for disaster situations where power may not be available for several days or even weeks. A good example of the requirements for short- and long-term backup power sources is the hurricane in 1989 that destroyed almost all land line communications in parts of Puerto Rico. Due to good planning, wireless communications were unaffected and became the primary communication link [3].

Backup power supplies are also required to ensure the equipment environment can be maintained. In most climates, the heat generated by the radio equipment in the base station shelter will require installation of air-conditioning equipment to prevent excessively high temperature in the shelter. If the base radio equipment is permitted to operate at higher than rated temperature (for example, due to a failure of the cooling equipment), it may malfunction temporarily (until the shelter temperature is lowered). Operating at excessive temperatures can increase the long-term costs due to higher failure rates. Operating at high temperatures can result in significantly shortening the "burn out" lifetime of many of the components, particularly the RF power amplifiers.

Maintenance and Diagnostics

Base station radio equipment must be maintained and repaired as equipment assemblies fail, and cell sites are often remote and scattered throughout a wireless network. In response to maintenance needs, advanced maintenance and diagnostic tools have been created.

Base stations require software to operate and can be installed at the factory or loaded by the maintenance technicians after the cell site's radio equipment has been installed. As base station software improves, the updated version of the software must be installed into the base station controllers and network switching equipment. Most systems allow downloading new software via the communication links. During the software download process, one or more communication link voice channels (time slots) are dedicated to transfer software programs instead of voice or data transmission.

The base station continuously monitors the status of its own operation and performance and sends report messages to the RNC and MSC. If spare equipment is available when a specific piece of base station equipment fails (e.g., backup controller or alternate radio channel), the controller can reconfigure to continue service. Other maintenance tasks include routine testing to detect faults before they affect service. Routine test functions operate in a background mode and are suspended when faults are detected. Diagnostics begin and status reports may be continuously printed to inform system operators that maintenance may be required.

If a system network equipment fails (e.g., radio transceiver), the suspect equipment assemblies must be tested to isolate faults. To verify equipment performance and monitor operational status, test signals are inserted at various points. Loop-back testing inserts test signals on one path (such as the forward direction) of the system and monitors the response of the signals on a return path.

Figure 8.6 illustrates two processes of loop-back test paths that are used to test a base station from the MSC. To test the communication link between the MSC and base station, the MSC sends an audio test signal to the base station on a voice channel (path 1). The line card then returns the test signal to the MSC via another voice path. If the return is unsuccessful, the fault is in one of the two voice channels or the voice channel card interface. To determine if the radio transmitter and receiver are working correctly, a second test path (path 2) routes a test audio signal through transmission and reception equipment. The test samples a portion of the output signal, shifts the frequency, and then redirects the signal to the receiver section. If the MSC receives the test signal, the RF transmission and reception equipment assemblies are assumed to be operational. Other loop-back paths can isolate other network equipment assemblies.

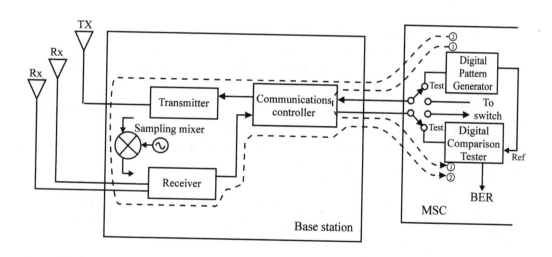

Figure 8.6. Wireless Network Loop-Back Testing.

Base stations can be equipped with a test transceiver (wireless telephone). This test transceiver can perform the same functions as a wireless telephone, but it is remotely controlled from a central test control location, usually at a MSC. A voice channel usually used for one of the normal base transceivers is temporarily reassigned to permit a conversation to be routed through the test transceiver. A technician or operator at the test desk can then place or receive a call at the cell site in question without the delay or requirement to first send a person to that site with a field test set. This will quickly indicate if there is no base transmitter signal, or if a particular base transmit carrier frequency is not functioning, and similar problems can be quickly diagnosed. When the test transceiver is operated remotely (possibly via a standard telephone voice channel), test signals that are transmitted by the base station can be sampled and verified (path 3).

Repeaters

Repeaters are radio amplifiers that can be used to extend or redirect radio coverage. Repeaters can be a simple remote amplifier or an intelligent device. Repeaters are located within the radio coverage area of another base station. The repeater amplifies desired incoming signals and retransmits the signal. The advantages are that the antennas can be located a longer distance from the base station and repeaters can also provide a greater link budget advantage. This translates into greater coverage - fewer cell sites required. A portion of the RF energy is received, processed and retransmitted.

Figure 8.7 shows a block diagram of an intelligent UTMS repeater. In this diagram, a receiver samples the radio signal from an adjacent base station (or another repeater). The intelligent repeater actually decodes the incoming signal, translates control commands, and remodulates the signals on another carrier frequency.

Radio Network Controller (RNC)

The RNC coordinates the overall operation of each of its base station equipment. The RNC also manages the connections of UEs that are operating within its radio subsystem. This means tracking the channel codes and assigning new codes when handoff is necessary.

The radio network controller (RNC) coordinates the radio resources of the base stations within its radio network subsystem. The RNCs perform control signal routing and message processing from commands that are received from the MSC

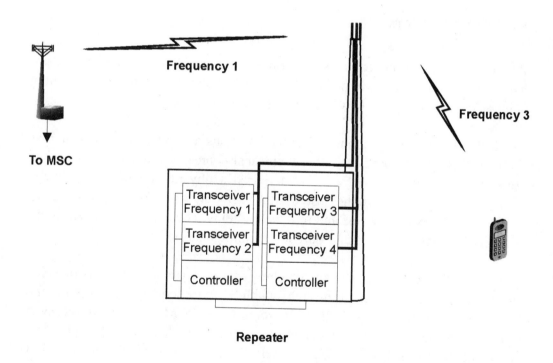

Figure 8.7. Intelligent UMTS Repeater Block Diagram.

(e.g., call setup). The RNC also adds additional control commands such as hand-off messages. Base station controllers insert control channel signaling messages, set up dedicated channels (for voice and data), and monitor the channels for channel quality levels that may indicate a need for handover. In addition, controllers monitor equipment status and report operational and failure status to the MSC.

An advanced feature of the UMTS system is to allow RNCs to communicate with other without the direct involvement of the MSC. This allows for distributed call processing that reduces the burden on the MSC, especially during the soft handover process.

Switching Centers

A switching center coordinates all communication channels and processes. There are two types of switches used in the UMTS system: a mobile switching center (MSC) and a packet switching system.

The switching assembly connects the base stations and other networks such as the PSTN or the Internet with either a physical connection (analog) or a logical path (digital). Early analog switches required a physical connection between switch paths. Today's switches use digital switching assemblies that are high-speed matrix memory storage and retrieval systems. These systems provide connections between incoming and outgoing communication lines.

Figure 8.8 illustrates a simplified switching matrix system. Time slots of voice channel information are input through switch S1 to be sequentially stored in the PCM data memory. Time slots that are stored in the PCM memory are retrieved and output through S2 to the slots that are routed to another network connection (such as a particular PSTN voice channel). Switch 1 (S1) is linked to switch 3 (S3) and switch 4 (S4), so that each moves to predetermined memory locations

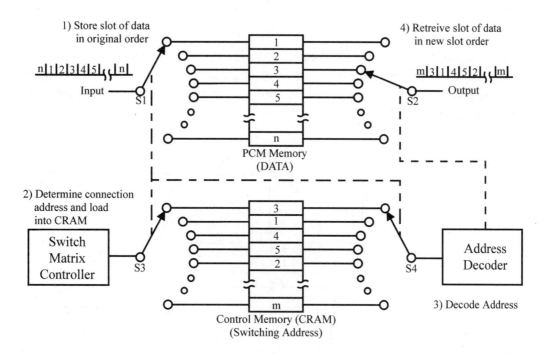

1) Store slot of data in original order

4) Retreive slot of data in new slot order

Input —— S1

Output

PCM Memory
(DATA)

2) Determine connection address and load into CRAM

Switch Matrix Controller

S3

Control Memory (CRAM)
(Switching Address)

Address Decoder

S4

3) Decode Address

Note: Switches (S1-S4) are electronic and do not use mechanical parts.

Figure 8.8. Time Slot Interchange (TSI) Block Diagram.

together (e.g., all at position 1). The address in the control memory determines the position of switch 2 (S2). The switch matrix controller determines which addresses to store in control memory slots. This address system matches input and output time slots.

Mobile Switching Center (MSC)

The mobile switching center (MSC), formerly called the mobile telephone switching office (MTSO), processes requests for service from wireless telephones and landline callers and routes calls between the base stations and the

PSTN. The MSC receives the dialed digits, creates and interprets call processing tones, and routes the call paths.

Figure 8.9 illustrates an MSC's basic components: system and communication controllers, switching assembly, operator terminals, primary and backup power supplies, wireless telephone database registers, and, in some cases, an authentication (subscriber validation) center.

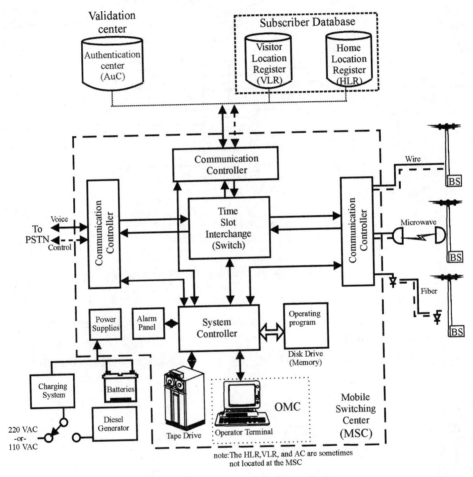

Figure 8.9. Mobile Switching Center Block Diagram.

A system controller coordinates the MSC's operations. A communications controller adapts voice signals and controls the communication links. The switching assembly connects the links between the base station and PSTN. Operator terminals are used to enter commands and display system information. Power supplies and backup energy sources power the equipment. Subscriber databases include a home location register (HLR), used to track home wireless telephones, and a visitor location register (VLR) for wireless telephones temporarily visiting or permanently operating in the system. The authentication center (AC) stores and processes secret keys required to validate the identity of wireless telephones.

The UMTS system defines two types of MSC: the serving mobile switching center (SMSC) and the gateway mobile switching center (GMSC). This is the logical separation of the MSC for directly controlling the mobile telephone and providing a bridge between other networks.

Serving Mobile Switching Center (SMSC)

The serving mobile switching center (SMSC) is the switch that is connected to the RNC that is providing service directly to the mobile telephone. The SMSC is responsible for coordinating the transfer of calls between different RNCs. When the call is transferred to RNCs that are connected to a different MSC, the role of SMSC will be transferred to the new MSC.

Gateway Mobile Switching Center (GMSC)

The gateway MSC (GMSC) is the point where the UMTS network is connected to the public circuit switched networks (typically the PSTN). All PSTN call connections must enter or leave through the GMSC. The GMSC maintains communication with the SMSC as calls are transferred from one system (or different MSCs within a system) to another.

General Packet Radio Service (GPRS) Support Node

A separate switching system is used for the transfer of packet data. This packet-switching network is composed of different types of support nodes that receive and transfer packets towards their destination. The general packet radio service (GPRS) support node performs a similar function as the MSC except it switches packets instead of maintaining a specific connection path. Packet nodes used in the network are divided into serving support nodes and gateway support nodes.

Serving GPRS Support Node (SGSN)

The serving GPRS service node maintains packet data communication with the mobile telephone via the radio network. The SGSN will sense, register and maintain information about packet data radios operating in its radio network. As the mobile telephone moves through the system, the SGSN will ensure packets are routed to the new base stations.

Gateway General Packet Radio Service (GGSN) Support Node

The gateway GPRS service node (GGSN) is a packet switch that routes packets between the UMTS core network and external data networks such as the Internet. The GGSN is the interworking function that is responsible for adapting and buffering the information between the systems.

Tandem Free Operation (TFO)

Mobile switching centers in the UMTS system have the capability of tandem free operation (TFO) to allow direct connection between MSCs without the need to decompress and recompress (transcoding) speech information. TFO overcomes the challenges of cascading the speech-coding process. Each time speech information is compressed and decompressed, some audio distortion occurs and time delay is added.

The logical function for coordinating TFO is the transcoder rate adaption unit (TRAU). The TRAU is usually located in the MSC (it is possible to put the TRAU in the base station) and it negotiates the ability of the MSC to use TFO with another MSC. The TRAU is also responsible for disabling TFO if the call is transferred to another MSC or system that is not capable of TFO.

Figure 8.10 shows tandem free operation. This diagram shows mobile telephone 1 communicating with another mobile telephone 2 in a different UMTS system. When the call is first established between systems, MSC 1 sends a message to MSC 2 indicating TFO is desired. MSC 2 responds and accepts the TFO request, and a dedicated data connection is created between MSC 1 and MSC 2 that allows coded speech information to be directly transferred.

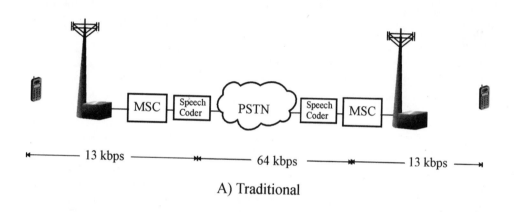

A) Traditional

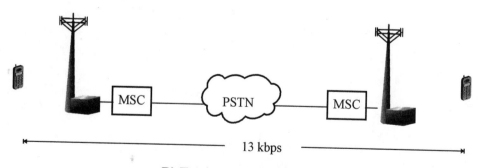

B) Tandem Free Operations

Figure 8.10. Tandem Free Operation (TFO).

One of the advantages of TFO is subrate multiplexing. Subrate multiplexing combines multiple compressed voice channels on a single communication channel. For example, four 12.2-kbps speech coder signals can share a 64-kbps DS0. Whatever transmission medium is used between cell sites and the MSC, maintaining the network's voice and data communication links is costly. Various methods, such as subrate multiplexing, can improve the efficiency of these links. Figure 8.11 illustrates how several subrate multiplexed channels can share a single DS0 channel.

Since the cost of the communication links between the MSC and cell sites can be a significant part of the system cost. More efficient use of each channel in a T1 or E1 communication link or increasing the number of channels on a given

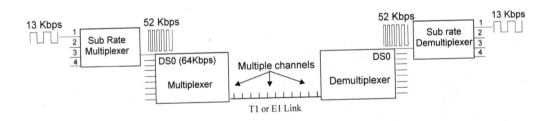

Figure 8.11. Subrate Multiplexing.

bandwidth allocated to an ATM channel is an important potential system cost reduction.

For analog cellular systems, the using 32 kbps ADPCM digital voice coding on each voice communications channel combines two conversations on each DS0/PCM channel. This increases the number of voice channels per communication link to 48 for T1 links and 60 for E1 links. Other systems use the VSELP coder at the MSC end to encode each voice channel at 13 kbps, and thus three voice channels can be combined in one DS0 channel over the T1 link (with some unused bits left over in each DS0 channel). It is not advisable to use ADPCM on the MSC-BS link and then convert it into another form of low bit-rate coding such as VSELP, since the quality of the speech is degraded due to the double transcoding digital coding conversion. However, 32 kbps ADPCM on the MSC-BS link is quite good for use with analog cellular.

Soft Capacity

Carriers frequently experience unexpected spikes in traffic levels and operators need to be able to respond immediately to relieve congestion. The AMR speech coder used in the UMTS is capable of adjusting its data rates that can maximize the capacity of their networks at the expense of reduced voice quality.

Political conventions, sporting events and natural disasters create traffic surges that temporarily exceed an operator's planned network performance. The UMTS system can change the speech coding process to a higher compression level (e.g., from the 12.2-kbps EHF speech coder to a 4.75-kbps speech coder). This allows operators to temporarily boost capacity on their systems by altering the system-wide vocoding rate. This also allows the service provider to balance the relationship between voice quality and capacity.

Backup Energy Sources

Backup energy sources are required to operate the UMTS network system equipment when the primary power is interrupted. Backup power that must be provided to switching equipment, subscriber databases, and cooling systems is usually a combination of batteries and diesel generators. During normal operations, batteries are charged with a charger using primary power. The batteries are directly connected to the UMTS system, and when outside power is interrupted, they immediately and continuously power the system. After a short period of power loss, a diesel generator automatically begins to power the battery charger.

Network Databases

There are many network databases in the UMTS network. Some of the key network databases include a master subscriber database (home location register), temporary active user subscriber database (visitor location register), unauthorized or suspect user database (equipment identity register), billing database, and authorization and validation center (authentication).

Home Location Register (HLR)

The home location register (HLR) is a subscriber database containing each customer's international mobile subscriber identity (IMSI) and international mobile equipment identifier (IMEI) to uniquely identify each customer. There is usually only one HLR for each carrier, even though each carrier may have many MSCs.

The HLR holds each customer's user profile which includes the selected long distance carrier, calling restrictions, service rates, and other selected network options. The subscriber can change and store the changes for some feature options in the HLR (such as call forwarding). The MSC system controller uses this information to authorize system access and process individual call billing.

The HLR is a magnetic storage device for a computer (commonly called a hard disk). Subscriber databases are critical, so they are usually regularly backed up, typically on tape or CDROM, to restore the information if the HLR system fails.

Visitor Location Register (VLR)

The visitor location register (VLR) contains a subset of a subscriber's HLR information for use while a mobile telephone is active on a particular MSC. The VLR holds both visiting and home customer's information. The VLR eliminates the need for the MSC to continually check with the mobile telephone's HLR each time access is attempted. The user's required HLR information is temporarily stored in the VLR memory, and then erased either when the wireless telephone registers with another MSC or in another system or after a specified period of inactivity.

Equipment Identity Register (EIR)

The equipment identity register is a database that contains the identity of telecommunications devices (such as wireless telephones) and the status of these devices in the network (such as authorized or not authorized). The EIR is primarily used to identify wireless telephones that may have been stolen or have questionable usage patterns that may indicate fraudulent use. The EIR has three types of lists: white, black, and gray. The white list holds known good IMEIs. The black list holds invalid (barred) IMEIs; and the gray list holds IMEIs that may be suspect for fraud or are being tested for validation.

Billing Center (BC)

A separate database, called the billing center, keeps records on billing. The billing center receives individual call records from MSCs and other network equipment. The switching records (connection and data transfer records) are converted into call detail records (CDRs) that hold the time, type of service, connection points, and other details about the network usage that are associated with a specific user identification code. The format of these CDRs is transferred account procedure (TAP) format. The TAP format CDR has evolved into the flexible TAP3 system. The TAP3 system (3rd generation TAP protocol) includes flexible billing record formats for voice and data usage. These billing records are then transferred via tape or data link to a separate computer typically by electronic data interchange (EDI) to a billing system or company that can settle bills between different service providers (a clearinghouse company).

Authentication Center (AC)

The authentication center (AC) stores and processes information that is required to validate of the identity (authenticate) of a wireless telephone before service is provided. During the authentication procedure, the AC processes information from the wireless telephone (e.g., IMSI, secret keys) along with a random number that is also used by the mobile telephone to produce an authentication response. The AC compares its authentication response results to the authentication response received from the mobile telephone. If the processed information matches, the wireless telephone passes.

Public Switched Telephone Network (PSTN)

The public switched telephone network (PSTN) is the landline telephone system connecting a wireless telephone to any telephone that is connected to it. Wireless telephones, landline plain old telephone service (POTS) dial tone, and other networks such as private automatic branch exchanges (PABX) all have different capabilities. Unfortunately, some control messages (such as calling line indicator) cannot be sent between the wireless telephone and different telephone networks, prohibiting some advanced features that digital systems could offer.

Figure 8.12 is an overview of the PSTN system. Two types of connections are shown: voice and signaling. End office (EO) or central office (CO) and tandem office (TO) switches route voice connections. The CO switch is nearest to the customer terminal (telephone) equipment. Tandem office switching systems connect CO switches when direct connection to an end office is not economically justified. Tandem office switches can be connected to other tandem office switches. Signaling connections are routed through a separate signaling network called signaling system number 7 (SS7). The SS7 network is composed of signaling transfer points (STPs) and signaling control points (SCPs). A STP is a telephone packet network switching point that routes control messages to other switching points. SCPs are databases that allow messages to be processed as they pass through the network (such as calling card information). SS7 messages are usually sent in a reserved voice grade channel (64 kbps) between the STP, SCP and other parts of the system. The messages in SS7 have the form of data packets similar to data packets used in other data communications systems such as X.25. SS7 messages permit control of a wide variety of network functions and are normally very reliable in their operation.

Two types of landline networks are shown: a local exchange carrier (LEC) and inter-exchange carrier (IXC) network. LEC providers furnish local telephone service to end-users. An interexchange carrier (IXC) is the long-distance service provider. In some countries, local and long distance providers are operated by the same company or government agency.

In the United States, the LEC and IEX businesses were legally separated due to an anti-trust legal settlement that took effect in 1984. Then the Telecommunications Act of 1996 has again permitted the same company to operate both IXC and LEC services, with a more open competition in both types of markets. It also allowed for the creation of competitive local exchange providers (CLECs) that can compete with incumbent LECs (ILECs). Before that new law became effective in the United States, government regulations prohibited direct-

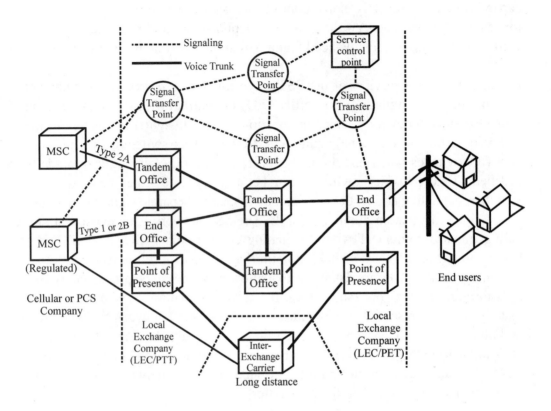

Figure 8.12. Public Switched Telephone Network (PSTN).

ly connecting an IXC to some end-user equipment, requiring a point-of-presence (POP) connection. The POP connection is a location within a local access and transport area (LATA) designated to connect a LEC and IXC. LATA is typically a geographic service area boundary for the Local Exchange Carriers (LECs). At the end of the 1990's, a global trend of telecommunications deregulation began.

Internet

The Internet is a network of networks that can understand a common data communication language. Although each network within the Internet may talk a different language between their elements (data nodes and switching points), they can receive and forward packets through their network to their destination. This is accomplished by a standard set of addressing and routing rules (protocols).

The most basic protocols used in the Internet are Transaction Capabilities Protocol/Internet Protocol (TCP/IP). TCP involves the tracking and confirmation of packets sent and received through the Internet. IP is only concerned with addressing and routing packets.

The Internet is primarily composed of routers that receive and forward packets towards their destination. Routers are smart switches that dynamically learn where to send packets they receive. Routers are initially programmed with routing tables that indicate where to send packets. After the router is connected to other routers, it informs its neighbors of its presence and the addresses of other routers that it is connected to. Neighboring routers update their routing tables with the information and begin to broadcast their new information to other routers. Over short period of time, many routers in the network have updated their routing table information, and packets will be more efficiently forwarded to their destinations.

Figure 8.13 shows a basic diagram of the Internet. This diagram shows that three packets are received from a UMTS wireless telephone have an Internet protocol (IP) destination address of 209.12.26.61. Each router in the network has its own unique IP address. Router 1 at the edge of the network determines that this packet can be routed through router 4 to its destination port on router 2. When router 1 receives the second packet, the link between router 1 and router 4 is temporarily busy. Router 1 makes the decision to forward the packet to router 3, which it knows is on an alternate path to router 2. When router 3 receives the packet, it forwards it on to router 5, and then it is forwarded to router 2. When packet 3 is received by router 1, the connection is available to router 4 and the packet is for-

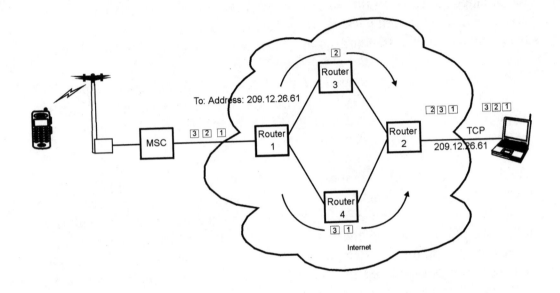

Figure 8.13. Internet.

warded through router 4 to router 2. This diagram also shows that, although the IP protocol has performed its job in full (all the packets arrived at their destination), packet 3 arrives before packet 2. In this example, the higher level TCP protocol automatically reorganizes the packets back into their correct order.

Wireless Network System Interconnection

Subscribers can only visit different wireless systems (roam) if the systems communicate with each other to use handover between systems, verify roamers, automatically deliver calls, and operate features uniformly. Fortunately, cellular systems can use standard protocols to directly communicate with each other. These intersystem communications use brief packets of data sent via the X.25 packet data network (PDN) or the SS7 PSTN signaling network. SS7 and X.25 are essentially private data communication networks. SS7 is available only to telephone companies for direct routing using telephone numbers. The X.25 network does not route directly using telephone numbers. Some MSCs also use other proprietary data connections. No voice information is sent on the SS7 or X.25 networks. Only intersystem signaling, such as SS7 mobile applications part (MAP) and intersystem signaling standard 41 (IS-41), is sent between networks to establish, authenticate, and maintain communication paths.

Ideally, intersystem signaling is independent of cellular network radio technology, but this can be difficult between systems where radio technologies differ. Consider intersystem handoff between a UMTS-capable and a GSM-capable cell site (assuming the wireless telephone capable of both). The UMTS system uses soft handover while GSM does not. As new features in wireless networks are added, intersystem signaling messages, standards that define them, and equipment that processes them must change.

Communication between MSCs is performed either by a proprietary or standard protocol. Standard protocols such as SS7 mobile applications part (MAP) or IS41 allow MSCs of different makes to communicate with few or no changes to the MSC. Regardless of whether a standard (e.g., IS-41) protocol or a manufacturer's private (proprietary) protocol is used, the underlying data transferred via inter-system signaling is the same. If changes are required to communicate with a different protocol, an interface (protocol converter) changes the proprietary protocol to standard protocol. The interface has a buffer that temporarily stores data elements being sent by the MSC and reformats it to the SS7 MAP or IS-41 protocol. Another buffer stores data until it can be sent via the control signaling network.

Intersystem Handover

Intersystem handover links the MSCs of adjacent cellular systems during the handover process. During intersystem handover, the MSCs involved continuously communicate their radio channel parameters with each other. Figure 8.14 illustrates intersystem handover between two different manufacturers' MSCs. The process begins when the serving base station (#1) informs the MSC (system A) that a handover is required. The MSC determines that a base station in an adjacent system is a potential candidate for handover. The MSC requests the adjacent MSC (system B) to measure the wireless telephone's signal quality. Both base stations (#1 and #2) measure the wireless telephone's signal quality until handover. In many cases, handover may be immediate. The serving MSC (system A) compares its measured signal strength with the signal strength that the MSC in system B measures. When the system B MSC measures a sufficient signal, the system A MSC requests the handover. Base station #1 issues the handover command, informing the wireless telephone to tune to another frequency, and base station #2 begins communicating to the wireless telephone on the new frequency. The voice path is then connected from the anchor (original) MSC to the system B MSC, and the call continues. After the anchor MSC receives a confirmation message that the wireless telephone is successfully operating in system B, the radio resources in the original cell site become available.

During intersystem handover, adjacent MSCs are typically connected by a T1 or E1 link or by fast ATM packet-switching system, providing both intersystem messaging and voice communications. An external landline connection between the MSCs is technically possible, but the setup time between them is slower.

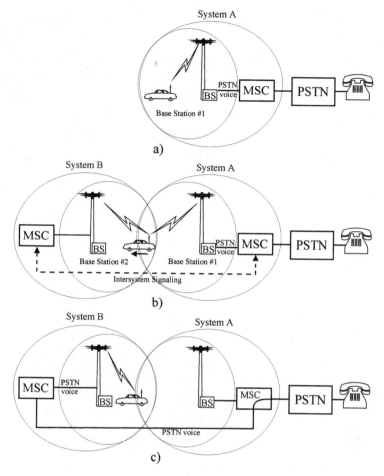

Figure 8.14. Intersystem Handover.

Roamer Validation

Roamer validation is the verification of a wireless telephone's identity using registered subscriber information. Validation is necessary to limit fraudulent use of cellular service. The two types of roamer validation are postcall and precall. Postcall validation occurs after a call is complete, and precall validation occurs before granting access to the system.

During the early deployment of cellular systems, the limited connections between systems resulted in delays of minutes or even hours before roaming cellular subscribers could be validated. To allow customers to use the phone immediately, early systems used postcall validation. Precall validation became possible when improved intersystem interconnection greatly reduced validation time.

Figure 8.15 illustrates roamer validation. When a wireless telephone initiates a call in a visited system (step 1), the cellular system attempts to find the wireless telephone's ID in its visitor location register (VLR). In this case, the visited system determines that the wireless telephone is not registered in its system (step 2).

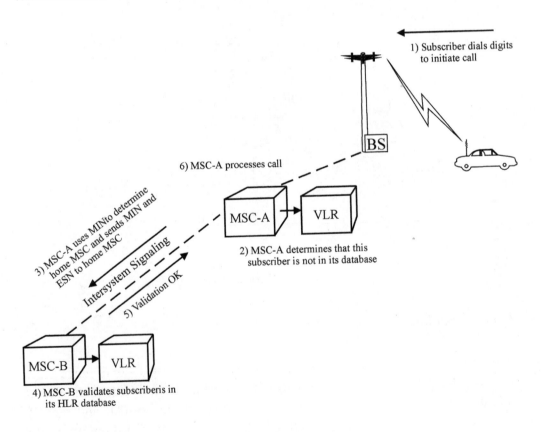

Figure 8.15. Roamer Validation.

Using the wireless telephone's ID (phone number), the visited cellular system sends a message to the wireless telephone's home system requesting validation (step 3). The HLR and AC compares the IMSI and authentication information to determine if it is valid (step 4). If the subscriber proves valid, the HLR responds to MSC-A to indicate that validation was successful (step 5). After MSC-A receives confirmation that the visiting wireless telephone is valid, the call is processed (step 6). MSC-A's VLR may then temporarily store the wireless telephone's registration information to validate the subscriber's identity rather than requesting validation from the home system again for the next call. After a predetermined period of wireless telephone inactivity, the information stored in the VLR will be erased. If the wireless telephone was recently operating in another cellular system, the home system informs the old visited system that the wireless telephone has left. This allows the old visited system to erase the wireless telephone's identification information.

Authentication

Authentication is the exchange and processing of stored information to confirm a wireless telephone's identity. Authentication is significant because roamer validation cannot detect illegally cloned (telephones not owned by the authentic customer but containing duplicated identification) wireless telephones.

New technologies offer a new authentication process to verify a subscriber's identity. The new process transfers stored information between the wireless telephone and an authentication center (AC). The two primary options for intersystem authentication are: (1) the visited MSC can use a temporary key, or (2) the MSC can request the AC to validate wireless telephones each time. If the AC validates the mobile telephone each time, the visited MSC must send all the authentication parameters. If the AC provides a temporary key, the visited MSC can use the key without validation from the home system for each call while the subscriber is in the system.

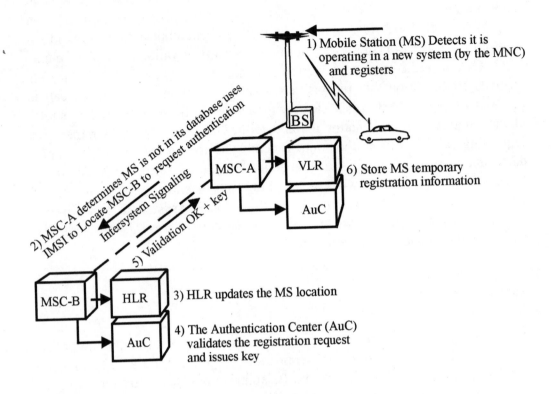

Figure 8.16. Authentication.

Figure 8.16 illustrates a wireless telephone's authentication process. When a wireless telephone detects a new cellular system (new system identifier), it attempts to register with the system (step 1). The visited system searches for the wireless telephone's ID in its visitor location register (VLR) and determines that the wireless telephone is not yet registered. The visited cellular system uses the wireless telephone's ID (phone number) to request authentication of identity (step 2) from the subscriber's home cellular system. If the home system information processes correctly, the authentication center (AC) validates the registration request (step 4). The AC either confirms validation or creates a key for future authentication using information received from the home system (step 5). MSC-

A's VLR then temporarily stores the subscriber's registration information (step 6) for future authentication without contacting the subscriber's home HLR for the next call. After a predetermined period of inactivity, the temporary authentication information stored in the VLR will be erased.

Automatic Call Delivery

Ideally, call delivery is completely automatic whether the wireless telephone is in its home system or visiting another system. Such automatic delivery requires the home system to continuously track the wireless telephone's location. Roamer validation is the means for providing this information back to the home system.

To enable voice connection between the home system and visited system, a temporary location directory number (TLDN) is assigned for each automatic call delivery request.

Figure 8.17 illustrates basic intersystem call delivery. When a home system (MSC-A) receives a call for its subscriber, the MSC checks its home location register (HLR) to determine if the wireless telephone is operating in another cellular system (step 1). The home MSC then sends a request to the visited MSC for a TLDN (step 2). The TLDN is cross-referenced with the IMSI in the VLR (step 3). The home system (MSC-H) then initiates a call to the TLDN (step 4). The visited system (MSC-A) receives the call and finds the TLDN number is listed in its VLR (step 5). It pages the wireless telephone using the IMSI that was previously stored in the VLR (step 6). When the subscriber answers, the call is connected (step 7). After a predefined interval of inactivity or notification that the roaming subscriber has entered another system, the TLDN is disassociated from that particular IMSI. The TLDN can be placed back into a pool of TLDNs to be used for other calls.

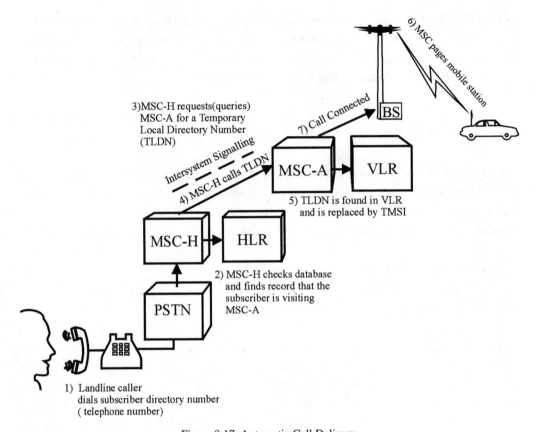

Figure 8.17. Automatic Call Delivery.

Network Planning

UMTS network design is a very intricate process. The cell site coverage areas are first designed. The individual cell sites must be positioned and configured so that they do not overlap too much while leaving no coverage gaps in the desired coverage objective. Antennas and transmission lines must be selected and positioned to perform adequately in the cell site coverage area's environment.

The radio coverage for wireless networks is usually simulated before investments are made in cell site locations and equipment. Cell site placement, signal propagation, traffic planning, system testing and optimization, and future expansion plans all play a role in system design. Signal propagation varies with terrain, morphology, and even the change of seasons and has a dramatic affect on a cell's coverage area. Traffic loading must be considered when positioning cell sites to ensure that the system capacity will not be exceeded to quickly. System testing and optimization will perfect the network by maximizing capacity and minimizing the occurrence of coverage holes.

Cell Site Placement

Cell site placement is a very complicated part of the network design process. Cell sites must be designed and selected carefully so that they conform to many government guidelines along with local zoning restrictions. Cell site radio coverage areas must overlap and the system must be designed so that cell sites work with each other (correctly handover) to cover the entire service area. To assist in the cell site placement process, radio propagation drive testing for cell site candidates and the use of network radio signal planning software can help.

The first step in the design process is to plan a theoretical cell site design, by geographically placing cell sites over the coverage objective area. Network planning software can be used to help with this stage of the design. This software can simulate the coverage properties of the cell sites. The next step is to find actual places near each of the theoretical cell sites to build real sites. This can be somewhat challenging because some of the theoretical sites may be located in areas where no sites can be constructed like densely populated residential areas. This is why the initial cell site design is so important.

Reviewing local zoning ordinances can help to make site candidate identification a much easier process. Once cell site candidates have been selected, the most suitable candidate is identified for further development. A drive test can be performed on the candidates to determine how the site will perform in the network. A crane can be used to raise a test transmitter to the height of the proposed site, and a vehicle can drive in the area to test the signal propagation properties of the site. This data is used to tune radio propagation models in the network planning software, to more accurately simulate the cell site's coverage. Radio regulatory guidelines must also be followed when designing the network. Other government regulations such as maximum tower height can be limited in certain areas (such as near airports).

Traffic Planning

Before designing the network, subscriber traffic loading must first be projected and analyzed. This is to ensure that the network that is built will be able of providing service to all its subscribers. Census information, wireless service market penetration, and other relevant data are analyzed and subscriber counts are formulated for the different parts of the service coverage area. Locations like downtown areas of cities and business parks are typically projected with a higher subscriber count than residential and highway areas. The network design takes these projections into account when planning the density of cell sites in these areas.

Strategic Planning

Strategic planning for a cellular service provider involves setting company goals, such as subscriber growth, quality of service, and cost objectives. It also involves making plans for obtaining those goals. Building and expanding a cellular system requires collecting demographic information, targeting key high traffic locations, selecting potential cell and MSC sites, conforming to government regulations, purchasing equipment, construction, and testing validation.

Most providers gather physical and demographic information first. For example, transportation thoroughfares, industrial parks, convention centers, railway centers, and airports may be identified as possible high-usage areas. Estimates of traffic patterns are used to help target coverage areas for major roadway corridors. Terrain maps, marketing data, and demographic data are all used to divide the cellular system into RF coverage areas. The object is to target gross areas where cell site towers may be located. The raw data needed might include system specifications, road maps, population density distribution maps, significant urban center locations, marketing demographic data, elevation data, and PSTN and switch center locations.

For the U.S. market, government regulations include quality of service (typical limiting the blocked call attempt ratio to 2%, or P02 grade of service) and time intervals for service offerings [4]. While business considerations may indicate that radio coverage is not necessary (e.g., an unpopulated rural area), government regulations may require that area to be covered within a specified period.

After systems are planned, equipment manufacturers and their systems are reviewed and purchase contracts are signed. During various stages of equipment installation, validation testing is performed to ensure that all of the planning goals are being realized.

After the system is planned and cell site locations are selected, RF simulation begins. Calculations based on antenna elevation and terrain data are used to estimate expected signal strengths and quality levels.

The results of such calculations are rendered graphically onto transparent overlays that can be placed over standard topographical maps (published by the U.S. Coast and Geodetic Survey, and by similar government agencies in other countries). Typically, different colors used on these overlays indicate different values of signal strength levels. System simulations may predict estimated signal coverage and performance levels, but to be certain, temporary cell sites are often tested using a crane to lift a temporary antenna to the planned tower height. Theoretical calculations are often imprecise everywhere by a relatively uniform dB error, which can be determined only by comparing theory and experimental measurement. Once the proper dB correction factor is known from this comparison, the theoretical calculation can be used for evaluation of other base antenna locations in the cell with considerably improved precision.

Code Planning

Unlike analog systems that use frequency and/or time slots to differentiate the channels, the UMTS system uses different code sequences. This means that UMTS channels use code plans instead of frequency plans. UMTS systems use short code offsets that appear to be unique codes for each radio channel in the cell sites. These offset values are assigned to each sector in each site. Cell sites can share the same code values, but must be separated by enough distance to ensure negligible interference. PN offsets identify the sector to a mobile and play an important role in handoff directions.

Signal Propagation Simulation

Radio simulation is used to select cell site locations and assign frequencies and code sequences. The types of radio simulation tools have dramatically changed due to the availability of computers and system needs.

Path loss describes the energy losses that a radio signal encounters during propagation between the transmitting and receiving devices. Many different factors have an effect on path loss, including terrain type, foliage density, and environmental clutter. Flat terrain allows signals to propagate freely without running into the ground, and they provide more even coverage. Signals can pass over valleys or be blocked by hills, which can create holes in system coverage. Dense foliage absorbs radio signals and significantly diminishes their strength. Environmental clutter refers to variations in the environment which include urban areas densely filled with large buildings, suburban areas scattered with shops and houses, and rural areas containing some widely spaced houses and highways.

Path loss models can be created to accurately predict how signals will propagate in each cell site's coverage area. They are usually generated with a software design tool and tuned with actual test data collected from sites. These path loss models are then used to make predictions of how the network will operate and can help forecast any coverage or interference problems.

The overall capacity of a wireless system depends on two key factors: spectral efficiency and interference levels. Spectral efficiency refers to how many simultaneous conversations can occur, in the same frequency band, at the same time. The other factor is the presence of interference in the same frequency band (co-channel interference).

In the UMTS system, all of the conversations occur in the same frequency band. This means that each cell site transmits on the same frequency and can create destructive interference to other adjacent cells. This process links capacity with coverage.

Through the late 1960s, terrestrial radio wave radiation (propagation) effects were predicted using charts and graphs and the prediction process was a recognized scholarly activity. These were fairly simplistic methods compared to the computer prediction models used in the 2000s.

The advent of computer-predicted propagation began in the United States first in Boulder, Colorado, in 1967 with Technical Note 101 and the Longley-Rice model then, shortly thereafter in Annapolis, Maryland, with the Electronic Countermeasures and Compatibility (ECAC) Terrain Integrated Rough Earth Model (TIREM). These first terrestrial models worked well between 20 MHz and 400 MHz in the land mobile radio services for base stations separated by tens of miles, with the mobile user always being in the far radiation field of a given station. Use of these models continued through the 1980s up to cellular systems at 800-900 MHz; however, the accuracy of these models began to fail as cellular stations became closer together (two-four miles apart). These models are even used today in some application software, although, there is little scientific justification for small-cell design at 1900 MHz in the personal communication service (PCS)

Computer simulation dramatically changed in the early 1980s. The character of terrestrial radio science began to change, in large part by the large demand for predictions brought on by cellular radio, and also by advances in computing technology making sophisticated computing practical for small groups of people.

The new needs of interference-limited cellular systems (rather than noise-limited regional systems) and new performance characteristics (BER and system capacity) still required propagation modeling, but there became a need for a new viewpoint of propagation. There was also a need to provide telecommunications professionals and computer programmers, rather than only experienced radio scientists, with simple simulation tools. This allowed a large number of rather unsophisticated practitioners to use and implement many networks quickly and economically.

An answer for a simpler propagation analysis view came in 1980 from M. Hata in his "Empirical Formula for Propagation Loss in Land Mobile Radio Services" [5]. The idea was that propagation could be represented graphically by one or more connected regression lines fit to measured data in distance away from a base station. Then, the computer could apply these over an area and also include a knife-edge diffraction calculation as well. Thus, along a radial path away from a base station, the location variations in the signal are averaged out, as is the spatial resolution afforded by the terrain due to terrain averaging.

The accuracy of predictions varies based on the type of radio propagation models used and the terrain information supplied to it. A well-performing and calibrated model can be expected to deliver a 9-14 dB standard deviation compared to accurate measurements with a spatial resolution of 200 meters (even with 30-meter terrain data) computed on a deterministic basis. The true signal location variability, typically in the 6-7 dB sigma range, is much less than the spatial accuracy of empirical modeling. This leads to the higher-order statistics of empirical modeling expanding without limit, making only median or mean computer simulations practical.

In the 2000s, the majority of propagation predictions are made (after extensive calibration of simple models with test data) using the "empirical method." And the very concept of predictive modeling not requiring such extensive calibration has been lost to both a generation of scientists and a generation of network developers.

It has been shown that the use of physical-optics theory in modeling can be applied to propagation simulation to produce more accurate modeling. In parallel with the rapid expansion of empirical modeling (and computerized planning tools using them), a modern physical-optics theory employs the Fresnel-Kirchoff method advanced by J.H. Whitteker of the Canadian Research Centre (CRC). The theory, reduced to practice, was visible to the academic community due to a paper in Radio Science in 1990 and a paper presented at an U.R.S.I. conference in Austin Texas in 1994. The Fresnel-Kirchoff method using special integration routines developed at CRC has produced an accuracy sigma of 5 dB or less in suburban morphologies using 30-meter terrain data and 250-meter clutter data. Of this 5 dB, orthogonal error components of temporal and algorithmic quantization error are estimated to be just over 3 dB each. The theory has been validated against a standard set of U.S. government measured data [the R data] and by network design in a growing number of applications.

The value of predictive network planning and design includes eliminating the costly implementation delays of test calibration. Predictive models are continually improving and the limit in accuracy (spatial resolution) has not been reached. It is expected to improve even more once high-resolution clutter and terrain data becomes the standard for use.

All wireless networks except those in very rural areas are interference-limited; that is, the success of communicating depends on the ratio of signal carrier to interference (and/or noise), generically called C/I, rather than on just the signal envelope C level alone. A statistical interference analysis computing the joint probability of interference of all chosen sectors for co-channel (or co-carrier) operation is needed. As a result, most propagation analysis tools include a C/I metric for the type of technology is available for analysis.

These new simulation tools have sufficient spatial accuracy to permit forward projections of network performance with increasing traffic load using simulation algorithms. An accurate prediction engine and a statistical interference engine are requisites for network performance simulation, The interference engine produces statistically significant results in the 95 percentile or greater range. The simulation process must provide for the interfering effects of traffic loading at a minimum, on a per-sector average basis.

Consider CDMA technology as an example. IS-95 CDMA is limited in performance in the forward (base-to-mobile) link, and the basic forward-link C/I metric is Ec/Io…the reference pilot channel signal level to the total interference, including self-interference of the multiple code-division channels appearing as broadband noise on the pilot "carrier." Preset (static) thresholds of Ec/Io determine the number of sectors (pilots) to be considered for soft handoff between nearby cell sectors and softer handoff between same-cell sectors.

The object of CDMA simulation is to maximize the network capacity under traffic load. This is accomplished by selecting proper initial site locations, heights, and antennas/orientations initially via computer optimization; then, postlaunch, to anticipate by forward projection when network additions (more sectors, carriers, or sites) are needed.

CDMA capacity is determined by how well traffic centers are targeted (cells close to traffic locations), how many sectors allocate a channel for each call (sectors per user in soft/softer handoff), and by the polluting effects of other pilots that are not contributing to handoff. The network is also assessed by how well it handles the available spatial traffic load. This includes coverage under loaded conditions as well. The capacity (albeit, sectors per user) of a well-designed CDMA network will vary only a little under the dynamics of traffic loading.

Figure 8.18 shows the true shape of a sector coverage core area, and of detached "rogue" coverage areas contributing generally to pilot pollution, far short of the largely circular "pie-shaped" sectors computed from terrain-averaged empirical models.

There are new simulation issues with regard to 3G implementation. Third generation systems are more complicated due to forward power control, turbo-coding improvements, and higher spectral efficiency with mode codes being available. In urban areas, the spatial resolution required will increase to the practical limitation of the computing machinery. Most certainly, 10-meter urban terrain and clutter resolutions are needed within the early 2000s, and 3-5 meter resolutions will be required before 2004 for 3G realistic simulations.

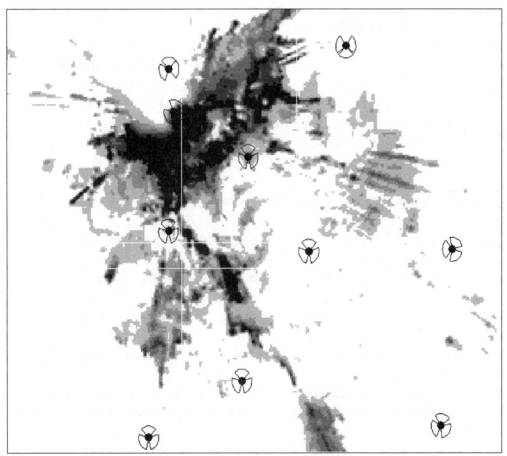

Figure 8.18. Sector Coverage Area (from Athena RF Propagation Tool).
Source: Wave Concepts International, Inc

The future of computed performance simulation to aid network capacity determination and network planning is expected to be much greater than the current use for initial implementation only. This is because the network operational performance is becoming more complex and also is becoming increasingly "unknowable" by practitioners due to the shear volume of data. The propagation simulation of performance must be placed on a scientific credible plane, and even the spatial resolution of these new predictive models must be improved in concert with the technology advances.

System Testing and Optimization

System testing and optimization is a process that measures the quality of the network and adjusts it to perform at maximum efficiency and quality. Specially designed software and hardware is used for test and analysis. Vehicles are loaded with test equipment and are driven through the coverage area to test the network quality. Data is collected on these drive tests and reviewed. The factors that are evaluated and their definitions include:

Forward Channel Signal Strength: The received power in the forward link channel.
Forward Frame Error Rate (FFER): The percentage of the forward transmitted frames that are corrupted.
Reverse Frame Error Rate (RFER): The percentage of the reverse transmitted frames that are corrupted.
Reverse Transmitted Power: The total power that the phone is transmitting. Forward and Reverse FER (Frame Error Rate).
Ec/Io: The CDMA signal quality defined as the CDMA chip energy divided by the present interference.
Soft Handoff Rate: The percentage of time a mobile participates in soft handoff.
Dropped Calls: The number of times the network drops communication with the mobile.

Areas of poor network performance are identified, and adjustments are implemented to fix the problems. These adjustments can include antenna changes, antenna tilting, antenna reorientation, or adjustment to a number of system parameters. The system is then tested again to ensure that the adjustments fixed the problems, without creating any new ones. This process is repeated until the network performs to the service provider's specifications.

System Expansion

As the number of UMTS service subscribers grows, the network must also grow to accommodate their additional traffic requirements. There are several options that can be considered when expanding the capacity of an existing network. These options include cell splitting and carrier addition. Cell splitting is making multiple new cell sites to aid an existing cell handle its traffic loading. Figure 8.19 depicts how cell splitting works.

First, the existing cell is altered to reduce its coverage area (lowering the amount of power or using directional antennas). One or more new cell sites are built to cover the areas that are not being covered by the altered existing cell site. The other typical solution to capacity problems is adding an additional carrier. Another frequency channel is deployed using the same cell site design. To use this method, you must own the license for additional frequency.

Intelligent Network

System features are usually sold as software modules. Adding system features (e.g., three-way calling) usually requires a download of new software. Ideally, this is easily done and is always backward compatible. As systems change and new, unskilled operators replace experienced ones, downloading and installing new features can be challenging. Carriers often desire to add unique features to better compete against their rivals. These features can be developed using customized applications for mobile network enhanced logic (CAMEL) or wireless

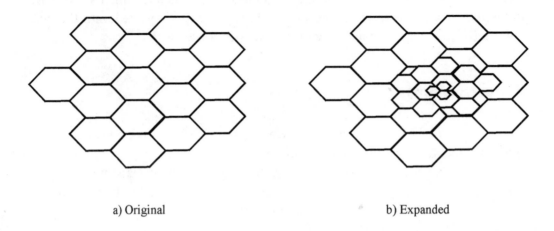

a) Original   b) Expanded

Figure 8.19. Cell Splitting.

intelligent network (WIN). CAMEL is an industry standard that uses the SS7 MAP to implement advanced features. WIN is an industry standard that allow carriers to implement new features and capabilities as needed by using IS-41 intersystem signaling.

Customized Applications for Mobile Network Enhanced Logic (CAMEL)

Applications that operate on a "services creation node" in a WCDMA or GSM network use CAMEL. CAMEL allows a network operator to develop specialized services using advanced intelligent network (AIN) systems.

CAMEL allows an operator to create a virtual home environment for the subscribers. As they use their mobile phone in different systems, the advanced features will continue to operate in a similar manner. This includes voice mail access and call forwarding features that could require that different or unusual access codes would be automatically converted using CAMEL signaling.

Call detection points (DP) identify possible transitions in call states (e.g., call initiation, special feature access request). The detection points are triggers that can request events. They may inform the home system of a special event and cause call processing at the remote location to be suspended during the modification of call processing. When the home system determines the correct sequence of operations for the call (e.g., add a string of access codes to a voice mail request), the call processing can be resumed with the new steps in place.

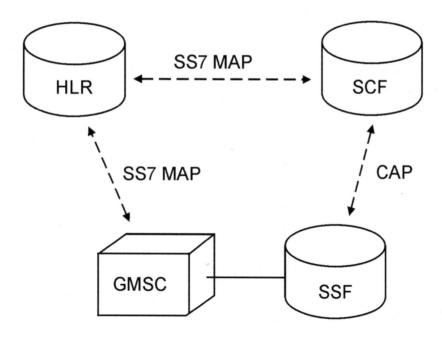

Figure 8.20. Customized Applications for Mobile network Enhanced Logic (CAMEL).

There are two key elements in the CAMEL system: the service control function (SCF) and the service switching function. The protocol between these functions is called the CAMEL applications part (CAP). The SSF holds features that are unique to the carrier (outside the normal UMTS feature set). The SCF contains the call processing steps for the advanced features. Figure 8.20 shows the key functional elements of the CAMEL system.

References

1 . CTIA Winter Exposition, "Disaster Experiences," Reno, Nevada, February 6, 1990.

2 . William Lee, "Mobile Cellular Telecommunications Systems," McGraw Hill, 1989, p.160.

3 . CTIA Winter Exposition, "Disaster Experiences," Reno Nevada, February 6, 1990.

4 . FCC Regulations, Part 22, Subpart K, "Domestic Public Cellular Radio Telecommunications Service," 22.903, (June 1981).

Chapter 9

Wireless Economics

Wireless telephone wholesale costs have dropped by approximately 20% per year over the past 7 to 10 years [1]. While the technology and mass production cost reductions for wireless telephones and systems are mature, new 3rd generation digital wireless telephones and systems are more complex. 3rd generation system equipment uses the same basic infrastructure as 2nd generation systems.

The economic goal of a wireless network system is to effectively serve many customers at the lowest possible cost. The ability to serve customers is determined by the capacity of the wireless system. Two key factors are used in determining the capacity of the system: the size of the cell sites and the spectral efficiency of the radio channels. When using any radio access technology, system capacity is increased by the addition of smaller cell site coverage areas, which allows more radio channels to be reused in a geographic area. If the number of cell sites remains constant, the efficiency of the radio access technology (e.g., the number of users that can share a single radio channel) determines the system capacity.

Wireless service providers usually strive to balance the system capacity with the needs of the customers. Running systems over their maximum capacity results in blocked calls to the customer, while running systems that have excess capacity results in the purchase of system equipment that is not required, which increases cost. Any wireless system (including analog cellular) can be designed for very high capacity through the use of very small cell site geographic coverage areas.

The objective of 3rd generation digital wireless systems are to achieve more cost-effective service capacity than 2nd generation systems. This is achieved by using techniques such as improved channel coding, efficient packet transmission, lower average data transfer rates through improved voice compression technology.

Purchasing and maintaining wireless system equipment is only a small portion of the cost of a wireless system. Administration, leased facilities, and tariffs may play significant roles in the success of cellular systems.

The wireless marketplace is undergoing a change. New service providers, such as specialized mobile radio (SMR) and personal communications service (PCS) carriers, are entering into the marketplace. This is likely to increase wireless services competition. Sales and distribution channels are becoming clogged with a variety of wireless product offerings. Advanced wireless digital technologies offer a variety of new features that may increase the total potential market and help service providers to compete. These new features may offer added revenue and provide a way to convert customers to more advanced digital services. The same digital radio channels that provide voice services also offer advanced messaging and multimedia applications.

Wireless Telephone Costs

The cost of 3rd generation digital mobile telephones is due to the following primary factors: development cost, production cost, patent royalty cost, marketing, postsales support, and manufacturer profit. Third generation mobile telephones are more complex than their 2nd generation cousins are. However, due to the economy of scale offered by mass production, it is expected that the cost of 3rd generation mobile telephones will eventually be similar to the cost of 2nd generation mobile telephones.

The average wholesale cost of analog mobile telephones (AMPS) has dropped from $307 in 1992 to approximately $104 in 1996 [2]. The initial cost of 2nd generation digital mobile telephones was 200% higher than the same size analog in 1992 [3]. By 2000, the average cost of single-band (single frequency) digital mobile telephones was only slightly higher than equivalent size analog telephones [4]. Although the introductory cost of 3rd generation mobile telephones in 2001 is more than 200% higher than 2nd generation digital mobile telephones, it is likely that the wholesale cost will rapidly decrease until they reach prices equivalent to similar size 2nd generation wireless telephones.

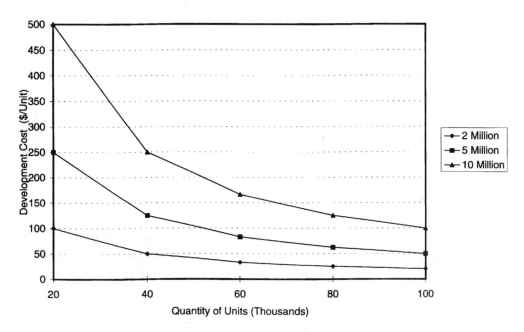

Figure 9.1. Mobile Telephone Development Cost.

Development Costs

Development costs are nonrecurring costs that are required to research, design, test, and produce a new product. Unlike well-established analog or 2nd generation digital technology, nonrecurring engineering (NRE) development costs for 3rd generation digital wireless telephones can be high, due to the added complexity of digital design. Several companies have spent millions of dollars developing digital wireless products.

Figure 9.1 shows how the nonrecurring development cost per unit varies as the quantity of production varies from 20,000 to 100,000 units. Even small development costs become a significant challenge if the volume of production of the digital wireless telephones is low (below 20,000 units). At this small production volume, NRE costs will be a high percentage of the wholesale price.

The introduction of a new technology presents many risks in terms of development costs. Some product development costs that need to be considered include: market research; technical trials and evaluations; industrial, electrical, and software design; prototyping; product and FCC testing; creation of packaging, brochures, user and service manuals; marketing promotion; sales and customer service training; industry standards participation; unique test equipment development; plastics tooling; special production equipment fabrication; and overall project coordination.

Using a reduced number of customized electronics components (custom integrated circuits) usually produces cost-effective product designs. To save product development time and reduce risk of developing completely new products (new generation of technology), companies may use readily available components. Custom integrated-circuit chip development is used to integrate many components into one low-cost part. Excluding the technology development effort, custom application specific integrated circuit (ASIC) development typically requires a development setup cost that ranges from $250,000 to $500,000. There may be more than one ASIC used in a digital wireless telephone.

Cost of Production

The cost to manufacture a mobile telephone includes the component parts (bill of materials), automated factory assembly equipment, and human labor. Digital wireless telephones are more complex than the older analog units. A digital mobile telephone is composed of a radio transceiver and a digital signal processing section. The primary hardware assemblies that affect the component cost for digital mobile telephones are digital signal processors (DSPs) and radio frequency assemblies. A single DSP, and several may be used, may cost between $15 and $28 [5]. The radio frequency (RF) assemblies used in digital wireless telephones often include more precise linear amplifiers and fast switching fre-

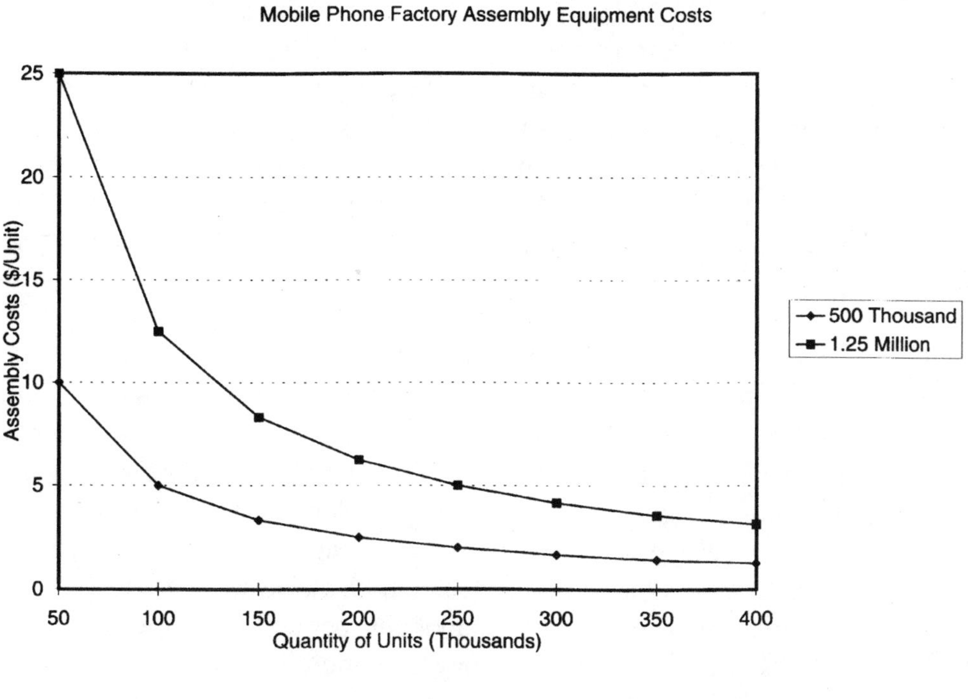

Mobile Phone Factory Assembly Equipment Costs

Figure 9.2. Factory Assembly Equipment Cost.

quency synthesizers. These RF components cost approximately $15-30. Other components that are included in the production of a mobile telephone include printed circuit boards, integrated circuits and electronic components, radio frequency filters, connectors, plastic case, a display assembly, a keypad, a speaker and microphone, and an antenna assembly. In 2001, the bill of materials (parts) for a 3rd generation digital mobile telephone was approximately $100 [6].

The assembly of wireless telephones requires a factory with automated assembly equipment. Each production line can cost between two and five million dollars. Typically, one production line can produce a maximum of 500-2,000 units per day (150,000-600,000 units per year). The number of units that can be produced per day depends on the speed of the automated component insertion machines and the number of components to be inserted. Typically, production lines are often shut down one day per week for routine maintenance and two weeks per year for major maintenance overhauls, which leaves about 300 days per year for the manufacturing line to produce products. Between interest cost (10-15% per year) and depreciation (10-15% per year), the cost to own such equipment is approximately 25% per year. This results in a production facility overhead of $500,000 to $1,250,000 per year for each production line. Figure 9.2 shows how the cost per unit drops dramatically from approximately $10-25 per unit to $1-3 per unit as volume increases from 50,000 units to 400,000 units per year.

While automated assembly is used in factories for the production of mobile telephones, there are some processes that require human assembly. Efficient assembly of a mobile telephone in a modern factory requires 1/2 to 1 hour of human labor. The amount of human labor is a combination of all workers involved with the plant, including administrative workers and plant managers. The average loaded cost of labor (wages, vacation, insurance) varies from approximately $20 to $40 per hour, which is based on the location of the factory and the average skill set of human labor. This results in a labor cost per unit that varies from $10-40. Because digital wireless telephones may have more parts to assemble due to the added complexity, the labor cost may increase.

Patent Royalty Cost

Another significant cost factor to be considered is patent royalties. Several companies have disclosed that they believe they have some proprietary technology that is required to implement the 3rd generation systems. Prior to the creation of the 3rd generation standards, companies agreed to fairly license the 3rd generation technology to other companies participating in the standards development process.

Some large manufacturing companies exchange the right to use their patented technology with other companies that have patented technology they want to use. As for manufacturers who do not exchange patent rights, in 1995, the combined royalties for IS-54 TDMA digital cellular phones was up to $70 per unit, and the combined royalties for IS-95 digital cellular phones was up to $100 per unit for companies that did not have cross-licensing agreements [7]. In addition to essential patents to implement 3rd generation technology that have been identified, patents from other companies may be desirable or essential to implement the standard specifications may not have been discovered or disclosed. Companies may discover that their products infringe patents after they are produced. Patent licensing costs can add substantial cost to the product.

Marketing Cost

Product marketing costs for wireless telephones include direct sales staff personnel, commissions to manufacturer's representatives, advertising costs, trade show fees, and support for industry seminars.

Wireless telephone manufacturers typically dedicate a highly paid representative or agents for key customers. Much as with the sales of other consumer electronics products, manufacturers employ several technical salespeople to answer a variety of technical questions prior to the sale.

There are wireless telephone manufacturers that use independent distributors to sell their products. This practice is more prevalent for smaller, lesser-known manufacturers who cannot afford to maintain sales staff who are dedicated to specific customers. These representatives typically receive up to 4% of the sales volume for their services.

Advertising programs used by the wireless telephone manufacturers involve broad promotion for brand recognition and advertisements targeted for specific products. The budget for brand recognition advertising typically ranges from less then 1% to over 4%. Product-specific advertising is often performed through cooperative advertising, which involves dedicating a percentage of the sales invoice (typically 2-4%) as an advertising allowance. When the advertising allowance meets the manufacturers' requirements, the allowance is paid back to the customer. This approach allows customers to determine the best type of advertising for their specific markets. The typical advertising budget for mobile telephone manufacturers varies from approximately 3% to 6%.

Cellular system manufacturers exhibit at trade shows, typically three to four times per year. Trade show costs are high. Cellular mobile telephone manufacturers exhibiting at trade shows typically have large trade show booths, gifts, and theme entertainment. To staff the trade show booth, wireless telephone manufacturers often bring 15 to 40 sales and engineering experts to a show to answer customers questions. Manufacturers often sponsor medium to large hospitality parties at the trade shows to allow existing and potential customers to meet with their staff in an informal environment.

To help promote the industry and gain publicity, wireless telephone manufacturers participate in a variety of industry seminars and associations. The manufacturers typically have a few select employees who write for magazines and speak at industry seminars.

All of these costs and others result in an estimated marketing cost for mobile telephone manufacturers of more than 15 percent of the wholesale selling price.

Postsales Support

The sale of cellular mobile telephones involves a variety of costs and services after the sale of the product, including warranty servicing, customer service, and training. Third generation products may involve multiple accessories such as computer interfaces and other intelligent devices. This added complexity is likely to increase the effort (and cost) for postsales support.

A customer service department is required for handling distributor and customer product related questions. Because the average customer for a wireless telephone is not technically trained in radio technology, the number of nontechnical questions can be significant. Fortunately, customer questions can typically be answered during normal business hours.

Distributors and retailers require training for product feature operation and servicing. The postsales support cost for wireless telephones is typically between 4 to 6%.

Manufacturers Profit

Manufacturers must make a profit as an incentive for producing products. The amount of profits a manufacturer can make typically depends on the risk involved with the manufacturing of products. As a general rule, the higher the risk, the higher the percentage of profit margin.

The wireless telephone market in the 1990s became very competitive due to the manufacturers' ability to reduce cost through mass production. To effectively compete, manufacturers had to invest in factories and technology, which increased the risk and the required profit margin. In 1995, the estimated gross profit in the wireless telephone manufacturing industry was 15 to 35% [8]. By 2001, several leading wireless telephone manufacturing companies were losing money.

System Equipment Costs

The cost for wireless system equipment is due to the following primary factors: development costs, production costs, patent royalty cost, marketing cost, post-sales support, and manufacturer profit.

Development Costs

These wireless network system equipment development costs are much higher than wireless telephone development costs. When a completely new technology is introduced, wireless network system development costs can exceed $500 million because the complexity of an entire wireless system is significantly greater than a mobile telephone. This is because there are many more assemblies in the network equipment, and significant testing and validation is required. Fortunately, 3rd generation systems can use most of the 2nd generation network equipment. This will reduce the overall cost of network development

Although base station radios perform similar tasks as a wireless telephone, the coordination of all the wireless telephones involves many additional electronic subsystems. Additional assemblies include communication controllers in the base station and switching center, scanning locating receivers, communication adapters, switching assemblies, and large databases to hold subscriber features and billing information. All of these assemblies require hardware and very complex software.

Unlike mobile telephones, when a wireless system develops a problem, the entire system can be affected. New hardware and features require extensive testing. Testing cellular systems can require thousands of hours of labor by highly skilled professionals. Introducing a new technology is much more complex than adding a single new feature.

Production Costs

It would appear that the physical hardware cost for 3rd generation wireless network system equipment should be more expensive than analog or 2nd generation network system equipment due to the added technological complexity. However, the physical hardware cost for digital network system equipment may actually be less than older analog equipment. This is a result of more standardized equipment, a more competitive market, and economies of scale.

The costs to manufacture a wireless network system include the component parts, automated factory equipment, and human labor. The number of wireless network system assemblies produced is much smaller than the number of wireless telephones. Setting up automated factory equipment is time consuming. For small production runs, much more human labor is used in the production of assemblies because setting up the automated assembly is not practical. The production of system equipment does involve a factory with automated assembly equipment for specific assemblies. However, because the number of units produced for system equipment is typically much smaller than wireless telephones, production lines used for cellular system equipment are often shared for the production of different assemblies, or remain idle for periods of time.

With over 200 countries developing and expanding their wireless systems, the demand for wireless system equipment is increasing exponentially. This increased demand allows for larger production runs, which reduce the average cost per unit. Large production runs also permit investment in cost-effective designs, such as using application-specific integrated circuits (ASICs) to replace several individual components.

Third generation systems have defined standardized interfaces between system equipment. This allows many different manufacturers to develop specific parts of the wireless system without having to develop all the different types of wireless network system components. It is possible in the 3rd generation wireless system for one manufacturer to supply the cellular system base station control equipment and another manufacturer to supply the base station radios. The ability for a manufacturer to focus on the high demand components without a large development investment increases competition and reduces prices to the wireless system customer.

Advanced digital technology is creating cost reductions through the use of cost-effective equipment design and low-cost commercially available electronic components. In the early 1990s, many technical system equipment changes were required due to changes in radio specifications. Manufacturers had to modify their equipment based on field test results. For example, complex echo cancellers were required due to the long delay time associated with digital speech compression. Manufacturers typically did not invest in cost-effective custom designs because of the rapid changes. As the technology has matured, the investment in custom designs is possible with less risk. In the early 1990s, it was also unclear which digital technologies would become commercially viable, which limited the availability of standard components. Today, the success of digital systems has created a market of low-cost digital signal processors and RF components for digital cellular systems.

Like the assembly of wireless telephones, the assembly of system radio and switching equipment involves a factory with automated assembly equipment. The primary difference is the smaller production runs, multiple assemblies, and more complex assembly.

The number of equipment units that are produced is much smaller than the number of mobile telephones produced because each radio channel produced can serve 20-32 subscribers. The result is much smaller production runs for wireless network system equipment. While a single production line can produce a maximum of 500-2,000 assemblies per day [9], several different assemblies for radio base stations are required. A change in the production line from one assembly process to another can take several hours or several days. Wireless system radio equipment requires a variety of different connectors, bulky RF radio parts, and large equipment case assemblies. Due to the low-production volumes and many unique parts, it is not usually cost effective to use automatic assembly equipment. For unique parts, there are no standard automatic assembly units available.

Because of this more complex assembly and the inability to automate many assembly steps, the amount of human labor is much higher than for wireless telephones.

Each automated production line can cost two to five million dollars. The number of units that can be produced per day on each production line varies. It primarily depends on the speed of the automated component insertion machines, the number of components to be inserted, the number of different electronic assemblies per equipment, and the amount of time it takes to change/setup the production line for different assemblies. If we assume there are four electronic assemblies per base station radio equipment (e.g., controller, RF section, baseband/diagnostic processing section, and power supply), the automated production cost for base station equipment should be over four times that of mobile telephones.

Figure 9.3 shows how the production cost per unit drops dramatically from approximately $400-1,000 per unit to $50-125 per unit as the volume of production increases from 5,000 units per year to 40,000 units per year. This chart assumes production cost is four times that of wireless telephones due to the added complexity and the use of multiple assemblies.

While automated assembly is used in factories for the production of wireless telephones, there are some processes that require human assembly. Efficient assembly of base station units in a modern factory requires between 5 and 10 hours of human labor. The amount of human labor includes all types of workers from administrative workers to plant managers. The average loaded cost of labor (wages, vacation, insurance) varies from approximately $20-40 per hour, which is based on the location of the factory and average workers skill set. The resultant labor cost per unit varies from $100-400, and there may be several units per network assembly.

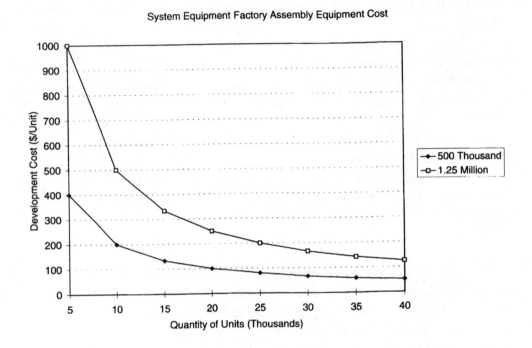

Figure 9.3. Factory Assembly Equipment Cost.

Patent Royalty Cost

There are only a few large manufacturers that produce wireless network system equipment due to the fact that the use of many different technologies is involved. Large manufacturers have a portfolio of patents that are commonly traded. Cross-licensing is common and tends to reduce the cost of patent rights. When patent licensing is required, the patent costs are sometimes based on the whole-sale price of the assemblies in which the licensed technology is used.

Marketing Cost

The marketing costs that are included in the wholesale cost of wireless system equipment include direct sales staff, sales engineers, advertising, trade shows, and industry seminars. Wireless system manufacturers often dedicate several highly paid representatives for key customers. Wireless system sales are much more technical than the sale of wireless telephones. Manufacturers employ several people to answer a variety of technical questions prior to the sale.

Advertising used by the cellular system equipment manufacturers involves broad promotion for brand recognition and advertisements targeted for specific products. The budget for brand recognition advertising is typically small (on the basis of the percentage of sales) and is targeted to specific communication channels because the sale of wireless system equipment involves only a small group of people who typically work for a wireless service provider. Product-specific advertising is also limited to industry specific trade journals. Much of the advertising promotion of wireless system equipment occurs at trade shows, industry associations, and on-site client presentations. The advertising budget for wireless system equipment manufacturers is typically less than 2%.

Wireless system manufacturers exhibit at trade shows typically three to four times per year. The trade shows costs for system manufacturers are usually much higher than the trade shows costs for wireless telephone manufacturers. Wireless system equipment manufacturers exhibiting at trade shows often have large hospitality parties that sometimes entertain thousands of people. Wireless system manufacturers often bring 60-100 sales and engineering experts to the trade shows to answer customer questions.

To help promote the industry and gain publicity, wireless system manufacturers participate in many industry seminars and associations. These manufacturers use trained experts to present at industry seminars.

All of these costs and others result in an estimated marketing cost for system equipment manufacturers of approximately 8-10% of the wholesale selling price.

Postsales Support

The sale of wireless systems involves a variety of costs and services after the sale of the product. This includes warranty service, customer service, and operation training. A 24-hour customer service department is required for handling customer questions. Customers require a significant amount of training for product operation and maintenance after a system is sold and installed. The postsales support costs for wireless system equipment is typically 3-5%.

Manufacturer Profit

Standardization of systems and components, particularly GSM, has led to a rapid drop in the wholesale price of system equipment. While the increased product volume of wireless system equipment has resulted in decreased manufacturing costs, the gross profit margin for wireless system equipment has decreased. The estimated gross profit in the wireless system equipment manufacturing industry is 10-15% [10].

Network Capital Costs

The wireless service provider's investment in network equipment includes cell sites, base station radio equipment, switching centers, and network databases. One of the primary objectives of the new technologies was to decrease the network cost per customer, which was made possible because the new technologies can serve more customers with less physical equipment.

In theory, existing analog cellular technology can serve almost an unlimited number of subscribers in a designated area by replacing large cell site areas with many microcells (small cell coverage areas). However, expanding the current analog systems in this way increases the average capital cost per subscriber due to the added cost of increasing the number of small cells and interconnection lines to replace a single large cell. For example, when cell sites with a 1/2-km radius replace a cell site with a 15-km radius, it will take over 700 small cells to cover the same area.

One of the reasons that digital cellular technologies were developed was to allow for cost-effective capacity expansion. Cost-effective capacity expansion results when existing cell sites can offer more communication channels, which allows more customers to be served by the same cell site. As systems based on such new technologies expand, the average cost per subscriber decreases.

Cell Site

The cell site is composed of a radio tower, antennas, a building, radio channels, system controllers, and a backup power supply. The cell site radio tower is typically 100-300 feet tall. The cost ranges between $30,000 and $300,000. While some of the largest towers can cost $300,000, an average cost of $70,000 is typical because, as systems expand, smaller towers can be used.

Many cell sites can be located on a very small area of land that is either purchased or leased. In some cases, existing tower space can be leased for $500-$1,000 per month. If the land is purchased, the estimated cost of the land is approximately $100,000.

A building on the cell site property is required to store the cell site radio equipment. This building is usually bulletproof, has climate control, and may contain various other nonstandard options. The estimated building cost is $40,000.

Cell sites are not usually located where high-speed telephone communication lines are available. Typically, it is necessary to install a T1 or E1 communications line to the cell site, which is leased from the local phone company. If a microwave link is used in place of a leased communication line, the communications line installation cost will be applied to the installation of the microwave antenna. The estimated cost of installing a T1 or E1 communications line is approximately $5,000.

The land where the cell site is to be located must be cleared, foundations poured, fencing installed, building and tower installed. A construction cost of $50,000 is estimated. Figure 9.4 shows the estimated cost for a typical cell site without the radio equipment.

Item	Cost x $1,000's
Radio Tower	$70
Building	$40
Land	$100
Install Comm Line	$5
Construction	$50
Antennas	$10
Backup Power Supply	$10
Total	$285

Figure 9.4. Estimated Cell Site Capital Cost Without Radio Equipment.

In addition to the tower and building cost, radio equipment must be purchased. The cost of the radio equipment usually varies based on technology and the number of customers that use the system.

After the total investment of each cell site is determined, the cell site capital cost per customer can be determined by dividing the total cell site cost by the number of subscribers that will share the resource (cell site). Because not everyone uses every radio channel at the same time, cellular systems typically add 20-32 subscribers per voice channel. For the different cellular technologies, each RF channel can supply one or more individual voice paths (may be a data channel). The number of radio channels per cell site multiplies the number of voice paths per radio channel. If 20 subscribers are added to the system for each voice path, the average number of subscribers per cell site varies from 1,000 to 18,000. This means a wireless system operator that has 500,000 customers requires between 500 sites (for analog) and only 27 sites (for 3rd generation).

Figure 9.5 shows a sample of system equipment costs as digital technology evolves. In column 1, we see analog FM technology that supports one voice channel per radio carrier. Because each subscriber will only access the cellular system for a few minutes each day, approximately 20 subscribers (customers) can share the service of a single radio channel. Narrowband AMPS (NAMPS) radio channels also provide one voice channel per carrier. The advantage of NAMPS is that more channels can be placed in each cell site. This is possible because the radio channels are one-third the width of 30 kHz AMPS channels. This increases the total number of subscribers per cell site to approximately 3,060. For the IS-54/IS-136 system, each RF channel supports up to three users (full rate), so each RF channel cost can be shared by 60 subscribers. For the IS-95 CDMA system, each RF channel supports approximately 20 users, so each RF channel cost can be shared by up to 400 subscribers. For GSM, each RF channel can provide service to eight simultaneous users. This allows up to 160 subscribers to share the radio channel cost. The WCDMA system allows approximately 100 full-rate (8 kbps) customers per radio channel. This means approximately 2,000 customers share the cost of a single WCDMA channel.

	AMPS/ ETACS	NAMPS	IS-54/IS-136 TDMA	IS-95 CDMA	GSM	WCDMA
Cost per RF Radio Channel (includes channel speech coders)	10,000	10,000	15,000	45,000	15,000	100,000
Number of Radio Channels per Cell Site (3 sector), assume 12.5 MHz	51	153	51	24	30	9
Total Radio Channel Cost	510,000	1,530,000	765,000	1,080,000	450,000	900,000
Tower and Building Cost	285,000	285,000	285,000	285,000	285,000	285,000
Total Cell Site Cost	795,000	1,815,000	1,050,000	1,365,000	735,000	1,185,000
Number of Voice Paths per Radio Channel	1	1	3	20(est)	8	100
Number of Voice Paths per Cell Site	51	153	153	480	240	900
Number of Subscribers per Voice Channel	20	20	20	20	20	20
Number of Subscribers per Cell Site	1020	3060	3060	9600	4800	18,000
Cell Site Capital Cost per Subscriber	$779	$593	$343	$142	$153	$66

Figure 9.5. Cell Site Capital Cost per Subscriber.

While it is not suggested that all of the available RF channels can be converted to digital channels within the system, the following table shows target costs that project the reasonable costs of a different cellular systems.

The multiplexing of several radio channels through one RF equipment reduces the number of required RF equipment assemblies, power consumption, and system-cooling requirements. Multiplexing in this way typically reduces cell site size and backup power supply (generator and battery) requirements and, ultimately, lowers the total cost.

Mobile Switching Center

Cell sites must be connected to an intelligent switching system (called the switch). An estimate of $25 per subscriber, used for the cellular switch equipment and its accessories, is based on one mobile switching center (MSC) costing $2.5 million that can serve up to 100,000 customers.

The switching center must be located in a long-term location (10-20 years) near a local exchange carrier (LEC) public switched telephone network (PSTN) central office connection. The building contains the switching and communication equipment. Commonly, a customer database called the home location register (HLR) is located in the main switching center. Large systems that have several MSCs only have one HLR. Each MSC has its own visitor location register (VLR). The VLR holds a list of all the active wireless telephones operating in its territory (both home customers and visiting customers). The switching center software and associated cellular system equipment typically contain basic software that allows normal mobile telephone operation (place and receive calls). Special software upgrades that allow advanced services are available at additional cost.

Operational Costs

The costs of operating a cellular system includes leasing and maintaining communication lines, local and long-distance tariffs, billing, administration (staffing), maintenance, and fraudulent use. The operational cost benefits of installing digital equipment includes a reduction in the total number of leased communication lines, a reduction in the number of cell sites, a reduction in maintenance costs, and a reduction of fraud due to advanced authentication procedures.

Leasing and Maintaining Communications Lines

Cell sites must be connected to the switching system by leased communication lines between radio towers, or by installing and maintaining microwave links between them. The typical cost for leasing a 24-channel line between cell sites in the United States in 1992 was $750/month [11]. Microwave radio equipment can cost from $20,000 to $100,000.

The number of subscribers that can share the cost of a communication line (loading of the line) varies with the type of service. For cellular-like subscribers who typically use the phone for two minutes per day, approximately 480 customers can share a T1 (20 subscriber per voice path x 24 voice paths per communication line) or 600 customers per E1 (20 subscribers per voice path x 30 voice paths per communication line). For residential-type service, where customers use the phone for approximately 30 minutes per day, approximately 120 customers can be loaded onto a T1 or 150 per E1. For office customers who use the phone for approximately 60 minutes per day, approximately 60 customers can be loaded onto a T1 or 75 for E1.

The monthly cost per subscriber is determined by dividing the monthly cost by the total number of subscribers. Figure 9.6 shows the estimated monthly cost for interconnection charges. The estimated monthly cost is based on 100% use of the communication lines. If the communication lines are not fully used (it is rare that communication lines are used at full capacity), the average cost per line increases.

Digital signal processing for all the proposed technologies allows for a reduction in the number of required communications links through the use of subrate multiplexing. Subrate multiplexing allows several users to share each 64K bit per second (kbps) communications (DS0/PCM) channel. This is possible because

Service	Line Cost per Month	No Chan	Load	Total Cost per Month
Cellular	750	24	20	1.56
LEC (residential)	750	24	5	6.25
Office	750	24	2.5	12.5

Figure 9.6. Monthly Communications Line Cost.

digital cellular voice information is compressed into a form much smaller than the existing communication channels. If 8-kbps speech information is subrate multiplexed, up to eight voice channels can be shared on a single 64-kbps channel, which can reduce the cost of leased lines significantly.

Local and Long-Distance Tariffs

Telephone calls in cellular systems are often connected to other local and long-distance telephone networks. When cellular systems are routed to existing land-line telephone customers, they are typically connected through the wired telephone network (usually via the local exchange company (LEC)). The local telephone company typically charges a small monthly fee and sometimes charges a usage fee of several cents per minute (approximately 1/2 to 3 cents per minute) for each line connected to the cellular carrier. Because each cellular subscriber uses the mobile telephone for only a few minutes per day, the cellular service provider can use a single connection (telephone line) to the PSTN to service hundreds of subscribers.

In the United States (and other countries that have separate long-distance service providers), when long-distance service is provided through a local telephone company (LEC), a tariff is paid from its cellular service provider to the local exchange company (LEC). These tariffs can be up to 45% of the per-minute long-distance charges. As a result of global telecommunications deregulation, wireless carriers may be permitted to bypass the LEC and not be required to pay the local interconnection tariffs.

Billing Services

Wireless system operators exist to provide services to customers and to collect revenue for those services. This involves billing systems that gather and distribute call charge information, organizing the charge information, producing invoices for the customer, and posting payments received from customers.

As customers initiate calls or use services, billing records are created. These records may be provided in the customer's home system or a visited system. Each billing record contains details of each billable call, including who initiated the call, where the call was initiated, the time and length of the call, and how the call was terminated. Each call record contains approximately 100-200 bytes of information [12]. If the calls and services are provided in the home system, the billing records can be stored in the company's own database. If they are provided in a visited system, the billing information must be transferred back to the home system.

Cellular systems are interconnected through a clearinghouse, which is used to accumulate and balance charges between different cellular service providers. Billing records from cellular systems are typically transferred via tape in a standard transferred accounting procedure (TAP) or cellular intercarrier billing exchange roamer (CIBER) format. These billing record formats contain information that is wireless-specific compared to the standard automatic message accounting (AMA) format that is used in traditional wired telephone systems.

In the 1990s, standard intersystem connection allowed billing records to be transferred automatically, which made advanced billing services such as advice of charging or debit account billing possible. Advice of charging provides the customer with an indication of the billing costs. Debit account billing allows a cellular service provider to accept a prepaid amount from a customer (perhaps a customer that has a poor credit rating) and decrease his or her account balance as calls are processed.

With the introduction of advanced services, billing issues continue to become more complicated. The service cost may vary between different systems. To overcome this difficulty, some service providers have agreed to bill customers at the billing rate established in their home system. In the United States, cellular digital packet data (CDPD) services are billed at the home subscriber's rate [13].

Each month, billing records must be totaled and printed for customer invoicing, invoices mailed, and checks received and posted. The estimated cost for billing services is $1-$3 per month. This billing cost includes routing and summarizing billing information, printing the bill, and the cost of mailing. To help offset the cost of billing, some wireless service providers have started to bundle advertising literature from other companies along with the invoice. To expedite the collection, some wireless service providers offer direct billing to bank accounts or charge cards.

Operations, Administration, and Maintenance

Running a wireless service company requires people with many different skill sets. Staffing requirements include executives, managers, engineers, sales, customer service, technicians, marketing, legal, finance, administrative, and other personnel to support vital business functions. The present staffing for local telephone companies is approximately 35 employees for each 10,000 customers. Wireless telephone companies have approximately 20-25 employees per 10,000 customers, and paging companies employ approximately 10 employees per 10,000 customers [14]. If we assume a loaded cost (salary, expenses, benefits, and facility costs) of $40,000 per employee, this results in a cost of $3.33 to $11.66 per month per customer ($40,000 x (10-35 employees)/10,000 customers/12 months).

Maintaining a wireless system requires calibration, repair, and testing. System growth involves radio coverage planning, testing, and system repair. Large wireless systems may have over 400 cell sites to maintain..

During the year, the geographic characteristics of a wireless system change (e.g., leaves fall off trees). This changes the radio coverage areas. Typically, a wireless carrier tests the radio signal strength in its entire system several times per year. Testing involves having a team of technicians drive throughout the system and record the signal strength.

Maintenance and repair of wireless systems is critical to the revenue of a wireless system. In large systems, several qualified technicians are kept on staff to perform routine testing. Smaller wireless systems often have an agreement with other wireless service providers or a system manufacturer to provide these technicians when needed. Wireless systems have automatic diagnostic capabilities to detect when a piece of equipment fails. Most wireless systems have an automatic backup system, which can provide service until the defective assembly is replaced.

Land and Site Leasing

In rural areas, exact locations for cell site towers are not required. The result is that the potentially high cost of leasing land in exact locations is not a significant problem. Several alternate sites may be considered. In urban areas and as systems mature, more exact locations for cell sites are required at sites that may be difficult to install and maintain. This generally results in increased land-leasing costs. By using a more efficient RF technology, fewer cell sites can be used to serve more customers.

Usually, leasing land for a cell site involves signing a long-term lease for a very small portion of land. The size of the land site may be 40-200 square meters, and the term may be for 20 years or longer. The cost of leasing land is dependent on location. Premium site locations such as sites on key buildings or in tunnels can exceed the gross revenue potential of the cell site.

Another option involves leasing space on an existing radio tower. Site leasing on an existing tower is approximately $500/month. Site leasing eliminates the requirement of building and maintaining a radio tower.

Cellular Fraud

It is estimated that cellular fraud in the United States during 1996 was in excess of $710 million [15]. This was approximately 3% of the $23.5 billion yearly gross revenue received [16]. Third generation wireless standards have the ability for advanced authentication capabilities which limits the ability to gain fraudulent access to the cellular network.

The type of cellular fraud has changed over the years. Initially, cellular fraud was subscription fraud. Subscription fraud occurs when a bandit registers a wireless telephone for service by using false identification. After a period of time, the bandit is sent bills that go unpaid, fraudulent activity is determined, and service is disconnected. Some cellular service providers now require valid identification and credit checks prior to service activation, which reduces subscription fraud.

As bandits learned more about wireless technology, the type of fraud has changed to access fraud. Access fraud is the unauthorized use of cellular service by changing or manipulating the electronic identification information stored inside of a mobile telephone.

In the mid-1980s, roamer fraud was possible. Roamer fraud occurs when a mobile telephone is programmed with an unauthorized telephone number and home system identifier so that it looks like a visiting customer. Because some of the cellular systems in the mid-1980s were not directly connected to each other, these systems could not immediately validate the visiting customer. In the 1990s, intersystem connection provides validation of the phone number, which limits (or eliminates) roamer fraud.

To allow fraudulent access to valid cellular customer accounts, criminals began to modify the electronic serial number (ESN) of mobile telephones to match a valid subscriber's ESN. This duplication of subscriber information is called "cloning." To enable the cloning process, mobile telephones have to be modified to accept a new ESN and a valid ESN must be acquired. ESNs are typically stored in a hard-to-get (secure) memory area of a mobile telephone. It typically takes a very technical person to be able to override the security system in the mobile telephone to modify the ESN. Obtaining valid ESNs is possible by reading the ESN on the label or using a commercially available test set that commands the mobile telephone to send its ESN. Cellular carriers are able to detect changing patterns of use when a cloned phone has been created. If the subscriber's billing account jumps dramatically, the cellular customer can be contacted to have his/her phone number changed. The original ESN is then marked invalid.

To overcome the barriers of ESNs becoming invalid, criminals designed their systems to change the ESN during each call. This changing ESN process, called "tumbling," uses valid ESNs that are prestored in the mobile telephone or captured from the radio channels during a valid subscriber's regular access. These valid ESNs are used by the modified mobile telephones either during each call or randomly each time they send or receive calls.

Most of these methods can be detected and blocked by the use of wireless telephone authentication information. Authentication is a process of using previously stored information to process keys that are transferred via the radio channel. Because the secret information is processed to create a key, the security information is not transferred on the radio channel. The secret information stored in the wireless telephone can be changed at random by either manual entry, the customer, or a command received from the wireless system. Authentication is supported in all of the digital technology specifications.

Marketing Considerations

The development of digital cellular technology allows cost-effective system capacity expansion and provides more revenues from advanced services. To obtain this cost savings and new feature service revenue, it is necessary to have a percentage of subscribers who have digital-capable equipment that can access the advanced technology. Second generation digital cellular marketing programs have focused on converting existing subscribers to digital service, enticing new customers to purchase digital over analog, and targeting new customers for advanced services. The key marketing factors that may determine the success of 3rd generation digital wireless includes the type of new services, system cost savings (carrier benefit), pricing of voice and data service (customer benefit), mobile telephone cost, consumer confidence, new features, retrofitting existing customer equipment, availability of equipment, and distribution channels.

Service Revenue Potential

At the beginning of 2001, there were over 700 million cellular telephone customers in the world [17]. The average cellular telephone bill is not much higher than the average wired residential telephone bill. The average usage charge per minute has not decreased much; however, the amount of usage has, because new customers entering into the market are consumers who do not use their wireless telephone very much.

The number of subscribers that operate on mobile wireless systems has been increasing by over 45% per year over the past five years [18]. Some of this growth is due to availability of new system service areas, reduction in the cost of service, and the decreased price of wireless telephones. It is not unreasonable to assume that a continued 45% yearly growth period for voice customers would exceed the total world population in only six years. However, the growth is actually in advanced services and nonhuman users (e.g., information services and electronic billboards).

The main revenue for wireless service providers has primarily been derived from providing voice telecommunications service. Digital wireless systems provide for increased service revenue that comes from a variety of sources such as advanced services and system cost reduction. Third generation wireless systems have broadband transmission capability to compete with wide area data networks, high-speed Internet access, and medium resolution video distribution (e.g., security monitoring).

System Cost to the Service Provider

One of the advantages of digital service is to allow more customers to share the same system equipment. Wireless system equipment costs account for approximately 10-15 % of the service provider's revenue. Digital wireless systems can offer a reduction of approximately 60% of system equipment cost per customer. Some of the advanced features of digital wireless (such as authentication to reduce fraud) also provide for reductions in operations, administration, and maintenance (OA&M) costs. These system cost reductions offered by digital wireless technology may be necessary to allow 3rd generation service providers to effectively compete against other wireless service providers. As more wireless companies (such as land mobile radio companies) begin to offer cellular-like services, the potential for a surplus of voice channel time exists.

Voice Service Cost to the Consumer

Over the past few years, the average cost of airtime usage to a cellular subscriber has been reduced by a significant amount. To help attract subscribers to migrate from 1st generation analog service to 2nd generation digital service, many cellular carriers have offered discounted airtime plans to high-usage customers with the requirement of using digital service. This discount provides a significant incentive to the high-usage customers. This same technique can be used by 3rd generation operators to convert 2nd generation customers to 3rd generation equipment and service. By shifting a small portion of these customers to 3rd generation digital service, the loading on the older analog radio channels and 2nd generation systems is reduced.

Data Service Cost to the Consumer

There are two types of data services that are available to customers: continuous (called circuit-switched data) or brief packets (called packet-switched data). Typically, continuous data transmission is charged at the same rate as voice transmission. Packet data transmission is often charged by the packet or by the total amount of data that has been transferred.

Circuit-switched data services are usually billed to the customer at the same rate as voice service. Packet data service can be billed by usage amount. A price of 7 to 23 cents per kilobyte of data is typical [19]. This results in an average cost to the customer of $3 to $10 per minute. The total revenue potential for packet data service is significantly higher than voice. The benefit to the customer is an over-all reduction in cost for transmission of small data packets. For example, an electronic credit card transaction requires approximately 200 bytes of data (0.2 kb). At a cost of 10 cents per kb, this would cost the subscriber approximately 2 cents. To process the credit card transaction by circuit-switched data, it would likely take 1-2 minutes of airtime (connection time). During most of the airtime usage, the equipment would be waiting for short messages to be passed between the bank and electronic credit card machine.

Wireless Telephone (Mobile Phone) Cost to the Consumer

In 1984-85, cellular mobile telephone prices varied from $2000-$2500 [20]. By 1991, you could get a free cellular phone with the purchase of a hamburger at selected Big Boy Restaurants in the United States [21]. One of the primary reasons for the continued penetration of the cellular market is the declining terminal equipment costs and stable airtime charges [22].

Wireless service providers often subsidize the sale of end-user telephones to help entice customers to subscribe to their service. This is called an "activation commission." As a result, wireless service providers do not usually anticipate revenues from the sale of basic telecommunications equipment. Some profit can be obtained from the sale of accessories such as extra batteries, portable hands-free kits. Many of the service providers are not concerned with the profit on wireless telephone equipment or accessories because their goal is to gain monthly service revenue.

To help introduce 3rd generation digital wireless telephones into the market-place, subsidies may be higher for 3rd generation digital wireless telephone equipment than 1st and 2nd generation wireless telephones. The wireless telephone service activation subsidy and the type of distribution channels used usually affects the retail price paid by the consumer. Figure 9.7 shows the wholesale mobile telephone cost in the United States over the past five years [23].

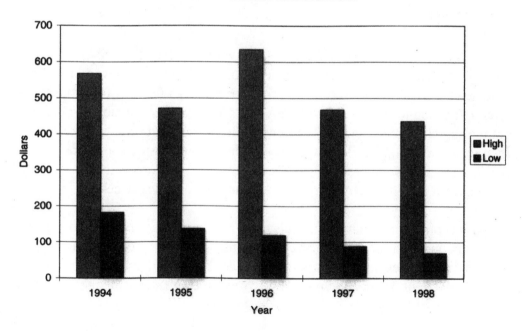

Figure 9.7. Wholesale Mobile Telephone Cost in the United States.
Source: Herschel Shosteck Associates, Wheaton, Maryland, USA

Consumer Confidence

To effectively deploy a new technology, the consumer must have confidence that the technology will endure. The next generation of wireless technology was required to be compatible the old and new systems to maintain this consumer confidence [24]. In most parts of the world, there are multiple digital technologies. These technologies offer different features, services, and radio coverage areas. Consumers must be willing to choose a technology that may not exist in future years. To help maintain consumer confidence, 3rd generation systems allow transfer to 2nd generation systems. Multimode wireless telephones will allow customers to maintain their confidence in 2nd generation systems while converting to new 3rd generation technology.

New Features

Customers purchase mobile telephones and wireless service based on their own value system, which estimates the benefits they will receive. New features provide new benefits to the consumer. These features can be used for product differentiation and to increase service revenue. New features available for 3rd generation digital wireless systems include multimedia capability, better access to Internet information services, high-speed data connections, and more reliable service. These new features may be used to persuade customers to convert to 3rd generation digital or to pay extra for these new advanced services.

While the first generation FM cellular telephone weighed over 80 pounds and required almost all the available vehicle trunk space. Second generation digital wireless telephones were only slightly larger than their analog predecessors were. The size of 3rd generation digital wireless telephones is likely to be similar to 2nd generation wireless telephones. Wireless telephone size continues to be reduced as production volumes allow for custom ASIC development, which integrates the analog and digital processing sections.

New features allow for different types of customers. With advanced data capabilities, cellular service may focus its products, services, and applications on nonhuman applications. Without a change in focus, wireless service providers could become limited to the voice services market that may eventually reach saturation.

Retrofitting

Retrofitting involves mobile telephone hardware conversion and equipment exchange programs. Due to the limited capability of analog mobile telephones, they cannot be easily converted to digital capability. While it may be possible to replace the analog mobile telephone (mobile car phone) transceiver with a digital transceiver, the retrofit market is considered small.

One of the easiest ways to reduce system blockage (system busy signals) and quickly increase system efficiency is by retrofitting high-usage subscribers. Retrofitting high-usage subscribers can increase the total demand for digital wireless telephones over several years. There have been many types of retrofit incentive programs created that allow a customer to exchange their analog mobile telephones for a digital mobile telephone. These programs have required the customer to exchange their older wireless telephone or designate another customer to receive the old unit prior to receiving a new digital unit. In return for this exchange, the digital mobile telephone would be provided to the customer at reduced cost or no cost. Higher commissions have been paid for digital wireless telephones to entice new customers to select digital mobile telephones over their analog equivalents.

Churn

Churn is the percentage of customers that discontinue cellular service. Churn is usually expressed as a percentage of the existing customers that disconnect over a one-month period. Churn is often the result of natural migration (customers relocating) and switching to other service providers. Because some wireless service providers contribute an activation commission incentive to help reduce the sale price of the phone, this can result in a significant cost if the churn rate is high. The percentage of churn in North America over the last five years has remained relatively constant at approximately 2.8% per month.

Wireless carriers and their agents have gone to various lengths to reduce churn. This includes programming in lockout-codes to lengthy service agreements. The programmer or wireless service provider can enter lockout codes (typically 4-8 digits) into some wireless telephones to keep the telephone from being reprogrammed by another wireless service provider. Wireless service providers sometimes require the customer to sign a service agreement that typically requires them to maintain service for a minimum of one or two years. These service agreements have a penalty fee in the event that the customer disconnects service before the end of the agreement period.

Distribution and Retail Channels

Products produced by manufacturers are distributed to consumers via several distribution and retail channels. The types of distribution channels include wholesalers, specialty stores, retail stores, power retailers, discount stores, and direct sales.

Wholesalers purchase large shipments from manufacturers and typically ship small quantities to retailers. Wholesalers will usually specialize in particular product groups, such as pagers or cellular phones.

Specialty retailers are stores that focus on a particular product category such as a cellular phone outlet. Specialty retailers know their products well and are able to educate the consumer on services and benefits. These retailers usually get an added premium via a higher sale price for this service.

Retail stores provide a convenient place for the consumers to view products and make purchases. Retailers often sell a wide variety of products, but a salesperson may not have an expert's understanding of or be willing to dedicate the time to explain the features and cellular service options. In the early 1990s, mass retailers began selling cellular phones. Mass retailers sell a very wide variety of products at a low profit margin. The ability to sell at low cost is made possible by limiting the amount of sales time spent providing customer education on new features.

Power retailers specialize in a particular product group such as consumer electronics and carry only a select group of products. Power retailers look for particular product features that match their target market. Because there are only a few products for the consumer to select from, the demand for a single product is higher than if several different models were on display. This tends to increase sales for a particular product, which leads to larger quantity purchases and discounts for the power retailer.

Discount stores sell products at a lower cost than their competitors. They achieve this by providing a lower level of customer service. Because there is limited customer service, many of the wireless telephones sold in discount stores are preprogrammed or are debit (prepaid) units.

Some wireless service providers employ a direct sales staff to service large customers. These direct sales experts can offer specialty service pricing programs. The sales staff may be well trained and typically sell at the customer's location.

Distribution channels are commonly involved in the activation process. The application for cellular service can take a few minutes to several hours. The wireless telephone must be programmed with information specific to the wireless customer. For 3rd generation systems, programming is stored in the UMTS subscriber identity module (USIM). Programming may be performed by the handset, preprogrammed in the USIM, or programmed using over-the-air activation (OTA).

Because there are several new technologies and different models of wireless telephones, access to particular distribution channels may be limited. In 2001, each retailer carried (stocked) approximately 3–4 different manufacturer's brands. Retailers can only dedicate a limited amount of shelf space for each product or service, which may limit the introduction of new digital products and services into the marketplace.

References
1. Herschel Shosteck, "The Retail Market of Cellular Telephones," Herschel Shosteck Associates, Wheaton, MD, 1996.
2. Ibid.
3. Personal interview, industry expert, March 2, 2001.
4. Ibid.
5. *Cellular Integration Magazine*, "Tech-niques," Argus Business, January 1996.
6. Personal interview, bill of materials for a 3rd generation mobile telephone.
7. Personal interview, industry expert, 1995 patent royalties.
8. Personal interview, "Jeffrey Schlesinger," UBS Securities, NY, February 12, 1996.
9. Personal interview, Bob Glen, Sparton Electronics, Raleigh, NC, January 1996.
10. Personal interview, "Jeffrey Schlesinger," UBS Securities, NY, February 12, 1996.
11. EMCI, "Digital Cellular, Economics and Comparative Analysis," Washington DC, 1993.
12. Balston, D.M., and Macario, R.V., "Cellular Radio Systems," Artech House, 1993, p. 223.
13. Wireless Internet conference, Council for Entrepreneurial Development, Raleigh, NC, September 1995.
14. Personal Interview, Elliott Hamilton, EMCI Consulting, Washington DC, February 25, 1996.
15. North Carolina Electronics Information Technologies Association, "Cellular Fraud," Raleigh, NC, November, 1995.
16. CTIA, "Wireless Factbook," Washington DC, Spring 1995.
17. GSM MOU, www.GSMWorld.com, February 22, 2001.
18. Ibid.
19. Sprint, Wireless Data Symposium, Raleigh, NC, December, 1995.

20. Dr. George Calhoun, "Digital Cellular Radio," Artech House, MA, 1988, p.69.

21. Crump, Stuart F., "Cellular Sales and Marketing," *Creative Communications Inc.*, Vol. 5, No. 8, p.2.

22. Chan, Hilbert, and Vinodrai, C., "The Transition to Digital Cellular," IEEE 1990 Vehicular Technology Conference, p.191.

23. Shosteck, Herschel, "The Retail Market of Cellular Telephones," Herschel Shosteck Associates, Wheaton, MD, 1996.

24. CTIA Winter Exposition, John Stupka, "Technology Update," Reno, NV, 1990.

Chapter 10

3rd Generation Wireless Applications

Third generation wireless applications are software programs that require wireless communication technology that can take advantage of the mobility and high-bit-rate data transmission offered by 3rd generation wireless systems. Many of the communications applications and services that were available for mobile communications in the 1990's were limited by low bit-rate (less than 10 kbps) data transmission. With 2nd generation mobile systems, it was not possible to offer streaming video, rapid image file transfer or high bit-rate data file transfer services.

The worldwide wireless communications market has grown from 190 million subscribers in 1996 to over 680 million by the end of the year 2000 [1]. The wireless market is expected to exceed one billion in 2003, approximately one phone for every seven people on earth! To sustain this high growth market trend and to persuade customers to upgrade to 3rd generation products and services, there must be new attractive and imaginative applications.

Third generation systems provide for two key advancements in mobile communication technology that allow for new advanced applications: packet data transmission and high bit-rate data services. Packet data transmission allows the wireless systems to transfer information only as the customer requires information transfer. This is compared to 2nd generation data transmission services that use a dedicated portion of a radio channel regardless of actual usage on the radio channel (amount of data transmission activity). Although the peak data transfer rate when a customer is browsing the web may be high, the average data transfer rate of the customer is low. Packet transmission allows a wireless service provider to cost-effectively provide service to many wireless data devices or customers. 3rd generation systems also allow high bit-rate data transmission (up to 2 Mb/s) that permits new services and applications such as video and high quality audio broadcast services. These services could not be provided on 1st or 2nd generation systems.

There are hundreds of key applications that require high-bit rate data transfer services that can be provided via 3rd generation wireless service. These include distance learning, high graphic online commerce, video and audio entertainment, interactive advertising, news and other information services, advanced manufacturing processes, media production, remote security, public safety, tele-medicine, utility management, and alternative (bypass) communication systems. If these applications become readily available and the cost of providing these services is low, the demand for 3rd generation products and services will be high.

Customers do not care or need to know how the underlying 3G communication technologies function. They just care that technology works for whatever application they want to use, and the benefit of using the application is perceived to be higher than the cost to use its service.

Much of the demand for wireless data access has come from the combination of availability of Internet information applications and low cost mobile communication. The Internet's standardized global collection of interconnected computer networks has allowed for access to information sources that provide significant benefits to those companies and individuals looking for knowledge. The Internet has created an awareness (culture change) of many new information services, and these new information services themselves.

In the late 1990s, new, low-cost, high bit-rate connections to the Internet became available. The rapid market growth of digital subscriber line (DSL) and cable modem technology has stimulated the development of new applications that are only possible via broadband high bit-rate connections. In the early 21st century, consumers are becoming aware of these new broadband multimedia applications and the transition back to low bit-rate information (text based) services is difficult.

Many consumers are already aware of benefits of wireless mobile service and are becoming aware of broadband applications. Potential 3rd generation customers may only need to be educated that these services can be delivered via rapid bit rate wireless data communication services to convert them from traditional wired (e.g., Internet access) to new wireless services. Of key importance for 3rd generation technologies are broadband applications that require mobility, low-cost installation or rapid deployment that competing wired broadband technologies cannot provide.

In 2001, the United States led the "information society" with over 100 million Internet and wireless users. In 1999, more than 33% of the households had on-line web access. [2]. Between 1997 and 2000, over 9% of household Internet customers (over 3 million customers) changed from narrowband to broadband access service providers (DSL and cable modem). The wireless Internet is in transition from point-to-point text based short messaging service (SMS) and digital audio broadcasting service to high-bandwidth wireless applications, such as audio and video streaming.

Distance Learning

Distance learning is a way to receive education or training at remote locations. Distance learning has been available for many years and can be categorized into public education (grades K-12), university and colleges, professional (industry), government, and military segments. In the early years, distance learning was provided through the use of books and other printed materials and was commonly referred to as a correspondence course.

Distance learning has evolved through the use of broadcast media (e.g., television) and moved onto individual or small group training through video-based training (VBT) or computer-based training (CBT). These systems have developed into interactive distance learning (IDL) as the computer allowed changes in the training.

Distance learning relies on communication systems (e.g., phone lines or mail) to connect students and teacher as an alternative to classroom training. Electronic learning (eLearning) is a form of distance learning that is becoming a viable alternative to traditional teaching methods and is poised for major growth over the next several years.

Through the use of broadband video and interactive graphic technologies, students are exposed to a far greater education stimulus than in the traditional learning environment. Integrated sound, motion, image, and text will all serve to create a rich new learning atmosphere and substantially increase student involvement in the learning process.

The rapidly changing global economy is forcing industry professionals to continually update their skills. Adults are now changing their occupations several times in a lifetime as technologies and skills become outdated. This requires continual learning for adults. Adults between the age of 35-45 are the fastest growing group of college learners [3]. To advance or consolidate their careers, over five million adults complete some form of distance learning each year [4]. This is one of the primary reasons why online learning is booming, especially among working adults with children. Distance learning via broadband connectivity allows adults to "attend" classes in the comfort of their living room or study, at their convenience.

Many of the online universities including training and professional specialty course programs, are catering to the rising demand from industry to deliver skill-development courses to the desktop at remote locations. These schools are offering Web-based professional certificates as well as associate and bachelor's degrees that are built around a solid core of business and computer classes. Companies rely on these certificates to ensure that employees are qualified for their new jobs.

In 1999, most online classes did not require that students have the latest high powered computer. However, they did require Internet access (via low bit rate analog modem). These distance learning courses were provided using low-resolution graphics or slow scan web video. As broadband services become more available and cost effective, it is predicted that distance learning courses will evolve to use high-resolution services such as high-resolution video conferencing [5]. Online distance learning courses can be accredited by regional accrediting agencies or via the Distance Education and Training Council.

Public (K-12) Education

Elementary education involves developing fundamental skills to children and young adults. Elementary education is normally funded and managed by government agencies, and it is the goal of many public education programs to provide the same education opportunity to all the members of a nation. This is provided regardless of the economic status of its students or regardless of whether the demographic structure of a community can support quality education programs.

The economics of traditional public education systems limit the offering of specific courses to regions that have a specific minimum density of students. To ensure that each student can be offered the same education opportunities, distance education can offer more courses to each student. Distance education also allows students to interact with other students with similar interests and needs at remote locations. Distance learning applications delivered through the Internet can provide access to standardized courses that provide equal education opportunities to most students in a nation.

By the end of 1998, approximately 89% of all public secondary schools and 76 % of elementary schools in the United States were connected to the Internet. Since then, public schools have continued to make progress toward meeting the goal of connecting every school to the Internet by the year 2000. (In 1994 only

35% of public schools in the United States were connected to the Internet.) In addition to having every school connected to the "information superhighway," the second goal is to have every classroom, library, and media-lab connected to the Internet. Schools are making great strides to achieve this and in 1998, 51% of instructional rooms in public schools were connected [6].

Connection bit rate is one of the key determinants to which extent schools make use of the Internet. In 1998, higher bit-rate connections using a dedicated line were used by 65 percent of public schools. Additionally, large schools with Internet access are more likely to connect using broadband access technology [7].

College and University Education

Since the Internet was pioneered at universities to facilitate information sharing, it's not surprising that an increasing number of them are creating Web-based universities. By 2002, 85% of two-year colleges (in 1999 there were a total of 847 two-year colleges in United States) are expected to be offering distance learning courses, which is up from 58% in 1998. It is projected that over 80% of the four year colleges (in 1999 there were a total of 1,472 four-year colleges and universities in the United States) will be offering distance learning courses in 2002, up from 62 % in 1998. Many of these will be Web-based. To put this into perspective, there are 15 million full-time and part-time college students in the United States, of which an estimated 90% are online, representing by far the most active single group on the Net. Moreover, in 1998, 21% of these students purchased $900 million in goods and services online [8].

It is estimated that 93% of distance learning programs in American colleges and universities use e-mail and almost 60% use the e-mail in conjunction with the Web [9].

When distance education is offered, campus visits are not required for most programs. Learners register online each semester, and may take single courses for personal enrichment or opt to enter a degree program. Textbooks and class syllabi can be mailed to learners or delivered via the Internet. Online classes run typically on a 16-week semester schedule, beginning and ending at the same time as on-campus classes. Students read their textbooks and visit online message boards weekly, posting class comments or questions whenever it is convenient for them. The back-and-forth commentary on the message boards simulates a classroom discussion. Midterm and final exams are usually taken under the watchful eye of an approved proctor at a local college, library, or human resources training center.

Figure 10.1 shows that the number of college students enrolled in distance learning courses in 1998 was approximately 710,000, and the number is estimated to reach 2.2 million in 2002, which will represent 15% of all higher education students [10].

Professional

Professional education is developed and provided for business firms, because it is necessary for them to remain competitive, especially because technology and business processes are constantly changing. Training budgets range from 1% to 5% of gross sales in many compaines, and a growing proportion of these funds is used for distance learning courses.

Government

Providing education for government workers is necessary to ensure that information-intensive systems (such as tax collection) can be operated effectively. In the United States in 1999, there were over three million government workers. The average government worker receives 1-2 weeks of training per year to use software and technology systems, learn standard processes, and develop leadership skills. This results in a requirement of over five million person-weeks of

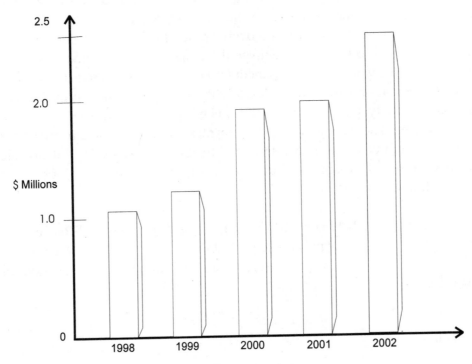

Figure 10.1. Growth of Distance Learning.

Source: IDC (International Data Corporation); UT Austin Web Central

training. To minimize costs such as travel, hotel, and lost work time, many government agencies are using distance learning programs.

Online Retail

Online retail selling involves the bartering and exchange of goods via a communication line to the Internet. In 1998, online retail sales in the United States exceeded $7.8 billion [11].

Online retail sales that occur via the wireless Internet Web provide far greater product selection, information, and convenience over traditional brick-and-mortar retailers. These applications may involve a wide range of products and services, such as books, compact disks (CDs), flowers, and airline tickets. Additionally, "intelligent personal search agents" are able to get best prices, last minute deals, and help in suggesting the appropriate gift.

Broadband multimedia access enhances online shopping. High-resolution catalog pictures, personalized animated modeling (to see how apparel looks on you), and video product display clips will increase the interest in online shopping. The number of online shoppers in the United States is projected to grow to 85 million, and the spending per shopper will double by 2003. Additionally, the time interval between going online and making the first purchase is down to an average of four months. In 1999, the median income for online households was 57 % higher than that of the average American household - $58,000 versus $37,005 [12].

Figure 10.2 shows that the most popular e-retail categories in 1999 include: books, music, videos, apparel, health & beauty, food & beverage, airline tickets, computer hardware, hotel reservations, and consumer electronics.

Travel

U.S. consumers booked $6.5 billion worth of leisure and unmanaged business travel online in 1999, almost triple the $2.2 billion booked in 1998, and representing 5% of total U.S. bookings in 1999. Online bookings are expected to increase significantly, to 14 percent of total bookings by 2005 ($28 billion), with key segments including lodging, cruise, tour, and rental car products [13].

Books

In 1999, over 50% of online shoppers indicated that they had purchased a book or CD online. The entertainment products category (books, video, and audio CDs) collectively will grow to almost $9 billion in 2003 [14]. Online toy shopping is expected to reach $1.6 billion in 2003, up from $300 million in 1999 [15]. The leading book retailer online in 1999 was Amazon.com, with over $1.2 billion in book and media sales [16].

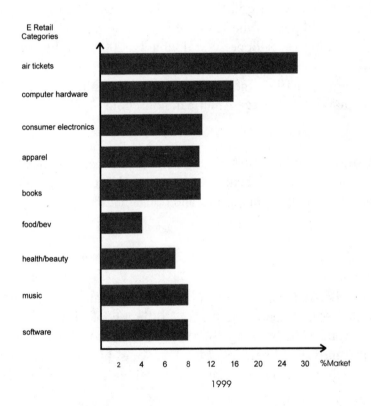

Figure 10.2. Division of E-Commerce Sales.
Source: The National Retail Federation/ Forrester Research Online Retail Index, March 2000

Mobile Commerce (m-commerce)

Mobile commerce (m-commerce) is the application of electronic commerce (e-commerce) via mobile wireless devices. M-commerce applications are used by consumers to increase convenience, improve timeliness, and allow purchases at almost any location. Using 3rd generation wireless technology, m-commerce applications such as content delivery and advertising present new revenue opportunities.

M-commerce applications will be linked to other types of applications, and in many cases will add value to them. For example, a free content application such as a directory service could be used to look up a local florist. A customer would then place an order with the shop, via the mobile terminal, for the purchase and delivery of flowers.

In 1998, e-commerce accounted for an estimated $57 billion in revenues, and analysts are forecasting that worldwide e-commerce will grow to $2.7 trillion by 2004, up from $740 billion in 2000. Accordingly, e-commerce transactions in business-to-business (B2B) will generate nearly $850 billion by 2004. Companies are expected to purchase on average 30 to 50% of goods and services online [17]. The key question is how much of e-commerce can be fulfilled by m-commerce on 3rd generation wireless systems? Some of the key m-commerce applications include online trading, mobile banking, and information content delivery.

Online Trading

Online trading allows customers to manage their personal investment transactions. Online trading customers will benefit greatly from the convenience and immediacy offered by wireless connectivity. Customers will be able to research companies, identify business trends, receive live quotes, join tip lists and stock forums/ chat rooms, and track their portfolio in real time. The online brokerage assets are expected to quadruple from more than $750 million in 1999 to over $3 trillion in 2003 [18].

Mobile Banking

Mobile banking services make it possible for a customer to track checking and savings account statements, balancing checkbooks, transfer funds, and pay bills — all with built-in security, from a wireless handset that is connected to the Internet. Mobile banking simulates having a bank teller in your pocket available any hour of the day.

Early mobile banking services have met with limited consumer acceptance in the United States. European consumers, especially those in the Nordic countries, have a higher consumer acceptance of the mobile channel as a way to manage personal finances. Iceland, with a cellular penetration of over 73%, is expected to be a virtually cashless society in the next five or so years. Since 1999, there has been a slowly growing increase in mobile banking features on bank sites.

By 2002, over 90% of banks are expected to allow users to track account balances by mobile phone. Stock and bond trading capabilities on bank sites are also increasing [19].

As more bills become available through banks, and more consumers adopt bill presentment as a standard format for bill payment, online management of personal finances, be it on the desktop or via a mobile device, will become increasingly important to consumers, and significant to financial services players.

Online bill payment services on bank sites increased 47% from 1998 to 1999. In 1998, approximately 15 billion monthly paper bills were sent to over one hundred million households in the United States. On an annual basis, the typical U.S. household spends on average 24 hours on bill management, $46 on postage, and $144 on check-writing fees as a result of having 12 recurring monthly bills.

This is expected to grow to 15 million by 2002 [20]. By 2002, it is estimated that some 60% of all online financial services households (defined as online households that trade or bank online) will be using online bill presentation and payment. These customers will be able to view on average 70% of their total bills, for a total of 1.4 billion bills presented to them online.

Online billing presents significant cost savings for vendors that bill their customers. Each paper bill costs vendors between $1.50 and $3.50, whereas electronically presented bills will cost only $0.35 to $0.10 [21]. Figure 10.3 shows the relative costs for online banking transactions.

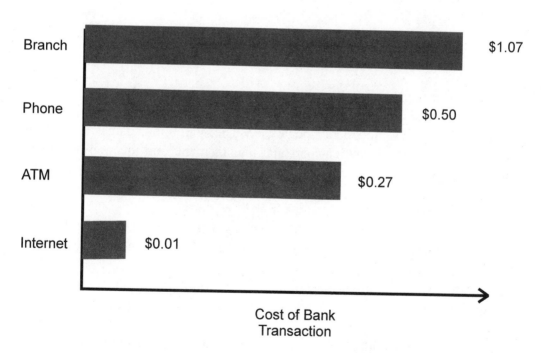

Figure 10.3. Cost of Online Bank Transactions.

Source: Merrill Lynch

Content Delivery

Content delivery involves the transporting of information from a source (content provider) to its destination (customer). The customer usually elects to receive content (such as travel directions or flight status information). The service provider may charge a fee for access or may receive a percentage of the fee paid by the recipient to the content provider (royalty fee). Some of the more popular content providers include mapping companies (for directions), music, flight status, weather information, and other real-time or near real-time information sources. The actual information content is often provided through an application service provider (ASP) transferred through an Internet portal (gateway). The ASP usually manages and updates the contents, and the 3rd generation wireless provider provides the transport to the end customer.

Entertainment and Lifestyle

Entertainment and lifestyle services cover applications that are primarily designed for leisure and entertainment, such as music and video movies, horoscopes, jokes, and soap opera updates. Music, gambling, games, television, movies, electronic information, personal management, and location-based services are in this category. Most of these applications are multifunctional, providing information, education, and advertising.

During 1999, over 19 million people worldwide used mobile phones to dowload or access online games or audio or video services. Entertainment will be one of the leading forms of content carried over wireless networks. Surveys of industry confidence indicate that entertainment is headed to be the second most popular mobile application after messaging i.e., e-mail and SMS [22].

In 2000, simple embedded games and ring-tone downloads were popular. Ring-tone downloads allow a cellular phone to ring with a distinctive melody chosen by the subscriber. As new, low-cost, broadband, wireless services become available, we will also see new applications. These include playing interactive mobile games, listening to music downloads (typically in MP3 format) via the wireless phone or attached accessory, and watching video clips (e.g., football highlights) on your wireless videophone.

Music

Online shopping allows customers to easily preview content or details of a product such as tracks on music albums. In 1998, music industry revenue topped $13.5 billion in the United States, with online sales totaling $157 million, up 315% from 1997's figure of $37 million. The online sales of CDs, tapes, and records is expected to grow to $2.6 billion (or 14% of total U.S. music sales of $18.4 billion) in 2003.

The sales of digital music software transferred via downloads have been very limited due to bandwidth constraints. Downloading a full-length CD, even in compressed form, is a formidable challenge for the average user with a dial-up modem. Regarding the market for digital distribution of music in the years 2002-2003, it is estimated that the revenue generated will be approximately $150 million. With 3G broadband wireless data, it will be possible to download entire music CDs in less than two minutes [23].

As an interim approach to music content delivery on the Internet, companies are offering digitally compressed music on the Internet in MP3 form. In 2000, a company named MP3.com launched subscription music channels on the Internet. For a monthly fee of less than $10, users have access to thousands of music tracks to choose from, which will be available for listening.

Figure 10.4 shows a wireless phone that has the ability to download and play MP3 music. With no moving parts to bump, users can play the high-quality music they downloaded from the Internet and do the jitterbug without getting the jitters. A device with 32 Mbytes of available memory can store and play up to eight songs

Gambling

Online gambling is the interactive process of allowing customers to wager money or credits in return for games that have standardized odds. Online gambling has the potential to be one of the largest interactive services. In 2000, the

Figure 10.4. Wireless Phone (model SGH-M110) With MP3 Download Capability.
Source: Samsung

global gambling market was valued at over $900 billion. A growing portion of the gambling industry is moving toward online gambling. Customers with a credit card and an Internet connection are able to gamble- casinos, lotteries and sports books (horse & dog racing, boxing, team sports betting, etc.) almost anywhere the world.

While there are some issues about the legality of gambling online, the majority of online gamblers are located in countries with regulations favorable to online gambling companies. Many of these companies are operating in places such as the Caribbean, Europe, Australia, and South Africa. It is projected that over $10 billion will be gambled online by 2002 as operators take advantage of the huge audience reach and cost savings of the Internet [24].

Networked Games

Since 1997, networked games have become a big opportunity on the Internet. Networked games allow users to play games against friends who are connected to the Internet. Almost any computer game that can be played by two or more people can be played online. It is estimated that by 2002, 60% of children online (over 16 million) will be playing games, and they will spend over $70.00 per year for game services. Adults will spend $140.00 per year, for an estimated total of $622 million, for online game services. 3G's high bandwidth services allow for substantially improved game services through streaming video and audio, and permit its players to engage in games virtually from anywhere.

And as low-cost home broadband services and equipment become more available, companies will create richer gaming applications. Major game vendors such as Nintendo, Sony, and Sega are beginning to enter the broadband market by selling game CDs and allowing potential customers to participate in online games for free. Alternatively, there are some games that can only be played online, including Ultima, Starseige, Quake Arena, and Unreal Tournament.

To use online games, customers pay a monthly access fee or pay-per-play to access online games. Networked games make it much easier for customers to find new opponents, or to find a partner to play at any time. 3G's wireless high-bit rate data access will provide for much better three dimensional (3D) graphics.

Interactive Toys

Interactive toys will utilize 3G wireless communication technology to better interact with other toys. Interactive toys have motors, sensors, infrared messaging, and speech recognition technologies that respond to communication signals and originate messages. The responses may be in the form of some mechanical action or audio message.

Interactive toys have been available for many years. Some of the first interactive toys responded to signals that were sent via broadcast television. These toys responded to colors or patterns appearing on the television screen.

Interactive technologies, specifically the user interface, are constantly improving. With wireless connectivity, for example, these interactive toys, such as virtual pets with artificial lives, will become more "alive" by exhibiting simultaneous physical, verbal and PC-like interactive behavior.

Video Access and Movie Rental

Video content delivery will be one of the leading drivers of the 3G broadband marketplace. Consumers have a voracious appetite for all types of media, particularly video (movie) content. In 1999, over 70% of households in the United States rented a movie — on an average 1.3 videos per week [25]. The statistics for movie rentals confirm the preference of movie viewers to stay at home to view movie content. Since 1980, when VCRs first emerged as a means of watching full-length motion pictures, the sales of prerecorded rental and sell through video cassettes has grown over 66,000% to 1998 as compared to box office theater growth of 22% over the same period [26]. The video rental business is projected to top $7 billion in 2000, growing to $19 billion by 2004 with video sales reaching $20 billion [27].

Adult entertainment content ordering and delivery has been one of the leading categories of early Internet usage. As such, adult entertainment was an early adopter of user interface augmentation due to streaming video, private access to sensitive material, and one-click ordering. In 1998, pay-per-view and subscription adult entertainment accounted for about 40% of the U.S. consumer paid online content market [28]. Adult entertainment, a multibillion dollar industry, will benefit from broadband access. Consumers will be able to download private content to their 3G handsets or wireless enabled viewers.

Music Content

Music content delivery involves the transporting of music content (usually in digital form) from managers of the content (music producers or their agents) to the end customer. Much of the music content was sold via the Internet in the 1990s, rather than delivered through it, due to the limited amount of bandwidth and devices to store and play downloaded music content. The sale of CDs and tapes via online services is expected to grow to $2.6 billion (or 14% of total U.S. music sales of $18.4 billion in 2003). As 3G wireless networks and other broadband systems are deployed, consumers will shift their acquisition from purchasing CDs or tapes to downloading their favorite music to their media player.

By 2000, more than half of the users on the Internet had listened to music audio on a personal computer (PC). Of these, 36% have download music and 5% have transferred unauthorized (pirated) music files to their hard disk drive.

Virtual Radio Stations

Virtual radio stations are digital audio sources that are connected to a network (typically the Internet). In 1999, there were over 2000 radio stations operating on the Internet. Virtual radio stations have a strong competitive advantage compared to standard radio broadcasts. Radio stations' Web sites can do more than simply rebroadcast their on-air signals. They can provide photos of disc jockeys, show contest prizes and their winners, and act as current news centers for entertainment events and weather services.

Broadcast radio stations have been offering content delivery by both radio and Web access in anticipation of a significant shift to Internet (virtual) radio. Internet radio offers the ability to customize (personalize) broadcast to groups or individual receivers of broadcast signals. By 2005, 41% of the population will listen to personalized, on-demand audio content at least once a week. Content providers will adopt genre-specific business models.

Radio stations are taking aggressive steps in developing a new breed of Web sites designed to offer fresh content and help the media outlets connect better with their target audience. This includes offering chat rooms, news updates, and music reviews, and other social-based services that make their web sites more appealing. Additionally, virtual radio stations can use their Web sites as research tools to determine listener preferences. The system serves up real-time information, providing details on the music being played by the radio station. Listeners then are asked to use the Web site to vote on the song being played, giving station programmers instant feedback on listener tastes. The radio stations then talk up their Web sites during radio broadcasting, driving more usage of the Internet service. The Internet is having positive and negative impacts on the radio station ratings and revenues [29].

Virtual Television Stations

Virtual television stations distribute digital video and audio through the Internet to groups of viewers. With broadband digital video access, the Internet will become a new avenue of distribution for broadcasters that hope to target previously unreachable mobile audiences.

Since 1999, there has been a growing public interest in interactive TV (iTV). This has been led by satellite and cable systems as they begin to deploy subscriber equipment and infrastructure capable of delivering a variety of interactive services. Some of the early interactive functions include an electronic program guide (EPG) and parental control through channel-locking features. A type of one-way datacasting on virtual television stations allows viewers to choose from limited, primarily text-based supplementary content.

Other virtual television features and functions may include game/quiz show audience participation. These features and functions all present new opportunities as well as challenges to programmers, advertisers, and providers of interactive services, as they navigate through a maze of complex platform landscapes defined by a complicated mix of networks, set-top boxes, and software. Its projected that 35% of U.S. households (over 25 million homes) will use some form of interactive TV services by the end of 2005 [30].

Virtual Books/ E-Books

Virtual books or electronic books (e-books) are books in digital form that can be displayed and navigated through by a user. Many virtual books are available through personal computers or personal digital assistants (PDAs) via CD ROM or a connection to the Internet. Some of the portable devices come with leather covers, built-in modem, and color screen.

Since 1998, some online publishers have offered electronic books in postscript descriptor file (PDF) format. E-books offer book publishers a mechanism to control distribution if they're able to tie content to a specific device, electronic books, or e-books. In 1999, the total U.S. book market was approximately $21 billion, and the e-books market share was less than 1% [31]. This is due in part to poor display devices and the lack of compelling content and in part to the limitations of the user's experience with the display device (which far outstrip those of digital music users.)

With the introduction of better display devices and more content available via the Internet, the marketplace for virtual books should dramatically increase. It is likely that e-book vendors will focus initially on vertical opportunity segments with time-sensitive content, such as mobile maintenance (service instructions), education (distance learning), healthcare (telemedicine), and law (case histories).

Virtual Newspapers and Magazines

Virtual newspapers and magazines use communications technology to deliver periodical and advertising information. In 1998, over 80% of consumers surveyed said they believed that the Internet is as reliable as offline (e.g., printed and television) media sources. Because of the proliferation of 24-hour cable news channels and the increase in online news services, the average daily newspaper readership has fallen to only 58% of the U. S. population in 1997. This is compared to over 80% in 1964. With only 31% of the 21- to 35- year age group reading the newspaper, traditional newspapers and broadcasters are using virtual newspapers and magazines via the Internet to reach a more affluent, younger demographic online audience [32].

Newspapers rarely duplicate their paper contents word-for-word online, but they often provide more than enough for the reader to live without the paper edition. When viewing online newspapers, readers are not limited to selections of local newspapers. They have access to newspapers around the globe. Almost all newspapers have an online version. Additionally, the online versions of newspaper are generally free (advertiser supported) and are available before the paper ones hit the stands. Online newspapers and magazines tend to offer expanded coverage into areas such as travel, entertainment, and culture. They provide exclusive content, such as breaking news, live sports coverage, online shopping, opinion polls, and discussion groups. However, probably the best advantage of online newspapers is that they provide advanced search and retrieve archives to the customer. With increased bandwidth access becoming available, virtual newspapers are more able to take advantage of video and audio media to add value to the news services.

Electronic Photo Album

Since the mid-1990s, low-cost digital cameras have been available that allow customers to capture and transmit digital photographs. Because digital cameras allow the customer to manipulate the digitized photos, they can be enhanced to remove red-eye (caused by reflection of flash lights by the retina of the eye), and unwanted areas can be cut out. These images can be used to create electronic postcards or greeting cards. A telecommunication network's high bit-rate data transfer combined with storage and forward service capabilities will allow customers to transmit and receive high-quality photographs. Furthermore, many wireless telephones already have the ability to attach a camera to their data port.

Digital camera revenue is expected to surpass that of film cameras in 2000 for the first time ever, with $1.9 billion worth of digital cameras to be sold in the United States. Digital camera unit sales are expected to grow from 6.7 million in 2002 to over 42 million in 2005 [33].

Personalized Communications

Personalized communication consists of applications and services that are based on access to and manipulation of a user's personal data. This includes services such as personal information management— calendar/scheduler, e-mail messaging, unified messaging, chat, and communities.

News and Information

News and information-based applications include the delivery of time-sensitive information along with access to directories and guides that users can access. Users will be able to customize their information service delivery according to their interests, such as headline news, business news, specific company news tracking, weather, sports results, and stock information.

Location Based Information Services

Wireless networks offer the ability to track the position of mobile phones (within a limited distance accuracy) and provide information services based on the determination of the location. Navigation and tracking services are highly valued services for users in key market sectors such as truck dispatch management and public vehicle management (e.g., buses). Location-based services can also be linked to advertising and commerce by providing, for example, directions to the nearest Italian cuisine restaurant, or a store with current sales promotions.

Business Applications

Mobile office and Intranet (internal company Internet) applications are essential for business and corporate users. Business users are usually the highest spending and highest-usage market segments.

The initial demand for 3G services will likely be generated by the business and vertical (specific industry applications that solve a business problem) sectors. This is because business customers have the largest need for the high bit-rate services. Business uesers demand time-critical delivery of data. Existing business users are frustrated by the slow bit rate of second generation cellular data. It is also easier to justify a financial benefit for business users compared to residential (entertainment) users.

Business users have the greatest need for applications such as file transfer or e-mail with attachments, along with mobile (location independent) delivery. These applications could be significantly improved with an increase in data bit rate as offered by 3G wireless systems. Mobile data applications are already being used in specific types of companies, such as utilities (electricity, water, gas, etc.), to operate and maintain critical facilities. Companies that use mobile data for these applications are committed heavy users.

Video Conferencing

Video conferencing is the combination of dedicated audio, video, and communication networking technology for real-time interaction. Companies use video conferencing to reduce or eliminate travel while allowing employees to interact face to face.

New applications, such as Microsoft's NetMeeting, offer real-time voice and video conferencing to conference attendees at two (or more) locations. In addition, many video-conferencing applications include collaborative application sharing (for shared presentations), multiperson document editing, background file transfer, and whiteboard (real-time, shared, interactive displays) to draw and paste on. The lower-cost and high-bandwidth capability of 3G wireless systems will allow more cost-effective and portable video conferencing services.

Remote Corporate Network Connections

Remote corporate network connections allow company employees to access company networks and receive similar services (e.g., rapid file transfer) as they would experience if they were located (working) at the corporation offices. The rise in "virtual corporations" has resulted from increased worker productivity, reduced facilities costs, and satisfaction of environmental and regulatory requirements for reduced number of commuters. It is estimated that over 7% of all workers in the United States spend a least some or all of their time as teleworkers. This growth in the home-based work environment has been a major driver of high interconnection bit rate for home and business networking.

Business Kiosks

Business kiosks are the remote location of business retail centers. Business kiosks may be unmanned or satellite offices that require connection to a head office or stand-alone information centers that require periodic information updating.

The use of business kiosks allows companies to expand their market territories without significant risk or capital investment. By utilizing wireless data connectivity, kiosks can be installed quickly and at low cost.

Public Internet kiosks are a type of payphone booth that contains a computer terminal that can access the Internet. For a nominal price, customers can check their e-mail or browse the Internet. Most public Internet kiosks are scattered throughout public places such as airports, train stations, convention centers, hotels, office building lobbies, and shopping malls. These public Internet kiosks can be used as a media center for information services.

Internet kiosks can also be multipurpose or adapted to satisfy specific needs. They can be used as automated teller machines, travel service providers, ticket centers or other business services.

In 1998, there were approximately 10,000 kiosks in the United States, and the number is predicted to rise to more than 100,000 by 2002. The typical cost of a kiosk is in the $35,000 to $55,000 range, in addition to monthly space rental fees [34].

Documentation Management

Documentation management includes the capture, storing, organizing, and coordinating of access to large amounts of text and image information. This information may be stored at one or more locations, and the information may be accessed or transferred to display devices (terminals), printers, or other repositories (for long term storage).

Documentation management allows manuals, procedures, specifications, and other vital information to be instantly accessible by authorized employees. Documentation management can save a company a considerable amount in printing reproduction costs, as all documentation is digital rather than paper.

Field Service

Field service personnel interact with clients or equipment in the field. In the past, these personnel have had limited access to company materials. Using 3G broadband communications systems, field service personnel can access documents (e.g., company catalogs and service manuals), example procedures (e.g., video clips), capture information (e.g., using a digital camera to record an insurance claim) and to assist in the repair of equipment (e.g., connect systems for remote diagnostics).

Customer Care

Customer care is the process of answering customer questions about a company's products or services. It is estimated that over 65% of the cost of providing customer support service originates from simple product and billing questions [35].

The cost of customer service is greatly reduced, and customer satisfaction is dramatically improved when customers and suppliers are able to satisfy their information need via the Internet. Furthermore, the capabilities as offered by 3G's wireless Internet provide for even greater flexibility and convenience from the field. The information gathered from a customer's browsing information services (areas regularly visited) allows companies to promote similar products and services.

Media Production

Media production involves the coordination of artistic content creation into image, video, and printed media forms prior to physical production.

Image and Video Production

Images and Video can be captured in electronic form and transferred to other locations. Because of the large file size of high resolution images, media transfer has primarily been in the form of high-density disks or video tape.

Although initial production of images or video occurs in a studio, edited images, video segments or computer animation may be performed at many different locations. Broadband connections allow for the editors and producers to interconnect without the delays of shipping storage media.

Printing Press

Printing presses transfer electronic media information (usually in the form of an image file) onto a print medium (usually paper for books, newspapers, or magazines). Since the early 1990s, printing presses have been converting their mechanical reproduction processes from mechanical to electronic (digital presses). In either case, printing presses require film or another medium that uses high-resolution images that are usually created by computers. High-bandwidth systems are now replacing film and other formats for transferring prepress images.

Security Video Monitoring

Security video monitoring applications help to visually assure that valuable assets that are owned by a company or by an individual will not be eroded or destroyed by unauthorized users of the asset. Traditionally, security video monitoring was limited to on-site video monitors that security personnel continuously viewed, or by delayed viewing of videotapes. The introduction of low-cost digital video cameras and data connections allows for remote location of video cameras. When these cameras are connected through the Internet, they are called Web cameras (WebCams.)

At the end of 2000, there were already in excess of 100,000 public WebCams in operation throughout the world [36] and private video monitoring systems have millions of privately installed video cameras. Although many of these video cameras are connected by wire, some are connected by wireless links.

The key applications for wireless security monitoring included traffic management (traffic cams), public access monitoring (public safety), law enforcement (cameras on police cars), and other applications that require cameras at remote locations where wired connections are not practical, or where mobility (video monitoring while moving) is important.

With 3rd generation wireless systems, images from police cars can be monitored at a central facility. This may dramatically increase the safety for police officers.

Telemedicine

Telemedicine is the providing of medical services with the assistance of telecommunications. Telemedicine does not completely replace medical expertise. Telemedicine is critical to providing quality and efficient healthcare services in many locations.

Telemedicine is a rapidly growing part of the medical information management market and is one of the largest and fastest growing segments of the healthcare device industry. The expected revenue by the end of 2000 is $21 billion.

In the United States, more than 60% of federal telemedicine projects were initiated since 1998. The concept of telemedicine captures much of what is developing in terms of technology implementations, especially if it is combined with the growth of the Internet and World Wide Web (WWW) [37]. The 3G networks will further guarantee a wireless extension of Internet-based services and technologies to the wireless device, thus contributing to lower operating costs and administration costs in communicating information from healthcare verticals such as insurance companies and streamlined processes. Furthermore, mobile medicine will enable healthcare workers to receive supply-on-demand content in a mobile environment.

Some of the advanced telemedicine applications include telecardiology, teleradiology, and telepsychiatry. Telecardiology services incorporate transmission of electrocardiogram (ECG) data, echocardiograms, heart sounds and murmurs, and cardiology images, and can be performed via both store-and-forward and interactive media. Teleradiology is the most widely adopted of all telemedicine applications. Clinical radiology requires prompt, near-real-time transmission of still-frame images, but may also demand live or full-motion video image communication and display. Telepsychiatry allows psychiatric care to be conducted at a distance and telepsychiatry can provide care more frequently to patients in outlying areas.

Telemedicine applications usually encompass computer, video, and telecommunications technologies-each with its own role to play in the acquisition, transport, and display of medical information. Some of the key areas related to telemedicine include patient record management and mobile clinics.

Patient Record Management

Patient record management involves the storage and retrieval of medical information related to a specific person. Patient information may be gathered electronically (such as an x-ray on film) or manually (such as a patient history data record). In any case, patent record management via telemedicine involves converting nonelectronic forms of information (such as the x-ray image on film) into electronic forms (data files) and managing these data files to integrate the data, voice, digitized images, or video. These files are stored in a computer (or several computers) and can be transmitted to workstations at a medical center, physician's office, or other site equipped to manage the telemedicine information request. Rapidly transporting image data and diagnoses between clinicians and medical doctors can add substantially to improved patient care.

Mobile Clinics

Mobile clinics are transportable facilities where healthcare specialists can treat patients using medical equipment. Figure 10.5 shows a mobile clinic vehicle. With the high-resolution video conferencing capabilities of 3G, mobile clinics in the form of a bus or a van can travel throughout rural areas to patients, with clinical technicians bringing hospital-type facilities to remote areas. The clinical technician coordinates communications with medical experts via wireless video-conferencing consultations.

These telemedicine video conference facilities allow hospital-based physicians to view, for example, patient wounds from a live video image. The traditional

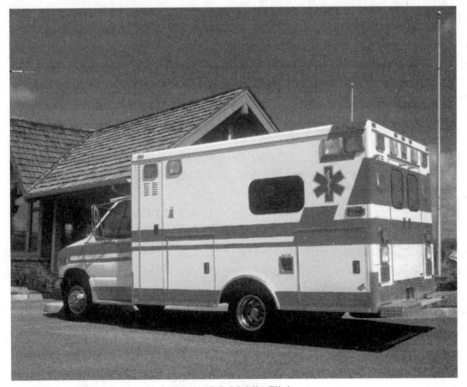

Figure 10.5. Mobile Clinic.

Source: American Emergency Vehicles

method requires visiting nurses to take Polaroid photographs of wounds and forward them to physicians for review. From the snapshot, the physician assesses how healing of the wound is progressing and determines whether changes in medication or treatment are needed. Using the mobile medicine clinic, visiting nurses dial the physician, forward the image in real time, and facilitate interaction between patients and hospital-based providers. Images can be captured and stored in an electronic medical record. The technology can help reduce the cost of continuing inappropriate therapy and shorten the time between data collection and decision.

Manufacturing

Telecommunication systems have long been used in manufacturing processes to monitor and control production to ensure the quality production of products. Manufacturing systems can benefit from wireless production monitoring and low-cost data communication systems.

Production monitoring is the process of using data devices or sensors (e.g., video cameras and keypads) that transfer information via communications lines to keep records of physical production. The Internet and other communication networks are moving onto the factory floor, providing companies with an inexpensive means to link workers and the machines they operate to remote repositories of information. Distant managers can watch what's going on, literally, from where ever they are, as sensors, tiny Web cameras and Web displays are being built directly into equipment deployed on assembly lines. Previously, these monitoring devices required physical, wired connections limiting their routing to production managers. By using the Internet or other wireless technologies, managers located in distant facilities can monitor production and ensure that problems are resolved long before the problem causes lost production or injury to personnel. Software that integrates Internet technologies into factory operations was a small percentage of the $4.8 billion market in 1999. Sales dollar volume of prepackaged manufacturing monitoring software is growing at a rate of 14.2 % per year [38].

Telephone Network Bypass

Telephone network bypass is the connection of customers' communications circuits (voice or data) via alternative telephone network providers. 3rd generation wireless providers offer the ability to provide low and moderate bit rate communication circuits directly to end customers. The key bypass services include wireless local loop (WLL), wireless office telephone systems (WOTS), and low bit rate data network connections (e.g., 56 kbps frame relay).

Mobile Electronic Mail

Electronic mail (e-mail) is the transferring of information messages via an electronic communications system. Initial versions of e-mail could send short text messages of one to three pages. E-mail technology has evolved (and standardized) to allow file attachments and new versions of e-mail (such as flash technology), and send animation or video clips as e-mail messages.

E-mail messaging is probably the best single reason for users to get connected to the Internet. There were over 400 million e-mail account users in 1998, and the number of e-mail accounts was expected to top 1 billion by the end of 2000.

E-mail messaging has been the leading application ("killer application") among online users aged 18 and younger. E-mail is used by more than 40% of online children under age 13, and almost 60% of online children between ages 13 and 18. A large proportion of older children spend their time online communicating with others via e-mail instant messaging.

Wireless e-mail will grow quickly as society adapts to e-mail as a more vital life-line of communications, especially as people begin to appreciate the convenience and freedom of being able to connect from anywhere. Additionally as the wireless e-mail landscape continues to mature, advanced capabilities such as voice-enabled text to speech, real-time synchronization with desktop and calendar, intelligent filtering and security will make wireless e-mail services a "need to have" rather than "want to have."

Targeted Advertising

Targeted advertising is the customizing and individual tracking of advertising to the specific recipient of the advertisement. 3rd generation wireless systems can customize, deliver and track multimedia advertising to specific groups of individuals.

Advertising is traditionally associated with the promotion of branded goods and services via printed ads (in magazines and newspapers), audio, and television (commercials). However, because of the intolerance issues of users in the wireless environment, advertising should be positioned differently, with different associations. Advertising over wireless should be linked to content, location and e-commerce, which will enable advertising to be positioned as a useful service.

Notes:

1. www.GSMobile.com, Dec 31, 2000.
2. Jupiter Communications.
3. Adults 35-45 are the most rapid growth education market.
4. Over 5 million adults complete distance learning courses each year.
5. Interview, industry expert, May 6, 2000.
6. U.S. Department of Education/ National Center for Education Statistics.
7. U.S. Department of Education.
8. e-Marketer; Student Monitor LLC.
9. "The Survey of Distance Learning Programs in Higher Education," 1999 edition.
10. IDC (International Data Corporation); UT Austin Web Central.
11. Jupiter Communications.

12. Activemedia 2000; e-Marketer.
13. Jupiter Communications.
14. Jupiter Communications.
15. Jupiter Communications.
16. 10k, Amazon, Dec 1999.
17. Yankee Group, 2000.
18. Jupiter Communications.
19. Jupiter WebTrack, Merrill Lynch.
20. Jupiter Communications.
21. Jupiter Communications; Morgan Stanley.
22. OVUM, 2000.
23. Jupiter Communications; The Recording Industry Association of America.
24. Datamonitor.
25. Video Store Magazine, January 1999.
26. Motion Picture Association.
27. Paul Kagan Associates.
28. Jupiter Communications.
29. www.electricvillage.com
30. Jupiter Communications.
31. Interview, publishing distribution industry expert, April 21, 2000.
32. Newspaper Association of America; Pew Research Center.
33. InfoTrends report.
34. Summit report.
35. Interview, Steve Kellogg, May 6, 2000.
36. APDG research, Broadband Applications, December 31, 2000.
37. Telemedicine Information Exchange (TIE).

Acronyms and Abbreviations

3GPP - third generation partnership project

3GPP2 - third generation partnership project 2

AAL 5 - ATM adaptation layer type 5

AAL2 - ATM adaptation layer type 2

AC - authentication center (also AuC) or administration center

ACCLOC - authentication center

ACELP - algebraic code excitation linear prediction

ACH - access channel

ACI - adjacent channel interference

ACK - (1) acknowledge (2) acknowledgment

ACLR - adjacent channel leakage ratio, caused by the transmitter nonidealities, the effect of receiver filtering is not included

ACM - (1) accumulated call meter (2) address complete message

ACSE - Association Control service element

ACT - analysis control terminal

ACTS - advance communication technologies and systems, EU research projects framework

ADPCM - adaptive differential pulse code modulation

AICH - acquisition indication channel

AM - (1) amplitude modulation; (2) ante meridian, before noon.

AMD - acknowledged mode data

AMPS - advanced Mobile Phone System

AMR - adaptive multirate (speech codec)

ANSI - American National Standards Institute

ARIB - Association of Radio Industries and Businesses (Japan)

ARQ - (1) Automatic Request to retransmit (2) Automatic Repeat Request

ASC - access service class

ASN.1 - abstract syntax notation one

AT - (1) access tandem (2) prefix for dialing using a modem

ATM - asynchronous transfer mode

AuC - authentication center (data base); associated with HLR

AWGN - additive white Gaussian noise

BB - baseband filter

BB SS7 - broadband signaling system #7

BBCCH - (1)broadcast channel (logical channel) (2) broadcast common control channel

BBCE - base band channel emulator

BCAG - bearer control agent function

BCCH - broadcast control channel

BCF - (1) base control function (2) bearer control function

BCFE - broadcast control functional entity

BCFr - bearer control function for radio bearer

BCH - broadcast channel (transport channel)

BDFE - block decision feedback equalizer

BER - bit error rate

BHCA - busy hour call attempts

BLE - block linear equalizer

BLER - block error rate

BMC - Broadcast/multicast control protocol

BoD - bandwidth on demand

bps - bits per second

BPSK - binary phase shift keying

BS - base station

BSAP - base station application part

BSC - base station controller

BSMAP - base station management application part

BSS - [1]-base station Subsystem (collective name for BSC + BTS); [2]-broadband switching system (3) base station system

BTS - base transceiver station (or system)

C-NBAP - common NBAP

C-PLANE - control PLANE

C-RNTI - cell-RNTI, radio network temporary identity

CA-ICH - channel assignment indication channel

CAP - (1) competitive access provider, carrierless amplitude and phase (2) CAMEL application part

CAPICH - common auxiliary pilot channel

CASE - common application service element

CB - cell broadcast

CBC - cell broadcast center

CBS - cell broadcast service

CBSEED - codebook seed

CC - (1) call control (2) conference calling (3) connection confirm (4) country code (5) congestion control

CCAF - call control agent function

CCAF' - call control agent function (enhanced)

CCCH - common control channel, can be AGCH, PCH or RACH

CCF - (1) conditional call forwarding (2) call control function

CCF' - call control function (enhanced)

CCH - common transport channel

CCR - commitment concurrency and recovery

Cct - (1) circuit (2) central control terminal

CD-ICH - collision detection indication channel

CDF - (1) cumulative distribution function. (2) cumulative density function

CDG - CDMA development group

CDMA - code division multiple access

CDPD - cellular digital packet data

CELP - (1) code excited linear predictive coding (2) code-excited linear predictor

CEPT - European Conference of Posts and Telecommunications (standards activities succeeded by ETSI), Conférence Européenne (des Administrations) des Postes et des Télécommunications

CF - (1) conversion facility (2) crest factor

CFN - connection frame number

CGI - cell global identification

CH - channel

CI - (1) cell identity (2) common interface (standard)

CIR - carrier to interference ratio

CK - cipher key

CLIP - (2) calling line identification presentation supplementary service (2) connectionless interworking protocol

cm - connection management

CN - core network

CODEC - coder-decoder

CODIT - (1) code division test bed, EU research project (2) code division multiple testbed

COST - (1) ETSI (previously CEPT) Council on Science and Technology, European Telecommunications Standards Institute (2) Committee on Standards and Technology

COUNT - call history parameter

CPCH - common packet channel

CPICH - common pilot channel

CR - (1) connection request (2) conventional receivers

CRC - (1) cyclic redundancy code/check; A cyclically generated field of parity bits (2) convolution redundancy check

CRFP - cordless radio fixed part

CRNC - controlling RNC

CS - circuit-switched

CSF - cell-site function. A MAC layer functional grouping

CSICH - CPCH status indication channel

CSMA/CA - carrier sense multiple access/collision avoid

CSPDN - circuit-switched public data network

CTA - cordless terminal adapter

CTCH - common traffic channel

CTM - cordless terminal mobility

CU - central unit

CWTS - China Wireless Telecommunications Standard Group

DAM - DECT authentication module

DAPICH - dedicated auxiliary pilot channel

DARPANET - Defense Advanced Research Projects Agency Network

dB - decibel

dBm - decibel level relative to a 1 milliwatt reference level.

DCA - dynamic channel allocation

DCCH - dedicated control channel (logical channel)

DCFE - dedicated control function entity

DCH - (1) dedicated channel (transport channel) (2) data channel

DCK - derived cipher key

DCPC - distributed constrained power control

DDTC - dedicated traffic channel

DECT - [1]-digital European (or enhanced) cordless telephone; [2]-digital European cordless telecommunications

DF - decision feedback

DL - downlink

DLCI - data link/line connection identifier

DMH - data message handler

DP - (1) dial/dialed pulse (2) detection point

DPC - destination point code

DPCCH - (1) dedicated physical control channel (2) dedicated packet control channel

DPDCH - (1) dedicated physical data channel (2) dedicated packet data channel

DQPSK - differential quadrature (four angle) phase shift keying (type of modulation)

DRNC - drift RNC

DRx - discontinuous reception

DS - direct sequence

DS-CDMA - direct spread code division multiple access

DSCH - downlink shared channel

DSP - digital signal processing

DSSS - direct sequence spread spectrum

DTAP - direct transfer application part

DTCH - dedicated traffic channel

DTMF - dual-tone multifrequency (signaling)

DTX - discontinuous transmission

EDGE - enhanced data rates for GSM evolution

EFR - enhanced full rate speech coder

EIR - equipment identity register

EIRP - equivalent isotropic radiated power

EP - elementary procedure

ES - end system

ESN - electronic serial number

ETSI - European Telecommunications Standards Institute

EVRC - enhanced variable rate code

FACH - forward access control channel

FAF - floor attenuation factor

FBI - feedback information

FCA - fixed channel allocation

FCC - Federal Communications Commission

FCH - fundamental channel

FDD - (1) frequency division duplex (2) full duplex

FDMA - frequency division multiple access

FE - functional entity

FEC - forward error correction

FER - (1) frame error rate (2) frame erasure rate

FFPC - fast-forward power control

FHSS - frequency hopping spread spectrum

FLPC - forward link power control

FMA1 - FRAMES multiple access 1

FMA2 - FRAMES multiple access 2

FP - (1) frame protocol (2) fixed part

FPICH - forward pilot channel

FPLMTS - future public land mobile telephone system

FRAMES - (1) future radio wideband multiple access system, EU research project (2) future radio multiple access scheme

FT - fixed radio termination

FTP - file transfer protocol

G - codebook gain

GAP - generic access profile

GFSK - Gaussian frequency shift keying

GGSN - gateway GPRS support node

GHz - gigahertz

GIP - DECT GSM interworking profile

GMSC - gateway MSC

GMSK - Gaussian minimum shift keying

GNB - go-back-n

GNW - global network

GOS - grade of service

GPRS - general packet radio service

GPS - Global Positioning System

GSIC - groupwise serial interference cancellation

GSM - Global System for Mobile communication (formerly Groupe Spècial Mobile)

GsmSCG - GSM service control function

GsmSSF - GSM service switching function

GTP-U - user plane part of GPRS tunneling protocol

HCM - handoff completion message

HCS - hierarchical cell structure

HD - half duplex

HDB - home database

HDLC - high-density/level data link control (not used over the radio link in GSM/PCS-1900)

HDM - handoff direction message
HLR - home location register
HO - handover
HSCSD - high-speed circuit switched data
Hz - hertz
IA5 - International Alphabet no. 5 (defined by CCITT)
IAM - initial address message
IC - interference cancellation
ICI - inter channel interference
ICMP - internet control message protocol
ID - identification identity identifier
IETF - Internet Engineering Task Force
IF - intermediate frequency
IFEI - international fixed equipment identity
IMSI - international mobile subscriber identity
IMT-2000 - (1) International Mobile Telephony, third generation networks are referred as IMT-200 within ITU (2) International Mobile Telecommunications in Year 2000
IN - (1)-interrogating node; (2)intelligent network
INAP - (1) intelligent network application protocol (2) IN application part
IP - (1)-intelligent peripheral; (2)-internet protocol
IPCP - internet protocol control protocol
IPEI - international portable equipment identity
IPI - inter-path interference
IPR - intellectual property rights
IPUI - international portable user identity
IRC - (1) international record carrier (2) interference rejection combining
IS-136 - US-TDMA, one of the second-generation systems, used mainly in Americas
IS-2000 - IS-95 evolution standard, (CDMA2000)
IS-95 - CDMAone, one of the second-generation systems, mainly in Americas and in Korea
ISDN - integrated services digital network
ISI - intersymbol interference
ISM - industrial, scientific and medical (frequency band)
ISO - (1) International Standards Organization
ISUP - ISDN user part
ITU - International Telecommunication Union
ITUN - SS7 ISUP tunneling
IWF - interWorking function
IWU - interWorking unit
J - Joules
K - (1) constraint length of the convolutional code (2) authentication key (3) Kelvin
kbps - kilobits per second
kHz - kilohertz
km - kilometer
km/h - kilometers per hour
L2 - Layer 2
LAC - (1) location area code (2) link access control
LAI - location area identity
LAN - local area network
LAPC - DLC layer C-plane protocol entity
LAPU - DLC layer U-plane protocol entity
LBT - listen-before-talk
LCD - long constraint delay
LCE - link control entity
LCP - logical control protocol

LCS - location services

LGMSK - linear Gaussian minimum shift keying

LLC - (1) low layer compatibility (2) logical link control

LMMSE - linear minimum mean square error

LOS - line-of-sight

LP - low pass

LPC - linear predictive code(r); Linear predictor-corrector

LPF - low pass filter

LS - least squares

LSP - linear spectral pairs

MA - (1) mobile allocation (2) midamble

MAC - (1) media access control (2) medium access control

MAI - (1) mobile allocation index (2) multiple access interference

MAN - metropolitan area network

MAP - (1) mobile access part (of CCS7, originally designed for use with GSM) (2) maximum a posteriori (3) mobile application part

MBC - multiple bearer control

Mbps - megabits per second

MBS - mobile broadband systems

MC - message center

MCC - mobile country code or miscellaneous common carrier

MCEI - MAC connection endpoint identification

Mcps - megachips per second

MCTD - (1) mean cell transfer delay (2) multicarrier transmit diversity

MCU - multipoint control unit

MDN - mobile director number

MDR - medium data rate

ME - mobile equipment

MF - (1) medium frequency or multifrequency (2) matched filter

MHz - megahertz

MIN - mobile identification number

MLSD - maximum likelihood sequence detection

MM - (1) man machine (2) millimeter (3) mobility management (4) multimedia

MMSE - minimum mean square error

MMSP - multimedia messaging service profile

MNC - mobile network code

MOS - mean opinion score

MPEG - Motion Picture Experts Group

MPH - (1) (mobile) management (entity) - physical (layer) {primitive} (2) miles per hour

MPL - mean path loss

MR-ACELP - multirate ACELP

MRRC - mobile radio resource control

MRTR - mobile radio transmission and reception

ms - (1) millisecond(s)(2) mobile station, mobile set

MSC - mobile service switching center

MSC/VLR - mobile services switching center/visitor location register

MSCR - multiple sensor conventional receivers

MSIN - mobile station identification number

MSISDN - (1) mobile station ISDN number (2) mobile subscriber ISDN number

MSS - (1) mobile satellite service (2) mobile switching subsystem

MT - (1) message type (2) mobile termination

MTP - message transfer protocol or part

MTP3b - message transfer part (broadband)

MUD - multiuser detection

MUX - (1) multiplexing (2) time multiplexor

mW - milliwatts

NAS - nonaccess stratum

NBAP - node B application part

NE - network element

NID - (1) network interface device (2) network identification

NLUM - neighbor list update message

NMSI - (1) national mobile station identifier (2) national mobile subscriber identity

NRT - nonreal-time

NWK - network; layer three of the DECT protocol stack

O&M - operations and maintenance

O-CSI - originating CAMEL subscription information

OA&M - operations, administration and maintenance

ODMA - opportunity-driven multiple access

OHG - operators harmonization group

OMC - operations and maintenance center.

OQPSK - offset quadrature phase shift keying

OS - Operating System

OSI - open system interconnection/integration

OSS - operator services system or operational support system, operation subsystem

OTAF - over-the-air function

OTASP - over-the-air service provisioning

OTD - orthogonal transmit diversity

OVSF - orthogonal variable spreading factor

P-TMSI - packet-TMSI

PA - 1) public address (system), 2) power amplifier (3) portable application

PACA - priority access channel assignment

PAD - (1) packet assembler/disassembler (2) padding

PARI - primary access rights identity

PARK - portable access rights key, states the access rights for a PP

PBX - Private (automatic) branch exchange

PC - (1) personal computer (2) power control

PCCC - parallel concatenated convolutional coder

PCCCH - physical common control channel

PCCH - paging channel (logical channel)

PCCPCH - primary common control physical channel

PCG - power control group

PCH - paging channel (logical channel)

PCM - pulse cod(ed) modulation

PCMCIA - (1) Personal Computer Memory Card Industry Association (2) Personal Computer Memory Card International Association

PCPCH - physical common packet channel

PCS - (1) Personal Communication Service (2) Personal communication systems, second-generation cellular systems mainly in Americas, operating partly on IMT-2000

PDA - personal digital assistant

PDC - (1) Pacific Digital Cellular (2) Personal Digital Cellular, second generation system in Japan

PDCP - packet data converge protocol

PDP - packet data protocol

PDSCH - physical downlink shared channel

PDU - protocol data unit

PER - packed encoding rules

PHL - physical layer one of the DECT protocol stack

PHS - personal handyphone system

PHY - physical layer

PI - (1) presentation indicator (2) page indicator

PIC - parallel interference cancellation

PICH - (1) paging indicator channel (2) pilot channel

PIN - (1) personal identification number (2) positive-intrinsic negative (photo-diode)

PINX - private integrated services network exchange

PISN - private integrated services network

PLMN - public land mobile network

PMRM - pilot strength measurement message

PN-PRBS - pseudo-noise, pseudo-random binary string/stream

PNFE - paging and notification control function entity

POT (S) - plain old telephone (service)

PP - (1) point-to-point (2) portable part

PPDN - public packet data network

PPP - point-to-point protocol

PRACH - physical random access channel

PRN - provide roaming number

Ps - (1) location probability (2) packet switched

PSCH - physical shared channel

PSD - power spectral density

PSI - provide subscriber information

PSK - phase shift keying

PSMM - power measurement report message

PSPDN - packet switched public data network

PSTN - public switched telephone network

PT - portable radio termination

PTN - (1) public telephone network (2) private telecommunication network

PU - payload unit

PUN - portable user number

PUT - portable user type

PVC - (1) permanent virtual circuit (2) predefined virtual connection

PWT - personal wireless telecommunications

QAM - quadrature amplitude modulation

QCELP - qualcomm code-excited linear prediction

QS - quality of service

QPSK - quadrature (four angle) phase shift keying (type of modulation)

RAB - (1) random access burst (2) radio access bearer

RACE - Research (and Development) of Advanced Communication (Technologies) in Europe

RACF - radio access control function

RACH - random access channel

RAI - routing area identify

RAM - random access memory

RAN - radio access network

RANAP - RAN application part

RAND - (1) random challenge value (2) random number

RAU - remote antenna unit

RB - radio bearer

RBC - radio bearer control

RBP - radio burst protocol

RCF - (1) read control filler (2) radio control function

RCH - resume call handling

RCLP - relaxed code-excited linear prediction

REL - release

REPI - radio fixed part identity

RF - radio frequency

RFTR - radio frequency transmission and reception

RLC - radio link control

RLP - Radio Link Protocol

rms - root mean square

RNC - radio network controller

RNP - radio fixed part number

RNS - radio network subsystem

RNSAP - RNS application part

RNTI - radio network temporary identity

ROLPC - reverse outer loop power control

ROSE - remote operation service element

RRC - radio resource control

RRM - radio resource management

RS - Reed-Solomon

RS1 - rate set 1

RS2 - rate set 2

RSE - radio system entity

RSSI - (1) received signal strength indicator (or indication) (2) radio signal strength indicator

RSVP - resource reservation protocol

RT - (1) radio telephone (2) real time (3) random time

RTCP - real time transport control protocol

RTF - radio terminal function

RTOS - real time operating system

RTP - real time protocol

RTSP - real time streaming protocol

RTT - radio transmission technology

RU - resource unit

SAAL-NNI - signaling ATM adaptation layer for network-to-network interfaces

SAAL-UNI - signaling ATM adaptation layer for user to network interfaces

SACF - service access control function

SAP - (1) service access point (2) session announcement protocol

SARI - secondary access rights identity

SASE - specific application service element

SBS - switched Beam System

SCCP - signaling connection control part

SCCPCH - secondary common control physical channel

SCF - service control function

SCH - (1) synchronization channel (2) supplementary channel

SCI - synchronized capsule indicator

SCP - (1) service/signal control point (2) switching control point

SCTP - simple control transmission protocol

SDCCH - (1) standalone dedicated control channel (2) stand-alone dedicated common control channel

SDD - space division duplex

SDF - service data function

SDP - (1) session description protocol (2) service data point

SDU - service data unit

SF - spreading factor

SFN - system frame number

SGSN - serving GPRS support node

SHO - soft handover

SIB - system information block

SIC - successive interference cancellation

SID - (1) system identification (2) silence indicator

SIFIC - send info for incoming call

SIFOC - send info for outgoing call

SINR - signal-to-noise ratio, where noise includes both thermal noise and interference

SIP - (1) SMDS interface protocol (2) session initiation protocol

SIR - signal to interference ratio

SLS - signaling link selection

SM - session management

SM MO - short message mobile originated

SM MT - short message mobile terminated

SMF - service management function

SMG - (1) Special Mode Group (2) Special Mobile Group

SMG2 - Special Mobile Group 2

SMRS - specialized mobile radio services

SMS - service management system or short messaging service

SMSCB - (1) short message service call broadcast (2) SMS cell broadcast

SN - (1) subscriber number (2) sequence number

SNDCF - subnetwork dependent convergence function

SNDCP - subnetwork dependent convergence protocol

SNMP - system network management protocol

SNR - Signal-to-Noise Ratio

SOM - start of message

SP - signaling point

SRB - signaling radio bearer

SRBP - signaling radio burst protocol

SRF - specialized resource function

SRI - send routing information

SRLP - signaling radio link protocol

SRNC - serving RNC

SRNS - serving RNS

SRP - (1) source routing protocol (2) selective repeat request

SRU - soft resource unit

SS - (1) supplementary service(s) (2) spread spectrum

SS7 - signaling system 7

SSCF - service specific coordination function

SSCOP - service specific connection oriented protocol

SSCR - single sensor conventional receivers

SSD - shared secret data

SSF - service switching function

SSP - (1) service switching point (2) service switching platform

STD - switched transmit diversity

STP - (1) signal transfer point; (2) shielded twisted pair; (3) spanning tree protocol

STTD - space-time transmit diversity

SYNC - sync channel

T-CSI - terminating CAMEL subscription information

TACAF - terminal access control agent function

TACF - terminal access control function

TARI - tertiary access rights identity

TBR - technical basic for regulation

TCAP - transaction capabilities application part

TCH - traffic channel

TCP - (1) transmission control protocol (2) transport control protocol

TCP/IP - transmission control

protocol/internet protocol

TCTF - target channel type field

TD/CDMA - time division CDMA, combined TDMA and CDMA

TDD - time division duplex

TDM - time division multiplexing

TDMA - time division multiple access

TE - terminal equipment

TF - transport format

TFCI - transport format combination indicator

TFCS - transport format combination set

TFI - transport format indicator

THSS - time-hopped spread spectrum

TI - transaction indicator (also Texas Instruments, in another context)

TIA - Telecommunications Industry Association

TIMF - terminal identification management function

TMA - telesystems micro-cellular architecture

TMSI - (1) temporary mobile service identity (2) temporary mobile subscriber identity

TPC - transmission power control

TPUI - temporary portable user identity

TR - transparent mode

TRAC - Telecommunication Research and Action Center

TS - (1) timeslot (2) technical specification

TSTD - time-switched transmit diversity

TTA - Telecommunications Technology Association (Korea)

TTC - Telecommunication Technology Commission (Japan)

TxAA - transmit adaptive antennas

U-PLANE - user PLANE

U-RNTI - UTRAN RNTI

UAK - user authentication key

UDP - user datagram protocol

UE - user equipment

UIMF - user identification management function

UL - (1) unnumbered information (frame) (2) uplink

UM - unacknowledged mode

UMTS - (1) Universal Mobile Telecommunications System (2) Universal Mobile Telephone Service

UPI - user personal identification

URA - UTRAN registration area

URL - universal service locator

USCH - uplink shared channel

USIM - USMTS subscriber identity module

UTRA - (1) UMTS terrestrial radio access (ETSI) (2) universal terrestrial radio access (3GP)

UTRAN - UMTS terrestrial radio access network

VAD - voice activity detection

VCI - (1) virtual channel identifier (2) virtual circuit identifier

VDB - visitors database

VLR - visited location register

VLSI - very large scale integrated circuits

VMSC - visited MSC, voice mail system

VOIP - (1) voice over internet protocol (2) voice over IP

VPI - virtual path identifier

W-CDMA - wideband CDMA

WARC - World Administration of Radio Conference

WCDMA - wideband CDMA, code division multiple access

WLAN - wireless local area network

WLL - wireless local loop
WMF - whitening matched filter
WORM - window control operation-based reception memory
WPBX - wireless PBX (power branch exchange)
WRS - wireless relay station
WWW - World Wide Web
XC - transcoder
ZF - zero forcing

Index